It's All in the Game

IT'S ALL IN THE GAME

A Nonfoundationalist Account of Law and Adjudication

Allan C. Hutchinson

Duke University Press Durham and London 2000

Printed in the United States of America on acid-free paper ∞

Typeset in Minion by Keystone Typesetting, Inc.

Library of Congress Cataloging-in-Publication Data

appear on the last printed page of this book.

To My Dad—Long May He Blow His Whistle

Contents

Preface

This book is an attempt to provide a sustained and convincing response to a very simple set of concerns: *What do/can/should judges do?* My focus is upon the interaction of law, politics, and adjudication as it occurs in the largely common law jurisdictions of industrialized nations. I attempt to move back and forth between jurisprudential debates of high theory and the daily practices of appellate judges. The aim is to develop a cogent account of adjudication as an engaged game of rhetorical justification that is both descriptively accurate and prescriptively realizable. As such, I provide an adequate description of what it is that judges do and what it is that jurists (and judges) claim that they are doing. Also, I offer a viable prescription of what it is that judges can and should do in fulfilling their professional roles and responsibilities. Throughout the book, my emphasis is on developing a better and more sophisticated elaboration of the claim that "law is politics." My account is meant to be both critical and constructive in equal measure.

The motivation behind this book is my felt need to take seriously the institutional and political implications of adopting a nonfoundational critique of law and adjudication. In particular, I grapple with the persistent charge that it is not possible to adopt such an ungrounded jurisprudential approach (or what is unhelpfully called a "postmodern" approach) and, at the same time, remain committed to a progressive kind of politics. As such, this project is a jurisprudential exercise in good faith—I try to follow these nonfoundational ideas to wherever they might lead me. My pressing concern has been to ensure that my critique did not turn into a pseudo or faux politics that was long on posturing and short on bite: a species of middle-class theorizing that paid only lip service to the progressive commitment to overcoming oppression and alleviating suffering. Whether I have succeeded in meeting that challenge is for the reader to judge, but I believe that I have provided a convincing response to those who view a nonfoundational account as reactionary and quietistic. While my account will not satisfy those who crave certainty and dogma in political struggle, I do insist that the turn to rhetoric need not be a turn away from politics. I commit to a suggested practice of adjudication and juristic critique that is thoroughly oppositional in both style and substance.

In writing this book, I have benefited from the critical support and intellectual friendship of many people. At the top of the list is David Fraser whose writing opened me up to the possibility of dealing with law and adjudication as playful games: the strength of his criticism will be a true measure of this book's success. It will be obvious to people who are familiar with the relevant theoretical literature that the work of Richard Rorty and Stanley Fish has been provocative and influential, although not always in ways that they would expect or prefer. Also, in law, I owe a debt to the insight and example of Duncan Kennedy and the late Mary Joe Frug—critical pioneers who made it easier for those who followed. Of course, there are many close colleagues and friends who have indulged me with their time, patience, and criticisms. These include Harry Arthurs, Lisa Philipps, Joel Bakan, Simon Fodden, David Vaver, David Cohen, Derek Morgan, Celia Wells, and my jurisprudence classes of '97 and '99. Special mention must be made of Patrick Macklem and Neil Duxbury, who read the whole final draft; although I did not always follow their advice, I benefited immeasurably from their comments and suggestions. For research, I am grateful to Simon Archer, Jennifer Blitz, Remy Boghossian, Peter Leva, Albert Wallrap, and Jim Smith. As well, I have had the opportunity and benefit of giving seminars on the book's theme at the Universities of Toronto, Cardiff, London, British Columbia, Sydney, and Manchester. Further, while the argumentative thread of this book is new, I do rely upon some earlier bits and pieces that I have published over the past few years. Various snippets and sections have been drawn from *Canadian Journal of Law and Jurisprudence*, *Harvard Law Review*, *Law and Society Review*, *McGill Law Journal*, *Modern Law Review*, *New England Law Review*, *Osgoode Hall Law Journal*, *Dalhousie Law Journal*, and *University of Toronto Law Journal*.

My family have provided all the proof that I need to confirm that life is a team game—my daughters, Katie, Emily, and Rachel, are a major source of pride and a constant check against complacency; my young son, Aaron, plays with an uninhibited exuberance that really does convince me of the genuine possibilities for him of a life in which "anything can go"; and my wife, Lisa, through her commitment and support, ensures that I have the confidence to *play the game* in the way I think it should be played. However, as my family knows too well, there are two other great passions in my life: soccer and Van Morrison. I wrote this book (and almost all other things) listening to the music of The Celtic Cowboy. While it is dangerous to dissect too closely the things that give one pleasure, I realize that, apart from the sheer delight of his music, what I most like about him is the way his performances reflect the kind of nonfoundational approach that this book defends and celebrates. His work embodies the passionately ludic attitude that plays with, as it plays within, different musical genres and motifs. He is not afraid to go his own way and "to take it where he finds it," as he sings. Always searching, but never finding, he suggests the productive restlessness and risk taking that are hallmarks of the great player; he does not let the fear of failure prevent him from striving for the glory of success. In the latter stages of completing this manuscript, he released a CD, fittingly entitled *The Healing Game*; it is his best in years. The words of the title track strike the right note: "Here I am again / Back on the corner again / Back where I belong / In the healing game."

In so many ways, playing soccer has been one of the defining threads and experiences of my life as a person, a professor, and a lawyer. In case this is seen as a sentimental overstatement, I should note that when I was first considered for a job at Osgoode Hall in 1978, the chair of the Recruitment Committee made the argument that "Allan is probably more at home on the soccer field than he is in the classroom, but we should take a chance on him." I took—and still take—that as a compliment. As some of my colleagues and students can attest, I am occasionally too combative for my own good. But over the years, I appreciate more and more that it really is the case that it is the playing as much as the winning that counts: you need to be a good winner as much as a good loser. Indeed, these days, it is the watching more than the playing that dominates my involvement; the couch has replaced the pitch in my not-so-sporting life. Nonetheless, I still thrill to the possibilities and magic of soccer's field of dreams, especially if it involves Manchester United, whose recent treble triumph confirms that dreams really can come true. As the gifted Danny Blanchflower reminded fans of all games, "the great fallacy is that the game is first and last about winning. It's nothing of the kind. The game is about glory. It is about doing things in style, with a flourish, about going out and beating the other lot, not waiting for them to die of boredom." I have tried to capture some of that glory in a popular book, entitled *Kicking the Habit: Life, Football, and Other Mysteries*.

Most important, it was through the language of soccer and a shared passion for the game that my dad and I established our relationship and still continue it today. He is a "blue" and I am a "red," but we managed to come together in our love of the game and each other. At 77, he is still blowing his whistle and has completed more than an astonishing fifty years as a referee. However, both my dad and I know that it is my mum who made it all possible: she is the one who has enabled us to live and play. While she has no particular love of soccer or law, she has plenty of love for both of us. She has more than tolerated our indulgences and has devoted herself to ensuring that we are able to play our respective games in the best way that we can. There are no thanks that are enough for that.

Last, but not least, I want to dedicate this book to the memory of Wendy Rambo, my administrative assistant during most of the time that this book was written and completed. After a brief illness, she died in early September 1998. Wendy was born in Manchester, like me, and exhibited many of the sterling qualities that the best of Mancunians embody—a forthright integrity, a mischievous sense of humor, an appetite for hard work, and a steadfast loyalty. She knew what it meant to *play the game*.

A game, a piece of sport, is valuable because it is unnecessary, unimportant, not just trivial but weightless. And because a game is all of those things, it can reach a profundity that the solemn events will never claim. A game can always be read as a metaphor for deeper conflicts, antagonisms, and violence—a game is a prelude to war, in that sense. But a game, or play, is also a way of passing time when time is all we have; it is an urge toward movement, action and maybe even grace as opposed to being stagnant and inert. And winning doesn't matter, because victory is always an illusion.

—David Thomson, *4–2*

1 Playing the Game: An Introduction

Imagine people amusing themselves in a field by playing with a ball. Throwing the ball aimlessly into the air, chasing one another with the ball. The whole time they are playing and following definite rules. Is there not also the case where we play and make up the rules as we go along?

—Ludwig Wittgenstein, *Philosophical Investigations I*

The business of judging has long engaged the attention and, in some cases, the imagination of legal theorists. Such curiosity is understandable because there is an almost universal conviction that something noble and fundamental is at stake in adjudication. Judges are not supposed to decide cases simply on a whim or the toss of a coin but are expected to act in such a way that their decisions are reached through a reflective process of reason and justification; they are judges, not tyrants or tricksters. Sadly, there is little more by way of general or uncontroversial introduction that can be said about what it is that judges actually do or should do when they are making decisions. Whether looking to the observations and opinions of lawyers, jurists, or judges themselves, the legal literature is all over the jurisprudential map—adjudication is variously thought to be an exercise in the simple application of existing rules, the stylized elucidation of just principles, a blunt tool of social engineering, a sophisticated rationalization of arbitrary power, an institutional practice of storytelling, a flawed distillation of formal justice, an elite hegemony of white men, a dialogic meditation on social fairness, and so on. Against such a backdrop, anyone who offers an account of adjudication, whether descriptive or prescriptive, would be well advised to resist the temptation to focus only on judging's technical features or to explain it solely as a peculiarly professional pursuit. Instead, adjudication needs to be situated in a much broader context in which law and its defining activities can be understood and assessed in terms of their connection and contribution to the political life of the social community that they help to constitute.

This book attempts such an ambitious undertaking. I insist that adjudication, like much of life itself, is best understood as a game—as a playful, yet serious attempt by judges to engage in law's language game of politics, which helps to constitute and regulate social life. In taking such an approach, I do not intend to trivialize adjudication by failing to appreciate that it is an exercise in power that has considerable effects on and is affected by the terms and conditions of people's lives. On the contrary, I hope to show that it is only by appreciating that "it's all in the game" that it will be possible to grasp fully the practical operation, the political determinants, and the transformative possibilities of adjudication. By depicting adjudication as a nonfoundational game of infinite dimensions, my account seeks to explain and evaluate adjudication in such a way that it captures its sense as a peculiar professional practice (in which it stands as something of its own thing) and as a profoundly ideological undertaking (in which it is organically related to the larger context of society). In this way, it might be possible to realize that law is not a site that is located aside or away from ordinary life and that adjudication is not an activity that can be appreciated as separate from ordinary living: law and adjudication are a part of, not apart from, life and represent one site and one way of playing the game of life. This means that the jurisprudential account that I offer is, as it should be, "a theory about the relation between law and life."[1]

Playing the Game

Soccer is my game. It has been part of my life (and, therefore, a part of me) since before I can remember. Many of my early years were spent kicking a ball around in one setting or another. Sleeping or waking, I was never far from a soccer ball. Some of my fondest memories can still be traced back to my grandparents' backyard or the local schoolyard as my friends and I whiled away the hours with only a soccer ball for company and dreams of our legendary favorite teams, players, and games. Even then, however, arguments over and about the game were commonplace. It did not seem to matter whether they involved "factual" disputes—was the ball in or out of play?; had elbows been used unfairly?; and, in particular, with coats as make-do goalposts, had the ball hit the post or gone over the bar?—or whether they involved the merits of a particular player or team: the contest was always as heated as it was inconclusive. Looking back, I realize that I was always near the center of these interpretative encounters, making sure that I had my twopennies' worth and that my team received what I considered its due. As so often, more was learned (good and bad) on soccer's field of dreams than the prosaic skills of how to kick and head the ball—friendship, competitiveness, fantasy, responsibility, sticking up for yourself, and, of course, basic argumentative techniques and maneuvers. It was always more than a game; we knew that FOOTBALL (or "soccer," as Americans would have it) was something larger than our own fledgling efforts. As I got older and played in more organized games, a childhood pastime became a juvenile obsession. In the immortal words of the legendary Bill Shankly, soccer did not become a matter of life and death: "It was much more important than that."[2]

Of course, the love of soccer (and games generally) is not shared by everyone. Some prefer the cooler charms of chess or more solitary pursuits, while others enjoy the more ordered and less physical sports of baseball or tennis. For me, though, the exhilaration of actually playing soccer was matched only by the heroic sense of what the game represented. Somewhat dated and very male in style, J. B. Priestley's description of a fictional English city of Bruddersford catches something of the magic that games of soccer meant to my friends and me:

> To say that these men paid their shillings to watch twenty-two hirelings kick a ball is merely to say that a violin is wood and catgut, that Hamlet is so much paper and ink. For a shilling the Bruddersford United A.F.C. offered you Conflict and Art; it turned you into a critic, happy in your judgment of fine points, ready in a second to estimate the worth of a well-judged pass, a run down the touchline, a lightning shot, a clearance kick by back or goalkeeper; it turned you into a partisan, holding your breath when the ball came sailing into your own goalmouth, ecstatic when your forwards raced away towards the opposite goal, elated, downcast, bitter, triumphant by turns at the fortunes of your side, watching the ball shape Iliads and Odysseys for you; and what is more, it turned you into a member of a new community, . . . cheering one another, thumping one another on the shoulders, swapping judgment like lords of the earth, having pushed your way through a turnstile into another and altogether more splendid kind of life, hurtling with Conflict and yet passionate and beautiful in its Art.[3]

While my soccer skills were developing, my rhetorical technique was also coming along apace. In all facets of the game, I was thoroughly committed in my approach, argumentative in my attitude, and combative in my actions; the game was the thing. As the playing became more sophisticated and more intense, so did the rhetorical exchanges over the rules and how the game should be played. Indeed, as the improvement in my playing skills began to flatten off, my penchant for argument began to flourish; my mouth was becoming faster than my feet. Much to my team's regret, I would often be as ready to dispute with coaches about how we should play or to argue the toss with the referee over his decision or interpretation of a rule as I was to play the game. Not surprisingly, my tendentious approach did not endear me to coaches, referees, or fellow players. Although I did play at a reasonably high level (even receiving the odd fiver stuffed in my shoe for my efforts), my playing days were numbered. When I was selected to play, I ended up too often in the referee's notebook and I found myself too often taking "an early bath." Through such encounters, I learned, but never really accepted, the fact that coaches and referees were always "right." This, of course, was not, to borrow Jackson's wisdom,[4] because they were infallible but because their decisions were final—they had the last say.

The fact that my father was (and remains) a soccer referee is important in more ways than one. He has spent a lifetime (over fifty years) blowing the whistle on playing fields that range from local parks to international stadiums. Indeed, my first exposure to the "big time" came in my weekly trips as a youngster with my dad when he was officiating in the major leagues. Not only did I get to rub shoulders with some of my playing heroes (I was literally dumbstruck when Bobby Charlton ruffled my hair in a gesture of greeting), but I saw firsthand what a difficult and thankless task that it was to be a referee—criticism, controversy, and the occasional meat pie or cup of tea thrown from the stands were the frequent rewards. Yet, through it all, my father and his colleagues in black took seriously their responsibility to apply the rules fairly and impartially: a job well done was its own reward. In conversation, my father was a stickler for upholding the letter of the rules; they might not always make perfect sense, he would say, but they were the official rules of the game and deserved to be followed by simple virtue of that fact. However, I came to realize that in the heat of the game, he never let the rules interfere with the flow of the game. He might have been the formalist in the dressing room, but he was the realist out on the field. Provided that the players had no malicious intent, he was prepared to ignore all but the most blatant infringements. Like most judges of law, he knew that good refereeing involved much more than a technical adherence to the rules for their own sake; it was the game that really mattered, not the rules. For him, if you played the game as it should be played, then he would let you get on and play the game. Of course, what it meant and means to *play the game*, whether in soccer or law, is what the larger game of life is all about.

With the considerable benefit of hindsight and over twenty years in law, I can now not only see the man in the boy and the boy in the man, but I can also detect the critical legal theorist in the ebullient soccer player—authority was to be challenged, rules were to be disputed, conventions were to be broken, facts and context were vital, neutrality was a pious pretense, and "right" and "wrong" were always situational. On reflection, I recognize that what is common to my sporting and jurisprudential involvements is the contentious issue of what it means to *play the game*. It is a phrase that is heard around any sporting event or performance. Sometimes offered as a cry of encouragement, it is more often uttered as both an implicit criticism of what is happening and a plea for the game to be played in a way that respects some general expectation of what it means to play it as it was meant to be played. As such, *play the game* invokes a general ideal of the game as a guide and standard for judging and disciplining its particular practice. In law, similar invocations echo around those multiple sites and venues wherever the game of law is played. Judges, lawyers, and law professors exhort themselves and others to *play the game* in accordance with a vision of law and adjudication that stands behind any particular manifestation of laws or performance of the judicial task. There are many performances in many places at many times, and they all embody and influence to different degrees and in different ways the constantly changing and contested notion of what it means to *play the game*. Indeed, as far as law is concerned, there are few more heated and demanding games than the jurisprudential one over what it means to *play the game*.

For most of my involvement in soccer and law, I have been a player rather than a referee or a judge. I played soccer until my late thirties and now play the game vicariously as a fan who still loves to watch and argue over what is the best way to *play the game*. As for my law career, I have been a law teacher, legal theorist, and occasionally a lawyer for more than twenty years. Committed to the enterprise as both participant and critic, I have spent the greatest part of that time speaking and writing about what law is all about and how it could be different or better than it is. In short, I have been arguing about what it means to *play the game* in law as much as soccer. However, while I am more comfortable being a player and critic, there have been two formal occasions on which I have been called on to apply rules rather than asked to follow or evaluate them. It should come as little surprise to learn that I have not experienced the role of judge as very different from the roles of player and critic. As far as I understand it, judging or refereeing is not qualitatively different from being a soccer or legal player: the rules and style of the game are different, but the art of judging or refereeing is no different for that. Indeed, each performance seems in its own way to be part of another game, albeit a special one of argument and justification, over what it means to *play the game*. The rules are less formal and the context is more open, but the experience is much the same—operating within a structure of constraints and expectations that are themselves both the basis of the game and the object of play. While the referee is relatively more constrained (in that some games are not soccer, whatever else they might be) than the judge (in that law consists of various games—sometimes soccer, sometimes chess, and sometimes something else entirely), they both participate in the game of what it means to *play the game*. As interpreters, judges and referees are free to do what they think best, not in spite of the enabling rules, but because of them. Indeed, the best of judges recognize that although the limitations on freedom are what make any game or freedom possible, "every limit is a beginning as well as an ending."[5]

In the Middle

The first occasion on which I experienced directly the peculiar demands and pressures of judicial responsibility was over twenty years ago when I was still in the middle of my soccer career and at the very beginning of my juristic one. I had received a serious injury and was unable to play soccer for an extended period. My father suggested that I do some refereeing in order to earn some extra money. Over a couple of months, I probably refereed about a dozen or so games. It was a difficult and, at times, harrowing experience. Apart from having to make almost instantaneous decisions on inadequate facts, it made me recognize that a full knowledge of the rules was only a small part of what was required to be a good or, at least, successful referee. The main responsibility was to work with and through the rules—a strict interpretation here; a generous interpretation there. Disagreements with the players and their coaches rarely arose from my knowledge of the rules, even though there were times when a more confident grasp of some details might have helped. The crucial challenge was to exercise judgment about how and when those rules should best be employed so as to ensure that everyone was permitted to *play the game* in the way that it was meant to be played. Needless to say, in many instances, there was no one way to do that, and there was certainly no way to make a decision that kept both teams and their supporters happy: their partisanship did not so much cloud judgment as stand in for it. While my view, as the referee, always prevailed over everyone else's, I was less confident about whether my decisions were right or, indeed, what it would mean to get them right in any objective or universal way. I could do no better (and no worse) than to call it as I saw it and hope for the best.

The other occasion on which I assumed the dubious responsibility of judicial authority was my three-year stint as associate dean of my law school. Being charged with the administration of the academic program, I had to interpret and apply a battery of rules and regulations that covered everything from course selection to grading profiles and plagiarism to sexual harassment. Although I only began to appreciate it later, on further reflection, my usual response was to begin with my intuitive sense of the situation and form a tentative judgment on the matter. Next, I would engage with the rules and confirm whether they justified my initial reaction. If they did, I would consider the likely and general effects of any decision on future requests or actions by students. As my experience in the job increased, I realized that my initial intuitions became more reliable: the clarity of the rules or the reasonableness of the students' arguments seemed to take on a more definite and less tentative shape as I worked regularly with a handful of basic rules. Of course, this had more to do with my own substantive preferences and values becoming more decided in these rule-based encounters than with my formal skills of rule interpretation becoming more polished and professional. Also, I recognized that my initial instinct was not something formed outside of the rules that I then tested against the rules, but was something that was actually influenced within and by the rules: a different set of substantive rules might have resulted in a different kind of judgmental instinct. It was my experience that my judgment was affected by the rules in much the same way that the rules were affected by my judgment.

Most students' requests for judgment or approval raised few difficulties—the rules seemed clear, and what the student wanted seemed reasonable and also seemed to fall squarely within those rules. I say "seemed" because my experience as player and referee or judge cautioned me against definitive or fixed notions of what was actually the case. However, not all requests and circumstances were quite so straightforward—sometimes the rules seemed unclear, the students' requests seemed unreasonable, or what they wanted did not seem to fall within the rules. Often, the rules gave me considerable discretion to do what was "just and reasonable in the circumstances." Other times, the rules were so obviously general and vague that they gave no clear answer. In both cases, I tended to take a similar approach. While I might have considered these situations to be invitations to do whatever seemed "just and reasonable" to me, I took them to demand something less subjective. I felt the very real need to be able to justify my own instincts as to what was "just and reasonable" by making some sort of reflective argument (if only in my own head) to others' sense of what was "just and reasonable." Even though most of my decisions were final and unappealable, I felt the compunction to be able to defend them as, at the very least, not being whimsical, capricious, or arbitrary. I was not concerned that others might not agree with my decision, but I did want them to agree that I had fulfilled my adjudicative function in a proper and responsible manner.

In order to meet this challenge of how best to exercise my discretion, I slipped into a way of proceeding that was also suitable for the most challenging of those occasions. These occurred when the rules seemed sufficiently clear in their meaning to mandate a rejection of a student's request, but the student had a reasonable argument (in that it seemed "reasonable" to me and was not a matter of simply trying to "get away with one") as to why the request ought not to be rejected. More than the exercise of broad discretion or the interpretation of unclear rules, this seemed to be the truly "hard case." In such circumstances, I asked the students to go away and write me a one-page explanation of why or how I could interpret the rules to reach the result that they required. Most important, I insisted that while creativity was enthusiastically encouraged, the students should only make arguments based on what they thought was a good faith reading of the relevant rules. Their suggested interpretation had to possess some plausible relation to the rules, or, at least, they had to make some argument that might convince me that such an interpretation was possible: the rules had to play more of a role than act as blatant rationalizations for what they wanted to do. In making my decision, I would grant their "reasonable" request provided that they could convince me that their interpretation of the rules was not so far "off the wall" that no one would recognize it as an interpretation of the rules at all. Accordingly, I did not need to be convinced that their suggestion was the best or most compelling interpretation of the rules but only that it counted as a plausible interpretation of the rules. It was not so much that "anything goes" but that "anything might go."

Of course, this did not mean that all disputes took care of themselves. While many students did not return (presumably unable to make a convincing argument), a number would come back with an argument to make. By then, I might have developed an argument of my own or have had a chance to reflect on the broader ramifications of acceding to their request. Either way, I fell back on my refereeing strategy—I could do no better (and no worse) than to call it as I saw it and hope for the best. Needless to say, this way of proceeding did not persuade all my colleagues or students that this was the best or even proper way to fulfill my decanal responsibilities of adjudicative integrity. The law school community has its fair share of card-carrying positivists—the rules were the rules and needed no more justification for their application than that. However, the commitment of such rule formalists was put to the test when they themselves were placed in a position where they were confronted with real people in real circumstances. Like my refereeing father, most of my colleagues were quick to soften or even ditch their resolute stance when it seemed prudent or expedient to do so. While this might say something good about their sense of justice or compassion, it did not place their professed theory of adjudication in a very good light if it could so easily be overlooked or discarded. Those colleagues who stuck to their formalist guns, whatever their motivations, at least were able to claim the virtue of consistency, even if it is the hobgoblin of little minds. It seemed that what it meant to *play the game* was less the fixed point by which to guide contingent practice and more a shifting ideal that was part and parcel of that contingent practice.

In both soccer and law, therefore, *play the game* is a simple instruction that relies upon a complex understanding of how a particular practice is to be carried out: it draws on a detailed and defensible ideal of play and participation. While the notion of what it means to *play the game* is crucial to all games in that they become unplayable without some shared understanding of what it is to *play the game*, that ideal is always a matter of contestation and conflict. What it means to *play the game* is always open and never closable. At times, disagreement is muted and marginal; this is when there is some general, if unstated, acceptance of a working fit between practice and ideal or when there is sufficient acceptance of some general ideal so that practical disagreements are easily spotted and condemned. At other times, the dispute is voluble and widespread; this is when there is little fit between practice and ideal or there is rampant disagreement over what the general ideal is supposed to be. In both soccer and law, there is a considerable correlation between two sets of claims—whether a particular instance of play or practice is a close approximation to a preferred ideal of what it is to *play the game* and whether the commentator liked the outcome of that particular play. Not surprisingly, the less that commentators like particular outcomes, the less likely they are to consider that their performance lived up to their ideal of what it means to *play the game*. The more that commentators like particular outcomes, the more likely they are to consider that their performance did live up to their ideal of what it means to *play the game*.

The Adjudication Game

That law can best be understood as a game is a matter of trite learning. Indeed, legal trials have their historical origins in sports and contests. Staged in official venues of courts, trials converted vulgar brawls into ceremonial games; ordeal and battle gave way to advocacy and adjudication as the sanctioned method of dispute resolution. Whether as a forum seeking God's intervention or searching for truth, the trial was a public occasion at which the private contest over justice could be resolved in a more mannered and conclusive way. However, in more recent times, the understanding of adjudication as a game has become more figurative and metaphorical. Law came to be viewed as a kind of practice that was similar to sports and pastimes or games, like chess or cricket. The critical advantage in treating adjudication as a game was seen to be that such a comparison would help to illuminate the way in which rules operated to affect participants' behavior and the way in which officials resolved playing disputes in accordance with the operative rules. Judges and referees were cast as neutral arbiters who stood outside the fray itself and dispensed impartial justice if and when the circumstances dictated. As one judge put it, "I can blow my judicial whistle when the ball goes out of play; but when the game restarts I must neither take part nor tell the players how to play."[6] While this simple image had obvious and convenient ideological appeal, it has tended to obfuscate as much as it has enlightened: understanding adjudication in such a crude and unsophisticated way served both to constrain the judicial practice itself and impoverish efforts to transform it.

However, with Hart's modern incorporation of Wittgensteinian insights into jurisprudence in the 1950s and 1960s, a new twist was added to this metaphorical relation between law and games. Adjudication came to be depicted as a language game in which judges act as creative, yet constrained hermeneutical arbiters in disputes over the meaning and application of rules. According to Hart, while language had a fixed core of meaning, there were penumbral areas that required the judge to confront important value-laden matters of principle and policy. Not surprisingly, this understanding of law and adjudication recommended itself to the practical mind of the common lawyer; there is felt to be an intuitive and reassuring fit between what lawyers and judges thought that they were doing and what Hart-inspired jurists told them that they were and should be doing. Although there has been considerable criticism of Hart's ideas in the last thirty years, much jurisprudential debate still takes place in and around this Hartian paradigm.[7] Nevertheless, while many valuable insights can be gleaned from such a theoretical treatment, most efforts to understand adjudication still remain beholden to a very traditional (what I will call "foundationalist") frame of reference—the understanding of language, law, and games has proceeded on the basis that each functions and can best be understood as largely grounded, complete, and certain modes of human interaction. The underlying claim is that it is possible to define the range of available moves and maneuvers with a sufficiently reliable degree of determinacy and detail, such that there are correct and incorrect ways of playing the legal game.

This jurisprudential ambition, of course, flows from an enduring commitment to the Rule of Law, which is seen to demand some division of constitutional labor between legal and political institutions. Although not as stark or crude as the unsophisticated idea that legislators make law and judges apply it, the prevailing liberal view remains that law must not be the same as politics and that adjudication must be qualitatively different from political decision making. In a democracy, it is argued that there must be some real difference between what adjudication entails and what ideological debate involves.[8] Of course, it is conceded that all legal activity occurs within specific historical contexts and has particular political consequences: law is not only a symbol and act of power, but it is also a major component of the social context in which those symbols and acts of power acquire meaning, significance, and effect. However, mainstream jurisprudence remains beholden to the view that while law is thoroughly political in context and consequence, it is possible to present an account of law in which adjudication not only should be but also can be and is largely performed in a qualitatively distinctive and democratically legitimate style. In a very important sense, it is insisted that law is very much its own thing. As put by a leading English law lord, while judges do not "confine their reasoning to the narrow inner logic of the law," judicial choice is "a rational, disciplined, and constrained process": law and adjudication address political issues and incorporate political values, but they are not reducible only to politics.[9]

In this book, I want to challenge that jurisprudential orthodoxy. The force of my critique is that such mainstream legal theory represents the triumph of hope over intellect; it is about faith, not argument. I argue that the claimed dispositive power of this "rational, disciplined, and constrained process" is illusory and overrated. Instead, I offer an account of language, law, and games that is thoroughly nonfoundationalist in purpose and performance. While many controversies in games are factual (was that ball over the line or who did the judge find in favor of?) or judgmental in nature (who was the best player or judge?), there are continuing and complex entanglements over the way particular rules are interpreted. Nonetheless, rather than construe law and adjudication as bounded and grounded exercises in rule application, I will emphasize the extent to which the language game of legal adjudication is indeterminate and ideological in that it inevitably and inescapably involves choosing among values in contingent circumstances; it is as much about playing with the rules as it about playing within the rules. As such, adjudication is an ideological game that is played within law's political stadiums. This does not mean that law is reduced to only the play of political forces but that legal intellectual interests mediate the ideological projects and impulses that are at large in society at any particular time. As such, adjudication is a game that must be appreciated from both an internal perspective (according to the professional self-understandings of its active participants) and an external perspective (according to the ideological lights of its social spectators).

In portraying law and adjudication as their own kind of games, I defend this not only as one way of looking at each activity but as something that is integral to their actual performance. Of course, I am not suggesting that law is an actual game—only that it helps to illuminate adjudicative practices if they are understood as if they were moves in a game. Understood in the sophisticated way that I recommend, the proposal of treating law and adjudication as a game is able to capture both the "routine" operation of the common law and the "radical" leaps that transform law. Most important, by viewing law and adjudication as playful activities, it can better be emphasized that "law is something we do, not something we have as a consequence of something we do."[10] This approach is not intended to essentialize law, soccer, and politics or to claim that, deep down and in their basics, there is Really Something that law, games, and politics are about. On the contrary, I insist that what is presently claimed to be the most favored way to *play the game* is simply a mélange of historical accident, human design, political affiliation, and economic interest. Nor is it intended to trivialize the importance of law as a social activity. Again, when understood in the innovative way that I recommend, the proposal of treating law and adjudication as a playful activity is intended to be neither a frivolous escape from harsh reality nor an indulgent entertainment for the privileged few. Instead, I argue that game playing can be viewed as a serious and creative way of engaging in and making sense of the world.

In understanding adjudication as a game, it is important to recognize that there are two sets or structures of rules in play. There are those rules that are the object and substance of the game. These are comparable to the equipment in cricket or the pieces in chess; they are the constitutional, common law and statutory rules that comprise the body of the legal system's substantive norms. However, there are also those often implicit and occasionally explicit rules that stipulate how the game of "playing with the rules" is to be played. These rules are interpretive in nature and provide judges with the basic maneuvers that they are allowed to make in deploying and applying the substantive legal rules; they include directions about precedential analysis and policy arguments. Of course, these interpretive rules are themselves open to constant reinterpretation and revision; they are never fixed or static in number or meaning. Indeed, the acceptance and weight given to these "adjudicative rules" vary from jurisdiction to jurisdiction and from time to time. As such, the legal game comprises a repertoire of arguments that combine to sustain a culture of legal reasoning. Viewed in this way, law is confirmed as a rhetorical activity; the different techniques of legal reasoning are to be treated less as "rules" and more as moves in a game in which its defining rules are always in play. In this vibrant and ever-changing game, there are a limited number of moves to be made, but they can be made in a bewildering combination and to unexpected effect. For every argument, there is a counterargument: they are not so much solutions to problems as they are probes into formulating a solution. Legal reasoning is about justification, not demonstration—a winning move is one where the cumulative effect of several different and often inconclusive strategies is enough, relative to a particular context and any other countermoves made, to convince someone to prefer one result or line of justification to another. In this way, law and legal reasoning are treated not so much as tools for extracting truth or data banks containing right answers as performative activities in the game of adjudicative interpretation; they are both technical and ideological in play and purpose.

The fact that judges (and jurists) vigorously resist the critical allegation that they are acting in an ideological way ought not to come as a surprise. It is surely the case that "nobody would claim that their own thinking was ideological just as nobody would habitually refer to themselves as Fatso; ideology like halitosis is in this sense what the other person has."[11] However, in emphasizing the ideological nature of law and adjudication, I do not subscribe to the critical (what I will call "antifoundationalist") claim that law is nothing more than the residual traces of the unbounded free play of the judicial mind. Whereas foundationalist jurists locate truth and authority primarily in legal doctrine, the antifoundationalist critics confer that interpretive privilege almost exclusively on judges. In contrast, while my nonfoundationalist critique destroys the possibility that law's legitimacy can be grounded in any account of adjudication as an objective exercise in the neutral application of given rules, it does not ignore the judges' experience of their task as "a rational, disciplined, and constrained process." Whatever else it is, adjudication is not only manipulation and posturing. By treating legal interpretation as a serious form of social activity, a nonfoundationalist approach better explains the felt necessities of law's rationality, discipline, and constraints on interpretive freedom. Far from loosening the political bite of the antifoundationalist's critique, this nonfoundational acknowledgment actually sharpens and deepens the critical force of the claim that "law is politics." By locating this "rational, disciplined, and constrained process" within contingent sociohistorical contexts, it becomes apparent that any foundational claims about the necessity or efficacy of its rationality, discipline, or constraints are unconvincing. Moreover, by concentrating attention on the informing contexts, it is possible to reveal and come to grips with their political character and corrigibility: the law's rationality, discipline, and constraints are never not part of the argumentative process that they are meant to ground and justify. In this way, my nonfoundationalist account is able to respect both the professional and ideological character of law and adjudication.

Nevertheless, although I insist upon the indeterminacy of legal reasoning, I can still agree with foundationalists that, at least in the short term and in the most general way, judicial decisions are predictable in that it is possible to guess with a plausible degree of operational accuracy what judges will and will not decide by way of actual outcomes. Nevertheless, this concession is by no means as damaging to my critical project as might at first be presumed. The force of a nonfoundational critique is that not only is there always room for the decisions in particular cases that will confirm that "anything might go" but that such a decision and such a case are never predictable and could occur at almost any time. As in soccer, an important aspect of legal play is that its course or unfolding cannot be predicted or controlled with any degree of confidence because there is always space both for innovation by individual players and for the intervention of luck, chance, or fate. Accordingly, I disagree entirely with the foundationalists' explanation that this predictability is connected to or justified by the rules of law or that any particular decision is predictable by any given judge on any given day. Insofar as there exist patterns and threads of legal doctrine, they are attributable to the judges' ideological commitments, which, as I will show, are far less determinate and far more developmental than is customarily conceded. Accordingly, it is crucial to understand that, from a nonfoundationalist point of view, the indeterminacy critique goes more to justifiability, whereas the predictability claim speaks more to outcomes.

The response to this kind of critical nonfoundationalist account has been almost universally negative. In a two-pronged strategy that has typified the progress of mainstream jurisprudence, the tendency has been to oscillate between an apocalyptic despair and a yawning indifference. The first response contends that such a jurisprudential initiative will be the death of the legal world as we have come to know it. Adopting an alarmist and occasionally hysterical tone, these jurists have sought to emphasize the radical and nihilistic implications of any disavowal of the foundationalist tradition. In direct contrast, the other tactic has been to point out that a nonfoundationalist approach, for all its huff and puff, makes nothing happen and has no necessary political consequences. Taking a complacent stance, these jurists argue that it results in a pleasant play of surfaces that offers little more by way of prescription than that judges ought to be more flexible and more open in doing whatever it is that they are trying to do. Accordingly, while pursuing very different tactics, these two lines of mainstream jurisprudential criticism have united in their insistence that a nonfoundationalist account is not to be taken seriously by anyone interested in a mature and productive critique of law and adjudication.[12]

Needless to say, I do not agree with such assessments. I maintain that a nonfoundational approach does not warrant despair or indifference; it is the most mature and productive challenge to the dominant strain of contemporary legal theory. While nothing necessarily follows from such a jurisprudential perspective, I will argue that it can have important and fundamental consequences for the understanding of law, the performance of adjudication, and the practice of politics. Those consequences can be radical without being nihilistic and can be reassuring without being quietistic. Throughout the book, I will work to demonstrate what it means to treat adjudication as an engaged game of rhetorical justification that is both descriptively accurate and prescriptively realizable. As such, I will highlight the gap between what it is that judges presently do and what it is that jurists (and judges) claim that they are doing. Also, in elaborating the critical and constructive force of the claim that "law is politics," I will emphasize what it is that judges can and should do in fulfilling their professional roles and democratic responsibilities. As continuing and active participants in law's language game of politics, judges might come to have the most profound and practical impacts on the form and substance of those politics. While it may be that in pursuing such a nonfoundationalist line of jurisprudential endeavor, "the end of all our exploring / Will be to arrive where we started," this will not signal a failure, but a triumph because in coming to "know the place for the first time,"[13] jurisprudence will have made a truly useful and radical contribution to the continuing debate over the theory and practice of law and adjudication.

If, as Oliver Wendell Holmes said, "lawyers spend a great deal of time shovelling smoke,"[14] then legal theorists continue to devote an even greater deal of time to producing it. Under the guise of elucidation, too much jurisprudential writing tends to mystify law and adjudication. On the other hand, a nonfoundationalist account of adjudication as a game works as a gust of fresh air to blow away much of the juristic fog that shrouds the doings of judges. It seeks to expose and lay bare the workings of the judicial performance. However, the ambition is not to junk or do away with the creative craft of playful judging. As part of a larger democratic project, dispelling the clouds of obfuscation that presently surround the adjudicative task is only a prelude to enabling a better understanding of judging so that judges (and critics) might be encouraged to turn their adjudicative energies to transformative effect. With a healthily skeptical attitude to the pretensions and pretenses of judicial theory and practice, judges might immunize themselves from the foundationalist contagion that afflicts efforts at improvement and reconstruction. By abandoning the limited and limiting confines of traditional jurisprudence, lawyers might begin to appreciate that they are engaged in a language game of rhetorical politics. Moreover, they might accept that adjudication and rule application are not supposed to be a convenient escape from political responsibility but are instead one of the most compelling occasions for its dutiful and satisfying discharge.

Finally, by way of introduction, it is worth emphasizing that it is not at all the case that a nonfoundational emphasis on indeterminacy is devoted to demonstrating the impossibility of establishing meaning or of communicating effectively. While it is concerned to undercut and invalidate the determinacy claims of mainstream jurists and judges, it is not engaged in such a frankly ludicrous project. Indeed, the contrary is entirely the case. A nonfoundationalist approach is dedicated to explaining exactly how the establishment of meaning and effective communication is possible. As such, I insist that by directing attention to the social circumstances and political conditions that language operates within and helps to constitute, it might oblige judges and jurists to address those sociopolitical contexts in order to understand how meaning comes about and how, therefore, it might be possible to transform both law's meanings and their informing contexts. Such an insistence ensures that the work of judges and jurists can become both relevant and radical. Rather than dissipate valuable intellectual energy in the futile search for some abstract and theoretical restraints on the interpretive instinct (because there is none that can claim any validity or force outside the very debate that it is intended to constrain), jurists and judges can concentrate on the valuable work of advancing the cause of social justice in a democratic society. While my account will not satisfy those who crave certainty and dogma in political struggle, I continue to insist that the turn to rhetoric need not be a turn away from politics and, most particularly, from a progressive politics.

The Game Plan

In order to carry through this project, I begin by sketching in chapter 2 what is involved in thinking about adjudication as a game. After surveying the constricted and flawed efforts of contemporary jurisprudence to appreciate adjudication as a game of rule playing, I defend a particular understanding of law as a game and, in the process, articulate and address some obvious criticisms—sociological, feminist, and Marxist—of such an approach. One important implication of this approach is that any viable theory of what a game is will itself have to be a game—a conclusion that is delightfully and directly consistent with the demands of a nonfoundationalist approach generally. Also, I offer a general introduction as to what is entailed in a genuine commitment to a nonfoundational critique. In the next chapter, I proceed to deepen and broaden this analysis by explaining more rigorously and illustrating more practically the philosophical character of understanding adjudication as a species of language game. Beginning with the pivotal work of H. L. A. Hart, chapter 3 introduces the cut and thrust of a nonfoundational approach to language and law in which the insights of Wittgenstein are given a critical and deconstructive twist. In providing such an account, I seek to develop a fuller and more convincing explanation of how a nonfoundationalist account of law and adjudication as a game is better able to capture both the experience of judges as they go about their daily business and the critical claim that law is a mode of politics in which "anything might go."

The next two chapters examine the viability of the foundationalist project in light of this view of law as a language game of infinitely playful possibilities. Chapter 4 looks at the different jurisprudential efforts to draw on literary theory in order to provide a method that can isolate and stamp particular interpretations with the imprimatur of interpretive correctness and legal validity. While presented as neutral interventions, these interpretive strategies operate as interested and aligned forms of political intervention and control. In contrast, a nonfoundationalist view emphasizes the rhetorical nature of reading in which legal theories of interpretation function as arguments and resources rather than as boundary markers for particular readings; the *who*s, *when*s, *why*s, and *wherefore*s of writing and reading are always socially contingent and therefore politically contestable. In chapter 5, I continue this exploration of foundationalist theories by concentrating on the efforts of two different but related naturalist attempts to ground adjudication in something more than the language of its extant rules. Focusing on the work of Ronald Dworkin and Ernest Weinrib, I accept that adjudication is as much about substantive fairness as it is about formal adequacy, but I undermine their claim that such a value-based mode of adjudication can be effected in a bounded or neutral way. As foundationalist accounts par excellence, the efforts of naturalist jurisprudence fail in terms of both descriptive and prescriptive merit; they provide further support to the claim that when it comes to law and adjudication, "interpretation is the only game in town."[15]

Having undermined the worth and viability of the foundationalist project, I explore further the different notions of "play" that inform the adjudicative enterprise. Chapter 6 looks at recent efforts by Cass Sunstein and others to re-present law as a practical activity in which legal reasoning holds a special place. However, while it is an improvement to abandon the idea of law and adjudication as a purely reflective exercise, this pragmatic turn is still too beholden to the foundationalist project: it tends to turn "play" into one more fixed and finite abstract category. In contrast, I insist that in law's language game there is nothing to ground the argumentative play of legal reasoning but more play; law is an engaged performance of rhetorical proportions. By way of further developing this understanding of judicial playfulness, chapter 7 seeks to demonstrate the extent to which such a nonfoundationalist account is different from antifoundationalist accounts of law. In the process of distinguishing my nonfoundationalist account from an "anything goes" critique, I clarify how it is possible both to take adjudication seriously as a bounded legal practice and, at the same time, to treat it as an ideological exercise—judges do "apply the rules," provided that it is understood that what the rules mean and what it means to follow them is never grounded and always contestable. This involves an important discussion about what it means for judges to act in "good faith."

The next two chapters of the book explore the notion of "politics" that is implicit in and made possible by a nonfoundationalist account of adjudication. Chapter 8 scrutinizes the foundationalist claims of those critics of law and adjudication who maintain that adjudication is less an independent field of intellectual endeavor and more the stylized product of material forces. While law cannot be made sense of or defended solely on its own terms, such theorists hold that it can be grounded and comprehended in a political dynamic that brings order to the seemingly arbitrary routines of adjudication. While acknowledging that such work is a welcome corrective to much traditional jurisprudence, a nonfoundationalist account insists that both society in general and the legal process in particular are far too messy in their patterns and practices to be reduced to neat equations of cause and effect; their importance is as much in the small details as in the grand design. The richness of social life cannot be crammed into one simplistic formula or once-and-for-all ideological narrative: the only outcome will be to impoverish both social life and any explanatory account that is forthcoming. Accordingly, in chapter 9 I suggest that a nonfoundationalist account does not so much blunt the edge of any political critique as sharpen it in important ways. It is not a question of being for or against Marxism, liberalism, or feminism but rather a matter of refusing to accept their more totalizing versions as all-encompassing theoretical statements of social and legal development or as universal programs for human emancipation and empowerment. A nonfoundationalist response is much more pragmatic, piecemeal, and eclectic: what it might be considered to lose in theoretical elegance, it gains in historical pertinence and political salience.

In the final two chapters, I draw together the different strands of my argument and suggest what it means for the future performance of legal adjudication. In chapter 10, I advance the idea and practice of a nonfoundational account of law and adjudication by fleshing out what is involved and by what standards it is possible to assess different renditions of the judicial game. Utilizing a particular notion of professional craft, I show how good judging is not a matter of getting it "right" or making it "true" but doing it well; great players are those who understand the worth of experiment, improvisation, and transformation. The constraints on being a good judge are the same as those on being a good soccer player—vision, technique, application, industry, conditioning, insight, and timing. Finally, in chapter 11, I look at the implications of my nonfoundational account of adjudication as a game within the broader context of democratic politics. In particular, I resist claims that such an account presages the death of law. While it might well ring the death knell for law and adjudication as it is presently perceived and defended, my account offers all the promise and potential to satisfy the democratic instinct for social justice that existing foundationalist theories vainly hope to serve and that antifoundationalist critiques condemn as illusory. As such, a nonfoundational account of law and adjudication recommends itself as the most effective way to meet the challenge of coming up with a jurisprudence that both incorporates the felt boundedness of judges as they go about their daily business and the critical claim that law is a mode of politics in which "anything might go."

Finally, I have deliberately chosen to call this "an account of law and adjudication." In particular, I have deliberately avoided the slippery and contested term "a theory of. . . ." This is because a theory indicates something that is too universal, complete, and comprehensive for my nonfoundationalist taste or sensibilities; it smacks of the kind of work—with its emphasis on grounded premises and guaranteed procedures—that is antithetical to my whole approach. The idea of a "theory" suggests that jurisprudence is a reflective and first-order enterprise that is to be set against and above a situated and second-order practice. It is exactly that kind of bifurcated thinking that I seek to challenge—theory is another kind of practice that cannot be entirely separated or fully appreciated apart from the historical conditions of its ideological production. As I will seek to demonstrate, all jurists exist in a post-Kuhnian world of scholarly inquiry and research. Although there remains considerable debate and disagreement around the precise import and intellectual implications of his work, Kuhn offered a challenge to the dominant analytical and positivist tradition that it is yet to be met or overcome.[16] By insisting that (legal) philosophy cannot be appreciated independent of its history, he ensured that the relation between an object and its interpretation will remain problematic and mediated; the neat distinction between the thing-to-be understood and the conceptual-apparatus-for-its-understanding cannot be maintained. As I insist throughout this book, law's language game and all efforts to understand it are playful and performative; there is no outside to adjudication's practical game that is not itself another game or practice.

2 It's All in the Game: Adjudication in a Nonfoundationalist Way

••••••

There are the rules, and what we make of them. It's the same with soccer and writing a book. . . . You've got to keep the ball on the island and the words on the page; and you've got to stay within the rules, or woo them till they bend.

—David Thomson, *4–2*

There are almost as many ways to define what makes something into a "game" as there are different ways of playing them. Games can be solitary or group pursuits, they can be physical or intellectual activities, and they can be regimented or improvisational performances. As Wittgenstein made plain, it is not that there is "something that is common to *all* [games], but similarities, relationships, and a whole series of them at that—'games' form a family."[1] And, it might be added, that, like families, what is a game and who can be players shifts over time and changes across societies. Similarly, there are many ways to approach the study of games generally and the playing of particular games—to the uninitiated, it might be a colossal bore; to the enthusiast, it might be the stuff of life; to the artistic, it might be a graceful dance; to the psychiatrist, it might be a healthy diversion; to the educator, it might be the complement to a healthy mind; to the cynic, it might be a contrived occasion for mass control; to the spiritualist, it might be a Zen experience of essential harmony; and whatever takes the observer's fancy. My own approach to games and, therefore, adjudication is, by and large, philosophical. It is an attempt to make sense of one particular game—the stylized activities of judges in common law countries in deciding cases—as an intelligent, self-conscious, and serious human endeavor that is part and in the service of a larger political context.

It seems to be the case that most people recognize that while games can be understood in terms of the formal rules that constitute or govern them, there is so much more involved; the existence of rules is a necessary but not sufficient condition to explain game playing in general or the actual performance of particular games. To try and understand cricket or baseball by reference to only the official rules of the game is to miss a vast amount of what is important or meaningful to any full account of what it means to *play the game*. As with most activities, it is the game within the game that makes the experience what it is or might be for both players and observers. Mindful, therefore, that games are as much about their informing ethos as their enabling rules, I emphasize the extent to which adjudication is about those informal conventions that determine how the formal rules of the games are to be applied and followed in concrete situations. This approach is by no means novel or special.[2] However, I go a step further than these traditional and broadly foundationalist accounts of games and what it means to play them. For me, adjudication is a special game of its own kind in that, because its operative conventions are not formally recorded and are practice based, the ethos of the game is never fixed or grounded; it is a game as much about deciding what is the game to be played as it is about playing that game. What it is to play the legal game of adjudication changes and develops as the game is played—the game is about the game because there is no one fixed or final Game of games. Adjudication is playful in the fullest sense of being ungrounded in anything but its own daily routines, rituals, and results.

In this chapter I explore and explain both what it means to treat adjudication as a game and what particular kind of game it is that judges play. In particular, this chapter introduces the idea of a nonfoundational approach to games, adjudication, and philosophy. After sketching the different theoretical allegiances and trends that comprise the contemporary jurisprudential scene, I highlight the foundationalist presumptions of most juristic efforts to explain and criticize the practice of adjudication. Using the adventurous (and neglected) work of David Fraser as an important bridge, the chapter lays out a contrasting account of adjudication that is informed by a less traditional and more nonfoundational understanding. In order to head off some possible objections to my critical claim that adjudication can best be appreciated and practiced as a special kind of game, I address the most obvious and fundamental criticisms of this gambit. Finally, I step back from the jurisprudential fray and offer a more technical account of what the adoption of a nonfoundational approach implies in terms of its overall relation to the traditional philosophical canon.

The Games That Jurists Play

Although it draws upon age-old themes and trends, modern jurisprudence is relatively young. Its birth can be traced to the publication in 1961 of

Herbert Hart's *The Concept of Law*. While this elegant monograph covered much more jurisprudential ground, jurists have tended to concentrate on the chapters about the nature of adjudication and, in particular, the operation and limits of rule application as a method of legal decision making—how is it possible to get beyond a discredited formalism without turning judging into an open-ended exercise in ideological wrangling? Hart's prominence in this debate is ironic, since he later concluded that he had said "far too little about the topic of adjudication and legal reasoning."[3] Indeed, the main thrust of his work was to present a more sophisticated theory of legal positivism than had hitherto been available, in which a formalist explanation of adjudication would only be a small part. As such, *The Concept of Law* captures a special kind of *soft* positivism. Rather than maintain that the truth of legal propositions is reducible to bare historical facts, Hart acknowledges that values can be fully implicated: "The existence and content of law can be identified by reference to the social sources of law . . . without reference to morality except where the law thus identified has itself incorporated moral criteria for the identification of law."[4] Within these positivistic parameters, Hart depicts law as a functional and sophisticated system of rules—the obligation-imposing primary rules that comprise the bulk of substantive legal doctrine, like criminal and contract law, and the authority-conferring secondary rules that distribute institutional power and jurisdiction, between legislatures and courts for example, over the creation and enforcement of the primary rules.

Against this analytical backdrop, Hart developed a suggestive account of adjudication. It is a description of what occurs, not a prescription for what might or should occur. In typical fashion, he made a virtue of compromise. Presenting a reasoned and reasonable account of modern judging, he unashamedly sought to inhabit a middle ground between formalist pitfalls and realist excesses. Almost all commentators accepted that the realist account of adjudication—"that judges always make and never find the law"—was a nightmare to be avoided. Instead, debate was joined over the extent to which the noble dream of a formalist faith—"that [judges] never make it"—could be revived and revised. Throughout his contribution, Hart accepted that while these "illusions . . . have much of value to teach the jurist in his waking hours,"[5] the sensible lawyer will settle for a good night's sleep. Hart's patented jurisprudential formula for a legal good night's sleep is prosaic and pragmatic. Because judges are empowered to apply rules in order to resolve disputes between conflicting citizens, the hallmark of "good" judges is their ability to identify the extant rules of the legal system and apply them to conrete situations. Nonetheless, for Hart this craft is not a purely technical or logical exercise. Because law, like language, is an entirely conventional affair and convention is neither gapless nor precise, some cases are "not merely . . . controversial in the sense that reasonable and informed lawyers may disagree about which answer is legally correct, but the law is fundamentally *incomplete*."[6]

Consequently, these so-called "hard cases" will invoke and require nonconventional decision-making processes. In fulfilling their duties, judges have to call on a variety of analytical skills and reasoning techniques: they act inductively when they extract rules from a line of past cases; they act deductively when they apply the inductively extracted rule to the case in point; and they act politically when the inductively extracted rule or its deductive application is uncertain or difficult. The challenge for both the judge and jurist is to strike an appropriate and manageable balance between the rule application of clear cases and the rule production of hard cases such that certainty is not sacrificed entirely to particularized flexibility. In this unpretentious account of judging, indeterminacy is something that pervades the judicial task, but it is always relative, marginal, and not to be exaggerated. Accordingly, Hartian judges are not mindless automatons, Delphic oracles, well-meaning simpletons, rampant legislators, or cynical manipulators; they struggle to do justice in a way that respects rules without becoming enslaved to them. To the chagrin of the dogmatist and the true believer, they are "men [and women], not god," nor, it might be added, beasts.[7] Hart's writings present judging as a balanced and judicious affair—it is rational without being scientific, flexible without being unbounded, judgmental without being arbitrary, and predictable without being predetermined.

In the thirty years since *The Concept of Law*'s original publication, the focus of jurisprudential attention has become (trans)fixed on the adjudicative function; what was once merely a small part of the juristic project has become its almost total concern. While Hart's more general jurisprudential ideas are no longer thought to be entirely pertinent to the contemporary agenda of pressing issues, legal theorists have not so much rejected Hart's rule-based positivistic account of adjudication as tried to qualify it in various ways. Taking a leaf from the litigator's notebook, they have sought both to confess (rules are important in law) and to avoid (rules are not exhaustive of law) the force of Hart's claims. Critics and defenders alike have retained Hartian positivism's central article of faith—namely, that rules are the basic currency of legal transactions and that they have a core meaning that can deal with and resolve most situations. Even the most antipositivistic jurist, like Dworkin, accepts that there are frequent occasions on which a rule "applies itself," and even the most pragmatic theorist, like Posner, embraces the idea that the skill to apply rules in a creative way and the ability to make that application persuasive to others are the hallmarks of good lawyers and judges.[8] However, the efforts to qualify and distinguish Hart have not been trivial. They can be grouped into two main trends—a naturalist resurgence and a positivistic retrenchment.

The great majority of jurists have sought to envelop an understanding of law and adjudication in a larger and more expansive moral universe. Although conceding that Hart was accurate in observing that rules were open-textured and their application did not exhaust the judicial function, these neonaturalist jurists argue that he failed to appreciate the extent to which the law consisted of more than rules. For them, behind and within the rules is a political morality that guides and constrains judges when the application of rules is unclear or undesirable. Law is about values and politics but not in any idiosyncratic or ideological way. In carrying out this jurisprudential maneuver, the primary task of theorists and judges is to detect and cultivate the politico-moral principles that breathe life into the dry husks of legal rules. However, while there is considerable methodological consensus, there is little agreement about the identity and substance of those principles. For some, the legal process is a subtle economic game in which the invisible hand of the market shapes and wields legal rules in the best approximation of wealth maximization; for others, legal doctrine is a morality play in which individual rights struggle with collective interests over the soul of constitutional justice; and for still others, the courts represent a privileged site for a continuing civic dialogue over the possibilities and parameters of democratic governance.[9]

What distinguishes each of these naturalist approaches is less their general methodology than their particular realization and application of it. In their own fashion, jurists argue that legal doctrine contains an implicit structure or latent ideal whose incomplete development is to be brought to institutional consciousness. However, in a hallmark move, the jurists then proceed to put that ideal to work as the basis for criticizing and reforming the recalcitrant portions of legal practice. The challenge for each theoretical endeavor is to ensure that the balance between the ideal-instantiated doctrine and its anomalous segments is maintained. Once the latter begins to compete with the former as a matter of descriptive accounting, the jurists' claims to be discovering the law's order rather than creating it will be confounded; it will begin to become obvious that the jurists' normative ideals are driving the whole process of jurisprudential explanation. Moreover, what began as the reassuring promise of incremental reform will be compromised by the opportunistic threat of wholesale transformation. In this fragile exercise of foundationalist jurisprudence, "deviations and contradictions become intellectual and political threats rather than intellectual and political opportunities."[10] Accordingly, the naturalist resurgents are obliged to tread an impossibly thin line between a valid practice of internal illumination and an invalid exercise in external projection.

A smaller group of jurisprudential scholars has maintained that Hart had gone too soft on the moral basis of law. They agreed with the naturalists that

Hart's attempt at compromise was not a triumph but a sellout: Hart was a radical in traditionalist's clothing who had reneged on the democratic compact by letting the political cat out of the legal bag. However, rather than try to salvage the legal enterprise by mixing in more morality, these archpositivists seek to redeem law's democratic legitimacy by purifying it of any moral entanglements at all. Such a *hard* variety of positivism treats law exclusively as a matter of social fact, not a moral ideal. While not everything judges say or do is law, their application of legal rules not only can but must be free of moralizing; to do more (or less) would be improper, unjudicial, and undemocratic. Satisfying people's presumed demand for clear and fixed rules, these jurists strive to maintain a sharp demarcation of judicial and legislative authority; judges are bound by the law's commands as much as any other private citizen or public official. This is not so much an amoral stance as a moral position that defends a legalism of strictly rule-bound adjudication as the most morally defensible account of law and adjudication in a constitutional democracy. It is a vision of judging that celebrates the systemic virtues of regularity, predictability, and certainty over the concern with substantive justice in particular instances: formal rules are the most efficacious and legitimate way to protect substantive values. In one of its most uncompromising incarnations, Justice Scalia (of the United States Supreme Court and a former jurist) insists that "there are times when even a bad rule is better than no rule at all."[11]

In spite of obvious differences, these conflicting naturalist and positivist trends are united in their shared and enduring formalistic belief that there must be a clear and defensible line between valid adjudication and ideological disputation. Both groups of adherents maintain that legal reasoning is a sufficiently detached and determinate enterprise that can generate correct and predictable answers to social disputes in a way that marks it off, in a nontrivial and meaningful sense, from open-ended political wrangling. While immersed in politics and history, law is claimed to be its own thing and not entirely reducible to anything else. Without such a possibility, the fear is that the Rule of Law will be subverted and democratic governance will succumb to the tyranny of special-interest groups. Moreover, without adequate determinacy in legal discourse, judicial arbitrariness will become the order of the day and adjudication will collapse into a series of ad hoc and unprincipled encounters; "muddling through" will be all that is left. Accordingly, positivists and naturalists agree that the preservation of the Rule of Law "has the value of promising to make politics safe, of preventing Leviathan from becoming Frankenstein's monster, . . . [of imposing] real restraints on arbitrariness or despotic conduct."[12]

Needless to say, not all jurists have been convinced by the basic Hartian claim that rule-based adjudication can (to a greater or lesser extent) place "restraints on arbitrariness or despotic conduct." A small disaffected group of critics insist that rules can never impose sufficient restraints on judges and that adjudication will always be an exercise in arbitrariness or despotism; adjudication is more about reason in the service of power than power in the service of reason. These so-called nihilists have exacerbated the formalist fear that without some plausible account of determinate rule following, there will be an official anarchy in which rules will count for nothing or simply be used as crude ex post rationalizations for ex ante decisions. For instance, Mark Tushnet contends that if he were appointed to the bench, he would adopt a "currently fashionable theory" of adjudication and then use it to advance the cause of socialism or whatever.[13] In a crucial sense, this fails to take the legal enterprise seriously and offers no real challenge to its theoretical legitimacy. After all, as Hart is at pains to insist, the judges' experience of actually applying rules must be incorporated into and explained by any cogent account of adjudication. On such a nihilist account, rules count for next to nothing in the fulfillment of judicial responsibility. Moreover, a nihilistic perspective persists in the error that judges can step out of themselves and adopt some view from a legal nowhere; judges are ideologues at large, who, unmoved by the siren song of Hartian judges, chart legal waters entirely to the eccentric promptings of their own political compass.

The important question for each and all of the positivist (whether of the hard or soft variety), the naturalist, and the nihilist accounts is not whether law in large part can be *represented* as the neutral application of clear rules wrapped up in intelligible doctrine but whether it ever can *be* so. Whereas positivists and naturalists believe that it can be, nihilists insist that it cannot; each is the flip side of the foundationalist coin. In contrast, I contend that the judges are both more and less constrained by rules than any of the positivists, naturalists, and nihilists believe. They are more constrained in the sense that they cannot get completely outside of rules and exercise an entirely free choice, but they are less constrained in the sense that they are not obliged to reach any particular decision as the result of a commitment to resolve disputes through rule application. It is not so much that rules do not exist as that they do not exist as canonical directives whose meaning is available without interpretation and which can impersonally dispose of cases. The meaning of a rule and its application never simply *is*—it is something to be argued for or about and not something to be argued from. As conventional and social matters, the meaning and application of rules are contextual and, therefore, open: the fear of rule-free choice is as contrived as faith in rule-bound choice. Any claim that judges are only being held back from a frenzy of arbitrariness by rules' restraining power is not only unrealistic but also does scant credit to the integrity and efforts of most judges.

Aside from their considerable differences, both traditional jurists and radical critics operate within the unnecessary confines of a jurisprudential project that is very foundationalist and, therefore, flawed in its critical claims for the present and future performance of the judicial enterprise. Naturalists and positivists strive to complete the foundationalist project of demonstrating that legal rules and their adjudicative application are grounded in something less contingent and more reliable than the shifting justificatory routines of present judicial incumbents. Although unalterably opposed to the worth or viability of the foundationalist project, nihilists remain in thrall to its all-or-nothing character; they insist that legal rules and their adjudicative application amount to only expedient window dressing for ideological manipulation. In contrast, I offer an account of adjudication that is thoroughly nonfoundationalist in ambition and accomplishment. Recognizing that "the questioning of foundations is neither foundationalist nor anti-foundationalist,"[14] I resist the temptation to deify or demonize the act of adjudication and, in the process, turn judges into demigods or demagogues. A nonfoundationalist account will not only serve to chastise those naturalists who are hubristic enough to project law as a seamless web of doctrinal filaments, but it will also act as a much-needed corrective to those nihilists who are driven to present rule application as nothing more than a transparent exercise in self-delusion.

In other words, I will articulate a critical account of law and jurisprudence that takes adjudication seriously in the only way that it can be taken seriously—as a special kind of activity or game that is defined by rules and roles, but in which the nature and effect of those rules and roles are themselves always in play. In this nonfoundational account, while judges are never not in a game, there is no one Game of games. Judges are neither entirely free nor completely constrained in what they can and cannot do because adjudication comprises a structure of constraints that makes possible simultaneously both the act of judging itself and the freedom to change the nature and effects of those constraints; the game changes as it is being played. While recognizing that play is an encounter with possibility within the context of closure, I emphasize the interplay of mutual readaptation between the judges and the rules: "Play is always playing with something that also plays with the player."[15] In the next section, I will develop this understanding of adjudication-as-game with particular reference to the nonfoundational nature of the practice.

A Different Spin

The suggestion that the idea and practice of adjudication can be illuminated through an analogical resort to games is not new. For instance, Hart makes frequent reference to games in his efforts to explain an account of law as a system of rules in which adjudication is largely exhausted by efforts to locate, define, and apply them. The analogy is simple and straightforward in that the judge is compared to the familiar and passive umpire of popular sports, like baseball and cricket.[16] Further, those theories that do not make explicit reference to game playing can be easily and usefully presented in such a way that both analogizes them to games and respects their theoretical integrity. However, while many valuable insights can be gleaned from this traditional treatment, the whole effort to understand adjudication as a game remains unnecessarily beholden to a very foundationalist frame of reference —the understanding of language, law, and games has proceeded on the basis that each functions and can best be understood as largely grounded, complete, and certain modes of human interaction. The underlying claim is that the range of available moves and maneuvers that are and might be made are capable, at least in theory, of being fixed with a reliable degree of determinacy and detail, such that there are correct and incorrect ways to play the legal game.

An explicit effort to understand law as a game in a way that eschews such foundationalist ambitions is offered by David Fraser. In *The Man in White Is Always Right: Cricket and the Law*, he offers an insightful meditation on the nature of rule-governed behavior and what it means to *play the game*. Although cricket might seem an unlikely activity through which to study the operation of contemporary adjudication, it is in fact an excellent choice. As a game that is encrusted with all manner and form of affectation, custom, convention, decorum, professionalism, ritual, and lore, it is a practice that should easily recommend its study to lawyers and critics. Indeed, professional and international cricket's rather mystical and mannered appearance hides a lived reality that is as contested and vital as any piece of litigation. The history of cricket, like that of law, is as riven with greed and venality as it is filled with the heroic exploits of the game's great players. As in law, the majesty and allure of cricket resides as much in people's romantic imagination as it does in the game's daily practice. Moreover, in his comparative study, Fraser engages in a style of analysis that rejects the traditional foundationalist focus of contemporary jurisprudence; the important comparison is not between umpires and judges but between players and judges. However, although his work does much to challenge prevailing thinking, Fraser does not have the full courage of his nonfoundational convictions: he hedges on the imperatives and implications of a thoroughly nonfoundational account. Consequently, after sketching Fraser's main ideas and insights, I carry through on the nonfoundationalist project that he begins but fails to complete.

In his extended meditation on the Duke of Dorset's 1777 quip, "What is human life but a game of cricket," Fraser has made a singular contribution to the literature on not only cricket but also law critical theory. Having written a work replete with references to philosophical and hermeneutical literature, Fraser is completely at ease in moving between the arcane worlds of hermeneutics, law, and cricket. His book is an attempt to demonstrate that "cricket, rather than being 'just a game,' offers a classic case study on how legal and ethical norms interact, are created, interpreted, and applied and how these examples can inform our understanding of other social phenomena." Fraser uses cricket as a medium through which to illustrate how issues of legality, ethics, and moral judgment inform all individuals' lives and their daily social practices. Like life, cricket raises debate "about the function of umpires and respect for the rule of law, about cheating and sharp practice, nationalism and racism and even basic human personal dislike." And, of course, Fraser proceeds to illustrate how issues of legality, ethics, and moral judgment in each person's life and daily social practices inform the performance and understanding of cricket. In traveling this two-way street, Fraser has to pass through and negotiate some of the central dilemmas that energize and trouble lawyers, cricketers, and citizens. In particular, he spends much time both reflecting theoretically on and engaging practically the issue of whether "the interests of justice are better served by uncritical devotion and respect for the ideal of judicial infallibility or by open, public critical debate."[17] Indeed, it is his exploration of what it means to *play the game* that threads together Fraser's analysis of law and cricket.

For Fraser, cricket is a social text. By this, he means to treat cricket as a social practice or performance that invites interpretation and obtains its meaning through its hermeneutical appreciation as a cultural artifact. As such, it can be interpreted and deconstructed in the same manner as any other social text, such as law or cockfighting.[18] While he denies the existence of any essence to cricket, he quite validly underlines the fact that frequent appeals are made to some transcendent archetype. However, unlike many players in the interpretive game, Fraser is acutely aware that any understanding of what it really means to *play the game* is constantly evolving and changing. As with law, cricket is "a more complex and contradictory social text than traditional scholarship would have us believe."[19] Throughout the book, Fraser reveals and explores how cricket and law, although ostensibly rule-based and rule-structured activities, are never quite what they seem; there is more to them than meets the eye, and what meets the eye is filtered through a host of interpretive filters. There is always a constant battle between claims to the letter and claims to the spirit of the law. In other words, the heart of cricket and law is the inconclusive and passionate game over what it means to *play the game.*

Moreover, in the taking of sides in this interpretive contest, there is little consistency in any particular person's approach and allegiance. Sometimes, there is an appeal to the letter of the law and, at other times, to its spirit. In both cases, there is some felt and shared understanding that there is something called *Cricket* that transcends its actual practice, but there is little agreement on what that might be in its local particulars. In the jurisprudential debate between formalism and naturalism, "the weapons of one discourse may be turned in a radical interpretive term against themselves or, in what may amount to the same thing, in favour of their apparent opponent."[20] Fraser emphasizes that in a game that is played internationally and therefore among and across different cultures, popular understandings of cricket come not so much from any rational study or understanding of the rules but from the lived experience of playing with and within them. There is a fluidity to interpretive interventions that renders the notion of a universal or objective understanding of cricket as hopelessly utopian (or, perhaps, dystopian). Accordingly, people are divided among, between, and within themselves as to what it means to *play the game*. As with so many things, the game goes on while plans are being made about how to *play the game*. The notion of what it means to *play the game* is always contested and contextual. Moreover, the tendency to characterize teams as having a peculiar and special national approach to playing is as often confounded by a team's most celebrated players as it is confirmed by its lesser lights. Like the game itself, national teams change in their attitudes and style as the exigencies of time and talent take their toll.

Yet, as cricket's farcical roots show, English efforts to see a particular sport or way of playing the game as an incarnation of a national *Geist* is fraudulent; it smacks of the most blatant ideology making. In cricket's case, as Fraser shows, it had much to do with the colonial attitude and the mission to spread the English way of life and thinking to the "uncivilized masses" of the New World. As its varied historical roots show, English cricket neither had nor has more a corner on fair play than any other country. The game of cricket came to prominence in the late eighteenth century as an excuse and occasion, along with pigeon shooting and ballooning, for gambling among the English aristocracy. Indeed, as early as 1787 and well before most other sports that continue to dominate world interest today, the modern laws of cricket had been largely regularized in order to satisfy the interests of gamblers. It was only in the middle of the nineteenth century that cricket became the preserve of the snobbish amateurs of public-school education; its subtlety and sophistication were considered to be well beyond the vulgar grasp of the merchant class, let alone the vast uneducated masses. Its seedy past conveniently obscured, it was held up as the embodiment of all that was great and good about the Englishman and his sense of fair play. It was a gentleman's game that rather than serving as an escape from the responsibility of maintaining superior standards of behavior, crystallized that code and elevated it from a mere pastime to an art form—sport as spectacle had been born.[21]

In adopting this kind of approach, Fraser takes an openly nonfoundationalist (what he terms "postmodern") approach to not only the study of law and cricket but to their practice and performance. He eschews any attempt to provide universal or metatheoretical explanations: "There is nothing pre-ordained or immutable about the orderings we do make." Instead, he replaces analyses of objective explanation with narratives of contextual and situated understanding. In this way, he is better placed to emphasize the contingency of history and to show that matters do not end as they must but as they have done and will continue doing. Unlike many critical commentators, Fraser never lets his readers forget that the ideas of context and history have to be understood in a contextual and historical way. What it means to *play the game*, whether it is cricket or law, is entirely experiential and situated. It is not a matter of abstract reflection but a practice of situated engagement. As such, his ruminations on cricket, law, and life are fully situated in the rich details and unpredictable twists of social living. Accordingly, Fraser is adamant that one thing is certain about such social practices—they are uncertain in the sense that "it is not always clear what the 'correct' legal or ethical decision or outcome should be."[22] While it is their informing context that gives meaning to rules, those contexts themselves are not a reliable or fixed ground for conclusive interpretation; there is no context of contexts through which to delineate the precise extent of any particular context. Interpretation is always context-bound, and contexts are always interpretively unbounded.

At the heart of Fraser's perspective—it would be mistaken, of course, to call it a method or theory—is the belief that there is nothing beyond, below, or besides interpretation but more interpretation. There is no privileged route or resort to know what it means to *play the game*. It is only by playing the game of what it is to *play the game* that people can reach some understanding, albeit provisional and revisable, of what it means to *play the game*. It is in this sense that "interpretation is the only game in town . . . [and] there are no moves that are not moves in the game."[23] The laws of cricket and the laws of the land are bats and balls in the hands of the cricketing and lawyering community, to be used with as much dexterity and ingenuity as each player can muster in the game of what it is to *play the game*. Notwithstanding this, the players are not free to act or play in whatever way they choose; they must always work to persuade and convince others of their performative interpretations within the game as it is presently played. Indeed, Fraser maintains that interpretations of rules are both free and constrained at one and the same time: "The story of law and legal education and cricket depends for its content and meaning on our decisions about what to remember, underline, exclude, or elevate in our reading of the particular text and all other social texts of which it is a part."[24] As such, what it means to play the game cannot be appreciated separately from the history of what it means to *play the game.*

Throughout his presentation, Fraser demonstrates that the interpretive strategies and rhetorical tactics brought into play—rules, history, ethics, reason, authority, nationalism, and so on—are not merely opportunistic by the participants but represent some deeply held views about what it means to *play the game* in accordance with the rules. As such, Fraser's account is not a simplistic theory that depicts judges, umpires, and players as either robotic operatives or wanton manipulators. Instead, it shows that interest always affects interpretation and that any claim to neutrality is always tainted. More pointedly, it highlights how actually playing the game is never separate from interpretive games over what it means to *play the game.* A game is always within the *game.* It is not that one informs or limits the other; it is that they are both played together and through each other at the same time. In the same way that one can never step outside the sporting game and play only the interpretive game, one can never stay inside the sporting game and take no part in the interpretive game. In both cases, what it is to *play the game* is always part of the game.

It's Not Cricket

Fraser's insistence and instruction about the lessons that lawyers can learn about law from a study of cricket are compelling and cogent. In so many ways, he succeeds in his ambition "to demonstrate that cricket is a text upon which are inscribed signs from other texts and experiences (like law) and, at the same time, to show how the lessons we learn from cricket are inscribed in other parts of our lives." Moreover, his examination of cricket does much to recommend a nonfoundationalist approach to law (and all facets of life) as the most illuminating and useful way for students of the law to proceed: "Cricket encapsulates the texture of life itself. In every ball, every stroke, every catch, every over, we can see, know, understand and give meaning not only 'to the game' but to our lives."[25] Nevertheless, as powerful and liberating as this insight is, I do not believe that the analogy between cricket and life will take as much intellectual weight as Fraser places on it. At some important point and in some crucial ways, it is no longer liberating or helpful to insist on the analogical equivalence of cricket and life as mediated through law. Indeed, Fraser seems to have abandoned his nonfoundationalist affiliations at exactly the point where a rigorous resort to them would be most useful and revealing. While adjudication is a legal game of life, it is no more cricket than it is soccer: adjudication is its own game that is soccer, cricket, and much else besides. Adjudication is both less foundational and less finite than that.

For Fraser, the critical dynamic at the heart of playing cricket and doing law is the existential tension between freedom and restraint. Rejecting facile distinctions between these two competing forces, his hermeneutic approach is anchored on the acceptance that people are always situated within a context of freedom and restraint—that people are never fully restrained nor are they ever fully free. People give meaning to their lives in the constant struggle to negotiate and change the forces of freedom and restraint that frame their lives: people are freely restrained and restrainedly free. Like bat and ball, freedom and restraint are mutually dependent and each can only be made sense of in light of the other. However, as much as I agree with Fraser that "we are not condemned or restrained except when and if we participate in our own restraint," I cannot accept the full force of his constructivist claim that "when we begin to see law and life as cricket, we can begin to take control over the construction of meaning in our daily existence."[26] On the contrary, it is only if we begin to see law and life as not *only* cricket (or any other game) that we can begin to participate *fully* in the construction of meaning in daily existence. Indeed, the fact that life is seen as the same kind of game as cricket is one potent and disabling way in which, as Fraser might put it, people participate in their own restraint. Life and adjudication are equally playful, though not in exactly the same way as games like cricket and soccer.

Accordingly, adjudication is not so much one particular type of game as it is a shifting multiplicity of competing games. One way of making this point is to draw upon a distinction made by James Carse between "finite" and "infinite" games. In his aphoristic writings, he defines finite games as those that involve temporal, spatial, and numerical boundaries and in which the aim of the players is to bring the game to what amounts to a successful rule-defined conclusion. However, in infinite games, play is not as much defined by rules and boundaries because the very rules and boundaries themselves are always in play. Also, the aim is not to bring the game to an end but to keep everyone in play. Of course, the rules of finite games can change, but not during the course of the game. The difference between infinite and finite players is that the former have begun to disabuse themselves of the perceived necessity of particular rules and to realize that rules are more a contingent expression of existing agreement rather than a fixed basis for enforced agreement. This does not mean that participants are free to do as they wish: they are always participating within their extant context, which they must struggle to change as they play within its constraints. In this sense, change and restraint are as much matters of imagination and persuasion as anything else. As such, in the infinite game of life, the players are vulnerable because, taking a self-consciously fluid attitude, they are always open to change and, therefore, rejuvenation.[27]

Clearly, cricket and soccer are finite games. Like most sports, they only have meaning within a certain set of rules and boundaries. Of course, there is obvious disagreement about those rules, but such debate is cabined and usually marginal. There is little or no space for discussion over whether soccer players can pick up the ball and run with it or whether cricketers must run every time that they hit the ball. While these might be possible or desirable rule changes, the games being played would no longer be what is now known as soccer or cricket; they would be more like the different sports of rugby and baseball. Indeed, the (apocryphal) story of rugby being created when William Webb Ellis picked up the ball during the course of a soccer match at Rugby Boys' School is the stuff of nonfoundationalist adventure and experimentation.[28] Life, on the other hand, is an infinite game within which a changing series of finite games are played. While it is governed by rules and boundaries at any particular time, life is a game as much about playing with the rules as playing within them. For instance, unlike soccer and cricket, life can have meaning in spite of or in contravention of prevailing laws: civil disobedients or criminals are still in the game of life even if they are not willing to *play the game* the way that others decree. Moreover, life goes on regardless of the particular rules in play: its informing rules and its informed practice may be radically changed, but life itself, unlike the playing of cricket, will still go on.

Law is and is not much the same as cricket. Lawyers learn about the law not from a detached and cool reflection on its rules and intricacies but through an immersion in the personalities and performances that comprise the legal community's canon; legal education is as much about "making moves" as it is about the learning of particular substantive rules. Despite what many continue to teach, but few actually believe, there is never such a thing as simply applying the legal rule to the facts in an entirely logical or value-free way. While David Fraser drives that insight home with a power and grace that a juristic Donald Bradman, cricket's (arguably) greatest batsman, might envy, he has allowed his focus on cricket to blind him to its shortcomings as well as its strengths as a compelling analogy for life and law. As important as his insight is that "like all other games, cricket involves a tension between the game as 'game' and the 'game' as an embodiment of cultural lessons and broader messages," he has fallen short of his ambition "to see law and life as cricket."[29] Cricket is only one way, among many, of living and doing law. As compared with traditional explanatory accounts of law and life, the advantage of a nonfoundationalist narrative about politics is that it is a story that shows that matters do not end as they must but as they have done. Fraser uses this advantage to great critical effect. Unfortunately (or fortunately), in cricket there is too much *must* for his own deconstructive good. Fraser compromises on his nonfoundationalist commitment in treating adjudication as cricket—it is context all the way up and down, and that context will not and need not be cricket.

At different times and in different ways, law is both a finite and infinite game, or, to put it another way, finite episodes of adjudication take place within the infinite possibilities of law. In each dispute that comes before courts, there is a winner and a loser: one litigant is able to claim victory over another in terms of the actual, even though temporary, definition given to particular rules in their application to the specific facts found to be in play at that time. Nevertheless, the broader game of law and adjudication continues unabated; the result in the finite occasion of individual litigation is one strategic episode whose general act of rule application becomes open to revision and reformulation at the very moment that it brings to a close that particular instance of litigated rule making. Moreover, not only is adjudication a game in which the performance of earlier encounters cannot be perfectly or mechanically repeated without the need to make new choices in new circumstances, but the details of the game being played can vary from one litigated fixture to another. In law as in life, there is no one Game of games. While lawyers, judges, and litigants are never not in a game, they are not necessarily always playing the same game—sometimes it is cricket, sometimes baseball, and sometimes neither. Consequently, in a nonfoundationalist account of law and adjudication, as well as there being no definitive instruction on how to *play the game* or on whether playing in one way is better than another, there is no fixed or final understanding of which is the best game to be played at any particular time.

This distinction between infinite and finite games and the limitations of treating cricket and law as thoroughly similar begin to bite when the issue of how political and moral values operate in adjudication is considered. If life is treated as a game of cricket and, therefore, as a finite game of traditional probabilities, politics has a very limited practice and understanding. Only certain moves are possible, the order of practice is regularized, and change becomes marginal. By presenting the game of cricket as analogous with the play of law and life, Fraser thereby trivializes politics and imposes unnecessary restraints on both lawyering and living generally. No matter how glorious the game (political or sporting) might be, it checks people's political imagination and limits the practical alternatives available to them; there is only so much one can do with a bat and ball. Unfortunately, in seeing law and adjudication as *only* cricket, Fraser comes unintentionally close to backing himself into the corner of those recent prognosticators who maintain that political history has come to an end, that the competition among competing political games has played itself out, and that the game of liberal democracy has established itself as the game of life par excellence.[30] While Fraser would be horrified at such a prospect, his enthusiasm "to see law and life as cricket" puts him in such politically disreputable company.[31] In contrast, if law and life are treated not as a game of cricket but as infinite games of endless possibilities and performances, politics and, therefore, law and adjudication might be viewed more expansively and the transformative possibilities might be increased. At the least, judge and jurists might be expected to explain why they are playing cricket rather than some other game.

Within this nonfoundationalist frame of reference, the qualities of the great judicial players in law's language game are not so different from those that are exhibited by judges who are traditionally acknowledged as part of law's judicial pantheon. While good judges are lauded for their technical abilities in parsing, great judges are celebrated for their vision and inventiveness: "Dealing with great tasks as play . . . is a sign of greatness."[32] What made Holmes, Cardozo, Denning, and Wilson into great judges is much the same as what made George Best, Dick Fosbury, Olga Korbut, and Muhammad Ali into great players: it is not whether they somehow got it right but that they played with a panache, a style that caught the imagination and changed people's understanding of what the game is about. By making moves, they played the game as much with the rules as within the rules. Great judges recognize that law is not something to be mastered, but that it is an infinite game of transformation in which experimentation and improvisation are valued above predictability and faithfulness to existing rules and ideas of what it is to *play the game*. At its most audacious, great judging demands "the willingness to stay in play, stay with the flux, without bailing out at the last moment . . . [and] keeping alive that indefiniteness, that possible-who-knows-when, may be-soon, maybe-now, that sense of working on thin ice, without assurance, keeping the play in play, keeping the exposure to the abyss in play, without arresting or tranquillizing it."[33] When played by such gifted players, adjudication is neither a hubristic effort to bring the game to a perfect conclusion nor an irresponsible attempt to foment chaos; it is an infinitely variable process in which there is never any ultimate victory or performance, but only the repeated and unrepeatable working of the space between order and chaos, freedom and constraint, and permanence and contingency.

Being a game of infinite possibilities, adjudication only has the present shape and style that it has because judges are satisfied with its extant practice or are unwilling to change it. There is nothing about adjudication today that should be thought of as The Way Adjudication Really Is. At best, it only amounts to a contingent understanding of what it means to *play the game*. From a nonfoundationalist perspective, efforts to isolate and define the essence of adjudication are mistaken and unrealizable. For instance, many commentators consider that the hallmark of adjudication as a special type of dispute resolution is its mode of participation and resolution through reasoned argument.[34] This, of course, says little by way of explanation or limitation: there is still almost limitless space to argue and reason about what amounts to "reason" and what amounts to "argument." For instance, there is still considerable debate over whether it is necessary for reasons to be given by judges. While there is an expectation that judges will give reasons for their decisions, particularly when asked by the litigants or where there are strongly disputed questions of fact, a failure to do so is not considered to rob a decision of its legitimacy or validity as an adjudicative act. In the language of appellate review, a trial judge's failure to give reasons will not necessarily amount to a reversible error because "to require trial judges charged with heavy caseloads . . . to deal in their reasons with every aspect of every case would slow the system of justice immediately."[35]

In developing my own account of law and adjudication, all that I intend (or need) to do is to begin from present understandings about adjudication in order to suggest what it might mean to take its practice seriously in a nonfoundational way. Of course, this means that what passes for adjudication or reasoned argument in the future might bear little or no resemblance to its present or past understanding; it is not that "anything will go" but that "anything might go." The recent trend toward Alternative Dispute Resolution hints at the possibilities for change and transformation. Moreover, what counts as adjudication will depend upon what people are persuaded to accept as being a proper or appropriate way to *play the game*: it is a matter of social fact and persuasion—not conceptual analysis and demonstration. Although many jurists seem incapable or unwilling to imagine a society committed to democracy and social justice that does not place courts and judges at its political epicenter, it ought to take little effort or imagination to conceive of a political proposal or state of affairs in which adjudication (as presently understood) plays no (or, at least, a much reduced) part.[36]

Not Playing the Game

The suggestion that adjudication can best be understood and undertaken as a legal game of interpretive playfulness will not strike everyone as appropriate or useful. Some critics will maintain that such a depiction creates more problems than it solves. Accordingly, while the idea and practice of adjudication as a legal game in the play of life will be developed and defended throughout the book, it is important to tackle early some of the main objections that might commonly be made about games both as useful practices in themselves and as devices through which to understand adjudication. Three particular and significant objections easily spring to mind—that even if adjudication is best understood as a game, it is a practice that does not deserve to be treated as significant or central in the overall operation of law as a mode of social regulation; that the values that lie at the core of all games and what it means to play them well are antithetical to a full and progressive understanding of adjudication and its political possibilities; and that the representation of adjudication as a playful game trivializes both the nature of adjudication and the issues that are often at stake in law. While each of these objections has considerable merit, none is fatal to my jurisprudential project. Indeed, when located within a nonfoundational context of inquiry, they can be seen to strengthen rather than weaken the relevance and force of understanding adjudication as a game.

For many scholars, the study of adjudication has become the study of jurisprudence *tout court*. By virtue of the way in which they conceive the project of theoretical reflection, legal theorists have tended to place adjudication at the center of law. As Ronald Dworkin puts it, "[the American] concept of law ties law to the present justification of coercive force and so ties law to adjudication: law is a matter of right tenable in court."[37] However, many critics of this approach contend that the concentration on the work of courts is not justified. Drawing from the growing empirical literature on the social operation of law, it is argued that courts are not only minor players in the socio-legal game but that adjudication may actually hinder rather that enhance social change. Insofar as judicial decisions must combine with broader social forces to be effective, any potential victories can be quickly neutralized by bureaucratic inertia, political intransigence, and judicial complacency. In short, adjudication is a special social activity that does not so much alter the status quo as help to hold it in place: "It is not so much that the court is the natural expression of popular justice, but rather that its historical function is to ensnare it, control it and to strangle it, by re-inscribing it within institutions which are typical of a state apparatus."[38] Such scholars do not so much dismiss adjudication as unimportant altogether as insist that claims about its centrality must become both more modest and more sophisticated: what significance adjudication has has less to do with its functional effect and more to do with its symbolic impact.

There is much force to this critical caution about the social importance of adjudication. It takes little critical imagination to recognize that the widespread aspirations for a truly democratic society might be better achieved through a legal system that allocates less rather than more work to courts in formulating and implementing public policy. Indeed, much of my own writing has been directed toward challenging the overblown claims of traditional jurists about the social utility and political efficacy of adjudication as a vehicle for social change.[39] Nevertheless, the force of this criticism does not so much invalidate this book's focus on adjudication as work as a guard against the tendency to treat adjudication as the be-all and end-all of jurisprudential analysis. The raison d'être of studying adjudication-as-a-game is quite simple and modest—to the extent that the great bulk of contemporary jurisprudential writing is devoted to understanding what judges can, should, and actually do when they judge, I offer an account that I believe to be more compelling both as a descriptive and prescriptive matter. Because the whole framework of legal education and scholarship is likely to remain centered on the adjudicative process for some time to come, I believe that a more instructive account of adjudication is helpful and necessary. As such, therefore, I do not intend to analyze the historical importance of adjudication as a political force or the sociological significance of courts as a strategic site of transformation. Such studies are vitally important, and my focus on adjudication should not be read as an implicit downgrading of their worth.

The second objection to treating adjudication as a game is that the values that lie at the core of all games and what it means to play them well are antithetical to a full and progressive understanding of adjudication and its political possibilities. The most insistent of these claims come from Marxists and feminists. For the Marxist, games (and adjudication) tend to inculcate the repressive morality of bourgeois capitalism; the good player is seen to embody and celebrate "the cult of duty for its own sake, the sense of sacrifice for the community, the ideology of the super-ego, obedience, discipline, etc."[40] While there is considerable force to this objection in that many games do reinforce and reward such ideal performances of what it is to *play the game*, there is no reason why it must necessarily be that way. Like all activities, games are not essentially one thing or another in moral and political terms; they generate and reflect values that can be both good and bad, depending on the context and the emphasis. There is nothing in the idea or practice of most games that requires that the dubious values of unquestioning obedience to authority, extreme competitiveness, intimidation, win-at-all-costs mentality, gamesmanship, and the like become the best or only way to *play the game*: friendship, sportsmanship, grace, finesse, self-esteem are also qualities that can constitute another sense of what it means to *play the game*. In adjudication no less than games generally, there are almost an infinite number of ways in which to play the game and *play the game*.

Drawing on a similar vein of critique, feminists argue that games reaffirm the dominance of patriarchal values; the qualities of competitiveness, domination, and bravado are favored over other values and ways to *play the game.* Moreover, the fact that games (or, at least, the more feted ones) are played largely by men weighs heavily in any assessment of the merit of using game playing as a paradigmatic practice for the understanding of other activities, such as adjudication. Again, while this objection is entirely valid under present circumstances, it does not so much invalidate the comparison between games, like cricket and law, as reinforce the insight that there is no one fixed or essential way to *play the game.* Although much sport is male in personnel and performance, not all games are sports and not all sports need be masculine in their orientation. There is little about game playing that suggests that a limitation on the participation of women is necessary or the infusion of a different set of informing values and motivations is inherently objectionable. Like women's exclusion from law, their exclusion from games and their sense of what a good game or play is impoverish not only women's lives but also the games that are played without them. Excluding women from games and sports "blunts and deforms [their] potential human significance."[41] As special kinds of games, many sports do have a male bias in terms of the physical prowess required to succeed—such as speed, strength, size. However, many games are also relational in nature such that what you do or can become is affected by those you are in play with. However, the objective must be not only to include women within men's games but also to transform the way those games are played and to proliferate the different kinds of games that are played. In so doing, it might be possible to transform both male and female views about the (un)importance and potential of games as an activity and metaphor for living. Again, in law, the move toward Alternative Dispute Resolution is suggestive of these possibilities.

Once people are disabused of the patronizing idea that women play an inferior version of cricket or soccer, it might be possible to appreciate that women's sports are simply one more way—no better or worse but simply a different way—to *play the game.* As such, women's sports contribute to the diversity and richness of the game's tradition as they reconfigure its most ingrained and narrow rites. When applied to law as a language game, this feminist reorientation can serve as a truly nonfoundationalist challenge to the very idea as well as practice of sport and life. Accordingly, in the same way that I reject the view that all games are irretrievably male in substance and style, I reject the claim that "modern legal theory . . . is essentially and irretrievably masculine."[42] While it is clearly the case that vast tracts of law and legal theory are masculinist in content and ambition, it is not the case that they are essentially or unavoidably so. A nonfoundational approach forgoes sharp distinctions between male and female ways of playing. Instead, I argue for a more fluid and open perspective on the possible and varied ways to play the game. I draw extensively on the work of much feminist literature to challenge the rigidity of traditional legal ways of proceeding and to incorporate new and previously excluded ways of performance. Indeed, my analysis is energized and informed by such recent work in legal theory. Consequently, I do not reject out of hand the traditional modes of legal reasoning but insist that they must be supplemented and transformed by an approach that is more thoroughly contextual and experiential; all methods shape substance and can never be politically neutral.[43]

Finally, there is the claim (which, of course, is the exact converse of the first claim that the impact of adjudication has been vastly overstated) that the representation of adjudication as a playful game trivializes both the nature of adjudication and the human interests that are often at stake: law is neither a frivolous escape from reality nor an entertainment for the privileged few. This, of course, is not my intention at all. While I do not contend that play is a fundamental feature of human existence without which life is incomplete, I do maintain that, like art and science, game playing can be important as part of the creative process of meaning giving; it is a serious way of engaging in and making sense of the world. To those who contend that a view of politics as "playful impertinence" might be seen to be indulgent and offensive from the vantage point of those who live under economic and social oppression, there is no better response than that the practice of "politics as play" offers the most serious and pertinent challenge to such suffering. Under the view of law and life as an infinite game, play ceases to be only a pastime and relief from the grinding earnestness of life. Instead, it becomes an activity of living that is intended to permeate all situations of social interaction and that strives to "open political spaces for agonistic relations of adversarial respect."[44] Within these patches of instability, conflicts of power might be challenged and robbed of their absolute and final predetermination in a way that ordinary politics and finite games cannot reasonably aspire to achieve.

The view that game playing is trivial is based on the assumption that there is a grounded world of foundational pursuits from which game playing is a welcome diversion. This notion of game playing is limited. A nonfoundational approach does not restrict itself to the operation of law and adjudication; this is only one location for its corrosive application. Instead, it insists that the search for and sighting of solid foundations throughout all social practices is a flawed enterprise. In a manner of speaking, mindful that there is no Context of contexts, it is contexts all the way down. Consequently, an account of adjudication-as-a-game takes seriously the need to ensure that all the social culture of people's lives is a playful context that can be constantly reshaped and in which people can constantly reshape themselves. Far from trivializing law or life, adjudication-as-a-game seeks to enlarge the space in which otherness can be encompassed and explored. In a social setting in which freedom and constraint are continually renegotiated and resituated, it might be possible to achieve a precarious but exhilarating experience of personal empowerment through which people can confirm themselves in their humanity and its limitless possibilities. For such players, there is no established playbook or script of acceptable moves, and they openly see the role of citizen "as theatrical, its style as poses, its clothing as costumes, its rules as conventional, its crisis as arranged, its conflicts as performed, and its metaphysics as ideology."[45] In this sense, adjudication is a playful game in the fullest and most serious sense of the term.

None of this, of course, is intended to suggest that there would be an anarchic lack of standards in the playing of law or life that would lead to chaos; there would be new and changing standards that combine the playful and the serious in a defiantly pluralistic amalgam of style and substance. Such political and legal players are capable of imagining and opening themselves up to possibilities other than those presently available. They are not fated to always be players in another's game or to play according to another's understanding of what it means to *play the game*. Within such a nonfoundational understanding, injustice occurs when people's life-chances or sense of self depends not on making a better move or changing the game but on being prevented from participating in the game over what it means to *play the game*. Democracy is about play because it ought to be committed to maximizing everyone's opportunity to play and replay life's game; it labels as unjust that which "prohibits that the question of the just and unjust be, and remain, raised."[46] People who are truly political are those who are empowered by their recognition that rules are always up for grabs and their struggles to change them are part of the essential fluidity of life. In such a society, the game playing of politics is not something that people care to do but something that people always live. By understanding adjudication as an infinite game whose performance both determines and is determined by the prevailing rules of play, a nonfoundational account ensures that its insights are far from trivial.

A Nonfoundational Understanding

The main thrust of my arguments so far has been that if adjudication is to be understood as a game, it must be done so in a thoroughly nonfoundationalist way. While I have suggested the general imperatives and implications of such an approach, I have not attempted to provide a structured or comprehensive statement of what is involved in such a philosophical commitment. In part, this is deliberate, not only because there are as many kinds of nonfoundational approaches as there are nonfoundationalists, but also because what amounts to a nonfoundationalist account of any particular subject is characteristically always open to question. Nevertheless, it would no doubt be helpful if I at least offered a short, albeit rather basic, introduction to some of the central claims that are commonly associated with such a general theoretical stance as they relate to law, politics, and adjudication. Of course, different writers do not necessarily subscribe to them all; nor do they explain them in exactly the same way or with the same emphasis. In short, in contrast to the implicit (and occasionally explicit) foundationalist conceit of traditional jurists, I want to initiate a shift from epistemology to politics by way of a nonfoundational critique.

If a nonfoundational approach has any particular hallmark, it is a thoroughgoing skepticism toward the belief that there are any essential, final, or foundational truths. Nonfoundational proponents join a flat rejection of universal knowledge with an outright denial of the existence of essential truths. In contrast to the foundationalist project, this approach begins with an implacable incredulity toward grand theories of social explanation and meta-narratives of ultimate knowledge. Rather than think of the individual as a unitary and sovereign subject whose inherent vocation is to bring the world to heel through the exacting discipline of rational inquiry, nonfoundationalists interrogate the whole idea of autonomous subjectivity and abstract reason by situating them within a continuing and contingent provisionality. Of course, this does not obliterate the experience of subjectivity nor the availability of reason, but it problematizes them in order to understand them as being multiple, contextual, and protean. Subjects and reason can never be entirely self-present in an unmediated and unsituated form. There is no escape from the historical fluidity of social living to the foundational imperatives of Destiny, History, Progress, Nature, Truth, or Whatever. In short, knowledge is always fragmentary, and truths are always plural. Subjects and reasons abound, but there is no Subject or Reason that can possess Knowledge or Truth.

It is not that truth is dispensed with entirely in the nonfoundationalist project but that different notions of truth are encouraged for the benefit of an intellectual endeavor that is nondogmatic and experimental. A nonfoundational perspective takes seriously the idea that truth is forever beholden to the discursive regimes through which it is apprehended and validated. Concepts such as truth, coherence, and objectivity are best understood as internal to historical debate over theory and not as some external set of discursive categories available to validate any such debate. Theorizing is not an escape to some realm of pure thinking but rather an effort to understand the social entanglement and situation of thinking itself. Neither detached nor impartial, truth always takes a stand and cannot be innocent of its informing context. Truth is not the reward of those who have taken to philosophical flight. It is of this world: it only makes sense in the sociohistorical context of power in which it arises. As such, the value of truth is never denied by nonfoundational critics, but it is always contextualized within a complex and fluid structure of sociohistorical arrangements for establishing and justifying power relations. As Derrida puts it, "The question can be raised, not whether a politics is implied (it always is), but which politics is implied in . . . a practice of contextualization."[47] Accordingly, the point of the nonfoundationalist exercise is to reveal the constant relation between economies of power and the production of truth: it is not to escape the context of power and speak from nowhere but to recognize the constraints of somewhere and confront the protocols of power.

Always attentive to its social situation and historical location, a nonfoundationalist approach harbors a deep mistrust of generalizations and encourages a preference for particularity. As Lyotard puts it, there is a need to cultivate "an incredulity towards meta-narratives," whether they are about History, Reason, Truth, Coherence, Reality, Oppression, Identity, or Whatever.[48] This is particularly the case in regard to Law. This docs not mean that those who adopt a nonfoundationalist approach disbelieve everything: this is as absurd as suggesting that absolutists believe everything. They have beliefs about history, reason, truth, coherence, reality, oppression, identity, or whatever, but they hold them in a conditional and provisional way. A nonfoundationalist denial of an absolute Truth is not tantamount to a commitment to a solipsistic relativism. Being nonmetaphysical rather than antimetaphysical, a nonfoundationalist stance does not reject the possibility of rational choice entirely, but it does abandon the belief that it can be rational in the sense of Right or Final. Instead, nonfoundationalists maintain that the rationality of discursive arrangements can only be validated by engaging with and through those arrangements rather than by claiming to retreat to an illusory vantage point outside of social history. More to the point, nothing is lost by this acknowledgment. A desultory nihilism is the bête noire of an unabashed absolutism: they are the Siamese twins of metaphysics.

Indeed, a nonfoundational critique rejects nihilism and relativism as much as absolutism; each suggests that truth and meaning can be understood apart from the customary, extant procedures of discursive justification. While the absolutist looks beyond society and its language to the imagined nature of things, the relativist reduces knowledge to the private opinion of particular persons. Whereas the relativist adopts a correspondence theory of truth, the nonfoundationalist does not claim to have a theory of truth, let alone a relativistic one. The desire for objectivity is nothing more (and nothing less) than the wish for the greatest possible intersubjective agreement and human cooperation. Such skeptics are not hoist by their own metaphysical petard, because "not having *any* epistemology, *a fortiori* [they do] not have a relativistic one."[49] Many foundationalists, of course, remain unpersuaded by this argument. They contend that such historicist claims for the truth of nonfoundationalism refute themselves because, contrary to their protestations, such skeptics do assume at least the absolute truth of their own skepticism. Yet this response begs the question. The charge that nonfoundationalism is thereby self-refuting presupposes the possibility of objective foundations for judgment that nonfoundationalist critics deny. Nonfoundational skeptics want to dispense with the privileged vocabulary of accuracy and representation, not retain it, replacing it with more prosaic standards of usefulness and acceptability.[50] For those who take a nonfoundationalist approach, there is no real difference between truth and what passes for truth. Their account of truth, not being metaphysical, is not about its approximation or correspondence to a transcendent order; nor is it a unique attribute of something. Truth does not exist apart from the social practices in which these assessments are made and understood. In this sense, there is "nothing more to the truth (the 'being true') of the occasional truth than the historical fact that there is an economy of knowledge in which what is said passes for true."[51] It would be absurd to deny that things pass for true or claim that nothing can pass for true—that is the true and absurd fate of the nihilist. Such an understanding about truth involves more than idiosyncratic belief because to "pass for true" something has to have an intersubjective and dialogic quality. Moreover, it is still possible to talk about "telling the truth" because it remains morally dubious to claim that something is true when it is believed not to be true. As such, the nonfoundational understanding of truth is practical and political in that it allows for reliance and change in sufficient measure to meet the democratic needs of a functioning society. Like water, though, truths move and reconfigure themselves as different historical currents and social agents pass through them: truths are in constant flux, not static at the water's edge.

Of course, an uncompromising nonfoundational perspective is skeptical about all things, especially skepticism itself. In a manner of speaking, nonfoundationalists are skeptical about what to be skeptical about; they hold beliefs about truth but in a skeptical and conditional way. Although their skepticism is general, it is also particularized in that it attaches to and permeates particular beliefs. Nonfoundational knowing is not about apprehending essence but about being convinced to hold a belief even while believing that belief is itself contingent and provisional. A primary task of nonfoundationalists, therefore, is not the search to fix truth but to establish convictions about rightness in certain contexts. These convictions and values are important and deeply held. However, as they are not the culmination of metaphysical revelation or epistemological refinement, the recognition of convictions must not become the basis for a hierarchy of principles deployed to adjudge the validity of other beliefs. While the holding of some beliefs as convictions is largely unavoidable, the ground—that constellation of partly sensed and barely articulated beliefs that are presently held—for making choices and decisions is always shaky. Accordingly, nonfoundationalists claim no deep knowledge that others lack; they offer only more and less useful beliefs about the way things are.

Accordingly, to be thoroughly nonfoundational, critics must resist the constant temptation of a philosophical nostalgia in which a lost age of idealistic certainties is sentimentalized. Instead, they must celebrate the fact that the notion of truth has been released from its metaphysical shackles and that truths are now open to human determination by specific people and specific historical circumstances. In the nonfoundationalist vocabulary, truth is no longer the ultimate value because it "has no power of its own, no utopian potential, no affinity for good, and will not make us free."[52] Like all other values, it must prove itself useful to the human project of improved social justice; what follows from truth is more important than what it is. Consequently, criticism is not an act of demonstration and revelation in an unfolding monologue of Truth and Knowledge validated from outside itself, but it is rather an exercise in rhetoric and persuasion in an active dialogue of competing voices that is grounded on its own terms within the debate itself.[53] This, of course, is a somewhat daunting process; it holds the prospect of tyranny as much as empowerment. While it is impossible to speak in the name of Truth, a more relevant and effective challenge is to relate what passes for truth to the present hegemonic practices that sustain it and are sustained by it. With this nonfoundational shift in theoretical focus, however, it might become possible to work toward a more democratic context in which all people can organize what is true for them or, at least, have a say in what is to pass for truth. Power is not resisted on behalf of or in the name of some absolute Freedom or essential Subject but in the political cause of alternative dispersions of power representing different freedoms and different selves. To recognize that power is everywhere is not to breed a social fatalism; it is intended to energize a political task that puts power forever under scrutiny. By deploying skeptical strategy, the political hope is to destabilize power, displace domination, and dismantle hierarchy.

It is important at this point to register and refute a possible criticism that might be brought against this nonfoundational account of the philosophical enterprise. Underlying my discussion is the important claim that there is something significant at stake in settling upon the appropriate role and status of legal theory. In short, I maintain that philosophy matters, but only provided that it is understood and practiced with a nonfoundational orientation. The critical rejoinder to this is that the larger questions of the law's philosophic or epistemic foundations have never been of much concern to jurists and judges. Contrary to Holmes's view that "theory is the most important part of the dogma of the law, as the architect is the most important person who takes part in the building of a house,"[54] lawyers and theorists do not choose the larger background theory against which they operate. Moreover, it is not that there are judges and jurists who, if only persuaded of their mistaken theoretical choice of foundationalism, would change in any significant way what they were actually doing as judges and jurists. Indeed, it might be suggested that I adopt an internally contradictory stance that takes a foundational approach to the worth and implications of a nonfoundational stance—arguing as if philosophy mattered, I argue that philosophy does not matter and then conclude that changing a philosophy will matter. Relying on the insights of Stanley Fish, it could be suggested that I fail to appreciate that legal theory has no implications for legal practice and that, although desperate to resist the foundationalist contagion, I perpetuate the foundationalist claim that theory matters.

If accurate, this is a powerful and debilitating critique. However, while I believe that this theory-has-no-consequences critique must be taken very seriously, it is wide of the mark as a criticism of my nonfoundationalist account. I am committed to the nonfoundational stance that nothing *will or must* follow from a nonfoundationalist approach to philosophy or law. However, I do believe that something *might* follow, depending on the particular practical context in which the critique is made. It is neither the case that changing philosophy always does nothing nor that changing philosophy always does something: what effects a particular way of thinking about philosophy will have is an empirical or political question. I agree that theory has no necessary or predictable consequences as a matter of theory, but maintain that it will likely have some consequences as a matter of practice; what those consequences will be, what their extent will be, and what their political spin will be will depend on the prevailing dynamics of the sociopolitical context. As such, in the present political circumstances of contemporary law and adjudication, I believe that the theoretical critique *might* (but only might) have significant consequences. In this sense, therefore, I insist that it is much more significant and interesting to ask in what contexts does a nonfoundational argument happen to lead to more play in judging and by what strategies might it be possible to facilitate such experimentation.[55]

Ironically, I believe that this nonfoundational position is also what Fish intended. Admittedly, there is a good deal of (deliberate?) uncertainty about what Fish is and is not claiming. His basic and typically contrarian claim is that there can be no position of theoretical innocence and that any theoretical position has no particular consequences for practice. As all interpretation is convention-bound, especially the debate over the interpretive conventions themselves, critics and readers can never escape to some nonconventional or theoretical grounds from where to map the conventional terrain. Moreover, he argues that nothing "turns on" his or anyone else's account of the relevant interpretive conventions. Theory as a generalized scheme to guide or reform practice is superfluous, for it is always and already "the helpless plaything of the practice it claimed to inform." For Fish, all attempts to construct theories, even purportedly antitheoretical ones, necessarily arise in concrete political settings. Any theory, therefore, "cannot help but borrow its terms and its content from that which it claims to transcend, the mutable world of practice, belief, assumptions, points of view and so forth."[56] While critics have latched on to his theory-has-no-consequences critique, they have overlooked the crucial riders that Fish attaches. Indeed, without these riders, Fish's insistence that "theory has no consequences" would itself be an example of the dogmatic kind of theoretical fiat that he is at pains to reject and invalidate.

For Fish, it is absolutely imperative that it be understood that his theory-has-no-consequences claim is itself a theoretical claim. He insists that any theoretical claim, including his own and any antitheoretical claim, does not matter in any necessary or purely theoretical way; all theory is a kind of practice and therefore only has consequences as a practice. What Fish does not say is that theory might not have any consequences at all. Unfortunately, Fish is almost begrudging in conceding that theory might well have consequences but that they will be political and contingent: "Theory goes nowhere (except in the wholly contingent ways of all rhetorics)." His most important claim, therefore, is not that theory has no consequences but that it might have very definite consequences as a rhetorical matter of contingent and political circumstances: "When theory has consequences, they will be rhetorical, not theoretical." Fish has hit upon an important nonfoundational insight but has downplayed its full force and meaning. It is not that with exposure of theory's lack of theoretical consequences, "nothing whatsoever will have been gained, and we will have lost any sense that theory is special." Rather, this loss and its revelation would have massive significance for the legal and governmental process: there may be no Supreme Court of legal theory, but there is a Supreme Court of law. Because legal theory is a prestigious feature of adjudication and law, challenges to prevailing theories might have a significant impact upon legal and judicial practice. The constitutional authority and prestige of the judiciary depends, at least in part, on the continuing belief by the community, including judges themselves, that judges are not simply ideologues at large but are, in some significant sense, constrained by the appropriate legal materials. As such, judges rely extensively on theory to preserve, disguise, and enhance their political power. Accordingly, while legal theory generally has no consequences as a theoretical matter, a nonfoundational critique "can be consequential in relation to configurations of interest and power already in place."[57]

For instance, legal discourse empowers certain speakers by granting them a license to establish meaning. In this sense, power protects itself by rendering its aspiring usurpers mute or, when it allows them to speak, by putting words in their mouths and depriving their words of significance. Most speakers whistle into the institutional wind, but a small few are privileged to speak with that wind at their backs. For instance, the force and meaning of the statement "you have broken the contract" is far from self-evident. It depends on an appreciation of and immersion in a whole sociohistorical context. Much will depend on the identity of the speaker: a statement's truth and force will increase proportionately with the speaker's authoritative status. In contemporary circumstances, its meaning will change and gain in communal strength depending on whether the speaker is an interested party, an officious bystander, a fledgling lawyer, a local politician, a law professor, a trial judge, an enacting legislator, or a Supreme Court justice.

In an important sense, therefore, I still maintain that there is some political force to the "Emperor's New Clothes" line of critique. Without some justificatory theoretical apparel, judges and jurists might be seen to stand naked or, perhaps more accurately, their uniforms in official establishment colors might be revealed for all to see. By declining to acknowledge the strength of theory's possible political consequences, Fish has designed and added his own diaphanous raiment to the Imperial collection. In contrast, I take the gamble that people, when made aware that the authority of others rests only on their own willingness to suspend critical judgment, might begin to assume responsibility for their own decisions and rely less on the putative authority of others. In the same way that a defense of foundationalism might in current circumstances tend to shore up the fragile authority of courts and their decisions, so might the critique of foundationalism tend to challenge them. In democracies, the claim that unrepresentative and unaccountable bodies are acting "politically, not legally," can be an important maneuver and *might* have important political consequences for the body and the citizenry. Of course, there is no guarantee that this will lead to any "progressive" changes or any agreement on what counts as a "progressive" change, but it might at least disturb the status quo and open up more opportunities for change. Disabused of foundationalist pretensions, judges and jurists *might* be less able to convince people and themselves that things must remain as they are or can only change in certain ways. None of these conclusions is made as a matter of theory or philosophy, but only as possible empirical outcomes and political observations in particular settings.

When understood in this way, the role of philosophers and, particularly, legal theorists in the nonfoundationalist project is not obsolete. As practical and political intervenors, they must abandon the long-standing belief that their worth and prestige derive from and depend on "knowing something about knowing which nobody else knows so well."[58] The notion that moral and social progress depends on unearthing the metaphysical bedrock of human existence and law has to be rejected. Such excavations are futile and feckless. Their alleged foundations are always contestable and contingent: their authority and meaning are part of, not apart from, the inquiry that they are intended to ground. The question, then, of how people should live or think about law is not a methodological puzzle of abstract dimensions but a substantive challenge of historical proportions. There is neither universal Truth nor suprahistorical Knowledge but a string of truth claims that establish a cluster of social practices through which knowledge is generated and by which it can be assessed in terms of its functions and usefulness. However, legal philosophers need not be shown the democratic door. Their work still has value provided that its insights are treated as rhetorical interventions in a continuing democratic conversation, not as authoritative conversation stoppers regarding eternal verities. Throughout the book, therefore, I suggest the different shapes and directions that the jurisprudential project might take if it were to be fired by the democratic imagination rather than instructed by the philosophical mind.

Once the blinkers of traditional epistemology have been removed, philosophers are more free to engage in a more open-ended conversation about the same matters. Their importance lies in developing alternative modes of discourse, so that philosophy comes to be less about efforts to legitimate existing claims to truth and more about attempts to encourage different ways of thinking. Based upon a hermeneutics of suspicion, philosophy might help to sweep away the confining limits of traditional epistemology and to open up spaces in which engaged and creative conversation can take place. Ever experimenting with new forms of knowledge, it might help persuade people to abandon the lingering attachment to a metaphysics of certainty. Rather than lay down authoritative blueprints for political or legal action in the name of some universal truth about the human condition or law, philosophers can seek out new possibilities and alternative openings, helping to unseat the belief that present sociohistorical arrangements are inevitable and frozen in place. In this way, philosophy and jurisprudence might become more a discourse of dissent than a monologue of reverence. Such a nonfoundationalist approach to law and life is the best complement to the aspirations of a plural and democratic society.[59] Once epistemology has lost authority, mob rule will not fill the theoretical void. Empowered with a new vocabulary, citizens might be able to reclaim authority over their own lives and participate more effectively in the civic elaboration of truths. Within such a nonfoundationalist society, jurists will not strive to reveal the essence of Law or Social Justice but will recognize that justice is nurtured in the hearts and minds of democratic citizens, where it was previously held hostage to epistemological fortune and languished for lack of articulate expression.

In a nonfoundationalist culture, the difference between, on the one hand, physicists and poets and, on the other, lawyers and politicians is sociological, not philosophical or methodological. The difference between knowledge and opinion is that between beliefs around which no community deviance is permitted and those around which community deviance is permitted. Indeed, Rorty suggests that the (legal) philosopher should imitate the poet rather than the physicist. As there is only language with which to understand language, there is no nonreferential escape to The Way Things Really Are: no form of life stands apart from language such that it can validate life, authenticate language, or vouchsafe reality. Relying on imagination, the jurist might seek to poeticize, not rationalize, culture and challenge the stereotypes and reductive thinking that help to limit human achievement. Life's rich ambiguity is not to be mastered but to be marveled at. In a world of incorrigible contingency, intellectuals must strive to rid themselves of the desire for an apocalyptic break with the past and the need to find a final vocabulary that would have the last word in humanity's conversation with history. Too often, radical critics turn out to be traditional metaphysicians in historicists' clothing. In contrast, the nonfoundationalist's challenge is to proliferate "an expanding repertoire of alternative descriptions rather than The One Right Description" and to celebrate the refusal "to play by the rules of someone else's final vocabulary."[60]

In this nonfoundationalist account, traditional modes of philosophy fail in the sense that there is no privileged ground that can account for or be taken as knowledge or meaning. The point is not to set poetry or rhetoric against philosophy but to show that philosophy is one form of rhetoric and that rhetoric is another form of philosophy. The general sense of rhetoric and poetry is that they amount to "artificial eloquence." However, in the nonfoundationalist vocabulary, their meaning goes back to its classical roots and implies the art of cogently presenting ideas and arguments in a way that does not insist upon their own superiority. As such, a nonfoundationalist approach is not a method or a program to replace the tradition of epistemology: it is more an opening of a space in which rhetoric and conversation can obtain.[61] A move to rhetoric would not dispense with the insights of philosophy but would require them to earn their spurs within a rhetorical exchange rather than claim them as revelatory truths. In such a poetic vision, reality is not the stuff of hard science: it is whatever is easily accepted as reality by people. Rather than seek to cabin and control reality, as philosophy does, rhetoric works within reality as it strives to rework itself and that reality. It is persuasion and, therefore, politics that drive discourse, not verification or falsification. As Fish characteristically expresses it, all rhetorical constructions are not equal, only equally rhetorical.[62] And this is doubly so for law, adjudication, and their operation.

Conclusion

In this chapter, I have sought to introduce and defend the idea that adjudication can best be understood as a game. Like most games, adjudication has a special character and style of its own. Like many games, judges play the dual role of player and referee—they officiate at the same time that they play. However, in contrast to the foundationalist ambitions of traditional jurists, the version of judging that I put forward maintains that law cannot be grounded in anything more ordered or scientific than the changing routines of its own prosaic practices as sites of political engagement. Because its operative conventions are not formally recorded and are practice-based, the ethos of the game of judging is never fixed or grounded. It is a game about playing with both the formal rules of law and the informal conventions that govern how those formal rules are to be interpreted. The great strength and appeal of thinking about adjudication in this way as a serious practice of playfulness, therefore, is that it captures the flow and movement of the common law. Each new performance is unique in that it can never simply repeat what has gone before. Moreover, what it means to *play the game* is as fluid as the play of the game itself. The values that the game of adjudication embodies and inculcates are contextual in that they take on meaning and are transformed through the playful practice of judging itself. Adjudication is a game that can be both disciplined and improvisational, competitive and cooperative, and constrained and creative in varying measures.

In presenting adjudication as a special kind of nonfoundational game, the account that I offer emphasizes two important features of its playful practice. First, adjudication is a language game in that it is played both through and with language: judges shape and are shaped by the discursive regimes that comprise law and the reality that it helps to make possible. Second, I place great weight on the fact that the language game of adjudication is played within a social and historical context that is never static but is always moving: while judges are never not in the game, there is no one Game of games. When these two features are understood in tandem, it becomes possible to grasp the full extent to which adjudication (and juristic efforts to explain and criticize it) is a truly nonfoundational game in both present performance and future possibility. I resist the traditional and hubristic view that judges and legal theorists are heirs to a foundationalist tradition. It is "as if all of a sudden [judges and jurists] had fallen in very deep water" of political conflict and realized that their only options were to "make certain of setting [their] feet on the bottom" or "swim and so support [themselves] on the top" by using language as a ground by which to walk on water.[63] Instead, I insist that as it is fluid contexts all the way down and around, the search for solid ground must be abandoned and replaced by efforts to adapt to a watery existence. It is to this idea of adjudication as a language game of contingent character and what that involves that I now turn.

3 The Language Game: From Ambiguity to Indeterminacy

The game of doubting itself presupposes certainty.

—Ludwig Wittgenstein, *On Certainty*

The fact that law is a language is no longer considered to be a revelatory observation. However, jurists were relatively slow to pursue the philosophical implications of this insight. The first and still most important jurist to pick up on this view was H. L. A. Hart, who offered a jurisprudential account that is derived from a particular understanding of law and adjudication as a language game. Hart's work was informed by the Wittgenstein imperative that good philosophy was simply making sense of people's daily linguistic practices and that the key to understanding was through the idea of language games. Wittgenstein's (later) view was that language consists of "countless" language games that are not "fixed, given once and for all" but that new ones "come into existence, and others become obsolete and get forgotten." However, he also argued that language itself is a game and, therefore, an activity that takes on shape and substance as a result of its social context: "The term 'language-*game*' is meant to bring into prominence the fact that the *speaking* of language is part of an activity, or of a form of life."[1] In line with this Wittgensteinian observation, adjudication can be thought of as a particular language game that takes place within the larger language games of law and society.

Working with Hart's mature theory, I will follow through, more fully than he did, on Wittgenstein's primary insight that legal language is a game of social activity that depends on convention and context for meaning. In particular, I will argue that because convention and context are never historically stable and always socially contestable, the meaning and application of legal rules cannot be put beyond the possibility of disputation or the need for defense. As such, the practice of adjudication becomes an incorrigibly indeterminate and political exercise. In defending this view of law and adjudication, I will not take Hart's theory lightly but actually will take more seriously than he did his remark that "rules cannot provide for their own application, and even in the clearest case a human being must apply them."[2] Viewing Hart from a nonfoundationalist perspective, I resist the claim that there is an abiding core meaning to rules that can be located and relied upon in applying them. While there is always a topical distinction between the core of a rule's meaning and its penumbral uncertainty at any particular moment, this relation between core and penumbra is contingent and cannot provide the stability and fixity that its proponents suggest and require; yesterday's penumbra might be today's core, which might be tomorrow's penumbra. People bring different experiences to rules and, therefore, interpret and follow them differently: there is no uniformity of experience and, therefore, no uniform experience of what is entailed in following a particular rule in a particular situation.

Accordingly, this chapter explains a nonfoundationalist account of law and adjudication as a language game. After introducing Hart's positivistic account of adjudication, I unearth the linguistic footings of Ordinary Language philosophy on which Hart built his juristic edifice. Next, I shift the critical emphasis from Hart's concern with "textual ambiguity" to a more radical exposure of law's "structural indeterminacy." Combining the ideas of Jacques Derrida with those of Ludwig Wittgenstein, I insist that it is insufficient to contextualize language without also recognizing the instability of all contextualizations. By reference to an extended doctrinal illustration, I show how law operates as a discursive framework through which to comprehend and construct the reality that lawyers take for granted as the ground for their own language games. Finally, the chapter closes with a return to Hart's theory of adjudication and its central idea of rule application in an attempt to drive home the subversive consequences of a nonfoundationalist account of language. Throughout the chapter, I emphasize that adjudication is best understood as an interpretive game in which the constraints are both always in place and never themselves outside of interpretation.

The Hart of the Matter

Throughout Hart's diverse oeuvre, the connecting thread is his positivistic insistence that law and morality are best kept separate if the study of either is to be profitable and instructive. Consequently he developed an account of adjudication that focuses upon the operation and limits of rule application as a method of legal decision making—how is it possible to get beyond a discredited formalism without turning judging into an open-ended exercise in ideological wrangling? In answering this question, Hart's concern is not with the internal perspective of how and why lawyers (and citizens) do what they do in particular legal cultures but with that of an external observer of law and legal systems generally. However, while he accepts that theorists need not endorse the viewpoint of participants in the system to be understood, he does recognize that it is essential that theorists record the participants' normative views and commitments: "Description may still be description, even when what is described is an evaluation."[3]

As such, although his theoretical stance is resolutely external, Hart's positivism is of a *soft* variety. He does not maintain that the truth of legal propositions is reducible to bare historical facts, but he acknowledges that values can be fully implicated: "The existence and content of law can be identified by reference to the social sources of law . . . without reference to morality except where the law thus identified has itself incorporated moral criteria for the identification of law." Within these positivistic parameters, Hart depicts law as a functional and sophisticated system of rules—the obligation-imposing primary rules that comprise the bulk of substantive legal doctrine, like criminal and contract law, and the authority-conferring secondary rules that distribute institutional power and jurisdiction, between legislatures and courts for example, over the creation and enforcement of the primary rules. In both cases, in keeping with his general theoretical perspective, Hart insists that rules had to be distinguished from merely observable regularities of behavior. For participants in the system, rules operate "as the basis for claims, demands, admissions, criticism, or punishment," and "the violation of a rule is not merely a basis for the prediction that a hostile reaction will follow but a *reason* for hostility."[4] Without reference to this internal attitude that lawyers and citizens exhibit toward rules, a vital element of jurisprudential understanding would be lost. In the Hartian scheme of things, therefore, a cogent explanation of legal obligation is as much about attitude and acceptance as it is about fate and fiat.

Against this analytical backdrop, Hart developed a reasoned and reasonable account of modern judging that unashamedly sought to inhabit a middle ground between formalist pitfalls and realist excesses. By seeking to avoid both the realist nightmare in which "judges always make and never find the law" and the formalist dream that "they never make it,"[5] he wanted to ensure that legal theory would abandon some of its more recent nocturnal fantasies so that legal practice would be able to get on with its day job in a refreshed and undistracted way. Hart's patented jurisprudential formula for a legal good night's sleep is prosaic and pragmatic. Because judges are empowered to apply rules in order to resolve disputes between conflicting citizens, the hallmark of "good" judges is their ability to identify the extant rules of the legal system and apply them to concrete situations. Nonetheless, this craft is not a purely technical or logical exercise. In a famous phrase, Hart argued that law has an "open texture." Because law, like language, is an entirely conventional affair in which convention is neither gapless nor precise, this system of rules cannot be complete or comprehensive: some cases, therefore, will be "not merely . . . controversial in the sense that reasonable and informed lawyers may disagree about which answer is legally correct, but the law is fundamentally *incomplete*."[6] Consequently, these so-called hard cases will invoke and require nonconventional decision-making processes. In fulfilling their duties, judges have to call on a variety of analytical skills and reasoning techniques: they act inductively when they extract rules from a line of past cases; they act deductively when they apply the inductively extracted rule to the case in point; and they act politically when the inductively extracted rule or its deductive application is uncertain or difficult. In this unpretentious account of judging, indeterminacy is an inescapable aspect of the judicial task, but it is always relative, marginal, and not to be exaggerated.

The first stage of Hartian adjudication is the inductive extraction of the appropriate rule; this is the precedential soul of the common law. Although there are "a vast number of determinate rules" and this exercise will be productive of "very little doubt," Hart concedes that "any honest description" will recognize considerable leeway for judicial involvement. Consequently, even at this first stage, indeterminacy is a characteristic feature of the adjudicative process—there is no one correct or authoritative method for determining the relevant precedent from among the many competing lines of cases, the rule for which a particular precedent stands, the precise verbal formulation of that rule, or the exceptions to that rule. As the history of the common law reveals, a flexible practice develops to soften the rigid theory of responsible adjudication. Also, Hart uses *rules* to encompass all the norms and standards that judges refer to and call in aid when determining the law and its application. For him, rules are a generic category of legal resource and principles are only a special and limited type: the difference between "all-or-nothing rules and nonconclusive principles . . . is a matter of degree."[7] Any contrast between rules and principles is only made to emphasize that certain legal standards function in slightly different ways in terms of weight and specificity. Hart maintains that nothing hangs on this distinction as regards the operation and legitimacy of adjudication.

Having formulated the relevant rule (and its exceptions) with sufficient precision, the judge must then set about applying that rule to the facts of the case. This is the dynamic hub of the judicial undertaking. Neither absolute faith in the dispositive force of rules nor arbitrary disregard of them is part of the Hartian dialectic. While rule application is not a purely mechanical or logical operation, a genuine commitment to its consistent practice means that "human conduct is made in some sense non-optional or obligatory." To apply a rule is not to make routine recourse to the consequences that attend such an application. Whenever one regularly does so, Hart argues that it undermines the practice and legitimacy of rule application generally: the judge ceases to be engaged in rule application but is instead making a post hoc resort to the rule as a justification for a particular consequence that is compatible with the rule and that is not offensive as a matter of justice. For Hart, although an attention to consequences may be required in some cases, this is better done openly rather than under the pretense of rule application:

> None the less, the life of the law consists to a very large extent in the guidance both of officials and private individuals by determinate rules which, unlike the applications of variable standards, do not require from them a fresh judgment from case to case. This salient fact of social life remains true, even though uncertainties may break out as to the applicability of any rule (whether written or communicated by precedent) to a concrete case. Here at the margin of rules and in the fields left open by the theory of precedents, the courts perform a rule-producing elaboration of variable standards.[8]

While the parameters and sources of this rule-producing responsibility have varied across the Hartian canon, Hart's mature advice was that this power to legislate interstitially is not to be performed in a vacuum or done in an arbitrary or ideological way. When legal rules fail or run out, judges are not somehow out on their own but are subject to "a wide variety of individual and social interests, social and political aims, and standards of morality and justice" that are encompassed in the working norms of legal doctrine. Indeed, it is the development and refinement of these "criteria of relevance and closeness of resemblance . . . [that] characterize whatever is specific or peculiar in legal reasoning." While there is no uniquely correct result, judicial choice is a rational and constrained process in which "many decisions can be clearly ruled out as incorrect,"[9] and in which the failure to ensure real or idealized unanimity among judges is not fatal.

While Hartian judges might become adept at the independent crafts of rule application and rule production, the acid test of the truly gifted Hartian judges is their astuteness at knowing when to move from rule application to rule production. While this does not lend itself to formulaic instruction or structured learning, the heuristic distinction between "clear cases" and "hard cases" is relied on by Hart to guide the perplexed judge through this critical maze and to maintain some chance of a good night's sleep. However, this instruction is somewhat empty, as he admits, because it is a matter of considerable difficulty to provide an exhaustive account of what makes a "clear case" clear and what makes a "hard case" hard. Nevertheless, he observes, somewhat tautologically, that clear cases are those occasions on which there is general agreement and very little doubt that the facts in issue obviously fall within the meaning and scope of a rule. Hard cases, therefore, must be those cases in which such general agreement is lacking and in which there exist real doubts about the applicability of a rule. As with nearly all of Hart's work, the distinction is not so much a matter of conceptual analysis as an observed fact about the empirical behavior of judges and the functional operation of language:

> Even when verbally formulated general rules are used, uncertainties as to the form of behaviour required by them may break out in particular concrete cases. Particular fact-situations do not await us already marked off from each other, and labelled as instances of the general rule, the application of which is in question; nor can the rule itself step forward to claim its own instances. In all fields of experience, not only that of rules, there is a limit, inherent in the nature of language, to the guidance which general language can provide. There will indeed be plain cases constantly recurring in similar contexts to which general expressions are clearly applicable ("If anything is a vehicle a motor-car is one") but there will also be cases where it is not clear whether they apply or not. ("Does 'vehicle' used here include bicycles, airplanes, roller skates?")[10]

Again, however, Hart has not been entirely consistent about the empirical distribution of these clear and hard cases or, therefore, about the extent to which judicial choice is present and unavoidable. He began with the opinion in 1958 of "how rare . . . [and] how exceptional is this feeling that one way of deciding a case is imposed upon us as the only natural or rational elaboration of some rule" and that the language of choice "better conveys the realities of the situation." Yet he appears to have repudiated that view by 1983 and settled on the conclusion that the standard resort to rule application occurred "very often" and was the primary device for legitimate adjudication.[11] It seems to follow, therefore, that while Hart contends that "a margin of uncertainty should be tolerated and indeed welcomed,"[12] he is also confirming that for the positivist claim to hold true, there must be a high degree of operational certainty. This conclusion seems vital if Hart is to maintain the integrity and validity of his accounts of law generally and judging particularly. Without a critical mass of standard meanings and settled rules, the very idea that rules would control judicial decisions, that there exists an actual body of workable rules, that such rules would command authoritative conformity, that judging is something less than legislative policy making, and that there is some meaningful distinction between the law as it is and the law as it ought to be, would all be lost. For Hart, therefore, while legal theory and training will understandably be occupied with the penumbra, "preoccupation with the penumbra is . . . as rich a source of confusion . . . as [preoccupation with] formalism."[13]

Of course, the fact that rules are not always dispositive of cases or that there is considerable scope for judicial choice and innovation is not presented by Hart as a matter of genuine concern. Indeed, he welcomes the fact that there is an inevitable and relative indeterminacy or open texture in the law: the loss of complete certainty and predictability is the price that has to be paid for the law being flexible enough to handle unanticipated cases in a fair and just manner. The challenge for both the judge and jurist is to strike an appropriate and manageable balance between the rule application of clear cases and the rule production of hard cases such that systemic certainty is not sacrificed entirely to particularized flexibility. On this issue, Hart is adamant that if clear cases did not comprise the bulk of adjudicated decisions, "we should not attach significance and value to them or think of such decisions as reached through a rational process."[14] Accordingly, Hart's writings present judging as a balanced and judicious affair—it is rational without being scientific, flexible without being unbounded, judgmental without being arbitrary, and predictable without being predetermined.

Playing with Wittgenstein

Hart's masterstroke was to introduce the linguistic lessons of Wittgenstein and his Ordinary Language colleagues to the study of law. Indeed, Hart was one of the first lawyers to take seriously the idea that law was a linguistic practice and that the jurist's task was to clarify and elucidate the social use of legal statements and linguistic practices. Consequently, his general jurisprudence and particular account of judging is driven, and given much of its intellectual shape, by his understanding of language's role. He thus shifted the focus of jurisprudential attention away from philosophical abstractions toward a more practical view of law-as-social-activity. In the Hartian canon, law was not a heavenly body but instead had feet of clay. However, in importing Wittgenstein's ideas into jurisprudence, Hart got more than he bargained for. Intended as mild correctives to jurisprudence's tendency to abstraction, the notions of *convention* and *context* are a strong form of theoretical purgative. Although Hart strives to confine their effects, such debilitating ideas are fatal to many of the basic concepts upon which Hart builds his theory of law. In short, because meaning is a function of context and context is itself contingent in that there is no Context of contexts, meaning is forever open to recontextualization and, therefore, is itself forever open—"anything might go."

Until the late nineteenth century, language had generally been taken for granted by philosophers. Treated as a transparent medium through which, if used properly, the light of meaning shone, it had eluded sustained or searching critique. Philosophers tended to proceed as if words were incorporeal elements that existed in an abstract realm whose unique meaning had to be revealed and refined. However, the advent of the "linguistic turn" in philosophy brought an end to such naïveté. While this concern with language took many forms and directions, the most important for English jurisprudence and Hart's positivism was the so-called Ordinary Language School of Philosophy, which drew its intellectual inspiration from the later writings of Wittgenstein. For Wittgenstein, many of philosophy's problems had been verbal and self-imposed because theorists insisted on taking words out of their context and separating them from their function: "Philosophical problems arise when language goes on holiday."[15] While his explicit target was the dominant Augustinian understanding of language as a "naming" device by which words stand as names for particular objects in the world and sentences are combinations of such names, his implicit focus was his own earlier idea that language operates as a picture that hooks on to the independent reality that it claims to describe. Accordingly, abandoning the idea that language had an enduring relation to the world and that words' meanings were simply pictures of that world, he was led to the major insight that language was a human activity and that words served different needs in different ways at different times; meaning was to be understood through the word's function and the rules that governed its use.

By way of the work of J. L. Austin and Gilbert Ryle,[16] Hart set out to introduce this bracing linguistic skepticism into the staid corner of juristic deliberation. In his inaugural Oxford lecture in 1953, he cast grave doubts on the adequacy and validity of attempts to supply a traditional definition *per genus et differentiam* of law and basic legal conceptions: it was simply not possible to provide a set of necessary and sufficient conditions for the use and meaning of a word. Instead, he emphasized that such words as "law" and "right" do not stand for any abstract entities or describe any preexisting factual reality.[17] For Hart, the relation between legal words and the world was neither straightforward nor mirrorlike. The adequacy of legal definitions is not to be found in their correctness but rather in their usefulness to achieve the particular aim in question. As such, the point of *The Concept of Law* was "to advance legal theory by providing an improved analysis of the distinctive structure of a municipal legal system and a better understanding of the resemblances and differences between law, coercion and morality, as types of social phenomena."[18] Accordingly, Hart is antireductionist in that he views legal terms as irreducible to nonlegal language or some nonlinguistic reality. Hartian jurisprudence is, therefore, touted to be as much about sociology as philosophy and as much about convention as universality.

Beginning from such a language-centered premise, Hart was persuaded that jurisprudence should consist of attempts to elucidate the underlying and recurrent themes of legal thinking through exposing the multitude of legal shadows and ambiguities in habitual legal usage. This approach did not do away with definitions entirely, but it recommended a much less abstract and more contextual analysis of legal language: definitions were to be general approximations rather than final explanations and could not be used as incontrovertible postulates from which conclusive axioms could be logically inferred. Consequently, words like "rule," "right," and "legal person" could not be defined by pointing to corresponding things or actions in the external world: they could only be understood in terms of their legal function and social usage. In his attempt to meet the objections of both formalists and realists, Hart urged that certain ground rules could be drafted and observed in giving meaning to legal constructs: first, put them into the context of the whole sentence; next, specify the conditions under which the whole sentence is true; and then, show how that sentence is used in drawing a conclusion from the rules in a particular case.

Nevertheless, Hart maintained that the social factness of law will confound efforts to construct a scientifically precise or purely abstract account of it. As a conventional linguistic practice, law shares the imprecision and messiness of social life. While there are better and worse ways to participate in and to practice legal language, there is no perfectible use of legal language. Any attempt to fix the meaning of particular words will be defeated by people's "relative ignorance of fact . . . [and] relative indeterminacy of aim." For Hart, people's inability to predict or anticipate the future with confidence ensures that the struggle to communicate in a clear and unambiguous manner is hubristic and, as such, is doomed to failure: "Uncertainty at the borderline is the price to be paid for the use of general classifying terms in any form of communication concerning matters of fact." Within the Hartian view of law, philosophical clarity is bought at the price of practical uncertainty and social determinacy at the expense of theoretical legitimacy. However, while words must be understood in their linguistic context and lack any absolutely determinate meaning, Hart maintained that words do have a *core* of settled meaning—there are some standard instances that guide their use. Without this sense that a particular string of words "fixes necessary conditions which anything must satisfy if it is to be within its scope and certain clear examples of what is certainly within its scope may be present to our minds,"[19] communication would not be possible. However, in Hart's view, outside their core of settled meaning or standard instances, general statements have a *penumbra* of indeterminacy—there is a fuzzy border in which the bewildering interaction of wordly flux and human ingenuity will confound attempts to give words sharp and clear-cut edges. In such peripheral regions of uncertainty, general agreement in judgments about meaning will have to be reached actively rather than simply recognized:

> The classifier must make a decision which is not dictated to him, for the facts and phenomena to which we fit our words and apply our rules are as it were dumb. Fact situations do not await us neatly labelled, creased, and folded, nor is their legal classification written on them to be simply read off by the judge. Instead, in applying legal rules, someone must take the responsibility of deciding that words do or do not cover some case in hand with all the practical consequences involved in this decision.[20]

Although Hart's resort to the themes of Wittgensteinian linguistic analysis appeared innovative and different in the 1950s and 1960s to the Anglo-American jurisprudential establishment, it was characteristically cautious and considered. In his inaugural lecture itself and later in *The Concept of Law*, Hart hedged on the importance and implications of context and function for linguistic analysis: they were more like helpful accessories than fundamental tools for moving beyond a strictly "representational" understanding of language. For instance, although he argued that legal terms were not used "to stand for or describe anything," they "[did] not have the straightforward connection with counterparts in the world of facts which most ordinary words have and to which we appeal in our definition of ordinary words."[21] Hart seemed to think that the dependence of meaning on function and context was a peculiarity of formal systems of language, such as law and games: law was an anomalous mode of expression. In view of this, he was fond of talking about the "natural expression" of certain concepts and points of view, as though their meaning were fixed and determinate across and among different contexts.[22] He failed to appreciate that the contextual and functional insight was as salient to the operation of the vast number of informal and overlapping practices that comprise language as a whole. Moreover, without such an acknowledgment, Hart's commitment to a truly functional and contextual understanding of language was seriously attenuated and fatally compromised. Insofar as the content of Hart's use-based *rules* and *rights* draw upon and connect to "ordinary language," the resort to context and function is rendered marginal and insignificant.

This debilitating tendency is reinforced by Hart's indication of what it means to take a contextual approach to legal language. Wittgenstein's treatment of sentences as the prime unit of meaning rather than as a series of isolated words was meant to be only a first step. However, Hart went no further in his embrace of a contextual analysis than to suggest that it was possible to attach meaning to legal constructs by putting them in their larger grammatical context and by recognizing "the cardinal principle that legal words can only be elucidated by considering the conditions under which statements in which they have their characteristic use are true."[23] This assertion is little more than a cursory nod in the direction of social usage; Hart remains indebted to a representational understanding of language. He most certainly does not escape the "picture" theory of language: he only extends its range of brushes and palette of colors. In so restricting contextual analysis, Hart comes almost as close to talking about the truth conditions for linguistic application as those traditional linguistic theories from which Wittgenstein was at pains to distinguish his own work. Indeed, Hart is caught between the "picture" theory of the early Wittgenstein and the "functional" skepticism of the later Wittgenstein.[24] While he dresses his theory in the fashionable Wittgensteinian trappings of social context and conventional usage, it is in its essentials a traditional and objectifying body of ideas. Static, technical, and ahistorical in its understanding of social convention, *The Concept of Law* lacks any real appreciation of social life as dynamic and contingent.

For instance, Hart seems to believe that, at least as a metaphysical possibility, language is capable of being unambiguous, provided that sufficient information could be generated to overcome "relative ignorance of fact . . . [and] relative indeterminacy of aim."[25] If such data were available, there would be a transparency between the words used to express speakers' intentions and the world described by those words so that hearers could not be confused or unsure in their understanding. In leaving open the possibility of such metaphysical perfectibility, Hart does not to live up to the skeptical expectations that his Wittgensteinian dalliance raises and encourages; *The Concept of Law* is a well-intended but unsuccessful attempt to contain the subversive implications of a thoroughly contextual and skeptical approach to law and language. Hart both fudges important questions about the historical and political dynamism of language and fails to understand that language is not only textually ambiguous but also structurally indeterminate. Because "a context, always, remains open, thus fallible and insufficient,"[26] context cannot do the explanatory and justificatory work that Hart and others ask of it. As much as context enables the possibility of any meaning at all, it disables the possibility of a fixed or settled meaning.

Consequently, the next section follows through on the skeptical process that Wittgenstein began (but did not finish) of unburdening language of its lingering metaphysical baggage and that Hart began (but did not finish) of flushing out law's epistemological pretensions. My critique begins (not ends) with the claim that meaning is ambiguous and multiple. From there it goes on to make a much more challenging set of claims about language and, therefore, law's attachment to rule application. The thrust of an uncompromising nonfoundationalist critique is to ensure that rules are never taken as the basis of agreements but that agreements are always understood as the basis of rules. In taking this line of critique, I intend to combine the insights of Ludwig Wittgenstein and Jacques Derrida—this is a risky but exciting prospect. However, while they derive from different traditions and write in a very different style, they are complementary in the important sense that they both maintain that the key to philosophy is language, they both are thoroughly skeptical about the possibility of a totalizing metaphysics, and they both hold that meaning is undecidable and unclosable. Accordingly, the work of Wittgenstein and Derrida are similar in that they locate meaning in the horizontal context of language as a self-contained Saussurean "play of differences" and in the vertical context of language as a contingent social practice.[27] The crucial difference is that whereas Wittgenstein found it sufficient to contextualize language, Derrida goes a step further by challenging the stability of such contextualizations.

Opening Up the Game

Central to the resort to linguistic analysis was the possibility that it might utilize language to plumb the epistemic depths of Reality and Necessity; Aristotelian "things" and Kantian "minds" had not proved equal to that task. The basic gamble was that philosophical problems could be resolved or, at least, eased by taking language and its everyday use more seriously. However, contrary to what Wittgenstein proclaimed, this endeavor only demonstrated that language was as likely to bewitch our intelligence as philosophy or anything else.[28] There is no literal language—one that is representational rather than constitutive and reflective rather than performative—against which other languages, such as law, can be contrasted. The study of language is not the last, best hope of philosophy, at least as traditionally understood, because it is itself shot through with all the contradictions and conundrums that philosophy strives to resolve: it is a case of out of the philosophical frying pan and into the linguistic microwave. Because truth and meaning are played out within the context of particular language games that are in social play at any given moment, there is no one vocabulary that somehow manages to capture a truer understanding of things than another vocabulary. There is no exit from particular language games that is also an entrance to the general language game that is privileged as the truer or better vocabulary of The Way Things Really Are. If philosophy has any particular mission or ambition (and I doubt that it has), it is not to isolate Truth, mirror Reality, or confirm The Way Things Really Are, but to challenge old shibboleths and generate new and interesting truths that better serve humanity's efforts to improve itself.

An old philosophical gloss does much to prick the balloon of philosophical conceit and to highlight the way that language does (and does not) work: "To do is to be"—Jean-Paul Sartre; "to be is to do"—Friedrich Nietzsche; and "do be do be do"—Frank Sinatra. Both the point and the recitation of this gloss, illustrating that language is very much a practice unto itself, contradict the claims and assumptions of many epistemologists. In particular, it highlights traditional philosophy's failure to grasp fully the implications of the critical idea that there might not be a transparency between the signifier and that to be signified—there may be all kinds of contextual forces in play that intervene. Discursive usage and practice are not the positivistic foundations that Hart and others claim them to be; they are riddled with political fissures and social cracks. Language is not something that is a mirror or window to reality but is always part of that reality: language is constitutive rather than designative. The relation of mind, language, and things is not about causal necessity but about functional adequacy. This is as much a matter of prescriptive fit as descriptive accuracy.

By way of undermining the foundationalist pretensions of much traditional philosophy, an important part of the nonfoundational project is to recognize and explore the profound connection between who people are and the communal language they speak. However, mindful of social history's inescapable contingency, language cannot be viewed as having an essential teleology or as acting as a medium between mind and reality. If language has a purpose, it is neither to represent an external reality nor to express an internal essence. Each language has its own purpose and helps to constitute reality and people's minds in different ways. The world and individuals do not decide between competing languages, because the world and individuals are not entirely separate from those languages: different languages are metaphoric creations that are contingently shaped and socially deployed. To treat such a project as worthwhile or possible slips back into the old metaphysical habit of seeking to emulate science when the scientific community itself has largely abandoned the view that the physical world is simply "out there" waiting to be noticed it in all its plenitude and detail. Treating something as true is a function of social practice, not a matter of objective proof. It is not that there is no difference between language and reality but that the difference is itself social and a matter of language. Within such a perspective, reality becomes largely a conventional construct and a matter of profound habit. Reality cannot be known outside of the discourse through which it is apprehended: "What we cannot speak about, we must pass over in silence."[29]

As Thomas Kuhn has made clear, there are no theory-independent facts that comprise an unambiguous starting point for scientific analysis. He contends that philosophy is learned by immersion in a professional practice, not by adherence to a universal set of formulaic rules. In the same way that he developed his idea of science as a paradigm-situated activity, it can be argued that language is a game that is determined by the conventional norms of social practice rather than logical criteria of objective validity. In short, there is no external object of inquiry or what Wittgenstein termed "superlative fact(s)" outside an internal context of inquiry.[30] Reality can be experienced differently depending on the discursive context and prevailing interpretive practices; there are no privileged descriptions or contexts that give ultimate grounding to all others. Moreover, it is not about moving an object from one context to another, because there is no object without context. As Rorty pithily suggests, there is "no way to divide the world between hard lumps and squishy texts."[31] *Mere observation* is neither mere nor observation. And this insight is doubly valid for studies and inquiries into society and law. There are no *facts* about the way that law-as-discourse works that are not themselves beholden to some theory about what counts as law, language, and social facts. Reality is not a foundation on which to ground any final or essential truths about the necessary constitution of society, because reality's status and meaning as discursive constructs are always inside social life and never beyond dispute. Of course, none of this means that people are free to construct any social world at all; the constraints of human vulnerability and the scarcity of different resources foreclose certain options. Although any world in which people live is not objective (in the sense of having a truth value and universal status that are somehow outside the contingent confines of human discourse), neither is it subjective (in the sense that each individual is free to sanction or abandon it as she or he chooses), nor relative (in the sense of being exclusively reducible to the commitments and interests of a particular group). Everything is "always already" contextualized.[32]

An example will help to concretize these abstract claims. In describing the world and the things that comprise it, there is a marked tendency to speak in terms that are taken to be value-neutral and that are thought to order, represent, or label a given physical world. Allowing for the peripheral and occasional dissonances between different language groups, it is assumed that there is a fixed and independent reality that is separate from people's attempt to give meaning to it. For instance, it seems commonsensical to claim that there are things called "trees" that are naturally separate from the flowers and shrubs surrounding them. Unfortunately (or fortunately), this claim is far from obvious or uncontroversial except if made within a particular discursive context. While there is a whole mass of *somethings* out there, they do not reveal themselves as particular *somethings* without human prompting. For instance, "vehicle" does not possess a positive presence by virtue of having an independent "vehicleness" within it. Its distinctiveness and meaning are a function of its relative location within a socially created scheme of discursive ordering. The language game in which "vehicle" takes on pertinence and relevance also endows certain attributes, such as wheels and transportive capacity, with a special significance in the overall meaning-giving enterprise. Within a another system of signification (or language game), a very different set of identifying attributes might be considered significant and meaningful. For instance, categorization of things in the world might depend on (a) whether it can talk; (b) its aesthetic appeal; (c) how much it weighs (d) whether it can be eaten; (e) etcetera; (f) how big it is from a distance; (g) the extent of its mathematical possibilities; (h) how much it is worth.[33]

Like all discourse, the language of the law is an engaged attempt to bring order and structure to an unruly and alien world. However, in time-honored fashion, the legal community has made a political virtue out of a taxonomic necessity. Classification is always evaluative and political in the sense that it functions as a hierarchy of signification; there is no form of pure taxonomy that passively catalogs instead of actively producing. While lawyers tend to experience the world as fixed and reified, law is not something that stands aside from reality but rather "is part of a distinctive manner of imagining the real."[34] Law divides social activity into a variety of doctrinal categories and develops different principles to understand and evaluate that categorized activity. In so doing, it confers the status of the real and concrete on the abstract and metaphorical. Accordingly, the task is not, as Hart seems to suggest, to amass more information; facts are never independent of the theory in which they achieve their status as facts. What is required is a more appropriate metaphor and intellectual structure for living. The worth of any scheme of conceptual ordering is not determined by its degree of fit with a pregiven world nor in terms of whether it is natural or artificial. Any taxonomic ordering is to be judged by its capacity to be more or less helpful in making the best of people's personal and collective lives. As such, legal taxonomy involves and can never escape the responsibility to take and defend a political stance: it is a major site for the political struggle over the kind of world we want to live in. A comparison between two Supreme Court of Canada decisions made only thirty-five days apart about the extent of collective responsibility for the welfare of particular individuals is instructive.

Whereas one upheld a claim for compensation by a property owner who had suffered substantial economic losses resulting from a provincial parks program, the other dismissed a claim for compensation by a five-year-old girl who had received traumatic personal injuries resulting from a publicly funded vaccination program.

A Tale of Two Cases

David Tener had invested considerable sums in the preliminary development of certain mineral resources that he and others owned in Wells Gray Park. In 1973, the British Columbia government passed legislation that made this land into a provincial park where no mining could take place without prior authorization. After five years of unsuccessful attempts to obtain the necessary approval, he sued the province for the capital value of the mineral resources, his wasted expenditures, and his anticipated profits from the exploitation of the mining claims. In the majority judgment in *Tener*, Justice Estey supported Tener's proposition that a property right included a right to minerals as well as a right of sufficient access to enable their development. Estey's focus and definition of the property right allowed him to invoke the nineteenth-century interpretive fiction that "a statute is not to be construed so as to take away the property of a subject without compensation."[35] He also held, as seemed consistent with the logic of the property structure, that the denial of access to the mineral resources constituted a recovery of part of the rights granted by the Crown in 1937 and that a taking occurred because the value of a state asset—the park—was enhanced. In a concurring judgment, Justice Wilson followed a similar course of argument and insisted that "the vice aimed at is expropriation without compensation." According to her lights, the denial of the access permit deprived Tener of his *profit à prendre* and constituted a taking because the deprivation effectively resulted in the Crown removing an encumbrance from its own property. In short, Tener's loss was the Crown's gain. With little sense of irony, she stated that "it would be quite unconscionable to say that this cannot constitute an expropriation in some technical, legalistic sense."[36]

While the conflict between Tener and the state could have been interpreted as a tale about the best way to deal with a situation where one person's welfare has been diminished as a result of government action to benefit the community, that is not the way the judgments read at all. The formalistic and analytical framework applied to the reality constructed by the judges transforms that idea (if it ever existed in the minds of the judges) into a claim for compensation on an expropriation of property. Attention is thus focused on historical and legal concepts of property, on the formal requirements of a taking, and on the interpretation of common law and statutory rights of compensation that *exist*. Given the pre-understanding of the judges and the internalized structure of law, the judicial exercise is to define property, establish its taking, and interpret the relevant legislation and common law cases to provide a right to compensation. The result is presented as flowing inexorably from the initial perception of Tener's welfare as involving a property right. The judges present their task and its accomplishment as about negotiating their way through a maze of legal concepts and language in order to arrive at a clear and given reality that dictates or, at least, recommends a definite and desirable result.

The courts' initial perception of *Lapierre* was radically different.[37] If *Tener* was a *property* case, *Lapierre* was a *torts* case. In 1972, a five-year-old Nathalie Lapierre received a measles inoculation under a mass government program. Nathalie began exhibiting symptoms within a week that were consistent with acute viral hepatitis, and consequently the illness had effects that left her in a condition of almost total permanent incapacity. On her behalf, Nathalie's father sued the Quebec government for damages under the Quebec Code Civil. As well as imposing liability for fault, Article 1057 provides that "no one can be compelled to give up his property, except for public utility, and in consideration of a just indemnity previously paid," and it had been used in earlier cases to indemnify individuals whose property had been damaged by government acting to benefit the community.[38] Giving the Supreme Court of Canada's judgment, Justice Chouinard expressed his sympathy for Nathalie, but little else.

Chouinard began by distinguishing a series of cases in which compensation was awarded when private homes were damaged or property revenues were diminished by state action because they involved instances of tacit expropriation; *Lapierre* was seemingly not amenable to such characterization. On top of that, he refused to construct a working theory of compensation from Article 1057. In light of the striking similarity between this provision and the doctrinal rhetoric in *Tener*, the court's failure to recognize even the slightest conceptual connection between *Tener* and *Lapierre* testifies to the hold that the legal structures of thought have over the collective judicial consciousness. Finally, without explanation, he held that Article 1057 could not be used to impose liability on the state since the article did not establish an independent source of obligation. Moreover, he did not recount why the argument that a "theory of risk" could be used to justify an award of compensation was rejected, notwithstanding the fact that several French administrative decisions had awarded compensation to those who had become immunization victims "as the result of efforts to protect the French public, in a pitiless game of chance."[39]

The episodes in *Tener* and *Lapierre* are illustrative of how lawyers (and laypeople) treat the law's conceptual apparatus and discursive categories as natural, and how, in the process, they confer the status of the real and concrete on the abstract and metaphorical. The legal notion of property does not comprise the tangible objects in the physical world but only the abstract relations between such visible effects and people. In legal terms, things like *property* are not really objects at all, but a bundle of forces that coalesce and disaggregate over time and space into recognizable entitlements or relations between people and objects.[40] Although born of historical expediency and sustained by political convenience, legal categories, like contract and property, take on a life of their own. Unlike what happens in the life of the so-called natural world, social activity responds to these conceptual metaphors and reproduces itself in accordance with them. This not only gives the law a patina of plausibility and coherence but also allows lawyers to refer to *reality* as confirmation of the naturalness and inevitability of prevailing legal structures and their underlying values. The fact that this process occurs unconsciously makes it no less political and much more socially effective.

The structure of legal taxonomy in *Lapierre* and *Tener* can best be explained by recognizing the intellectual constructs that the judges used (and were used by) to understand and categorize the social events that led to the two cases. *Lapierre* was a *tort* case—a personal injury claim with no evidence of a deliberate bureaucratic sacrifice of Nathalie's welfare. *Tener* was a *property* case—the devaluation of an economic resource with considerable evidence of a deliberate executive choice to sacrifice Tener's property. The legal way that the judges constructed the different universes of *Tener* and *Lapierre* conditioned their whole response to the claims. The operative legal structures were so ingrained that they became a matter of first nature to them, almost beyond reflection or reappraisal. The judges mistook the taxonomic structure for that-to-be-structured. Insofar as classification is a powerful intellectual device that consists of a purposive aim and a series of associative criteria,[41] the judges ignored those vital purposive dimensions and treated the legal categories in play as permanent technical descriptions of a fixed reality rather than contingent normative prescriptions of contingent realities. They managed to follow and perpetuate a doctrinal schema that places property above persons. Whereas the notion of strict liability is standard in property, losses lie where they fall in tort unless there is a finding of fault. Consequently, through the vehicle of doctrinal principles and legal classifications, not only are the values of the past sustained in the present, but the judges are also able to disclaim responsibility for this state of affairs. However, the conditions for entry into any doctrinal category are neither fixed nor certain; they are as fluid and constructed as the doctrinal rules within the category itself. It is entirely possible for events or categories to be redescribed and reworked to contain what is presently considered irrelevant or incompatible. In so doing, it is not that the visage of *natural reality* is being masked by a more palatable and expedient face but that an earlier constructed reality is being replaced by another: the familiarity of the earlier reality has lent to it an appearance that seems more natural and given. The constraints on law and reality are as much imaginative as they are material.

There were, of course, several options open to the deciding judges. One obvious response was to have retained the familiar legal structures and simply reclassified Nathalie's body as her property. It is hardly a novel move; people have been and continue to be treated as property for much less benign reasons.[42] However, the recategorization of bodily well-being from a personal right to a property right is merely a strategic calculation and simply effects an instrumental restructuring of present thinking. The worth of such a strategy is hopelessly transparent; the approach is facile and self-defeating. Not only does shifting Nathalie's welfare into the *property* room of the taxonomic castle retain and actually strengthen the existing intellectual structure of legal discourse, but it also can bring about only modest improvements in social welfare. While legal reality has been reconfigured by such alterations in conceptualization and classification, the changes are marginal and stopgap. The point is that the choice is purposive. It must be framed and made in terms of political values and social usefulness; it is not simply about the accuracy or validity of technical descriptions about The Way Things Really Are.

It should be understood, therefore, that the criticisms made of *Tener* and *Lapierre* are not simply criticisms of particular judges or judgments. The critique is intended to cut much deeper and touch on the whole legal way of thinking about the world and ourselves. As a language, law does not simply serve society; it defines and helps to constitute that society and its members: law is one of the discursive practices, institutional structures, and intellectual media for organizing and acting in the world. The belief in a possible rendezvous with an ultimate reality, unmediated by discourse, is mistaken. It is too simplistic to presume that lawyers stand outside the world and can understand, evaluate, and control the world without being part of it. By being in the world, they are frontline combatants, whether they like it or not, in the political struggle to resist, reproduce, or change that world. Once the power of discursive assumptions and taxonomic classifications—the existing ideas and language that are used to think about events like David Tener's economic well-being in British Columbia in 1973 and Nathalie Lapierre's physical and emotional well-being in Quebec in 1972—are more fully recognized, it might be possible to begin the essential project of beginning to talk differently and, in doing so, change what passes for truth and reality in people's lives. While some discursive commitment is necessary, no one particular structure is inevitable. There are other possible ways to think about and engage in the world. While the legal structures of the conceptual status quo are disciplining, lawyers, judges, and laypersons are not entirely disciplined; there always exists room for renegotiation and reconstruction. In the nonfoundational sense that I have tried to evoke, law is a language game in which there is no one Game of games and which lawyers are obliged to play while they work to reconfigure it.

Staying Real

By pursuing this critique, I do not subscribe to the absurdly idealistic view that there is no world that functions outside of language—that reality is "begot of nothing but vain fantasy / Which is as thin of substance as the air / And more inconstant than the wind."[43] The nonfoundationalist response is not that there is nothing that is denoted by the word "vehicle" or that all are free to create their own personal reality. It is that what is known as "vehicles" and their nature as "vehicles" is only meaningful and apprehensible in the language that brings them into human consciousness. Consequently, beyond immediate and personal sensations of the physical environment, the world is only accessible and knowable through language; life is an interpretive activity. While communicative practices are not the only kind of practices, they do frame and give meaning to other practices and are important for that reason. Thus, Hart's insistence that the meaning of certain words, like "vehicle," is somehow a fact, that its definition simply *is* and its authority is self-evident, is not tenable: language and meaning are always hostage to their historical and theoretical context.

Understanding language, therefore, is not about abstract reflection, but it is about social activity. The key relation is between speakers rather than between words and things: "If language is to be a means of communication, there must be agreements not only in definitions but also (queer as this may sound) in judgments," and, therefore, "the speaking of language is part of an activity, or a form of life."[44] For all his good intentions, Hart fails to follow through on this fundamental Wittgensteinian insight. He treats ordinary language as not only the first word but also—and this is the problem—as the last word on its philosophical significance. However, contrary to Hart's view, ambiguity in language is not the result of inadequate or imprecise attempts at definition; it is a result of the systemic and structural problem that as meaning depends upon agreement, there is no sufficient or adequate common ground among users of the language as to what particular words mean in particular circumstances. The worlds of people and, therefore, of language are contingent; neither stands still long enough to maintain any final social consensus or historical closure. This view of language does not deny the possibility of meaning, but it is fundamentally skeptical about the status and stability of any meaning reached. Thus, it is more easily understood that while context manages to account for the operation and intelligibility of language, it simultaneously manages to undermine the possibility of grounding it in anything but context itself.

While this nonfoundational approach to language rejects the notion of language as an exercise in representational precision, it does not obliterate or essentialize the distinction between discursive representation and reality. Instead, it blurs that distinction and renders it organically unstable and normatively volatile. However, the fact that reality is socially constructed does not mean that it is somehow *unreal*—socially constructed is as real as it gets. There is no *absolute* reality that is outside our ways of construing reality and against which supposed pseudo-realities can be scrutinized. This is only fitting because, being thoroughly skeptical, a nonfoundational perspective is skeptical about what to be skeptical about and how to be skeptical about it. A nonfoundationalist account recognizes that people hold beliefs about truth and reality, but they are just that—beliefs that are held in a provisional and conditional way. Accordingly, in the nonfoundationalists' vocabulary, to be skeptical is not to be relativistic; their notions of truths are pluralistic and, cutting across and within social cultures, are not reductive in epistemological provenance.[45] Moreover, as Hart again recognized but did not fully grasp, it is not possible to develop a *theory of meaning* from such a pragmatic conception of language. The ascertainment of meaning is never reducible to some formulaic or fixed process of abstract reflection but is always susceptible to the vicissitudes of flawed and incomplete social practices. A nonfoundationalist inquiry abandons entirely a transcendental attachment to or ambition to fix foundational conditions for language. Instead, its task is to expose the dynamic fluidity and changing character of those foundations. In this way, it is appropriately *non*foundational rather than dogmatically *anti*-foundational.

One substantial danger of this nonfoundationalist position is thought to be that it can easily reduce to a hollow solipsism in which language has some theological drive or reason that places it beyond reflection or control. As language is a world to itself, then what is it that language is mediating when there is no language-external reality? The answer is not that there is no reality but that it is only possible to obtain access to it through language. A nonfoundational perspective does not so much obliterate as blur the distinction between discursive representation and reality. In the same way that it rejects the traditional view that the world and the language used to comprehend it are totally separate, it also denies that they are one and the same. It is never possible to ascertain in any conclusive or definitive way the demarcation between the world and discourse: their relation is dynamic and contingent. As Bruner contends, "We create realities by warning, by encouraging, by dubbing with titles, by naming, and by the manner in which words invite us to create 'realities' in the world to correspond with them: constitutiveness gives an externality and an appropriate ontological status to the concepts that words embody."[46] The nonfoundational challenge, therefore, is not to repudiate entirely external reality or to invalidate efforts at rational judgment but to place them under constant scrutiny, to recognize their contextual configuration, and to never take them for granted.

However, those who subscribe to a nonfoundationalist critique are not condemned to idolize the existing discursive practices in their literalness or to engage in a demoralizing solipsism. Judges and jurists must begin to assume responsibility for the existing world and its discursive and taxonomic supports. Insofar as these structures and categories have been made, they can be remade. However, before that can occur, there must be a greater understanding and appreciation of how they were made, why they were made that way, and how they function. While it is not possible to get entirely outside the world's abstractions, it might be feasible to "smash the semantic box in which current thinking is locked . . . [and] craft a better cabinet out of materials readily available in a real world."[47] Such knowledge is a form of empowerment in itself because it gives perspective and purchase on the "fabricatedness" and "nonnaturalness" of present arrangements. Social justice can be realized through and in the process of world-(re)making once the accent of truth has been detached and emancipated from the particular social, economic, and cultural relations that comprise the status quo. While the judgments that are contained within language are not always reflected on, adjudication provides an important occasion when they can be subjected to intellectual and political scrutiny in a formalized institutional setting. Because law and adjudication are never only descriptive, judges and lawyers cannot evade responsibility for the prescriptive organization of the world. Hart's positivistic claim that a satisfactory jurisprudence can finesse moral or political controversy and confine itself to being "an essay in descriptive sociology" is untenable.[48] Accordingly, the theoretical enterprise must undergo a radical reorientation in which philosophy (of law) will cease to be only a technical task of refined description and will also become a political project of engaged construction. Replacing epistemology with hermeneutics, the jurist will not seek to pin down foundational truths but will strive instead to open up the essential dialogue of world making.

Consequently, Hart's claims about the "relative indeterminacy"of law, in the sense of rules being vague, ambiguous, and competing, are misplaced, because language is constitutive rather than designative, contextual rather than abstract, and political rather than metaphysical.[49] Law and language are thoroughly and pervasively indeterminate. Whereas ambiguity suggests a textural property that is capable of final resolution, indeterminacy represents a discursive or linguistic property that pervades the whole interpretive act so that any final resolution or interpretation is unavailable. Structural indeterminacy gives rise to a hermeneutical undecidability in the sense that there can be no final closure to any claim for meaning.[50] Nevertheless, while law is indeterminate, this is not tantamount to contending that adjudication is a game in which "anything goes" at any time. While meaning is always available, it is never socially stable or historically fixed; historical contingency confounds linguistic certainty. The settled possibility of establishing meaning at any particular time is always haunted by the impossibility of settling on established meaning for all time. A nonfoundational account recognizes that it is entirely plausible to believe in indeterminacy and, at the same time, still have confidence in particular interpretations of particular rules at particular times in particular circumstances—provided that such confidence is based upon rhetorical cogency and not epistemological truth value. In Hartian terms, the attempt to define "vehicle" is not only periodically hampered by the word or rule's textual ambiguity but is permanently incapacitated by language's structural indeterminacy.

In introducing a nonfoundationalist account of language and, therefore, adjudication, I hope to have calmed implicit Hartian fears that without the hard core of settled meaning, there cannot be law "in some centrally important sense" and that "the notion of rules controlling courts' decisions is senseless"; this is an unwarranted indictment of responsible skepticism and participatory democracy.[51] It is simply not the case that unless words have a context-transcendent meaning, the possibility of governance according to law will have vanished and anarchy will be loosed on an unsuspecting populace. Under an apparent hard shell of settled meaning, there always lies a soft center of temporary meaning. There are, no doubt, instances of cynical rule manipulation by judges and lawyers in which they treat rules as "playthings." Yet there is nothing in a nonfoundational refocusing of rule-based adjudication that denies or compromises Hart's observation that "for the most part decisions . . . are reached . . . by genuine effort to conform to rules consciously taken as guiding standards of decision." However, a nonfoundational approach does insist that nothing necessarily follows from making a "genuine effort to conform to rules consciously taken as guiding standards of decision."[52]

Moreover, I have explained the extent to which law and adjudication help to create the reality to which lawyers and judges merely claim to respond. As Stanley Fish puts it, they "construct the (verbal) ground upon which they then confidently walk."[53] Among other things, this means that lawyers and judges are always implicated in the politics of reality, because they cannot avoid participating in the ideological struggle to establish, maintain, and change meaning. Always part of, but never entirely reducible to, their historical and social context, judges and jurists can never escape the taking of sides. As intellectual reality brokers, they are part and parcel of the events that they claim to interpret and change. As such, lawyering as well as criticism is an active intervention in the struggle for social control rather than a passive reflection on that struggle. Within this nonfoundational understanding, interpretation is not a matter of indisputable proofs that establish the term and conditions of legal language but rather a series of rhetorical probes in a continuing conversation about and within legal discourse. This demands a refocusing of critical attention away from a Hartian preoccupation with epistemological *concepts* to a deconstructive concern with political *contexts*. In the next section, therefore, I explain that while a nonfoundationalist account of law and adjudication does insist upon the instability and undecidability of legal meaning as historical and political phenomena, it does so in a very particular and careful way.

Between Core and Penumbra

In 1978, MacCormick felt confident enough to state that "no one has ever advanced" an assault upon easy cases.[54] By this he meant that there existed cases in which the application of the rules to the facts was beyond reasonable dispute; the jurisprudential action was more around the incidence, identity, and resolution of hard cases. However, a nonfoundationalist account of legal language launches exactly that kind of full frontal assault. It challenges the distinction between hard and easy cases by contending that all cases are vulnerable to deconstructive disruption. In no uncertain terms, a nonfoundational account insists that there never is simply an easy fact of the legal matter; it is indeterminacy all the way up and down. The skeptical life of the law is both the indeterminate logic of its own contingent experience and the indeterminate experience of its own contingent logic. Indeed, an uncompromising skepticism is devastating to traditional jurists' intellectual peace of mind, because it strikes at a central claim of the positivist thesis that there are "a vast number" of determinate rules whose application will be obvious and unproblematic in the bulk of cases. For Hartian positivists, if there were not a considerable number of easy cases, law could not be considered as a social fact, independent of moral considerations; it would be entirely a matter of judgment and an occasion for the exercise of strong discretion. Although absolute certainty is not an achievable goal and "a margin of uncertainty should be tolerated and indeed welcomed," Hart concedes that for the positivist claim to hold true, there must be an operational degree of certainty or else "there is no central element of actual law to be seen in the core of settled meaning which rules have."[55] While Hart is right to point out the experience that lawyers and judges have of "the core of settled meaning," he is mistaken to treat "the core of settled meaning" as a feature "that rules have" and to consider that core or meaning as "settled" in anything but the most temporary, provisional, or contingent way. "The core of settled meaning" is only central, settled, and meaningful until the next performance or play of the judicial game.

As Hart so compellingly shows, the formulation and application of rules are fraught with uncertainty and difficulty. In his three-step process of inductive, deductive, and discretionary decision, judges have plenty of institutional room to maneuver. However, once it is recognized that this takes place within the structural and endemic indeterminacy of discursive practice, a depiction of rule-based adjudication as factual and easy is far wide of the scholarly mark. The appeal of rules is also their greatest weakness. By trying to generalize inductively from particular circumstances and then later to particularize deductively from general statements, rule-based theories of law overlook the main nonfoundational insight that judging is "all in the details" and that those details are constantly being reconfigured. Rules arise from and speak to social relations that are always subject to change and only have any particular meaning as a result of their consideration within a specific politico-historical context. Moreover, that context, never self-evident, demands an act of delineation that implicates values and power: "The question can be raised, not whether a politics is implied (it always is), but which politics is implied in . . . a practice of contextualization."[56]

It takes little effort or imagination to illustrate this contingent and shifting relation between the core and penumbral meaning of "vehicle." For Hart, it is clear that "if anything is a vehicle a motor-car is one," but it is equally unclear whether "vehicle" includes "bicycles, airplanes, roller skates."[57] At any particular time in any particular place for any particular purpose for any particular community, this delineation of vehicle's core and penumbra may accurately track the prevailing consensus. However, it is difficult to sustain and defend this precise division as an enduring account of vehicle's meaning. Even within a particularized context, there will be debate and disagreement not only over whether penumbral cases sufficiently resemble core instances to warrant inclusion as vehicles but also where the line between core and penumbra is to be drawn: Does a motorcar include a police car, ambulance, or maintenance vehicle? Does it encompass a child's toy, a wheelchair, a child's stroller, a lawn mower, or a statue of a motorcar? Moreover, Hart's injunction to consider words in their grammatical context is as likely to result in further confusion as improved clarification: Does "park" include an industrial estate, a marine park, an amusement park, as well as a recreational enclosure? Does it include a car park?

An extended historical example underlines the extent to which the core and penumbra of words, like "vehicle," shift and reconfigure in the effort to apply the rule "no vehicle may be taken into the park." In the early part of the eighteenth century (or before), the core and penumbra of vehicle clearly did not include motorcars; they were not yet invented. It was animals and animal-drawn conveyances, like wagons and sleds, that dominated the vehicular scene. For instance, in 1868, pre-car London introduced traffic controls and pedestrian crossing signals. The police notice warned that a manually operated semaphore would indicate *Stop* or *Caution* to "all persons in charge of vehicles and horses."[58] Indeed, as late as 1925 in Washington, it was unclear whether the power "to regulate vehicles on public streets" encompassed automobiles, as they were unknown as a practical means of conveyance at the time of the regulation's original enactment in 1887.[59] Ironically, by 1922 in Alabama, an animal unattached to a conveyance had been held not to be a vehicle for the purposes of a statute authorizing the confiscation of vehicles used for criminal activities and, by 1925 in Virginia, animal-drawn conveyances were not considered to be included within the ambit of vehicles.[60] Projecting forward a few decades into the next century, it is not inconceivable that the motorcar will have had its social day and have moved back into the penumbral regions of linguistic usage: it might be replaced by an environmentally friendly return to animals and animal-drawn carriages or by some futuristic means of transport that has only begun to register faintly on the present social consciousness.

In such matters, it is important that the question of law's indeterminacy is not confused with its predictability. Much is made by foundationalists of law's relative predictability in their rejoinder to the critical charge about law's indeterminacy. However, contrary to the foundationalists' claims, there is nothing contradictory about arguing simultaneously that law is thoroughly indeterminate but relatively predictable. A nonfoundationalist account is concerned as much with the general justificatory basis for judicial decisions as the outcomes in particular cases; it is both a philosophical inquiry into adjudication and a sociological one. Consequently, I can agree with foundationalists that, at least over a reasonable period and for a sizable series of judgments, decisions are predictable in the sense that it is possible to estimate with a plausible degree of accuracy what judges will and will not decide by way of outcomes. However, I disagree strongly with foundationalists that this predictability is connected to or justified by the rules of law or that any particular decision by any given judge is predictable on any given day. In a nonfoundationalist account, indeterminacy and predictability are different notions—indeterminacy is concerned with questions of justifiability, whereas predictability is addressed to discussions of outcomes.[61]

For instance, Kent Greenawalt proposes, as a justification for his claim that the law has a workable level of determinacy, that "virtually any lawyer . . . would conclude, after careful study, that the law provides [a particular] answer."[62] Even this modest and pragmatic standard is problematic and self-serving; it mistakes predictability for determinacy. If "virtually any lawyer" includes those lawyers of a critical or deconstructive disposition, it will be extremely difficult to ever "conclude, after careful study, that the law provides [any determinate] answer." If such lawyers are not included, determinacy will have been achieved by hypothetically polling only those lawyers who already believe that determinacy is possible. Intended as a noncontroversial and itself neutral standard of determinacy, Greenawalt's proposal falls afoul of the indeterminacy critique: it confirms rather than refutes the contingent and inescapable politics of law. Meaning and determinacy are not properties of the law itself but a function of agreement among lawyers about its relevant informing contexts. Indeed, as the example of a professional legal community confirms, many of the judgments and much of the agreement that Wittgenstein argues make language work are brought about "through training, drill and the forms of our life."[63] To be a lawyer is to talk like a lawyer, and to talk like a lawyer is as much about the inculcation of social values and attitudes as it is about the learning of legal rules and technical words.

As a matter of professional training and social custom, rule application does not lend itself to a definitive account of what it is to follow a rule. To declare that someone has followed or obeyed a rule *correctly* is to say little more than that they did something the same "as we do it."[64] The question is not whether there are rules or whether they are relied upon—they clearly are. However, they do not exist as canonical directives that can impersonally dispose of cases without interpretive intervention; the meaning of a rule and its application never simply *are*. Rules determine nothing except customary reactions and dominant practices. As a social practice, rule application is not an analytical issue of formal realizability or causal necessity; *conformity with* is not the same as *caused by*. This agnosticism is what distinguishes the skeptic from the positivists and the nihilists. Simply providing the next number in a series is not the same as justifying this maneuver as a necessary following of a particular rule. In the same way that Newton's law of gravity did not cause or account for the apple falling, rules do not cause anything to happen. In matters of social behavior, the most that a rule can do is to help one understand whether the participants in such behavior believe that they are following such a rule. As Wittgenstein concluded, in justifying behavior, "The rule is . . . what is explained, not what does the explaining."[65] Rules are rough-and-ready indicators or markers of earlier values that other judges have been persuaded had sufficient agreement within or appeal to the relevant discursive community. In a nontrivial sense, therefore, every application of a rule is a remaking of the rule. Rule application is an occasion on which judges acknowledge, consciously or unconsciously, the values that hold certain social practices in place. As such, adjudication, no less than lawyering, is through and through about values, not facts and about persuasion, not demonstration. Applying rules is a political matter of taking sides: the only questions are *which* and *when*.

Not So Easy

As regards the traditional distinction between easy and hard cases, it should by now be clear that a skeptical account of law has no truck with it or need for it. In short, there are no hard cases or easy cases: there are only cases. "Easiness" is not a property or quality that inheres within a case or rule. Rules and their application do not arise or make sense outside of an interpretive context. The easiness or hardness of cases derives from background facts about agreements in judgments, historical contexts, and social stability. What goes on in easy cases is the same as in hard cases; it is only that their context is less contested and more taken for granted. In this sense, Hart is correct when he states that easy cases occur where "there is general agreement that they fall within the scope of a rule,"[66] provided that the emphasis is firmly on the fact of "general agreement" and not, as Hart seems to put it, on "the scope of the rule." The fact of this general agreement (whether a matter of social consensus or social hierarchy) is important—the greater its extent and strength, the greater the existential experience of easy cases and legal certainty.[67] When it comes to language, there is simply no fact of the matter; what any term or rule refers to or means is always an interpretive and, therefore, contestable issue. Indeed, in understanding language and law as functional instruments, it is important to see them less as individual tools, like ratchets and screwdrivers, and more as a social device, like a manufacturing process or assembly line, that demands a high degree of collaboration and integration. It is in this sense that "general agreement" is to be understood.

Nevertheless, no matter how extensive or deep the agreement is, it does not alter the fact that easiness can never become an intrinsic feature of the rule itself. The temptation to mistake dominant ways of thinking for natural necessity must be studiously resisted; the process is so ingrained and uncontroversial as to *appear* as if the process did not occur. My claim, therefore, that many cases are easy and that, as Hart says, "general terms would be useless to us as a medium of communication unless there were such familiar, generally unchallenged cases"[68] requires that "unchallenged" be understood in the nonfoundational sense as *unchallenged in the present social circumstances*. After all, easy cases are as much a product of hermeneutical interpretation as hard cases. They are not an occasion to forgo the need for such interpretation but only an occasion upon which there is considered to be no political reason or political will to disturb prevailing understandings. However, some critics still continue to insist that there are easy cases. Their critical response to the nonfoundational account of easy cases and what it means to take rules seriously has taken two related forms—the "weird and bizarre" and the "obvious and trite."

The first response claims that there are some factual applications of rules that are so far-fetched and ludicrous as to be clearly outside the scope of the rule and thus never reasonably count as potential interpretations of the rule. For instance, Greenawalt observes that "no plausible formulation of the statutory crime of theft, under present social conditions, will include the ordinary act of scratching one's nose."[69] But examples like this seem to miss the whole point of the nonfoundational account. It is not the rule or its formulation that is determinative but rather the social context and what is considered relevant in it that is significant. The constraints are more on people's imagination (who but a da Vinci could have imagined cars, computers, or spaceships in centuries of old?) than on the interpretive possibilities imposed by a rule's linguistic expression. In actual social circumstances in which the "bizarre" or "weird" situation would actually arise, the reasonableness of the interpretation would be much less implausible and much more contestable.[70] Greenawalt himself underscores this point by qualifying his observation as only being plausible "under present social conditions." However, even "under present social conditions," it might be possible to bring nose scratching within the crime of theft, at least if this includes accessories before the fact—a thief's accomplice might use a nose scratch as the signal that the coast is clear. In other words, the resort to outrageous examples actually underlines the force and extent of the indeterminacy critique—if, in matters of theft, everything else goes, other than acts like scratching one's nose, then the extent of determinate and plausible meaning is so great as to offer no fixed or reliable constraints on rule application at all.

The second response insists that there are some circumstances that are so obvious and trite that even "under present social conditions," their status as easy cases cannot seriously be challenged: the appropriate outcome of applying a rule is beyond serious dispute. For instance, when contemplating Hart's rule that "no vehicles may be taken into the park," even a critical Fuller agrees that there is "no need to worry about the difference between Fords and Cadillacs."[71] Such a bold pronouncement is premature. While it may well be that in most situations and for most people, the make of car will not be relevant, it does not follow that it will be so in all possible situations. Again, it is the determination of context that is vital, not the rule's formulation. There are a number of circumstances in which the make of car might be treated as significant in the application of the rule. At a Ford factory or recreational facility, "vehicles" might have come to be interpreted as prohibiting only those cars that are not made by Ford, such as Cadillacs, the obvious rationale being that there is an important difference between cars made by the park's owner and anyone else and that Ford wants to encourage its employees to drive only its own cars. After all, any language game—of which law is the example par excellence—that could once refuse to count women as persons and later make women into men seems a strange arena of human communication within which to insist and rely upon the determinacy, relative or otherwise, of language. Furthermore, there is a rich history in the English common law of judges making what appear to be counterintuitive and bizarre findings. When almost all petty thefts were punishable by mandatory capital punishment, judges resorted to all kinds of odd distinctions and interpretations to avoid the imposition of draconian penalties: no one now considers those judges to have acted unjudicially.[72]

Accordingly, both these critical responses to a nonfoundational account of so-called easy cases only serve to confirm that which they claim to condemn—the difference between the resolution of easy and hard cases is not one of intrinsic identity or separate processes but rather one of relative obviousness based on situated assessments of relevant social contexts and agreements. Whether a case is hard or easy has little to do with the particular rule itself; all rules are potentially easy and hard. What determines the perception or treatment of a case as hard or easy is to be found in a complex appreciation of the contextual and interrelated positionings of the rule(s) to be applied, the facts to be ascertained, and the parties and judges involved. None of this will be configurable in any fixed or formulaic way; the overall combination defies the kind of confident or simple prediction on which traditional accounts of adjudication depend. As with almost all games, no one game is ever exactly like another, as the conditions and circumstances under which any particular performance takes place change in such small and large ways that mechanical replication is not possible or viable. Consequently, the limits on judges are not imposed by the external force of the legal rules but by the internal pressure of the judges' own imaginative strengths and political convictions; judges are situated within a context of constraints that shape as much as limit their freedom. As Justice Cardozo rather grandly and perhaps too generally stated, "There is emancipation . . . in our very bonds."[73]

Although my nonfoundational account stresses imagination over technique and persuasion over demonstration, it does not commit me to the untenable or nihilistic position that it will always be possible to make the application of a rule come out in the way that the judge wants it to. Sometimes cars are vehicles and horses are not. But this is a matter of imaginative insight or rhetorical achievement, not objective truth or ahistorical determinacy; "anything might go," but not "anything goes." In such circumstances, it does not mean that the skeptical account has failed to give a cogent or realistic account of law and judging. On the contrary, the very fact that skepticism accepts the existential experience of rule boundedness is what makes it cogent and realistic. Without some explanation or place for that fact, a nonfoundational view of law would be sadly deficient in terms of its own commitment to situated and engaged forms of understanding and evaluation. Moreover, as almost all theorists and lawyers will agree, because a case cannot be brought within a rule, it does not follow that the case must fail. Even under archformalist accounts of law, judges can either fashion an exception to a rule or amend the rule. As Hart states, "A rule that ends with the word 'unless . . .' is still a rule."[74]

Conclusion

In this chapter, I have contended that language is not so much textually ambiguous as structurally indeterminate: different meanings are brought about by differences in context. Using the important work of Hart as a foil, I have made the central claim that adjudication is better understood as an interpretive game in which the constraints are both always in place and never themselves outside of interpretation. Despite the confidence of Wittgenstein, there is no context of contexts in that there will always be disagreement about what the proper context of any law or rule is. It is the disagreement over context that creates the ineradicable presence of indeterminacy. However, although insistence on the endemic instability of law does not dictate that meaning is always elusive, it does hold that meaning's continuous slippage and instability prevent the establishment of any meaning that is fixed and beyond further interpretive contestation. While meaning is always parenthetical and can never be grounded, the possibility of meaningful dialogue is always available: it is the theoretical status of such practical meaning that is debatable. Needless to say, most mainstream jurists have sought to resist this radical account of how law and adjudication are unable to exercise or claim the authority for their operation that a foundationalist approach promises. I now turn to recent efforts to salvage the adjudicative enterprise from the implications of this indeterminacy critique.

4 Playing with Authority: Interpretation and Identity

"You know, I like you less and less the more I know you."

"Madame, it is always a mistake to know an author."

—Ernest Hemingway, *Death in the Afternoon*

As a site for interpretive activity, law is both a reflective and reflexive effort to make sense of human struggle. In almost all its manifestations, the practice and skills of interpretation lie at the dynamic heart of the legal enterprise, whether this involves the prosaic writing and rereading of parochial legal texts or the more expansive reading and rewriting of sprawling social situations. But in all cases, unable to escape the creative opportunities and constraining responsibilities of interpretive activity, lawyers function on the contested territory of discursive practice. As such, they are engaged as active participants in the mediation and negotiation of political meaning through legal interpretation. However, uncomfortable with the open-ended possibilities of such an interpretive task, judges and jurists have been anxious to establish a suitable and disciplining hermeneutics. In their different ways, they have sought to avoid the specter of linguistic indeterminacy that has threatened the jurisprudential enterprise since Hart's work on legal language. Influenced by their own institutional history and political needs, judges and jurists have opted to preserve the notion that the *author* can act as a principled marker of hermeneutical thrift in the unruly proliferation of interpretive possibilities: "[The author] is the measure and evaluator of all juridical actions."[1] Ranging across individual judges and academic commentators through constitutional conferences and legislative assemblies to the Rule of Law and the common law itself, traditional jurists look for an authoritative way to *play the game* that is able to bring a workable degree of stability to the potential frenzy of legal interpretation.

In meeting this challenge, legal theorists have sought the assistance of their literary colleagues. However, as events have tended to confirm, the literary enterprise is a strange place to look for reassurance about the possibility of hermeneutical authority—literature tends to be celebrated more for its richness of interpretive possibilities than its capacity to generate authoritative meanings. Far from facilitating the process of fixing law with a determinate meaning, the literary diversion has highlighted the desperation of jurisprudence's attempt to fix legal meaning and to ground the judicial enterprise in something outside of itself. If contemporary literary theory has any message, it is that to ask about meaning is to ask about everything; there is no formal place or process that can ground legal interpretation such that the debate about law's meaning and substance can proceed in a neutral or nonideological way. Both adjudication and literary criticism tend to be interpretive activities that are dominated almost exclusively by elite professionals who are intent upon ignoring the historical contexts in which both take place and upon hiding the political agendas in the service of which both are done. As such, there is no *Theory of Interpretation* that can govern or underwrite the particular interpretation of specific texts. Texts only mean in concrete settings, and theoretical understandings about the significance of the contexts in which writing and reading take place are part of that setting. The text can never be read in its own abstraction or generality but must always be read against and within the complex codes of power in which it arises and receives attention.[2]

In this chapter, therefore, I will criticize efforts to defend the foundationalist claim that, among the many different ways of playing law's language game, there are some performances that are more authoritative than others. After introducing the accepted modes of legal interpretation, I explain the theoretical and practical obstacles that stand in the way of establishing the authors' intent with any degree of confidence or certainty. Next, I show how a nonfoundationalist critique does not dispense with the idea of authorial intention but rather destabilizes it and robs it of authoritative force; there must be a shift from understanding interpretation and identity in metaphysical terms to engaging them as part of a political endeavor. However, in insisting on the "death of the author," I do not mean to suggest that the identity of judges is unimportant. Accordingly, in the next couple of sections, I go on to defend the claim that not only is interpretation important but that the identity of those who interpret is important. Of course, in the process, I will make sure that *identity* is understood and utilized in a suitably nonfoundational sense. In so doing, it might become possible to grasp that it does matter who is playing law's language game. But it does so in a way that is very different from the traditional view. Finally, the chapter closes by exploring the implications of a nonfoundationalist critique for the actual practice and performance of adjudication. In particular, I emphasize that there is no vantage point available from which to survey interpretive strategies that is itself not political.

The word "author" is derived from the Latin *auctor*. As traditionally used, it tended to operate to preserve a text's cultural precedence rather than to highlight the process of creative reinvention. It draws upon a whole etymological tradition that centers upon the concept of "authority." Although it was not until the Enlightenment that the idea of authors as the authoritative source for their own words replaced the *auctor*, there was still an implicit acceptance that writers drew their authority from that of a divine Creator. While this tendency is less marked today, foundationalist jurists still hanker after such interpretive validation and hermeneutical legitimacy. Yet, much critical literature has sought to post the obituary of the author (and, therefore, Authority) as the interpretive source and hermeneutical guarantor of meaning. The main thrust of those who insist upon "death of the author" is that there is no one to challenge or to speak in the name of, because "to refuse to arrest meaning is finally to refuse God and his hypostases, reason, science, the law."[3] Nonetheless, not all jurists have been prepared to throw in the foundationalist towel. While they accept that language is a game in which meaning is not fully determinate, they do not accept that efforts at authoritative interpretation are doomed to failure. With the help of literary theory, there has been a concerted effort to ground or trace back an interpretation to a foundational or ultimate source that can confer authority on one particular interpretation over another—*the author*.

In both law and literary criticism, the fear is that without a reliable and grounded mode of interpretation, the possibilities for ascribing meaning to texts will be limitless: the interpretive critic will have little alternative than "to surrender to the flux, the gossip, the muddle and the motley."[4] The unsettling threat of indeterminacy is that without the possibility of a right or wrong interpretation that can be certified as authoritative, the possibility of knowledge and, therefore, goodness is subverted and lost. This fear is felt to be especially troubling in law. In contrast to literary criticism, jurisprudence is not considered to be a study through which to celebrate a text's contradictions and playfulness; legal answers to questions of textual authority and interpretive validity can have devastating consequences for individuals and society generally. In particular, legal theorists worry that, divested of a disciplining protocol, adjudication will be revealed as an inescapably creative and self-referential act, which, in turn, will engender "the deepest and darkest of all nihilisms"—a demeaning vision of social existence in which the very idea of not only the Rule of Law but life in general is rendered meaningless and right becomes simply a function of might.[5]

In the study of both law and literature, therefore, theorists have been energized by the felt need to negotiate between the competing claims of authors and interpreters as the ultimate location of hermeneutical authority over disputed texts. In addressing this task, the jurisprudential establishment has clearly thrown its institutional and intellectual weight on the side of authorial authority as the linchpin in the interpretive process. In this effort to ground law's interpretive ministrations, there are three general approaches to establishing the locus of authorial authority—the *textual*, the *intentional*, and the *communalist*. Although they each offer different and often conflicting accounts of the sources and techniques for arriving at a certifiable meaning, they have the same foundationalist ambition as well as the same interpretive faith in the centrality of author-ity—that there are authoritative ways to *play the game* that can ground adjudication in something more neutral and less political than each judge's situated efforts to ascribe meaning to legal texts. Not surprisingly, a nonfoundationalist critique argues that this ambition is as unnecessary as it is unrealizable.

While the textualist account of interpretation is the most traditional and longest established approach in law and jurisprudence, it received a relatively recent and sophisticated confirmation in the literary theories of the so-called New Critics. They maintain that the text is best understood as an organic artifact whose meaning is contained within its structured whole and can be grasped without reference to historical, social, or biographical circumstances: the meaning of the text is ascertained by reference to universal criteria of value and is entirely internal to the text itself, which is established "as an object of specifically critical judgement."[6] Therefore, the textualists' special claim is that what counts as evidence of the author's intention should be limited to the text itself. As such, the text *is* the intention of the author: "Language is the very condition of intention and intention is the vehicle of meaning."[7] Accordingly, under the textualist approach, it is not that the author ceases to exist but only that the legal or literary work stands in entirely for the author's ideas and intentions. Once produced and put into circulation, texts are considered to possess an objective status that exists independently of their authors and their declared intention. However, a text's meaning does not disclose itself easily to the casual reader; it can only be elicited by a close and professional study of its overall structure and thematic unity.

In law, the adjudicative enterprise proceeds as if statutory texts and constitutional words had an independent existence; they are treated as incorporeal elements, existing in a realm of abstract reality and possessing exclusive meaning. In short, such textualists resist a "living" approach as being undemocratic and insist that the legal text is the best source of the legislators' intent; judges are the humble servants of the document's framers. Under such an interpretive approach, the genius of judges lies in their ability to winkle the correct meaning out of a legal text and to apply that meaning to the facts of a particular case. Until recently, judicial efforts to construe constitutions and statutes were dominated by the textualist approach, albeit in an undertheorized and overconfident manner. Under the *literal* rule, courts follow the plain and ordinary meaning of the statute's words as understood at the time of the enactment without concerning themselves with the social impact or desirability of their decision; a judge might interpret an old statutory provision that "no vehicles are allowed in the park" to cover an ambulance or a bicycle but not a horse or an airplane. Alternatively, under the *golden* rule, courts strive to follow the plain and ordinary meaning of the statute's words, unless that would lead to obvious absurdity or injustice, in which case the court will construe the statute's words in such a way as to avoid such absurdity or injustice. In assessing "absurdity or injustice," courts will be guided by the larger context of the overall statute, such that in interpreting the rule that "no vehicles are allowed in the park," a judge might decide that it is absurd to treat an ambulance as a vehicle and an airplane not as one. Indeed, the received view in England and Canada remains that courts cannot use legislative debates to elicit legislative intent; it is to be gleaned from the overall text and structure of the statute.[8]

Despite its institutional tenacity, the textualist stance is difficult to take seriously as a convincing solution to the hermeneutical problematic. Even the most traditional of lawyers and judges concede that in cases of difficulty or ambiguity, a strictly textualist analysis is, at best, incomplete. In those hard cases when there is genuine disagreement over what the text recommends, textualism seems singularly unhelpful; it acts more as an invitation to readers to make choices than as a realistic restraint on those interpretive choices. Under any rudimentary theory of language, including Hart's conventionalist approach, the text does not have an absolutely objective content or exclusively self-contained meaning; the text does not so much speak for itself as has to be spoken for. There is no beginning to a text and there is no end; the boundaries to reading and writing are constructed around the text, not imposed by the text itself. The text does not announce or present itself but emerges in the course of interpretive practice: "Linguistic and textual facts, rather than being the objects of interpretation, are its products."[9] Under the guise of valid and impersonal interpretation, a textualist approach smuggles in surreptitiously through the back door that which it ceremoniously denies entry at the front door—the personal preferences of the reader or judge. Textualists do not so much surrender to "the flux, the gossip, the muddle and the motley" as proceed as if it were simply not a problem. Like the Emperor, such theorists are only sustained in their nakedness by the complicity or fear of the legal colleagues.

Conceding the open-endedness of literary and legal texts, another group of legal theorists adopt an intentionalist approach to constitutional and statutory interpretation. As a hedge against the threat of reader anarchy, they propose that the meaning of any disputed text can be fixed by retrieving the intent of its author; the hermeneutical exercise is most decidedly a matter of discovery, not creation. The theoretical basis of this claim is that authorship is a communicative act that brings into being a text that functions as a medium through which its writer attempts to convey a discrete experience or idea to the text's potential readers. In such a scheme, meaning is something akin to a precious gem that is secreted in the text by its author, to be uncovered and treasured by diligent and discriminating readers. For example, E. D. Hirsch maintains that interpretation can only be grounded in the intention of an author, who, "as represented by his text, is unchanging and reproducible."[10] To answer the obvious objections to this seemingly simple-minded proposal, a critical distinction is made between a text's meaning and its significance. Whereas a text's meaning is what its earlier writer meant and is synonymous with the author's intention, a text's significance is what the later reader makes out of that meaning and so, unlike a text's meaning, can change with historical circumstance and personal predilection. Accordingly, the intentionalist approach assumes that any interpretation of the text must comport with the explicit, implicit, or reconstructed intention of its makers, even if that intention is to create an ambiguous or indeterminate text.

In law, the intentionalist approach has been most vigorously applied in constitutional law. The basic claim is essentially normative. Judicial interpretation can be legitimate only so long as it seeks to give democratic effect to the original act of consent by the people to the Constitution as a document to limit governmental power. Most important, it is recognized that the best evidence of the Constitution's meaning is the framers' intentions. It is the task of the judge to elicit that intention from the available material and to resolve present disputes in light of that understanding. Such proponents maintain that any other approach would convert interpretation into amendment and blur further the already hazy line between the judiciary's law-applying responsibility and the citizenry's lawmaking role.[11] However, the resort to an intentionalist approach has also found favor in statutory interpretation. The strict intentionalist approach recommends that the law is not the legislative text but rather the intent of the legislators. At best, the statute offers evidence of what that legislative intent might be. The interpreter's task is to engage in archaeological fieldwork by sifting appropriate historical sources in order to excavate the authors' intentions. The difference between the intentionalist and textualist approaches is more one of emphasis than kind. Whereas the latter views the text as the only legitimate and reliable evidence of legislative intent, the former treats the text as only one of the possible and legitimate sources for eliciting legislative intent. Nevertheless, both gain their hermeneutical purchase from a commitment to the priority of authorial authority in the interpretive hierarchy—authors trump readers in the debate over what it means to play the game properly.

A more sophisticated and modern version of the intentionalist approach is offered by Richard Posner. He views interpretation as less an act of obedience to a command from a superior to a subordinate than a communicative dialogue over time between the senior (legislative) and junior (judicial) partners in the practice of government. Wherever there is no ascertainable or clear intent following a rigorous inquiry, Posner maintains that judges should put themselves in the legislature's shoes and determine what it would have done had it squarely faced the new problem. On this view, legal interpretation is about imaginatively reconstructing authors' intentions in order to assess how they might have answered any question of interpretation if it had been put to them: "The reader's task is to open a channel to the mind of the author."[12] However, unlike traditional intentionalists, Posner recommends that judges should not only "fill the gaps" in the legislative text but also in legislative intent: judges better fulfill their democratic mandate when they engage in such "imaginative reconstruction" than when they refuse to act without the benefit of the legislature's actual and expressed guidance. In this view, the recoverability of authorial intent, actual or imagined, works as a point of fixity in a world of flux; it is a hermeneutical haven in an anarchic world.

The intentionalist approach retains considerable support among legal theorists; it is the interpretive common sense of the legal and literary community—although the text governs meaning, resort to the author's intent is both permissible and determinative where that text is unclear or ambiguous. For instance, courts will strive to interpret the statute's words in light of the legislature's purpose for enacting the legislation such that the mischief to be addressed is effectively remedied. In interpreting the rule that "no vehicles are allowed in the park," a judge might conclude that as the purpose of the enactment was to permit people to relax or play in the park without worrying about their safety, the use of skateboards and roller blades falls within the spirit of the prohibition. However, in both its strict and more sophisticated forms, the intentionalist approach is predicated on the operating assumption that there is an actual and fixed authorial intent or legislative design that can be located and articulated with sufficient clarity such that courts can respect and implement it. While the search for legislative or constitutional intent can serve some important and useful purposes (e.g., contextualizing the specific problem and its possible resolution at the time of enactment and generally improving the present understanding of politics by a better acquaintance with its past),[13] it cannot anchor legal interpretation. As both a philosophical and practical matter, there is little to suggest that it is possible to identify a particular intent that is capable of grounding and authorizing textual interpretation over time and in specific circumstances.

As a practical matter, even if courts were correct in their assumption that an application of legislative intent would best fulfill their democratic mandate, it is difficult to know how it would be possible to locate such intent. The initial step of distinguishing intention from aspiration, expectation, and the like is apt to prove insurmountable: there is no reason to assume that everything that legislators say is what they mean or intend. Further, the attempt to generate a finding of what a large group of legislators would have wanted over time, after circumstances have changed and in unanticipated disputes, seems destined to be frustrated; the identification of past intentions, particularly of collective entities, remains doggedly resistant to present interpretation. Legislators very rarely have a specific or exact intention in mind across a range of potential future disputes. To remedy such shortcoming, the courts are obliged to engage in the most speculative of "what if" investigations—if legislators had thought about or been able to anticipate this problem, which they did not, how would they most likely have answered the problem? Moreover, if it is not naive to believe that the legislature is filled with reasonable politicians who are engaged in pursuing reasonable goals reasonably and in saying what they mean, it is most definitely wishful to think that they agree on what *reasonable* means. Also, in hard cases, it is difficult to understand how an imagined refinement of legislative purpose can yield determinate answers. Any purpose or objective that is consistently attributable to legislatures is likely to be so general that it will be of little help in specific circumstances.[14]

As a theoretical matter, it is not easy to see how the intentionalist approach can overcome the considerable historiographical and ideological barriers that stand in the way of its practical realization. Rather than a simple fact that stands antecedent to interpretation, intention is itself in need of interpretation; it can never be retrieved in an accurate or faithful fashion and, therefore, must always be reconstructed. The fact is that the attempt to retrieve intent is doomed to failure because the historical venture is itself as open to interpretation as the text's interpretation that history seeks to limit. While there are considerable commonalities between the present and the past, intention is never retrievable in some pure sense because the past must always be viewed through a filter of operative assumptions that make some tentative retrieval possible and, at the same time, render any absolute retrieval impossible. Moreover, it is by no means self-evident that democracy is best served by giving effect to the views of long-dead politicians who received only indirect consent from the enfranchised few; this is an ideological claim that must be argued for rather than argued from without further justification. In short, therefore, intentionalist interpretation is "frequently historically uncertain, practically indeterminate, politically repugnant, conceptually incoherent, and contradicted by the evidence that the Framers' intent was that the Framers' intent should not bind future generations."[15]

A Scholarly Community

With both the textualist and intentionalist strategies found practically and theoretically wanting, the prospects for relying upon the idea of the author as the locus of interpretive authority appear dim; each seems to serve as a weak cover for the undisciplined imposition of interpretive choice. Nevertheless, with considerable ingenuity, legal theorists have refused to accept that there is no legitimate and appropriate form of adjudication in a democratic polity. As a hedge against the imagined twin threats of an overbearing authorial constraint and an undisciplined interpretive freedom, mainstream jurists have constructed a *communalist* account of legal interpretation. Positing the extant community as a collective author, they have sought to cabin the textual search for meaning in some communal precepts of interpretive regularity or in the establishment of an interpretive practice of institutional integrity. For example, Ronald Dworkin maintains that legal interpretation should proceed on the basis that legal rights and duties "were all created by a single author—the community personified—expressing a coherent conception of justice and fairness."[16] In this way, legal interpretation is constructed as a dynamic exercise that inculcates a respect for texts as well as allowing for their developing interpretation in line with changing social mores. Within this framework of understanding law as one evolving and communal text, the emerging pragmatic understanding holds that interpretive authority is generated in the organic, sophisticated, and responsive interaction between legal texts and their professional interpreters.

In an essay that explicitly draws on recent developments in literary criticism, Owen Fiss argues that adjudication is "neither a wholly discretionary nor a wholly mechanical activity."[17] Striving to avoid a deified text as well as an unruly solipsism, he rejects both a crude textualism in which the text speaks with a clear and single voice and a textual nihilism that celebrates the multiple and anarchic voices of the text. Fiss proposes a set of interpretive devices that mediate and constrain the encounter between text and reader. While he acknowledges the presence of strong and irreducible personal elements in the acts of understanding and expression that constitute interpretation, he relies upon the notions of disciplining rules, which constrain the interpreter, and an interpretive community, which recognizes these rules as authoritative, to import an element of objectivity into the process. Interpreters are not free to assign any meaning that they wish to the text because they must establish a meaning that will be persuasive to the prevailing community and conform to its relevant standards. Fiss acknowledges that this element of objectivity will be present only if there is a single interpretive community whose standards of interpretation are universally accepted. Accordingly, he maintains that the existence of this unitary interpretive community is demonstrated by the shared judicial commitment to uphold and advance the ideal of the Rule of Law: "In legal interpretation there is only one school and attendance is mandatory."[18]

For Fiss, therefore, adjudicative legitimacy is not based on the substantive correctness of a decision but on a bounded objectivity achieved through the authorized and authoritative use of the extant interpretive rules. However, his emphasis on the existence of a hierarchy of courts and his confidence in the Rule of Law as offering workable constraints on interpretive freedom seem misplaced. There are two main problems with this jurisprudential initiative. First, because it makes meaning dependent upon the prior existence of consensus, Fiss's theory has nothing to say in exactly those circumstances where interpretive relief is most needed—in those hard cases when there is no consensus available. The existence of procedures for resolving interpretive disputes does not resolve the issue of how such procedural rules themselves are to be given determinate meaning and application. In need of interpretation themselves, those very same "interpretive rules" cannot provide the desired foundation on which interpretive authority can be based. Fiss's account is for the already-converted, not the yet-to-be-persuaded. Second, this communalist idea actually makes the critical point rather than refutes it. Fiss implicitly concedes that judicial decisions are less explained by legal doctrine and precedential rules, and more determined by the political views and institutional commitments of the community. Ultimately, when the persuasiveness of his arguments falls short, Fiss can only make his interpretive claims stick by demanding enforced allegiance. After all, in Fiss's scheme of things, the judge is not only a combination of literary critic and moral philosopher, but he "also speaks with the authority of the Pope."[19]

Despite the best efforts of contemporary jurists, Hart and Sacks's assessment is as accurate now as it was in 1958—"The hard truth of the matter is that . . . courts have no intelligible, generally accepted, and consistently applied theory of statutory interpretation."[20] Insofar as jurists have viewed their role as, at least in large part, offering an intellectually compelling and practically viable account of legal interpretation, the mainstream jurisprudential project is an unmitigated disaster. Nonetheless, across the broad spectrum of efforts to establish such a theory, there still exists a profound commitment to the possibility of establishing an authoritative mode of interpretation. Of course, there are considerable differences between the various offerings. Whereas some judges and jurists maintain that statutory meaning is fixed and retrievable, others hold that it is always in flux and in need of reconstruction. And whereas some consider that the judiciary ought to act as the honest agents of the legislature, others contend that the judiciary and the legislature ought to engage in a dialogic collaboration for the public benefit. Yet, despite these differences, all the traditionalists agree that there must be a viable theory of statutory interpretation, because, without one, the practice of statutory interpretation will be unintelligible, unconstrained, and undemocratic—the rogue judge will be rampant and, what is worse, will be known to be so.

While this fear is understandable, it is overrated and overstated. The realization that there is no authorial authority does not lead to an irresistible slide into "the flux, the gossip, the muddle and the motley." Although no meaning is ever entirely reducible to intention, it does not follow that intention is irrelevant to the meaning-giving exercise. It is surely the case that any reading of a text requires some resort to an idea of the author's intention. In its most general sense, interpretation is about intention, because all interpretation is based upon some acceptance of the notion that texts are the product of human intention rather than, for example, the random outcome of the proverbial bunch of monkeys playing with typewriters. Any act of reading is premised on the idea that it involves reference to an author's intent, even if that intent is being constructed as reading occurs.[21] However, to accept this premise has no necessary conclusions for the interpretive task. In particular, it does not entail any commitment to a particular or substantive account of that intention; it merely recognizes that all texts are written somewhere by someone for some purpose. The author's intention is not so much unavailable as incomplete; it is a slippery item that evades capture. As Jack Balkin puts it, "Once the signifier leaves the author's creation and is let loose upon the world, it takes on a life of its own in the other contexts in which it can be repeated."[22] Intention, therefore, is not something that can fully or exclusively account for meaning in any determinative or definitive manner. The nonfoundationalist point is that authorial intention, like any and every other construct, is insufficient to ground the hermeneutical project. It is never possible to close or elide the gap between what is intended and what is taken from text. Paradoxically, all meaning is about intent, but that intent is never fully available and is always in need of creative reconstruction.

However, in casting interpretation as a playful practice of creative reconstruction, a nonfoundationalist approach is not to be taken as claiming that the identity of judicial players in law's language game is somehow unimportant or irrelevant. To ignore entirely the fact that *someone* is speaking is as much a mistake as to depend exclusively on who is speaking to determine meaning.

In insisting that "writing is that neutral, composite, oblique space where our subject slips away" and where "the author enters into his own death,"[23] there is nothing incompatible with arguing both that the author has ceased to function as a source and guarantor of interpretive meaning and that the identity of writers (and readers) remains vitally important. While there is no value at all in trying to reinstall the author as the authoritative linchpin in the interpretive process, it is possible and desirable to ensure that the identity of judges and jurists makes a difference in how the adjudicative game is understood and played. Notwithstanding "the death of the author," the writer as a historical figure remains relevant: its particular importance and role will shift and vary with the task at hand. Within such a critical understanding that accepts that there is no Theory of Interpretation that can govern or underwrite the particular interpretation of specific texts and that texts only mean in concrete settings, it becomes possible to grasp that it does matter who is reading and writing. But it does so in a way that is very different from the traditional view. Who is speaking is not a matter of indifference. But the difference is not metaphysical or ontological; it is political and historical.

From a nonfoundationalist perspective, it must be emphasized that nothing necessarily follows from the political identity or historical location of the speaker or hearer. Certainly, there is no necessary connection between the speaker's intentions and the meaning of what is said; the idea of authorial authority as an ultimate source or grounding is consigned to the trash can of failed foundationalist theories. However, the social identity and historical placing of who speaks and who listens is not completely irrelevant or of no effect. The practice of speaking will not cease to be an intentional act and its status will demand attention as such. The person who writes cannot control what is read or understood and how it is to be heard or understood. As Jacques Derrida puts it, intention "will have its place, but from that place it will no longer be able to govern the entire scene and system of utterance."[24] The nature, salience, and consequence of that intention is hermeneutically relevant in that it is always open to interpretation and reinterpretation, but it will never be the final word on or of interpretation. In contrast to traditional understandings of hermeneutical practice, a nonfoundational critique works to problematize rather than prioritize any claim to authoritative interpretation. My hermeneutical ambition, therefore, is not to obliterate authors but to reorient them as one—and only one among many—nonprivileged participants in the continuing process of negotiating texts and giving meaning to them in the context of people's lives.

Accordingly, in the next couple of sections, I will defend the claim that not only are writing and reading important but that the identity of those who write and read is important. Of course, in the process, I will make sure that *identity* is understood and utilized in a suitably nonfoundational sense. In order to get at and explicate the difference between authors and writers, I will re-pose and re-answer Michel Foucault's famous and characteristically enigmatic question: "What difference does it make who is speaking?"[25] His whole essay can be read as an outright dismissal of the need for or relevance of authors in the hermeneutical enterprise—in effect, an indifference to the difference that difference might make, if any, in who is writing or speaking. Foucault's primary interest is in the operation of discourse more as a productive process of subject formation than as the formed process of productive subjects; discourse creates as much as it is created. While I want to hold on to the general import of that account, I also want to supplement it by showing that there is a different notion of difference that is at work in understanding fully the hermeneutical problematic—a serious interest in the kind of difference that difference might make in who is writing or reading. In short, by way of a nonfoundationalist critique, I will draw a distinction between the metaphysical claim of "difference" and a political understanding of "difference." It is through the metaphysical death of the author that the political writer (and reader) comes to life. It is in this important sense that it matters and makes a difference who is speaking (and reading).

Making the Difference

In 1982, Bertha Wilson was the first woman appointed to the Supreme Court of Canada (she is still only the fourth). In a later influential essay in which she confirmed the importance of judicial impartiality, she sought to answer a pressing question for the legal and general community: will women judges really make a difference? Surveying a considerable amount of legal literature, she came to the opinion that "a distinctly male perspective is clearly discernible" in many areas of law, especially criminal law, which is "based on presuppositions about the nature of women . . . that are little short of ludicrous." In order to combat this bias, she endorses institutional efforts to reeducate and sensitize male judges to these problems. However, she insists that it would be necessary to appoint increasing numbers of women judges if any genuine or substantial progress was to be made. Wilson argues that the appointment of women judges will not only provide important role models for women and alter the dynamics of courtroom demeanor, but it also could "establish judicial neutrality through a countervailing female perspective." Drawing on Gilligan's idea that women have a "different voice" and frame moral decisions differently from men, Wilson suggests that women judges would bring a different experience to the task and responsibility of judging:

> The universalistic doctrine of human rights must include a realistic concept of masculine and feminine humanity regarded as a whole, that human kind *is* dual and must be represented in dual form if the trap of an asexual abstraction in which *human being* is always defined in the masculine is to be avoided. If women lawyers and judges through their differing perspectives on life can bring a new humanity to bear on the decision-making process, perhaps they *will* make a difference. Perhaps they will succeed in infusing the law with an understanding of what it means to be fully human.[26]

From a nonfoundationalist perspective, I want both to agree and disagree with Wilson's impassioned and confident belief in the transformative power of women judges (and, by implication, judges who are from other excluded or disadvantaged minorities). If Wilson is making the metaphysical claim that women will have a necessary and consistent impact on the law and craft of judging by virtue of their ontological status and essential experience as women, I want to disagree—this is simply one more way to rehabilitate the discredited author as the authoritative pivot in the interpretive game of law. However, if Wilson is making the very different political claim that the appointment of women judges will increase the likelihood that women's different social experiences will be brought to bear on judicial decision making, I want to agree—this abandons the search for interpretive foundations and emphasizes the social context in which writing and reading take place. In nonfoundationalist terms, the identity of those involved in the interpretive process is neither the beginning nor end of the fixing of meaning; context will influence and be influenced by such participation. It is not the *will* in "perhaps they will make a difference" that should be stressed but rather the *perhaps*.

For some, Wilson's initial claim that the identity of the judge has any relevance at all will be very controversial. While they might concede that certain judges have allowed their own particular biases and prejudices to intrude into their decision making, they will view this as a perversion of the requirement that judges act with impartiality. For them, the solution to bad judges who allow their male (or any other) perspective or presuppositions to affect their judgment is not to appoint more bad judges who will only be able to counteract that partiality by introducing countervailing perspectives and presuppositions of their own; impartiality demands that judges be appointed who understand that their duty is to apply legal rules in an objective and detached manner. As I have been at pains to argue, this stance is thoroughly discredited. What "rules" mean and what it means to "apply" them is always contestable and never innocent of the judge's values and involvement: adjudication is a political practice. However, Wilson's retort to the traditionalists' charge is equally problematic. While she deserves to be applauded for her commitment to appoint more women judges, she is mistaken in her justification for doing so; it is as flawed to treat the identity of judges as being all-important as it is to contend that their identity is unimportant.

For Wilson, the identity of the judges seems to be paramount because the authority of their performance will be derived from the authenticity of the experience from which it arises: the silenced voice of oppression will speak truth to a complacent or complicit world. Apart from the fact that identity is not fixed or identical across and within gender (or any other different category), the difficulty with such a foundationalist position is that it falls back on a very crude notion of interpretation in which identity is entirely determinative of interpretation. It suggests that texts or judgments need not be read in any serious or engaged way but that they can be assessed and authorized by reference to the identity of their author. In the same way that judgments by women or blacks can be valorized and praised, so judgments by men or whites can be stigmatized and dismissed. The problem with this so-called identity politics is that it depoliticizes politics by turning it into a metaphysical issue; it repeats the essentialist error of creating a world based on the timeless and global truths of black, female, and gay lives. While to deny entirely racial or sexual identities is to fool ourselves and court complicity, to accept them entirely is to ignore their ideological production and, therefore, the possibilities for their political transformation. It is not useful to claim that there is a "women's point of view" and a "women's voice," which must be released if society is to give women "really what they want" and "on [their] own terms."[27] This is likely to ensure the continued dominance of white and male voices against which other voices will always vie for attention and whose importance will be reinforced at the very moment of their greatest threat.

In making this argument, it is important to understand "identity" in a nonfoundationalist sense. In contrast to Wilson's Gilliganesque understanding, identity is performative, and, therefore, it is not a foundational base from which expressive excursions are made and made meaningful; a constituted identity is (re)shaped by and through its continuing performances. Identity or difference is not indifferent to the context of time and place. Identity is relative, not intrinsic; fluid, not fixed; perspectival, not neutral; and protean, not perfected. Nevertheless while people are not fundamentally fixed by their experience of race, gender, and class, they are distinctively marked by such social categorizations. As such, identity is a temporary location in the interplay of difference that comprises life's game. As people (re)constitute themselves in their lived relations with others, so judges (re)constitute themselves in their participation in law's language game. However, like everything else, that experience is itself always and already the product and subject of interpretation. It cannot escape interrogation by masquerading as its own grounding: "Belief in the truth of Experience is as much an ideological production as belief in the experience of Truth."[28] Consequently, while it may be true that oppressed groups have an understanding about oppression that others do not have, that is no reason for privileging that account as a more truthful representation of reality. However, it is still vital to include the standpoint of the oppressed, "not because it has any special access to the truth, but because what is taken as truth is incomplete or distorted without the views of the oppressed."[29] Having lived a life of exclusion, the oppressed are likely to understand oppression better.

In some circumstances and locations, identity alone may speak louder than any words of explanation or indignation. The influence that more women and black judges can have as role models in law and society generally should not be underestimated. Moreover, as Wilson insists, the fact that women become a more regular presence in the courtroom will help to transform the demeanor and dynamics of legal advocacy. But the ineffable impact of identity cannot always be relied upon to get the job done: it can only be one tactic in a more complex strategy of politicization. The force of identity is important but only when it is understood as a contingent and dynamic distillation of what has been done, is being done, and will be done. While identities affect people's choices and actions, the choices made and actions taken affect people's identities. As an important site for social discipline, identities are to be constantly struggled over and frequently transformed; it is not a psychic space of authentic self to be repaired to or moved toward. In understanding action and identity as inseparable and mutually reconstituting, it becomes possible to grasp race, gender, sexual orientation, and class as thoroughly historical and, therefore, inescapably political in character. There is nothing essential or natural about people's identities. While experienced as real, they are always constructed and, therefore, always reconstructible. In a nonfoundational account, therefore, the political challenge is to transform relations "by continually rethinking who we are and why we are making the choices we make so we can free ourselves from the belief that our selves are constructed by our sexual identities."[30]

Accordingly, the claims that identity is or is not essential to an informed interpretation misses the point. While they do not collapse into each other (for this would truly be a perversion of any institutional ideal), it is simply not the case that the identity and background of people are irrelevant to their interpretive activity as writers and readers. Who people are cannot be entirely divorced from what they do or say. It is a conceit of established groups (white, male, heterosexual, etc.) to maintain that a cold objectivity is the only touchstone of true knowledge. Too often that objectivity has turned out to be little more than these groups' own partial interest in philosophical garb. The privileging of abstraction over experience, detachment over commitment, and objectivity over situatedness has not served to generate neutral knowledge but rather to neutralize challenges to existing orthodoxy. Of course, I do not suggest that political identity always supersedes reflective rigor in assessments of interpretive meaning and effect. As a nonfoundationalist, I only want to make the otherwise neglected point that ideas and interests are neither unrelated nor related in any fixed or general way. The problem lies in the vain effort to deny such affiliation between ideas and identity rather than in efforts to negotiate its implications. Effective judges and jurists are neither hubristic philosopher kings nor enslaved courtesans—they dwell on the threshold between apartness and alignment.[31]

In all debate around interpretation and identity, the mistake is to maintain that one is superior to or negates the other. The real challenge is to recognize and fathom their relation: making personal identity into the trump card of the legal interpretation debate is no better than pretending that identity can only have a corrupting influence. In today's society, identity and difference ought neither to be deified nor demonized in the name of authoritative interpretation or social justice. Furthermore, insofar as this debate tends to center upon so-called "political correctness," it cannot itself be allowed to take place in a historical or political context. While it might be possible someday and in some place to ignore the question of identity, this is most certainly not possible today in North America generally and the legal community particularly. If society were rid of discrimination and had achieved a genuine state of equality, the appointment of women (visible minorities, gays, etc.) to elite institutions (white, male, etc.), like the Supreme Court of Canada, might not be so urgent or desirable. However, the fact is, of course, that society is still very much marked by discrimination and inequality. Accordingly, to be a woman (visible minority, gay, etc.) is still to be the object of persecution because, and not in spite, of one's identity. Unfortunately, the courts are no less culpable than any other institutions in this history. Consequently, the experience of being a woman (visible minority, gay, etc.) remains critical to a full understanding of what it is to be a woman (visible minority, gay, etc.) and to why women (visible minority, gay, etc.) judges are required in today's society.

Of course, the proof of the pudding is in the eating; theoretical reflection needs to be accompanied by practical illustration. There is no better supporting evidence for the nonfoundationalist account of the relation between personal identity and judicial performance than the careers of Bertha Wilson herself and her colleagues, Beverly MacLachlin and Claire L'Heureux-

Dubé, on the Supreme Court of Canada. While there is nothing that they have done interpretively as judges that could not have been done by their male counterparts, the fact that they have done them as women judges cannot be politically underestimated. Their identities as women have never been entirely irrelevant, but their precise effect and importance have varied tremendously, depending on the context, among them and within themselves. At times, their identities as women have been important; at other times, their separate politics have weighed more heavily than their shared identities. While each of them has occasionally brought her own identity as a woman directly into the judicial performance, each has deployed it in different ways. Indeed, a survey of their judgments underlines the extent to which their experience as women and their own understanding of what it means to be both a woman and a judge are very different.[32] From a nonfoundationalist perspective, none of this is surprising. Identity is consistent neither among people nor across contexts, nor are its effects on interpretation generalizable: it is a matter of politics and practice, not philosophy and theory.

It can be concluded, therefore, that the relation between writers and their work is contextual in the sense that it will vary depending upon the historical circumstances and social conditions of its reading. The fact that "the author is dead" does not mean that writers of texts are no longer vital or relevant but only that they are no longer God. Biography still counts, but not in a predetermined or formulaic way. The life and texts of judges (and jurists) interact in complex and unstable ways. The value of any contribution to the struggle for a better world can never be fixed by its maker's identity: there is no one authentic experience of anything that deserves authority purely by dint of that experience alone. The weight to be attached to any contribution may well be affected by the circumstances of its making and reception: identity is neither entirely dispensable nor completely determinative. All writers, judicial or otherwise, are cultural impostors if they claim to write for or on behalf of their social class or group. As a nonfoundationalist critic, I have sought to deny any *necessary* connection between identity and interpretation but not to efface the historical and contingent relation between identity and interpretation. This is the difference between "writing" and "authorship." Such a claim is not a slight to racial identity or, more important, to racial suffering. It is a recognition of identity, but an identity that is contingent and therefore transformable, not certain and fixed.

Reading Differently

Although bitterly regretted in most traditional quarters, the Barthian notion that "writing is that neutral, composite, oblique space where our subject slips away" and where "the author enters into his own death" is to be welcomed.[33] The fact that the author of a text (or the text itself) cannot authoritatively control or constrain the meaning-giving exercise can be put to practical and arguably radical effect. Texts—like the Constitution or statutory enactments—that appear to carry a narrow and conservative meaning can (but not must) be shown to be capable of giving rise to transformative and expansive interpretations. Similarly, texts authored by reactionary writers, such as legislators or judges, can be liberated to serve progressive ends. By taking interpretation seriously and, at the same time, recognizing that interpretation is a dynamic occasion for creative reinvention, even the darkest textual cloud might be found to contain its own silver political lining. This state of affairs is achieved by insisting that the inevitable interpretive choice be exercised for the benefit of those who are presently excluded by entrenched patterns of oppression: "The task of constitutional theory ought no longer be to rationalize the real in one way or another, . . . [but] should be to contribute to a political movement that may begin to bring about a society in which civic virtue may flourish."[34] In playing law's language game, the limits on the judge or critic are more those of the imagination than of the rules themselves.

However, mainstream jurists have not been left dumbstruck by the critical challenge. They respond by arguing that the critics have become political victims of their own hermeneutical success. At bottom, the spirited rebuttal to critical attempts to sabotage the mainstream hermeneutical project rests on the argument that the theoretical rout of authorial tyranny and textual certainty has been bought at the bankrupting price of reader anarchy. It is claimed that when push comes to shove, critical skepticism leads to the conclusion that texts mean everything and, therefore, nothing. If any text can mean anything, all interpretations are equally valid and any interpretation is as valid as any other. The only constraints on interpretation are imaginative ingenuity and political cunning. The text becomes a blank check that can be written in the readers' political currency of choice. For the mainstream critic, this amounts to no interpretation at all: it is reduced to *only* the crudity of ideological appropriation. This point is amusingly made by Don Herzog in his punishing critique of Mark Tushnet's work:

> I have a distressingly large library, one that keeps growing. I lug books from my apartment to my office, from one library to another, from New York to Michigan. I pile them up and occasionally face the incredibly dreary task of loading them into boxes. Why do I bother? Why don't I have just one text, say a large piece of paper with the tantalizing word "TEXT" inscribed in the middle in Gothic lettering? I could then inter-

> pret it in any way I wanted: I could read Henry James into it, or out of it, or Joyce, or Simmel, or . . . . And why does Tushnet publish so much? Could he hold the sceptical view about his own work? Would he never complain that he had been misread? Suppose I read Tushnet's article—or the Constitution—as the story of a small boy growing up in Kansas during the Great Depression. (Suppose I read all texts that way.) Is that just a view the community is not likely to endorse, or is it wrong?[35]

These questions raise difficult issues, and mainstream jurists' criticisms are not entirely without merit. Indeed, some critics themselves are partly responsible for bringing something of this on themselves. In the enthusiasm to uncover false claims to privileged status at every turn, there has been an understandable temptation to herald the demise of authorial authority and its replacement by the empowered reader as a necessarily progressive achievement by critical workers in the name of democratic revolution. While this opens up some political opportunities, such a critical move is very problematic, as it simply shifts power from one group and is content to confer it on another. Whereas authors were once privileged, readers now assume the exalted role of meaning fixers.[36] While this might open fresh opportunities for progressive reinterpretation of legal texts, it will not necessarily impact on or change the substance of existing choices; it does not reduce the possibility of conservative decisions by conservative judges. More important, however, the whole critical endeavor takes place within the very same framework of foundational hermeneutical assumptions as the traditional agenda that it is intended to subvert; it works with the notion of interpretive authority rather than dispensing with it altogether. As elaborated by some of its alleged champions, the deconstructive critique is content to topple the old king in order to coronate a new queen. Yet it is the very institution of monarchic authority that needs to be overthrown. As such, a nonfoundationalist critique ought not to be taken to confer interpretive authority on readers but rather to be seen as a total challenge to the project of locating hermeneutical authorization in any grounded way at all.

A nonfoundational approach counsels a flat rejection of universal knowledge and an outright denial of essential truths. In contrast to the foundationalist project, it begins with an implacable incredulity toward grand theories of social explanation and metanarratives of ultimate emancipation. Rather than think of the individual subject as a unitary and sovereign subject whose self-directed vocation is to bring the world to heel through the exacting discipline of rational inquiry, a nonfoundationalist critique interrogates the whole idea of autonomous subjectivity and abstract reason; it places them in a constantly contingent condition of provisionality.[37] Of course, a nonfoundational approach does not obliterate the experience of subjectivity nor the availability of reason but rather problematizes them in order to understand them as being multiple, contextual, and protean. Within this broader understanding, it should be clear that a nonfoundationalist critique does not offer itself as one more interpretive methodology in locating textual meaning. Instead, it insists that there is no escape from the historical horizons of social living to the transcending imperatives of Destiny, History, Progress, Nature, or whatever. In short, knowledge, truth, and meaning are always fragmentary. Subjects and reasons abound, but there is no Subject nor Reason. By deploying such a skeptical strategy, the political hope is to destabilize power, displace domination, and dismantle hierarchy.

In contrast to the traditional view that "expression is the dress of thought,"[38] a nonfoundational approach maintains that language is not a jumble of accumulated vestments but rather a system that neither labels nor represents the world of reality. Meaning is a differentiating function within that linguistic structure itself; reality cannot be apprehended from outside its discursive standpoint. Being internal to it, meaningful thinking does not precede nor can it be the precondition of communication and expression. Meaning is not transmitted through language by independent subjects, possessed of prelinguistic thought, but the communicating subjects are themselves constituted in and through that discourse itself. When this insight is combined with the fact that the discourse is itself dynamic and contingent and, therefore, never outside attempts at political appropriation, the hermeneutical exercise becomes fraught with difficulty. The idea that there could be *authoritative interpretation* of that fixed meaning in any final, contestable, or objective way becomes dubious, if not altogether oxymoronic. None of this denies the possibility of meaning or widespread agreement on the particular products of interpretive processes at a particular time and place. A nonfoundational way of reading does not destruct the idea or practice of meaning, but it does disrupt any hermeneutical exercise that claims to offer standards of ultimate decidability or closure. It views meaning as always contestable. As such, meaning can never be a ground for law's language game, because that game itself encloses meaning. Moreover, law's language is itself never a grounding for anything, because it is the very activity through which interested attempts at hermeneutical acquisition are played out.

A nonfoundationalist approach calls into question not only the metaphysics of interpretive presence but the very idea of a metaphysics itself. Its self-defined task is not to work within the extant matrix of interpretation but to decenter, disconcert, destabilize, and disorder that framework. While it is devoted to exploring the revealed terrain of interpretive ambiguity, paradox, and multiplicity, a nonfoundationalist account of reading does not seek to wreak interpretive havoc for its own sake. As such, its threat is not found in its claim to produce alternative and unconventional meanings (although it does that in abundance) but in the unrelenting challenge to the claimed establishment of authoritative claims of meaning. It rejects entirely the notion of meaning as property that can be circulated in perpetuity between authors and readers over time. Performed within a nonfoundationalist context, reading ends not in a final affixing of meaning but in a temporary respite from a lasting indeterminacy. In adopting such a stance, the understanding of what "the death of the author" means and its implications for legal theory take on a very different hue. Indeed, its most significant consequence is that the death of the author does not give birth to the autocratic life of the reader-critic. The image of the scepter of divinely sanctioned authority being passed along the hermeneutical line is misleading. The challenge to hermeneutical authority and the notion of subjectivity as a fixed, unified, and bounded identity applies equally to the newly crowned reader. Embedded in a constitutive discourse of power, readers are also disciplined by the extant protocols of power—they are subjects in subjection. There is neither a transcendent author nor a transcending reader. Neither texts nor lives can ever be recovered or understood in their separateness or entirety: they can never be placed outside of history nor put beyond interpretation in history. Although intention offers itself as the authoritative and determinate constraint upon interpretation, the fact is that "intention must itself be interpretively established."[39]

The "death of the author" is the effect of an antimetaphysical contagion that attacks all claims to hermeneutical authority, including the designation of an empowered reader as the seat of interpretive power. The reader is no more free (and no less constrained) to confer meaning and effect closure than the author. The text always says more than both the author *and reader* can determine or dictate. In the same way that the author "cannot choose to write *what will not be read*,"[40] the reader cannot choose not to read what has not been written. The reader is no more an originator than the author; not simply subjective and narcissistic, the meaning-giving process is constrained in the same way that all individuals are constrained and constituted by the context of readership within which they find themselves. In reading as in writing, there is always the inescapable element of the parasitic or the plagiarized. Situated in and sanctioned by an informing context, authoritative readers are also a projection of the same metaphysics that breathes life into the idea of the creative author: each is a cultural, historical, and political construct rather than a natural category. Like the author, the reader cannot be a firm foundation for hermeneutical authority because the reading subject is the product of discourse as much as its producer. The reading subject is as implicated in the powerful webs of social discourse as the writing subject: the distance between the two is historical and, therefore, is itself unbreachable in any final or fixed manner. Accordingly, in the same way that a nonfoundationalist critique relieves authors of the burden of authority, it also reminds readers of the weight of context. While notions of Author, Text, and Interpreter wither and die on the metaphysical vine, writers, writing, and readers are nourished and come to political life in the rich soil of social living.

Interpretation is not a static act that places the authoritative seal of hermeneutical approval on a finished textual product. Instead, it is a fluid and dynamic negotiation that remakes the text to be interpreted in the very act of interpretation. Moreover, that interpretive engagement is situated in a historical context that is itself never outside the interpretive engagement. While reading always overwhelms intention, the reader is never "free" to reach any conclusion; meaning and readers are always located within an institutional context of interpretive constraints. On such a nonfoundationalist account, meaning is less a piece of property to be surveyed and filed in an authoritative register than a fiery challenge that melts the cold charms of the traditional hermeneutical enterprise. On the far side of meaning, it might be possible for future generations of writers and readers to establish an interpretive practice that will have relinquished the urge to locate truth and fix meaning. As a playful performance in law's language game, this practice will be more interested in cultivating fresh insights and stimulating further senses of wonder that can conceive of the text as "a tissue of citations, resulting from the thousand sources of culture."[41] Stepping out of the shadow of dead Authors and the godlike Interpreters, judicial players must remain vibrant writers and readers in the interpretive contest. As active participants in the meaning-giving process, they do not stand off to the side but are instead always at the heart of the hermeneutic action.

By deflating the pretensions of any contending candidate for interpretive honors, a nonfoundationalist critique roots out privilege and reveals it as a masquerade for false expertise. However, it does not pretend to wipe the historical text clean and bestow untrammeled scrawling rights on all comers. Each practical act of interpretation implies a particular theoretical understanding of interpretation. Such a theory takes a stand, provisional and contingent, on the contested writings of authors, texts, contexts, and the like. There is not only never an ending to the interpretive responsibility, but there is also never a beginning that can act as stable foundation on which to build. Beneath each new seam that is mined and excavated, there is no final bedrock to be reached. This is as true for theories of interpretation as it is for interpretation itself; it is not possible to settle arguments about interpretation with arguments that are themselves beyond interpretation. Theories of interpretation are part of the debate over meaning, not guides to the resolution of contested meaning. Interpretation is an exercise in persuasion in which different theoretical maneuvers are deployed in order to attain the agreement of the contesting community. Any meaning that does actually stick is a function of that agreement, no matter how temporary or fragile, and not some recognition of a preexisting or external state of interpretive truth.

The Politics of Interpretation

Each mainstream theory of interpretation—*textualist*, *intentionalist*, and *communalist*—attempts to provide a foundation for the constrained relationship between author, reader, and text. Such foundationalist theories operate as guides as to how to interpret generally and what particular interpretations are to be arrived at if they are to warrant the stamp of interpretive correctness and legal validity. If the resort to literary theory was intended to resolve these efforts, it was a forlorn hope. While the vocabulary has changed, much else remains the same. If anything, this literary turn of events has simply served to emphasize the extent to which legal interpretation is thoroughly permeated by political interests. While presented as neutral interventions, these interpretive strategies are not so much disinterested as totally interested forms of political intervention and control. In contrast, a nonfoundationalist view maintains that there is no metahermeneutical method that is itself outside the play of contingent interests and contextual circumstances; it emphasizes the rhetorical nature of reading and emphasizes its political determinants and context. In this move from hermeneutic philosophy to rhetorical politics, legal theories of interpretation function as arguments and resources rather than as boundary markers for reading.

In an important sense, the force of the nonfoundationalist critique is that rhetoric works to give the appearance that there are foundations in place that can guarantee truth, coherence, and the like. People conveniently forget that the foundations themselves are merely provisional and contingent, but no less real for that. These transient grounds and foundational arguments are rhetorical in nature and function. In a manner of speaking, it is interpretation all the way down. Accordingly, the purpose of a nonfoundational critique is not to show that any particular interpretation is illegitimate or that all interpretations are equally legitimate. On the contrary, the purpose is to call into question the grounds on which a particular interpretation is claimed to be authoritative or determinative. While the author's intent or the legislation's purpose will provide guidance to the meaning of any particular text, it will not be sufficient to foreclose or limit other interpretations as legitimate. To this end, a nonfoundational critique is not something that can be used in the practice of interpretation: it has no particular substantive or political agenda that can be simply followed or enforced. Recognizing that politics is itself ungroundable in any final or definitive way, all it can do is to underline the fact that all interpretations involve choice and that all meaning is provisional and unstable. Rather than being a full and final commitment to one school of thought, such as socialism or liberalism, taking sides "develops over time, through a series of decisions and commitments in specific reading situations that develop into a cultural style, a way of negotiating experience."[42] As such, a nonfoundational approach does not constitute a method by which texts can be interpreted; it is more of a critical reminder of how the closure of textual meaning is not possible. It cannot tell judges or jurists what to do; it can only caution them against claims that they make for what they do.

Any appreciation of what is involved in the familiar acts of reading and writing entails some political sensibility as much as a talent for analytical rigor. The *who*s, *when*s, *why*s, and *wherefore*s of writing and reading will always be contestable. Written and read in an irretrievable whirl of social circumstances and personal intentions, meaning's only destiny is to be multiple and irresolvable. This does not mean that interpretation is wholly reduced to politics; writing and reading are to be correlated to rather than collapsed into the politics of their history. In the same way that any hermeneutical endeavor cannot slip free of history, so must jurisprudential reflection always be politically charged; legal theories are not an evasion of ideology but a relocation of it. Even the most intransigent claim that legal interpretation can and must proceed apolitically is of utmost political and ideological significance; no interpretation stands innocent of the charge of political involvement. Interpretation cannot be grounded on empirical facts nor validated by any metaphysical truth; each is never beyond interpretation but only takes on meaning within an interpretive context.

However, the conclusion that a text is never reducible to one meaning and is always open to multiple interpretations does not mean that critical debate or interpretive activity is pointless. What it does mean is that there has to be a shift in analysis and focus from the issue of what is the right or wrong meaning of a text to what is the better or worse meaning to be ascribed to the text in light of a particular context of reading. For instance, the question may arise as to whether I have given a fair/objective/correct/or valid reading to Foucault's, Barthes's, or Wilson's essays. Apart from the obvious ironies of this inquiry, there are some pertinent lessons to be learned from it. First of all, provided that I have acted in good faith, the nature of such a challenge is beside the point in the nonfoundational critique that I have offered. The merit of an interpretation is not judged by its formal approximation of faithfulness to some model of interpretive integrity but rather by its usefulness and power to illuminate the task at hand. As Foucault himself may have concluded, "The only valid tribute to thought . . . is precisely to use it, to deform it, to make it groan and protest."[43] To think or interpret otherwise is to fall back on the discredited and defunct idea that there is a metaphysical distinction between explication and creation that can be made and is worth defending. As a rhetorical act, interpretation is political and involves a taking of sides. Consequently, any challenge to my interpretation will be, like the interpretation itself, as much a matter of politics as anything else. Not that this reduces interpretation to only politics—only that it can never be meaningfully understood apart from politics, which, of course, is itself never a ground for anything.

What such a nonfoundational perspective implies for the practice of judging in actual cases is, of course, open to interpretation. But it does suggest certain intimations. Because politics and history are always the context for theoretical engagement, it is the case that hermeneutical strategies have implications for politics and history. At the least, a nonfoundational critique might oblige judges and jurists to assume greater responsibility for their interpretations; there is no theory of interpretation that can relieve them of the burden of choice and justification. Mindful that it "is impossible, now more than ever, to disassociate the work we do . . . from a reflection on the political or institutional conditions of that work,"[44] judges and lawyers might begin to rethink and rework the expectations and performances of their judicial task. Recognizing adjudication for the playful activity it is, judges and jurists might experiment further with both the substance of decisions made and the way that the judicial game is played. Of course, none of this in itself will necessarily occasion an institutional conversion to a progressive politics. However, it might embolden or embarrass some into assuming a judicial posture that is more willing to address the real issues that divide and plague society—economic deprivation, public illiteracy, sexual violence, education, racial hatred, and other such issues. While unrelenting analyses of oppression and performances of textual radicalism will not in themselves bring an end to such problems, they can contribute to that cause. By opening up legal texts and social contexts from the hold of traditional interpretive strategies, it might be possible to make them available for interested attempts at more democratic appropriation. Furthermore, establishing an alliance between lawyers and the dispossessed might create public openings for the dispossessed to reestablish their own culture in their own lives. This, in turn, might enrich and transform the lives of judges and lawyers.

There are, of course, risks with such a nonfoundationalist strategy that insists that no political action can be vouchsafed and no particular consequences can be promised. The major risk is that it will be seen to harm the cause of racial, feminist, or gay justice. By deconstructing authorial authority and intention, it might be seen "to remove the very levels against power at the moment that they have been seized by those who have lacked them."[45] However, the hazards of clinging to a foundationalist faith—for that is what it is—are much greater and more damaging than the risk of taking a nonfoundationalist gamble. If some special authenticity and derivative authority are to be bestowed upon the black judge as black judge, there is no consistent or logical way that the same authority cannot be claimed by the white judge as white judge: consistency and logic are vital standards in the metaphysical almanac. In a world in which the vast majority of judges remain white, male, and heterosexual, this would be counterproductive, for it would undermine the excellent critical work done in prying judicial texts free of their limiting authorial circumstances and making them available for transformative reading. To return to the traditional hermeneutical practice of author-based interpretation would be regressive. It devalues and trivializes the crucial role of the black, woman, or gay critic, reducing it to that of faithful decoding and technical retrieval. Traditional hermeneutics has to leave the critic to stand obediently aside and allow the authoritative voice of (white, male, heterosexual) authorial experience to speak for itself in imparting Truth to the world.

This is a foundationalist trap that a nonfoundational sensibility can help critics of racism, sexism, and homophobia to avoid. There is little to be gained and much to be lost in re-inscribing the epistemology of transcendence that is the hallmark of traditional hermeneutics.[46] The idea of transmitting authentic human experience through a transparent textual medium for direct and respectful consumption by the popular masses is a travesty of any emancipatory project. By claiming authenticity and authority for previously excluded voices in the name of a transformative politics, the debilitating metaphysics of ontology is given precedence over the politics of struggle. Not only will the interpretive monarch be returned to power, but such a restoration will have been effected with the help and blessings of democratic critics. Yet it is only in the dark kingdom of the blind that such one-eyed upstarts can feign regal right. At best, the author (and readers) is a puppet-monarch whose every move is choreographed and staged by the dominant elite. The triumph of a truly democratic politics will only occur when the interpretive monarchy is finally deposed and, in its place, a polity of truly equal readers and engaged writers is established.

To be clear, none of this is to be taken to imply that women, black, and gay judges will not make a difference. It is that any difference will be political, not metaphysical, in orientation and consequence. While there are not, nor can there be, any metaphysical certainties, the institutional chances of transforming law and judging are greatly improved. The appointment of women judges, black judges, and gay judges will increase the likelihood that a different perspective will be brought to bear upon the adjudicative process: "Outcasts invent new moral identities for themselves by getting semantic authority over themselves."[47] In the same way that there is nothing to prevent white, male, heterosexual judges from acting to transform themselves and the law, there is nothing to guarantee that female judges, black judges, and gay judges will not continue the existing traditions of law and judging. But the more likely impact will be that the experience of such traditional outsiders will work its way into the adjudicative exercise and, in one way or another, its doctrinal product. Moreover, the very existence of these diverse judges within the ranks of judicial authority might well have important political consequences for the overall perception as well as for the practice of the courts' work. As with any game, the introduction of new and different players will begin in different, inconsistent, and unpredictable ways not only to influence the style in which the existing game is played but also to transform the kind of game that adjudication is and becomes.

For example, the impact of Thurgood Marshall on the American Supreme Court has been enormous: his presence and self-identification as a black man were a huge part of that impact. Yet this effect was never assured. In strictly doctrinal terms, there is nothing that he did that could not have been effected by a white judge, blessed with a similar political imagination and political will. However, it was the fact that he did it that was so important. His experience as a black man meant that it was more likely (not certain) that he would understand and champion the history and hopes of black Americans. It was more likely, because of that experience, that he would possess the political vision that he had. Moreover, it meant that his judgments would be more likely to be received differently (in positive and negative ways) than those of white judges. In short, the significance of his judicial career is not the result of his ontological identity as a metaphysical Black Author or Reader and the hermeneutical authority that his judicial text worked in sway of that fact. It is a political story about a political writer in a political world whose signification will always be political: he played the game, as much as he could, on his terms, not those of others.

Of course, it is ludicrous to suggest that race or ethnicity ought to be the *sole* criterion of judicial merit or achievement. But it is equally mistaken to believe that it should not count at all. Race should not prevent a contribution, but it affects its weighting and interpretation. As recent events have shown, while Thurgood Marshall was a black man, not all black men are Thurgood Marshall. The debacle of the appointment of Clarence Thomas and his subsequent judicial career underlines this. In contrast to the Du Bois–Marshall orthodoxy of affirmative action that prevails, Thomas opts for the out-of-favor Booker T. Washington line that it is equal opportunity, not equal treatment, that blacks need. In a developing series of judgments, Thomas has articulated a reading of the Constitution that draws little or no distinction between laws designed to subjugate a race and those that favor a race in order to make up for past discrimination. While a couple of his white colleagues, Justices Stevens and Ginsburg, have tended to uphold the legacy of Marshall, Thomas has drawn upon his own experience to argue that "government-sponsored racial discrimination based on benign prejudice is just as noxious as discrimination inspired by malicious prejudice."[48] Nevertheless, whatever the political evaluation of his developing and distinct judicial position, Thomas's career ought to have demonstrated emphatically the weakness of identity politics: there is no necessary connection between identity and interpretation. Nonetheless, it also ought to have shown that the appointment of black, women, and gay judges will at the very least put questions of identity under the public and intellectual spotlight. In this way, what it means to play the judicial game "with authority" will always be open to political contestation.

Conclusion

Most people will remember the classic Marshall McLuhan scene in Woody Allen's movie *Annie Hall*. Alvy and Annie are waiting in line for a movie. Behind them there is a verbose academic trying to impress his bored date with his cinematographic erudition. An exasperated Alvy cannot resist intervening when the man begins to pontificate on the views of Marshall McLuhan. When Alvy tells him that his version of McLuhanian thinking is nonsense, the man defends its validity by offering his credentials as a teacher of a communications class at Columbia University. In his comic coup de grâce, Alvy brings into the scene from off-camera McLuhan himself, who promptly puts the flabbergasted academic in his place: "You know nothing of my work. How you ever got to teach a course in anything is totally amazing." To end this vignette, Alvy turns to the camera and laments: "Boy, if only life were like this."[49] There are many instructive and insightful lessons for academics in this wonderfully funny scene, including warnings about their propensity to pretension and the dangers of losing contact with the commonsensical intuitions of everyday living. But what is more pertinent, Allen's acerbic humor touches a raw nerve in the body of jurisprudential scholarship, particularly the concerns with the relevance, importance, and status, if any, of the author. While his cinematic text offers an instinctively reasonable critique of overzealous efforts to deny that authorial intention has any special privilege in the interpretive task of fixing textual meaning, it also carries (at least, to me) a more subversive insinuation—that, along with the wistful hope that authors could provide authoritative resolution to interpretive disputes over their texts and stave off surrender to "the flux, the gossip, the muddle and the motley," there is an unshakable sense of existential resignation about the elusiveness of authoritative meaning. As Allen concedes, "*If only* life were like this."

In this chapter, therefore, I have tried to show that while the understanding that language is a social activity has largely been conceded by the jurisprudential establishment, jurists still strive to claim that there is "an interpretive process which claims for itself the solidity of a thing."[50] As such, judges and jurists look for authority in all the wrong places when they seek to constrain interpretive practice with interpretive theories. Interpretive authority is not something that readers or lawyers must or need look for outside of themselves. Rather, it comes with the political responsibility of engaging in present efforts to make sense of the past as a way of coping with the future. As a historical endeavor, it already has all the possibilities and parameters that legal interpretation could ever want or need. Insofar as authority is something that remains important, it is something that judges have simply by virtue of the fact that they are designated as players in law's language game. As practitioners of legal interpretation, the only question for them, therefore, is not where they find authority but how they respectfully earn and usefully exercise it.

5 A Pure Way of Playing: The Naturalist Revival

I saw it all. Depth beyond depth was revealed to me—the byss and the abyss. I saw—as one might see the transit of Venus or the Lord Mayor's Show—exactly how it happened and why the tergiversation was inevitable—but it was after dinner and I let it go.

—Winston Churchill, *My Early Life*

Hart's elevation of legal common sense to the status of jurisprudential insight is considered by many to be the greatest strength of his work. With deceptive ease and elegant simplicity, he offered a plebeian account of law that gave prominence to the prosaic routines of its judicial personnel; there was little room for grand judicial gestures or jurisprudential posturings. Acknowledging that law contains some irreducible dimension of discretion, he made a positive virtue of compromise and found room for formalists and realists alike in his humble jurisprudential arrangement. In playing the language game of law, good Hartian judges were thought able to combine strong technical proficiency with an occasional measure of political judgment. However, Hart's rule-based depiction of law and adjudication has not swept all before it. For theorists of a more naturalist persuasion, law is about rules, but it is about much more as well; the existence of rules is a necessary but not sufficient condition for an accurate description of a just legal system. By drawing a sharp line between legal validity and political morality, Hart is considered to have deprived law's language game of its most basic and ennobling source of adjudicative guidance. In short, these jurists maintain that law is as much about substantive values as it is about formal rules. They insist that good judging requires that the technical skills of the adjudicative decision maker be placed squarely within the service of a very definite political mandate of social justice: "Law . . . is deeply and thoroughly political . . . but not a matter of personal or partisan politics."[1]

At the heart of this naturalist revival is the enduring belief that inasmuch as adjudication is a language game, it is also a noble sport of political import. While language is indeed a social activity that is largely indeterminate in application, there is a way of playing law's adjudicative game that is *natural* in the sense of capturing and expressing the law's quintessential and most just performance. To a greater and lesser extent, the jurists holding this view have been unable to resist the temptation to claim that they are "voicing the dictates of a vague divinity."[2] By striving to identify or interpose something between the best efforts of judges to develop the law justly in specific cases and the resulting general system of norms, these naturalists see the invisible hand of some foundationalist ghost at work; law always manages to be more than and never only what judges say it is. However, this naturalist tendency to pass off philosophical hubris as political humility cannot be justified in either ambition or performance. There is no perfect or perfectible way to play law's adjudicative game that is not itself part of its continuing political performance; law is grounded in nothing more (or less) ordered and stable than the changing routines of its prosaic practices. Contrary to naturalists' recommendations, lawyers and judges are not fated to become philosophy's disciples in order to fulfill their democratic mandate. Adjudication does not correspond with an elusive metanarrative of legal propriety, but rather it determines it own standards of political competence within and through its engaged practice.

In this chapter, therefore, I will take to task those jurists who maintain that there is a natural and, therefore, superior and compelling way to play law's adjudicative game. After introducing the tradition from which the modern naturalist revival comes and its jurisprudential aspirations, I concentrate on the foundationalist work of two leading theorists, Ronald Dworkin and Ernest Weinrib. My discussion around Dworkin's ideal of law-as-integrity is intended to show that although it advances the understanding of adjudication as a political practice that works the space between law's institutional past and its future possibilities, his account is unable to ground the law in anything more foundational than the general commitments of his own brand of liberal morality. In grappling with Weinrib's ideal of law-as-justice-ensouled, I not only expose the foundationalist conceit of mistaking personal insight for universal insight but also focus on the naturalists' tendency to treat law and its adjudicative elaboration as proceeding as if it had a life of its own, separate from its judicial operatives. Throughout the chapter, I emphasize how a nonfoundationalist account both highlights the failings of such accounts and explains more successfully the operations of the judicial enterprise as a dynamic activity that incorporates the continual debate over the better and worse ways to *play the game*.

Working Law Pure

The naturalist effort to identify an ideal of justice that can best direct the shape and substance of a legal system is as old as law itself. Although such theoretical attempts have taken a bewildering variety of guises, the abiding claim has been that there is a necessary and significant connection between law and political morality; the validity and value of law is to be measured against something more than a positivistic standard of formal adequacy. In their classical appearance, naturalist theories of law have insisted that there are universal principles of abstract justice that inhere in the nature of society or humanity that must be respected by law. However, in their modern manifestations, naturalists' accounts of law have become more modest in ambition and less expansive in orientation; they have concentrated on the particular difficulties of judging rather than on the general problematic of defining law. Consequently, instead of seeking to locate an external set of objective moral criteria that law must reflect and instantiate, contemporary theorists have devoted themselves to uncovering the morality that is internal to law itself.[3] In their different ways, all jurists claim to look deep into the traditions and themes of the law in order to highlight a common thread of morality that binds legal doctrine together as a coherent and just enterprise. Because this political morality was drawn from law's raw materials, it might have helped to allay fears that judges would usurp the legislative function and also might have ensured that just results would not be eclipsed by legalistic concerns. As such, many contemporary jurists considered that Hart had given the democratic game away by conceding that the constraints on judges were never sufficiently complete or clear enough to expunge entirely the need for the judicial exercise of political choice. Accordingly, although naturalists play up the inevitable political dimension to performances of law's adjudicative game, they do maintain that the judicial task must and can be performed without turning law into an ideological venue in which not only "anything goes" but "anything might go."

One of the most enduring tropes of this naturalist tradition is that the common law is constantly working on and through itself to satisfy better its own self-transforming ambitions. This assertion can be traced back over 250 years to the arguments of a young solicitor general, Mr. Murray (later to become the legendary Lord Mansfield), in a relatively unimportant Chancery case about testimonial competence. Contending that the law moves generally from one particular occasion to another, he concluded that "a statute very seldom can take in all cases; therefore the common law, *that works itself pure* by rules drawn from the fountain of justice, is for that reason superior to an act of parliament."[4] Always traveling but never arriving, the common law is portrayed as continuing process that fulfills and refreshes itself from its own self-generated resources. Under this depiction of the adjudicative enterprise, judges are cast very much as the latter-day heirs of the Platonic tradition and make no apology for their performance as philosopher kings and queens. As such, despite their regular incantation that "the life of the law has not been logic but experience," lawyers and judges are still captive to a very abstract and detached understanding of philosophical inquiry. Insofar as *experience* counts in law's existence, it is that of law's own workings and judges' own wiles.

Although this metaphysical ideal seems to speak in the mystical tones of bygone days, its influence remains strong today. The contemporary jurisprudential establishment coheres around the received wisdom that law is more than the sum total of its extant rules and decisions. Indeed, the sentiment remains strong that there is something called *Law* that is felt to be both the expression and repository of a political wisdom that transcends the bounds of its temporary articulation. In insisting that adjudication is a practice of bounded objectivity, even the most pragmatic of juristic commentators insist that law "has both boundaries and moral significance not wholly reducible to, although never independent of, the ends for which it is deployed."[5] As such, it is generally agreed that even the most conscientious judges cannot be left entirely to their own promptings but must be guided in their endeavors by the need to ensure that individual decisions conform to the dictates of a higher law. References to law's transcendent qualities are muted and tempered by concessions that, whatever else it might be, law is a human activity that is inevitably flawed in its performance. In playing the legal game of adjudication, the judicial agonists are disciplined by an ideal of what it means to *play the game* that they articulate as they actualize it. Contemporary legal theorists strive, therefore, to explain and justify the delicate (and elusive) relation between law's immanence—the idea of law as the rational embodiment of an indwelling necessity—and law's instrumentality—the practice of using law as a democratic tool for social engineering.

In the forefront of this naturalist revival is Ronald Dworkin, who has placed the notion that *the law works itself pure* at the dynamic core of his legal theory. Dworkin lionizes judges as princes of law's realm who are charged with the duty of applying and transforming the extant law in line with its own purer ambitions. In the Dworkinian Empire of Law, although these noble judges bear the brunt of that responsibility, they must leave it to philosophical "seers and prophets . . . to work out law's ambitions for itself, the purer form of law within and beyond the law we have." While such work and inspiration may elude rank-and-file lawyers, they are not left to their own devices, for their "god is the adjudicative principle of integrity."[6] However, this romantic vision of judicial practice is not itself philosophically pure, as it attempts to adapt the law's doctrinal essence to the changing context of social politics. This attempt at jurisprudential compromise around law's philosophical immanence and political instrumentality has not only failed to persuade naturalists' critics, but it has disaffected other naturalists. For instance, maintaining that Dworkin and his ilk have failed "to make sense of legal thinking and discourse in their own terms," Ernest Weinrib offers an Aristotelian account of law-as-justice-ensouled that defends and extols the objective truth of law's coherence and rationality. By attributing to law its own immanent theoretical intelligence that transcends and informs all its instrumental practical instances, Weinrib hopes to show that contemporary law is a deserving philosophical object of democratic allegiance precisely because the essence of law is its capacity to "work itself pure."[7]

In both its more modest and less qualified forms, the naturalist effort to isolate a pure or privileged way of what it means to *play the game* capable of guiding prosaic efforts at judicial decision making is flawed. Although Dworkin and Weinrib are to be commended for highlighting the pervasive political nature of adjudication and for insisting that judges draw upon a substantive ideal of what it is to *play the game* in order to fulfill their institutional responsibilities, they are foundationalists of an even more uncompromising and fundamentalist kind than their positivist counterparts. Not only do they maintain that law is its own determinate thing that is not entirely reducible to anything else, but they also believe that there is actually one best way to *play the game*. Having mastered that special modus operandi, all that judges need do is to follow it as best as they can in every new fixture and venue. However, on closer scrutiny, such recommendations are little more than thinly disguised proposals to *play the game* the way that Dworkin and Weinrib like it or want it to be played. While law can indeed be a noble pursuit and judges can turn in truly heroic performances, there is little need to depict law and adjudication in such essentialist and elitist terms. In my nonfoundationalist critique, I maintain that such a hubristic rendition of the jurisprudential project is neither accurate as a descriptive matter nor possible as a prescriptive issue. In contrast to the naturalists' almost mystical account of the law's development and its judicial elaboration, I argue that the practice of law and adjudication is never more (and never less) than a human activity—contextualized, contingent, and constructed. Law is a political game, but it is much more open and much less rarefied than such naturalists propose or pretend.

However, a demonstration that the ideals of a naturalist Dworkin or Weinrib do not flow inexorably from the law does not, of course, dispense entirely with their claim on jurisprudential attention. While it robs them of their claimed authority as objective truth tellers or conversation stoppers, their work can still be treated as rhetorical interventions in a continuing conversation about how to *play the game*. However, their proposals must only be judged as one more contingent proposal for making sense of the world and its transformative possibilities.[8] The notion that jurisprudential theory and adjudicative practice depend on grounding law and adjudication in the metaphysical bedrock of Truth and Knowledge has to be resisted. The alleged foundations of the judicial game are always contestable and contingent: their authority and meaning are part of, not apart from, the inquiry that they are intended to ground. If legal theorists are to be effective or useful, they must abandon the belief that their task is to lay down authoritative blueprints for legal and adjudicative action in the name of some universal truth about the nature of the human condition or its legal manifestation. Disabused of the foundationalist pretense that their worth and prestige derive from and depend upon "knowing something about knowing which nobody else knows so well,"[9] such legal theorists might recognize that there are more possibilities for social justice than its stunted articulation in their naturalist accounts. Indeed, they might be able to concede that justice is not a staid matter of philosophical insight but a vigorous practice of political engagement.

Hard Cases

In the early days of his theory building, Dworkin paid considerable and close attention to so-called hard cases. He made much of the distinction between *hard cases*, in which the relevant law is unclear, unsettled, or unjust, and *easy cases*, in which the relevant law is clear, settled, and just. However, in the face of sustained criticism,[10] Dworkin has effected a considerable shift in his original position. While he has retained the experiential differentiation between hard and easy cases, he has abandoned the claim that judges approach and decide each case differently. Moving to a more constructivist account of legal interpretation, he now considers that there is no need to develop a theory about when cases are hard; the alleged difficulty in distinguishing hard and easy cases is "a pseudoproblem" because "the distinction between easy and hard cases at law is neither so clear nor so important as critics assume."[11] For Dworkin, all cases require judges to resort to moral or political principles. However, as "the noblest dreamer of them all," Dworkin is committed to the view that even in the most difficult or novel case, judges must confine themselves to the task of declaring what the law *is,* not what it *shall* be; there is never an occasion when they should, as Hart puts it, act like "a conscientious legislator, on [their] sense of what is best" in terms of their own moral instincts and political beliefs. Dworkinian judges are to treat the law as if it were a seamless web—complete, consistent, and determinate. Insofar as there is uncertainty, it is not in the law itself but in individual judges' capacity to ascertain and articulate the applicable law.[12]

For Dworkin, adjudication (and legal theory) is not so much about the legal materials as about the reading of them. While Dworkin admits that such an adjudicative feat requires a Herculean effort of "superhuman intellectual power and patience," he offers a constructivist hermeneutics that asks judges to breathe political life into the dormant words of legal texts. This is not to be thought of as "an algorithm for the courtroom," but it is intended to provide an appropriate blend of interpretive freedom and textual constraint. This is done by adhering to and applying the twin tests of *formal fit* and *substantive justice*. Any interpretation of the legal materials must be able to demonstrate some plausible connection to society's legal history. However, the better theory is not necessarily the one that accounts for the most decisions or opinions; the doctrinal fit is only a heuristic device or rule of thumb. The requirement of *formal fit* interacts with the second requirement of *substantive justice* and merely acts as a rough threshold. This requirement obliges judges to develop—albeit in a partial, piecemeal, and provisional way—a scheme of rights that a just state would establish and enforce. The conscious striving for such a perfected theory is the distinguishing hallmark of Dworkinian adjudication, as it demonstrates that judges, as members of a political community, "accept that they are governed by common principles, not just by rules hammered out in political compromise" or massaged to fit "any judge's personal convictions of justice." Moreover, when constructing their theories of political morality, judges are further to be guided by the fact that they operate within a democratic regime of governance and ought not to be satisfied by a vulgar reliance on conventional morality. For Dworkin, a true democracy is found in the egalitarian principle that "government must treat its citizens as equals": judicial power is legitimated by a commitment to uphold the existing political order of rights, even if a particular government is committed to legislative policies of utilitarian welfare or material equality, and to extending them only in some equal manner.[13]

In this way, Dworkin strives to demonstrate how the judicial elaboration of law can manage to be both rational and just: "Propositions of law are true if they figure in or follow from the principles of justice . . . that provide the best constructive interpretation of the community's legal practice." By engaging in this limited public formulation of substantive values, Dworkin concludes that his naturalist theory of adjudication actualizes the ideal of adjudication in a democratic polity better than an exclusively rule-based account. Accordingly, in his view of law-as-integrity, judges and jurists best fulfill their democratic mandate by adopting a professional discipline that constructs as it celebrates the communal practice of law working itself pure:

> Law is not exhausted by any catalogue of rules or principles, each with its own dominion over some discrete theatre of behaviour. Nor by any roster of officials and their power each over part of our lives. Law's empire is defined by attitude, not territory or power or process. . . . It is an interpretive, self-reflective attitude addressed to politics in the broadest sense. . . . The protestant character of law is confirmed, and the creative role of private decisions acknowledged, by the backward-looking, judgmental nature of judicial decisions, and also by the regulative assumption that though judges must have the last word, their word is not for that reason the best word. Law's attitude is constructive: it aims, in the interpretive spirit, to lay principle over practice to show the best route to a better future, keeping the right faith with the past. It is, finally, a fraternal attitude, an expression of how we are united in community though divided in project, interest, and conviction. That is, anyway, what law is for us: for the people we want to be and the community we aim to have.[14]

In line with this revised naturalist account of law-as-integrity, Dworkin insists that all cases are to be adjudicated in the same way, and, therefore, the difficulty of distinguishing hard and easy cases is "a pseudoproblem." From the judges' point of view, an easy case occurs when the relevant rule is clear such that the judge "has nothing more to do," and a hard case occurs when the relevant rule "does not . . . enforce itself." A hard case will present itself to judges when the test of formal fit cannot discriminate sufficiently between two competing lines of argument and a choice has to be made "by asking which shows the community's structure of institutions and decisions . . . in a better light from the standpoint of political morality." For a critically informed Dworkin, easy cases are only special cases of hard ones and are disposed of by the same method of interpretive integrity. Nevertheless, he does concede that the felt experience of judges in dealing with easy and hard cases will be different: "Since the answers to the questions [an easy case] put are then obvious, or at least seem to be so, [judges and jurists] are not aware that any theory is at work at all."[15] Consequently, while Dworkin acknowledges that judges have a different sense of easy and hard cases, he insists that there is no philosophically deep or interesting difference between them in terms of the method for their proper resolution. For Dworkin, cases are easy or hard in terms of the facility or difficulty with which the interpretive ideal of integrity can be achieved; they are not easy or hard in some pre-interpretive or independent sense. While this maneuver is intended to insulate his naturalist theory from further critical damage, it does not so much deflect criticism as deepen its overall import and effect. Dworkin's proposals are not so much salvaged as sabotaged.

Along with the idea of legal continuity, Dworkin maintains that the judges should treat the law as if it were a seamless web, providing complete and determinate guidance on all legal disputes; there is no need or justification to leave the law behind and engage in unconstrained choice. However, if all cases are hard cases, it follows that rules can only dispose of cases so long as the results that their application recommends are compatible with the principles sanctioned by a judge's best reading of law-as-integrity. In reality, therefore, rules are nothing more than a function of principles. Their relationship is wholly unequal; it is a relationship of one-sided dependence. On Dworkin's analysis, legal rules are not rules of law but rules *about* law. Rules are nothing more than the articulated conclusions resulting from an appeal to those principles identified by reference to the interpretive ideal of law-as-integrity at any particular historical moment; they are merely historic plots on the doctrinal graph that describes the linear development of the law. Consequently, rules are only evidence of the controlling principles at the time of particular disputes, and as those principles shift and change, the rules will become an inaccurate representation of the soundest theory. This revelation that rules are parasitic entities is confirmed and reinforced by Dworkin's own statement of what it is for law to exist: law comprises "standards binding upon the officials of a community, controlling their decisions of legal right and obligation." Since, on this analysis of Dworkin's jurisprudence, law exists only as a body of principles, the law is only certain, discoverable, and settled insofar as those principles are certain, discoverable, and settled. At an early stage in the development of his theory, critics were not slow to seize upon Dworkin's apparent concession that there are practical and theoretical problems involved in isolating and cataloging those principles that are of a legal nature. In reply, Dworkin put forward the ingenious proposal that this apparent failing in his theory is remedied by deposing to, as he now calls it, "the interpretive ideal of integrity."[16] However, by falling back onto this interpretive device, Dworkin exposes Hercules's Achilles' heel.

Dworkin explains that understanding law-as-integrity requires that a judge—in order to ascertain the appropriate principles that will dispose of a case—consult the body of settled rules that amount to "the brute facts of legal history." But what are these "brute facts"? Are they rules? If so, what are these rules other than functions of the very same principles? For Dworkin, the notion of a law-as-integrity—whereby principles emanate from and are substantiated by appeal to rules—presupposes the independent existence of rules. Yet, as he is at pains to emphasize in the most recent renditions of his theory, rules do not have such a separate hermeneutical existence; their meaning and valence are wholly dependent on their interpretation in line with law's dominant principles. As Dworkin starkly states, insofar as an easy case is one in which the relevant law is unclear, "the description 'unclear' is the *result* rather than the *occasion* of Hercules' method." Dworkin is committed, therefore, to the baffling conclusion that rules derive from principles that, in turn, derive from rules. In truth, Dworkin has enticed and trapped Hercules within a juristic hall of mirrors. In seeking to implement the demands of the interpretive ideal of judicial integrity, Hercules is faced with an image of infinite reflection that his efforts to fix only serve to refract further. The only way to escape such an unnerving prospect is for Hercules to look inside himself. It is only by giving overriding and special consideration to his own values that Hercules will be able to reach any interpretive resolution or decision. But in so doing, Hercules will have obliged Dworkin to abandon the interpretive ideal that is touted to provide the necessary grounding for pure claims to legal truth and knowledge such that they can be vouchsafed from the polluting influence of ideological politics. Intended as a check on judicial subjectivity, Dworkin's "interpretive ideal of integrity" allows judges to pass off their partisan values as objective legal truths.[17]

Dworkin's legal theory has provided a welcome antidote to exclusively rule-based theories of law and adjudication. Yet it must be remembered that even so, the model of rules retains a focal prominence for Dworkin. Not only is the trigger for Herculean adjudication to be found in the ambivalence or absence of rules, but the settled body of rules is claimed to be the motor force of principled adjudication. By taking a nonfoundationalist approach, I have sought to challenge Dworkin's foundationalist claims. The logic of recognizing that all cases are hard cases is to deny the separate existence of rules as a source of settled meaning without which Hercules cannot begin to respect and meet "the interpretive ideal of integrity." With the conclusion that rules cannot be a reliable or firm grounding arises a task that imposes labors even beyond Hercules's superhuman talents, let alone the limited abilities of lesser judicial mortals. As one of the few judges who has come close to emulating such mythical feats, Cardozo once stated that "the labour of judges would be increased almost to the breaking-point if every past decision could be reopened in every case."[18] It is ironic, therefore, that while Dworkin does capture certain important insights about adjudicative aspirations and actualities, he remains in a deep jurisprudential sleep in which the figments of his liberal imagination amount to more of an ignoble nightmare than a noble dream. To avoid such a fate, Dworkin must awake from his jurisprudential slumbers and come to terms with working reality as judicially lived. In doing so, he will realize that while he is correct in his claim that judges have no real option but to make a moral reading of constitutions and laws, he is mistaken in believing that either their texts or precedential history can provide the kind of foundationalist constraints that he craves. A text and its precedential history, as part of law's adjudicative game, are never themselves beyond political contestation; they are both the source and the object of judges' interpretive performances.

In the next two sections, I want to concentrate on two related criticisms of Dworkin's naturalist account—contradiction and conservatism. I have already emphasized the philosophical emptiness of Dworkin's postulated ideal of adjudicative integrity and how he traps himself in a vicious circle of operational arguments that can only be broken by personal and partisan intervention. From there, it is a small step to criticize his theoretical account, which is structurally unable to capture and accommodate the overflowing practice of adjudicative reality—he glosses over the confusion and contradiction that is at the existential heart of law. Furthermore, in opting for a distinctly imperial account of law and adjudication as an elitist practice, Dworkin commits himself to an unhealthy degree of conservatism that is inimical to any truly democratic polity. All in all, these criticisms underscore the fact that, notwithstanding Dworkin's insistence to the contrary, law is not only "deeply and thoroughly political," but it is so as "a matter of personal or partisan politics."[19] When played under Dworkinian tutelage, law's adjudicative game is limited to a restricted set of moves that artificially stem the contingent flow of political possibilities. Rather than join issue with Dworkin at an exclusively abstract level, I will ensure that my criticisms are given practical context and legal confirmation by revisiting one of Dworkin's favorite problems—*Elmer's Case*.

One Will and Many Ways

The facts of *Riggs* v. *Palmer* are straightforward and uncontroversial. In 1880 Francis Palmer, a widower, made a will. After giving two small legacies to his daughters, he left his residuary estate to his sixteen-year-old grandson, Elmer; this included considerable personal property and the farm on which Elmer and his grandfather lived. In 1882, the grandfather married Mrs. Bressee; unlike in many jurisdictions, this marriage did not have the effect of automatically revoking the will. In order to prevent the making of a new will in favor of his grandfather's second wife, Elmer poisoned his grandfather. He was convicted of second-degree murder and imprisoned. The two daughters, Mrs. Riggs and Mrs. Preston, brought an action to prevent Elmer from enjoying the disposition made in his favor. The only issue for resolution was how the statutory rule should be interpreted and applied: "All persons, except idiots, persons of unsound mind and infants, may devise their real estate, by a last will and testament, duly executed, according to the provision of this article." The statute also went on to state that "no will in writing, except in the cases hereinafter mentioned, shall be revoked or altered otherwise"; none of those exceptions was triggered by the facts of the case.[20]

At first instance, the court decided in Elmer's favor and allowed him to inherit the property. On appeal, counsel for the daughters made two principal arguments: first, since a will is revocable until death, Elmer's murder had deprived his grandfather of this right (which he surely would have exercised), and, second, it could not have been the legislature's intention that the statute should be interpreted literally in such extraordinary circumstances without reference to established principles of law and equity. Counsel for Elmer responded with two contending arguments: this was a case in which the words of the statute should receive their plain and ordinary meaning, and, second, as Elmer had been imprisoned for his grandfather's murder, it would amount to punishing him twice for the same act if he was also deprived of the legacy. The case was finely balanced and, apart from the competing equities of the substantive dispute, brought into play important jurisprudential questions about the proper nature and scope of adjudication. In particular, it provides a convenient and compelling practical site at which to test Dworkin's claims about the possibility and desirability of adjudication as a principled and constrained exercise in legal choice.

Having had the benefit of counsel's arguments, it would be for Hercules to decide whether the parties' disagreement was genuine. Both counsels regarded the statutory rule giving effect to testamentary intention as the starting point of their arguments; whereas the appellants argued that the rule should not apply, the respondent argued that the rule should apply. The question for Hercules, therefore, was to decide on the applicability of that rule or, as Dworkin later put it, "what the real statute the legislators enacted really said." Mindful that "the description 'unclear' is the *result* rather than the *occasion* of Hercules' method," he would not restrict himself to meditating on whether the words of the statute were clear or unclear in an acontextual sense; the fact that "there are decent arguments for each of two competing interpretations of it" was sufficient to determine that it was.[21] Consequently, Hercules would not follow the lead of Judge Gray, who, in his dissenting judgment, took the view that as the practice conditions of the rule had been met (i.e., the existence of a valid and unrevoked will and the death of the testator), this was an easy case and could be disposed of syllogistically:

> If I believed that the decision of the question could be effected by considerations of an equitable nature, I should not hesitate to assent to views which commend themselves to the conscience. But the matter does not lie within the domain of conscience. We are bound by the

rigid rules of law, which have been established by the legislature, and within the limits of which the determination of this question is confined. The question we are dealing with is whether a testamentary disposition can be altered, or a will revoked, after the testator's death, through an appeal to the courts, when the legislature has by its enactments prescribed exactly when and how wills may be made, altered, and revoked, and apparently, as it seems to me, when they have been fully complied with, has left no room for the exercise of an equitable jurisdiction by courts over such matters. . . . I concede that rules of law which annul testamentary provisions made for the benefit of those who have become unworthy of them may be based on principles of equity and of natural justice. It is quite reasonable to suppose that a testator would revoke or alter his will, where his mind has been so angered and changed as to make him unwilling to have his will executed as it stood. But these principles only suggest sufficient reason for the enactment of laws to meet such cases.[22]

It is clear that Hercules, like the majority of judges in *Riggs*, would not feel constrained in the same way as Mr. Justice Gray. He would step back from the particular context and look to the principles of substantive justice that best formally fit and substantively justify the law in general. Having isolated a salient and overarching principle, Hercules would read the statutory rule against this particular interpretive backdrop and find against Elmer. This was much the line taken in the leading judgment of Judge Earl, who maintained that equitable principles (adverted to but ignored by Judge Gray) circumscribed the operation of the statutory rule:

> We need not, therefore, be much troubled by the general language contained in the laws. Besides, all laws, as well as all contracts, may be controlled in their operation and effect by general, fundamental maxims of the common law. No one shall be permitted to profit by his own fraud, or to take advantage of his own wrong, or to found any claim upon his own iniquity, or to acquire property by his own crime. These maxims are dictated by public policy, have their foundation in universal law administered in all civilized countries, and have nowhere been superseded by statutes.[23]

In arriving at this conclusion, Dworkin shows that he has traveled a long way since his early encounters with *Riggs*. In particular, he has embraced the idea that all meaning is context-specific; ambiguity is not a property of a sentence but arises out of the context in which it is to be interpreted. Nevertheless, in terms of his own jurisprudential agenda, Dworkin has managed to travel both too far and not far enough. On the one hand, he has come too far in that, by recognizing that principles play a vital role in judicial reasoning, he has obliged judges to recognize and consult more sources of adjudicative guidance than they ever could handle or want; there are always competing and contradictory principles in play. On the other hand, he has not come far enough in that he still is unable to explain why it is that legal principles should or can be any more clear and dispositive in the adjudicative direction that they give than the rules that they are intended to clarify and inform; the meaning of principles is not the source of legal meaning but simply another occasion for the struggle to establish meaning. I will deal with each of these points separately.

First, Dworkin offers no real explanation of how principles are any more likely to lead to interpretive closure than rules. Indeed, as principles are usually pitched at an even higher level of generality than rules, it is likely that they will be not only in as much need of interpretation as rules but that they will be a very unreliable source from which to effect interpretive closure around rules. As Dworkin well knows, there are no "brute facts of history" that stand outside or above the interpretive process such that their meaning can be grasped as self-evident and beyond controversy; principles do not reduce or bring to an end the interpretive encounter but amount to another occasion for its continuance. As Dworkin himself admits, principles are not self-executing and will often provide intimations that are decidedly indecisive; unlike rules, "a principle like 'No man may profit from his own wrong' does not even purport to set out conditions that make its application necessary."[24] Accordingly, Dworkin's resort to principles as interpretive aids simply pushes back the inquiry rather than resolves it. Hercules is once again drawn down another hermeneutical blind alley. It is difficult enough to decide what the equitable principle that "no person shall profit from his or her own wrongdoing" means, let alone to expect that it can bring interpretive clarity to a penumbral uncertainty in a legal rule. What does "person" mean? What does "profit" mean? What does "wrongdoing" mean?

Second, as well as pointing up the extent to which Dworkin's theory of law and adjudication collapses in on itself and becomes an empty shell, *Riggs* neatly demonstrates the extent to which law is full of confusing and contradictory principles that prevent the establishment of any legal certainty. Dworkin assumes that once it has been demonstrated that Hercules's resort to principles is superior as a matter of analytical description and substantive prescription, the decision to be reached is self-evident and certain. Indeed, he concludes that "Elmer's fate will depend on the interpretive convictions of the particular panel of judges that decides his case";[25] it is a straight and simple choice between the contrasting approaches of Judges Earl and Gray.

Yet Dworkin makes this facile assumption too quickly. Even if judges shared the same interpretive convictions about the general responsibility of adjudication, they could still decide very differently in the same circumstances. A determination that proper adjudication involves reference to those moral principles that are embedded in the law does not resolve the equally pressing question of which principles among the many on offer are to be chosen and applied. Contrary to Dworkin's wishful thinking, the resort to principles does not so much narrow or reduce the scope for legal uncertainty as actually broaden and deepen it. In striving to counteract the positivist claim that judicial reasoning is empty of moral principle, Dworkin has only succeeded in showing that it is so full of competing and contradictory principles as to be of little practical help in generating certain or settled results.

Assuming that a judge follows the lead of Judge Earl or Hercules and begins to sift through the law to identify possible principles in light of which the statutory rule is to be read, it will soon become clear that there are at least two general principles and that they point in very different directions. While the principle that "no person shall benefit from his or her own wrongdoing" works against Elmer, the principle that "no person shall be punished twice for the same act" works in Elmer's favor. Both readings are entirely plausible interpretations of the common law tradition and both can claim a similarly high degree of threshold doctrinal fit. Even as a matter of substantive justice, there is no legal way to determine which is the best or better account of the law; there is a standoff. In a case like *Riggs* (and, by implication, many others), impartial logic or reasoning only goes so far. At some point, a choice is required that might in the final analysis only be traceable to "a semi-intuitive apprehension of the pervading spirit of our law."[26] It is very disturbing that Dworkin responds to such eventualities with the banal conclusion that "different judges will disagree about each of these issues and will accordingly take different views of what the law of their community, properly understood, really is."[27] While such rare or occasional differences will have little lasting effect, it is surely the case that anything more than the occasional aberrant or idiosyncratic decision will wreak havoc on the law's development and Dworkin's theory. And the fact is that in almost all cases there will exist contradictory principles that can plausibly be brought into adjudicative play. In such circumstances, the task of trying to make sense of legal doctrine as an exercise in interpretive integrity will exceed even the superhuman efforts of Hercules; it will become more of a hopeless aspiration than a realizable goal.

The courts and legal doctrine are venues for the ceaseless negotiation of this conflict between principles. As there are many different principles and similar norms at work in its formulation and interpretation, even one judge's contribution to legal doctrine is not a reflected embodiment of one indwelling and integrated vision of legal justice but is the formal site for the attempted but elusive blending and reconciliation of competing principles. The temporary accommodations made are more a result of political expediency than moral integrity. Although one set of principles may tend to dominate and infuse the law with its guiding values, competing principles will constantly challenge it and provide a debilitating set of counterprinciples. At times, the tension will precipitate doctrinal crisis; at other times, the friction will be subdued and less disruptive. Yet, muted or manifest, this antagonism fuels and informs doctrinal development. There is no overarching metaprinciple that is available to synthesize the competing general and theoretical attachments in particular and concrete circumstances. In each situation, it is possible to demonstrate that a choice of either principle is fully justified as a matter of formal fit and substantive justice. Once Hercules has made that choice, Dworkin has nothing to say *as a matter of legal argument* by way of persuasion to anyone who disagrees with him. At this point, the engagement is open and ideological. While this does not mean that persuasion and reason have run their course and that raw power is all that remains, it does mean that law has been left behind in the sense of the appropriate adjudicative attitude in which Dworkin insists and requires that law should be conducted. To be blunt, he translates his sectarian preferences into a universal truth and gives credence to the severe claim that "the status of the bourgeoisie is particular, historical; man as represented by it is universal, eternal."[28]

One of Dworkin's arguments in response to the criticism that there are multiple principles at work in the law is that these moral indicators are "competitive" rather than "contradictory" and that "mistakes" can be isolated in a noncontroversial manner. Yet the main thrust of Dworkin's response is unpersuasive:

> These principles are sometimes competitive, but they are not contradictory. [Hercules] asks whether past decisions in cases in which they do conflict have resolved them coherently. Perhaps they have, though whatever account he accepts of that resolution will probably require him to treat some past decisions, those that fall on the wrong side of the line, as mistakes. Perhaps not: perhaps a coherent legal system must treat all cases of this kind of conflict in the same way. Then he must ask, in the way now becoming familiar, whether one of the choices the system might make between the principles is ruled out on grounds of fit; if neither is, he must decide which is superior in personal and political morality, and though others would decide differently, that in itself is no objection to his choice.

With characteristic opacity, Dworkin seems to concede the point rather than refute it. Of course, judges who make "choices differently in different kinds of circumstances" are not necessarily "morally schizophrenic"; judges need to adapt their general political commitments in order to apply them to the different and detailed contexts that demand decision. However, this insight is cold comfort to Dworkin's openly foundationalist ambition to distinguish the constrained act of adjudication from the more open-ended play of political morality. It is only within his naturalist account of adjudication (which unjustifiably insists that there is available a discoverable *and legal* metaprinciple of differentiation, capable of identifying one kind of circumstance from another) that judges run the real risk of becoming "morally schizophrenic."[29] However, in a nonfoundationalist account, "contradiction" is less a debilitating occurrence that must be explained away or resolved in order to salvage the legitimacy of the adjudicative enterprise than a source of doctrinal energy that provides law with its transformative potential.

Moreover, Dworkin's concession that if neither principle is ruled out on the grounds of fit, judges must decide "which is superior in personal and political morality," can hardly claim to resolve the debate in his favor, especially when combined with his closing remark that the fact that other judges would decide differently "in itself is no objection to [one judge's particular] choice." Any critic can surely be excused from thinking that if this is the best defense that Dworkin can muster for the claim that judges are constrained by the interpretive ideal of judicial integrity, this is no defense at all; it is all confession and no avoidance. The only way to arbitrate such claims is to engage in the doctrinal trenches and to show how particular interpretive methods and their critical deconstructions work out disputes at something other than "the level of abstract principle." Typically, Dworkin and his heroic disciples eschew such good sense; their analyses are almost entirely ahistorical and nonsubstantive in character. In elaborating how the common law has moved from one doctrinal phase to another, Dworkin wants to believe that principled integrity has been both the motivation and the guide. However, the common law's rich and long tradition bears eloquent testimony to the absence of any metaprinciple capable of resolving the contests of principles. Indeed, it is the very absence of such an all-embracing algorithm that is both the blessing and the curse of adjudication in a common law system. When viewed from a nonfoundationalist perspective, legal progress is revealed more accurately as the contingent choices of the judicial personnel among the contradictory principles of legal doctrine. It is to this issue that I now turn.

Back to the Future

One of the most intractable and pervasive problems for traditional jurists is to explain the undoubted phenomenon of legal evolution and progress. Such an explanation has so far eluded the grasp of countless jurists. The ability of a theory to explicate the operation of the judicial enterprise through standard instances is not the full measure of its worth. The metewand of any theory is its genius to transcend the commonplace and to comprehend the judicial resolution of novel or extraordinary instances: "How can a system of law, a system of ideas whose hypothesis it is that rules are constant, adapt itself to a changing world?"[30] For all the wisdom and common sense of its central insights, Hart's *The Concept of Law* failed to provide an adequate or satisfying explanation of this phenomenon. However, in part because of the central place assigned to the role of principles and their flexible dimensions, Dworkin's theory of adjudication has a better chance at capturing the momentum of legal change and explaining its dynamics. The scheme of principles is forever changing in order to reflect the sense of appropriateness developed in the public and the legal profession over a period of time. However, it should not be assumed that this scheme is amorphous or lacks continuity. Dworkin's account of law and adjudication attempts to straddle a middle position between a conventionalist account that demands that all present decisions are fully compatible with past decisions and a pragmatist account that instructs judges to make the best present decisions without regard to past decisions. In short, his interpretive ideal of judicial integrity seeks to combine both backward-looking and forward-looking elements by insisting that judges view what they do as "an unfolding political narrative" that "begins in the present and pursues the past only so far as and in the way . . . that present practice can be organized by and justified in principles sufficiently attractive to provide an honorable future."[31]

Until now, my focus has been on the extent to which Dworkin's theoretical account places no real check upon the judges in their efforts to reach just results and, therefore, *on his own terms*, fails to present a convincing account of law and adjudication. However, I now want to change tack and take at face value Dworkin's claims about the restraining effect that the past decisions that comprise legal doctrine have upon the resolution of present decisions. It will be remembered that his difficulty has been to demonstrate that Hercules can make resort to values without reducing adjudication to only the political or moral values that Hercules believes are paramount as a matter of personal conviction or ideological commitment; the law must in some way place a check on Hercules such that while his values have a role to play and while there may well be some consistency between his views and those of the law, he is not legislating his own views under the institutional guise of judicial reasoning. Accordingly, if this check or sense of restraint is to be more than illusory, Hercules must be required to pay more than lip service to law's past. Indeed, the essential thrust of Dworkin's account is that what marks those principles that are to guide and bind him as *legal* is their interpretive authorization by "the brute facts of legal history." Since "the best constructive interpretation" is one that expresses as a coherent whole as much of the community's legal doctrine as possible, it is clear that this theory, if it is to be credible, will require judges to forgo their own views occasionally and, instead, to perpetuate the general ideology that underpins the common law.

As a descriptive account of the law, Dworkin's offspring seems to be close to the mark; he concedes that law does not move forward in quantum leaps but is content to creep forward in incremental stages. As one of the leading English common law judges of the modern era opined, "The common law evolves not merely by breeding new principles but also, when they are fully grown, by burying their progenitors."[32] However, if his theory is taken seriously as a prescriptive matter, Dworkin seems to be saddled with an account of law that commits him to decisions that will by necessity be profoundly conservative; it will be incapable of accommodating wholesale change and will ensure a preservation of the general status quo. Indeed, Dworkin confesses that "any plausible working theory would disqualify an interpretation of [Anglo-American] law that . . . claimed a general principle of private law requiring the rich to share their wealth with the poor."[33] Notwithstanding the fact that there are occasional counterprinciples in the law that demand such a sharing, this conclusion underlines the extent to which a commitment to Dworkin's account of law and adjudication demands a commitment to the basic structure and fairness of the existing legal system. While this will not be a problem for many observers most of the time, it certainly will be for a few most of the time and for some part of the time.

The full force of this conservative failing is underlined in Dworkin's discussion of patently unjust laws. The central question is whether wicked legal systems generate legal rights and whether judges must enforce such rights. Did slave owners have the right to the return of their escaped slaves? Did a judge have to confiscate the property of Jews at the request of Aryans? Dworkin is sorely and genuinely troubled by these cases. This is not simply because he finds them intolerable as matters of substantive justice but because his own attachment to law-as-integrity seems to warrant their answer in the affirmative. Indeed, a good faith reading of the relevant legal materials in early-nineteenth-century America and mid-twentieth-century Germany points to the existence of such rights and, therefore, to their judicial enforcement in the name of democratic justice. However, Dworkin seems undaunted and offers a distinction that is intended to finesse these ignominious outcomes:

> A full political theory of law . . . includes at least two main parts; it speaks to both the grounds of law—circumstances in which particular

> propositions of law should be taken to be sound or true—and to the force of law—the relative power of any true proposition of law to justify coercion in different sorts of exceptional circumstance. . . . If a judge's own sense of justice condemned [the grounds of law] as deeply immoral . . . , he would have to consider whether he should actually enforce it . . . , or whether he should lie and say that this was not the law after all, or whether he should resign. The principle of integrity in adjudication, therefore, does not necessarily have the last word about how the coercive power of the state should be used. But it does have the first word, and normally there is nothing to add to what it says.[34]

Accordingly, while Hercules will normally follow the law, he can ignore the law where and when he considers it to be "deeply immoral." While this might seem to extricate Hercules from a tight spot, it actually undermines the whole basis of Dworkin's account of adjudication: he has bought this victory at too high a price. Shaved so thin, legal integrity will be so transparent as to be of little use in future skirmishes. The "judges's own sense of justice" is regnant and trumps the community's legal consensus. This means that judges are unconstrained by past judicial and legislative decisions if they consider them sufficiently wicked or "deeply immoral." Yet wickedness is a notoriously contested concept; one judge's iniquity can be another's equity. The history of the common law is redolent with judicial pronouncements that reveal the ephemeral character of such moralistic designations. Moreover, the threshold requirement of "exceptional circumstances" operates as no check at all, and it would be logically impossible to ask "the principle of integrity" to determine the conditions of its own applicability. According to Dworkin, the primacy of the judge's conscience is not fatal in circumstances that are not "exceptional" because "the principle of integrity" will provide the necessary institutional constraint. However, in "exceptional circumstances," the judge's "own sense of justice" will be irresistibly paramount. Accordingly, provided that judges have a sincerely held belief that a showing of wickedness has been made, they are free to "lie," "resign," or "refuse to enforce the law." This is a profoundly disturbing conclusion for a foundationalist like Dworkin who is devoted to justifying the self-sustaining legitimacy and moral force of the judicial enterprise. In such circumstances, the touchstone of good judging is the strength and sincerity of a judge's moral and political beliefs, not the the moral force of the extant law or particular judges' fidelity to it. While this insight is fatal to the foundationalist exercise, it is untroubling to a nonfoundationalist account—the quality of law's adjudicative game is openly and inevitably determined by the moral commitments of its judicial players.

The law of torts provides a more mundane but equally compelling example of this failing. Suppose a judge believed that any system that did not provide full compensation for all victims of misfortune in all circumstances was wicked, because failing to compensate would be to treat people's lives as mere commodities to be traded in the market of accidents. Or imagine a judge who believed that no one should ever be required to compensate another for injury unless it was deliberately caused, because to do otherwise would be to curtail people's liberty. In his "morally pluralistic society," Dworkin has little comeback against such judges. Sadly, he ensures that such radical critics of the system will have little role to play because "neither a Marxist nor a fascist" [nor feminist nor Crit or whoever?] "could find enough present law distinctively explained by his political philosophy to qualify for the contest."[35] Yet, presumably, that was exactly the case for progressive judges in early-nineteenth-century America and mid-twentieth-century Germany; they could not find sufficient support for their own views in the extant rules. It would seem that in law's empire, some views count for more than others simply by virtue of the persons that hold them. This, of course, is the essence of elitism and the very antithesis of democracy.

To give his theory any historical or political purchase, Dworkin must rely on the fact that "legal argument takes place on a plateau of rough consensus." When that fragile consensus breaks down, law's empire will begin to crumble. Yet Dworkin's complacency about the political validity and voluntariness of that consensus is very troubling. Despite his constant reference to and reliance upon "the brute facts of legal history," he is almost willfully blind to the suffering that has been perpetuated in the name of Law. In an admission of breathtaking naïveté, Dworkin depends on the moral inertia of the undifferentiated political center and the tyranny of the familiar when he asserts that "no one really thinks the law wicked or its authors tyrants." Yet the modern history of law and adjudication suggests, at the least, a less roseate assessment of the Rule of Law. After all, slavery, anti-Semitism, and racism are as much the creatures of law as antiracist initiatives to eradicate them; the judiciary cannot claim to be the consistent champions of the oppressed.[36] Not surprisingly, judges have favored the status quo, whether good or bad, over most challenges to it. In so doing, judges have acted in exactly the way that Dworkin's ideal of law-as-integrity recommends—they have given especial significance to the law's institutional morality and authority. In contrast, a nonfoundational explanation recognizes that the judges' allegiance to the status quo is less a matter of precedential pressure than a political commitment. Because what it means to "follow the rules" is always contestable, judges are as political in following the existing rules as they are in changing them. In law's adjudicative game, the experience of being both free and bound is at the heart of judicial play.

Justice Ensouled

One jurist who happily concedes that naturalists like Dworkin have failed to deliver on the foundationalist promise "to make sense of legal thinking and discourse in its own terms" is Ernest Weinrib. However, his prescription for jurisprudential success is no less foundationalist. In classical tradition, Weinrib's aim is to bring a moral order of coherent unity to what would otherwise be the chaos of human life. Concentrating on private law, he argues that law possesses an immanent moral rationality that, like love and friendship, must be understood purely in terms of itself; it is less than a positive instrument at the ideological disposal of its temporary guardians and more than an empty vessel waiting to be filled by its future inheritors. Within such a philosophical schema, Weinrib insists that it is nonsensical to talk of external purposes and ideals because private law is a justificatory enterprise that "tends toward its own coherence" and seeks "to realize a self-adjusting harmony of principles, rules and standards." For Weinrib, therefore, legal formalism is the normative truth of legal history and "embodies a profound and inescapable truth about law's inner coherence," without which the law's defense would be arbitrary and fail as an exercise in normative justification. Law has a unified and immanent intelligence in which coherence is understood as an internal achievement that "has no external referent." Weinrib insists, therefore, that instrumentalist and moralistic accounts fail because they treat private law as something less than complete in its own terms and less than justified on its own conditions. In what has become a signature phrase, he concludes that "if we must express this intelligibility in terms of purpose, the only thing to be said is that *the purpose of private law is to be private law*."[37]

In this Weinribian scheme of things, law reaches its fullest perfection when its form and substance are conjoined in harmonious unity. Although inseparable and constitutive of each other, form has theoretical primacy as the regulative and ordering mode of content. However, unlike its Platonic counterpart, the Weinribian form is not discoverable a priori but is beholden to the historical context of its legal content; form is content made pure and content is form made contingent. The quality of universality is attached to the method and not the results of its contingent application. The route to justice is through reflective self-consciousness and not immersion in empirical detail. In this philosophical way, private law is claimed to *work itself pure*, because "although manifested in circumstances that are socially and historically conditioned, the forms of justice . . . transcend particular social and historical contexts . . . ; the forms of justice are universals." For Weinrib, it is the Aristotelian notion of corrective justice, understood not as the imposition of a convenient extralegal moral purpose, that represents the analytic device through which private law is able "to realize its own immanent rationality." Accordingly, he surveys tort law's terrain and explains how its conceptual apparatus—duty of care, proximate and factual cause, misfeasance, and the standard of the reasonable person—capture and contain "the normative correlativity of doing and suffering harm."[38]

Throughout his work, Weinrib insists that the task of the judge is to actualize the justificatory structure latent in private law's intelligible potentiality. Although adjudication is "neither deductive nor determinate," Weinrib maintains that this difficulty need not be cured by resort to extraneous political values but by an act of legal judgment that is based on precedent, professional training, the constraints of the judicial role, and an acute "awareness of the need for systemic coherence." In this way, Weinrib claims to operationalize a legal formalism that achieves a rational, immanent, and normative governance of juridical relationships that is neither instrumental nor ideological in character and content:

> The forms of justice are both determinate and indeterminate. They are indeterminate in that they do not predetermine exhaustively the particular results they govern. They are determinate in that they establish the bounds of coherence for the particulars that fall under them. In determining the character, kind, and unity of juridical relationships, the forms of justice determine all that they need to, or can, determine as forms.[39]

Behind the intimidating facade of philosophical rigor and academic erudition, Weinrib's legal theory is theoretically fragile and historically suspect. As both a plausible description of past legal practice and convincing prescription for future legal development, Weinrib's account fails to support the foundationalist claim that private law "works itself pure." While there are many criticisms that can be leveled at Weinrib's account of "universality with a variable content,"[40] I restrict myself to its two emblematic failings as a prototypical foundationalist account of law and adjudication. First, in a maneuver typical of all foundationalists, Weinrib smuggles in personal preference in the guise of universal insight; he insists that his version of adjudication and jurisprudence is the only and best way to *play the game*. Second, he presents a jurisprudential account that depicts law as having a dynamic life of its own that seems to proceed while not only oblivious to what its judicial expositors think that they are doing but also frequently in complete opposition to what they think that they are doing. Indeed, for all its lofty ambitions, Weinrib's jurisprudential account manages to confirm the modest claim that the practices of law and philosophy are no more (and no less) than a human pursuit—situated, fragmentary, and flawed.

At the heart of Weinrib's critical methodology is the injunction to move back and forth between law and theory in "a circle of thought that feeds upon its own unfolding theoretical explicitness." Accordingly, he takes the extant historical materials of legal practice, identifies their implicit structure of justificatory coherence, elucidates that structure's normative standpoint, and examines the extent to which the law's substantive doctrines reflect those formal ideas. In this important sense, Weinrib accepts "the principal doctrinal and institutional components of . . . law more or less as given and then works back from them to the structure they embody." Although this Kantian methodology has much to recommend it, it runs the considerable risk of too readily collapsing critical analysis into a series of empty tautologies. If the interpenetration of form and content is taken at face value, there is no possibility that there can be a poor fit between law's content and its internal structure. Form will always be the intelligible order of its content and content will always be the contingent embodiment of its form: "Juridical intelligibility emerges from a mutually reinforcing movement between form and content." In the Weinribian scheme, private law is and could never be other than it is. Even if there were "pure forms" of legal thought, they would contain only so much information about what is the case and nothing about what ought to be the case. Of course, this conclusion is as profoundly empty and uninteresting as the discovery by Molière's physician that opium puts people to sleep because it contains a sedative principle.[41]

However, there is a more disturbing possibility that flows from Weinrib's attachment to such a critical methodology. If intelligibility is concerned exclusively and exhaustively with notions of coherence, character, unity, and genericness, the best that internal understanding and criticism can do is to adjudge practices to be "mistaken to the extent that they do not adequately reflect the whole ensemble of institutional and conceptual features that must cohere if the law is to truly make sense." Always beholden to its experiential matter, the moral fiber of form can never deviate from the normative substance of its contingent content. Accordingly, for a perfectly critical Weinrib, the law's moral worth would consist of nothing more than being the most coherent and consistent exemplar of whatever it happens to be at any particular time: "The formalist's concern is not with whether a given exercise of state power is desirable on its merits . . . , but with whether it is intelligible as part of a coherent structure of justification." This kind of internal and complacent inquiry trivializes not only the object of study but also the scholarly enterprise that claims to be its very apotheosis. As with Fuller's attempts to articulate an "inner morality of law," the best that a rigorous

Weinribian naturalist can offer is a morality of technical efficiency in which consistency and rigor are the normative virtues par excellence; methodical and conscientious torturers come to be as deserving of moral approbation as methodical and conscientious surgeons.[42]

Weinrib, of course, is not content to offer a legal theory that can be dismissed as an empty tautology and a hollow morality: he does not intend to be an apologist for torturers. After all, Weinrib's defense is of private law as "justice ensouled." Indeed, he is adamant that his foundationalist account provides a regulative ideal that has normative and necessary implications for the law's content and development: law's form is also a form of justice and operates as a qualitative metewand against which to measure law's quantitative performance. Consequently, in order to defend himself against such charges, he acknowledges that "not every decision is a felicitous expression of the system's coherence" and that "internal to the process of law is the incremental transformation or reinterpretation or even the repudiation of specific decisions so as to make them conform to a wider pattern of coherence."[43] While there will always likely be a gap between aspiration and achievement, that gap will be ascribable, in light of law's inner normativity, to analytical mistake, not substantive error. Notwithstanding this, Weinrib's strange ambition seems to be to perform an inductive extrapolation of one principle from decisions and then a deductive demonstration of its explanatory power over those same decisions in order to—and this is the kicker—predict and underwrite future decisions. To achieve such a result, he has to perform the formidable philosophical task of pulling himself up substantively by his own formal bootstraps.

However, at some point in the historical development of the law's substantive content, Weinrib must determine which of "private law's massive complex of cases, doctrines, principles, concepts, procedures, policies, and standards" do and do not have special significance in the sense that "their systemic absence would mean the disappearance of private law as a recognizable mode of ordering." To give his theory any chance at all of having operational relevance and ethical credibility, Weinrib has to introduce the very sociopolitical values that his philosophical method is intended to banish from legal theorizing. In short, Weinrib falls back on the same illegitimate maneuver as the reviled instrumentalists and the failed formalists—he passes off personal preference as universal insight. The critical move in Weinrib's shift from internal analysis to external values is when he plays the Aristotelian card of corrective justice. After a lengthy statement of why law's content secures its intelligibility by being an adequate example of the most abstract conceptions of juridical relationships, Weinrib speeds to his conclusion that "in the history of legal philosophy, private law is Aristotle's discovery." Yet there is nothing in the long history of law's content or of law's form that dictates either the inevitability or necessity of that conclusion. Indeed, Weinrib concedes as much when he states that "negligence law . . . can be understood as expressing" corrective justice: he seems not prepared to make the claim that it *must*. Moreover, in making the blatant assertion that if it turns out "that the hypothesis of the law's coherence cannot be sustained, then the law will have failed to live up to its own aspirations to be a truly justificatory phenomenon," Weinrib confirms that law's normativity will not be established by looking at legal materials alone: it is a question of moral allegiance as much as analytical accuracy.[44] Accordingly, while Weinrib's pure forms of law can offer themselves as *one* abstract distillation of law's contingent content, they cannot claim an exclusive insight nor assert hegemonic authority. The acclaimed "immanent moral rationality" of the law amounts to Weinribian politics in philosophical costume.

It is equally plausible that tort law's internal rationality could be traced to an array of possibilities—wealth maximization, resource egalitarianism, or capitalist exploitation are a few of the contending candidates.[45] There is nothing in Weinrib's argument that explains why corrective justice *must* comprise the internal rationality of tort law or why it is the most morally intelligible explanation of tort law. It is not that the Aristotelian conception of corrective justice cannot plausibly be posited as the abiding moral dynamic of private law but that it can never be declared to be the only and necessary form of law. Moreover, corrective justice is itself a contested territory, of which many different normative maps have been drawn: some take it to give rise to a regime of strict liability; others utilize it to support a shift to no-fault liability.[46] The most we can say by way of formal generalization about the law of torts is that it deals with the determination of liability in situations of risk and injury. Any attempt to go beyond this by identifying a particular mode of determining liability (i.e., negligence as the actual embodiment of corrective justice) from among the plethora of historically specific modes (intention, strict liability, negligence, etc.) must forsake its claim to universal and formal validity. Indeed, within the foundationalist canon, loss of generality is the price of specificity and the cost of generality is the loss of specificity. It is only by introducing a host of mediating values that are neither exclusively formal nor relentlessly actual that Weinrib can span the crucial gap between pure form and substantive content. Yet in so doing, Weinrib gives the game away and reveals that the foundations of his theory are far less secure and stable than he claims or requires.

Having chosen negligence liability as the true substantive embodiment of corrective justice's formal intelligibility, Weinrib is left with the daunting task of accounting for the continuing, sizable presence of strict liability in tort law. In an audacious move, he argues that some of the more important doctrines that are often thought of as being based on strict liability (vicarious liability, abnormally dangerous activities, nuisance, and defense of property) are only improper and imperfect instantiations of corrective justice. For Weinrib, therefore, such "strict liability" doctrines do not stand as areas of recalcitrant resistance to the historical unfolding of law's immanent intelligibility but are, again when properly understood, exemplary testaments to corrective justice and law's capacity to *work itself pure*. Yet in making this move, Weinrib has surely overextended himself. Insofar as he is prepared to justify competing doctrines as compatible with the law's immanent rationality and, thereby, instantiating corrective justice, he has demonstrated the vacuity of his critical methodology, not its explanatory power. If the idea of corrective justice is capable of accommodating and reconciling negligence and nuisance, standard of care and vicarious liability, proximate cause and *Rylands* v. *Fletcher*, it is surely and truly indeterminate. Far from being the regulative ideal that Weinrib posits it to be, the idea of corrective justice is revealed as empty and transparent. In Weinrib's hands, corrective justice is capable of explaining almost everything and, therefore, justifying almost nothing.

The crux of the matter is that any foundationalist theory of private law is ultimately called to account at the bar of history, where it must sooner or later explain itself in terms of the broad sweep of legal change. To put it bluntly, history has a bad habit of confounding even the most sophisticated of philosophical theories. In the twentieth century, whether on the American turnpike from *MacPherson* to *Sindell* and beyond or the Anglo-Canadian road from *Donoghue* to *Junior Books* and beyond, the doctrinal regime for unintentional injuries has been thoroughly transformed. Even if tort law once approximated Weinrib's standards of corrective justice, it is now thoroughly dominated by talk of distributive policies and instrumentalist concerns. As in other areas of the law, there has been a marked shift in emphasis from the attribution of blame to the apportionment of risk; the ascription of liability is based more on a broadly utilitarian accounting of social welfare than on a moral definition of individual responsibility. Although Weinrib is not blind to these developments, he seems unperturbed by them. As with his treatment of strict liability generally, he makes his way through tort law pointing out those doctrines that do (i.e., "but for" causation, reasonable care, and reasonable foreseeability) and do not (i.e., probabilistic causation, punitive damages, pure economic loss, and illegality) reflect the demands of corrective justice. In typical fashion, where there is little or no fit between extant doctrines and justificatory principles, he announces that the law has failed "to live up to its own aspirations as a truly justificatory phenomenon."[47]

On the whole, however, Weinrib seems committed to the conclusion that in its refusal to follow the American shift toward strict liability, Anglo-Canadian law retains a more pristine conception of private law that better embodies tort law's underlying commitment to a pure form of corrective justice. It is presumably not Weinrib's claim that his "universally valid" theory of formalism is applicable only to contemporary Anglo-Canadian law and not to modern American or old Anglo-Canadian law. While it is plausible to suggest that pockets of American law may be in "error" or "ignorance," it is less than persuasive and more than a little embarrassing for Weinrib to declare that the bulk of American tort law is so mistaken as not to amount to tort law at all. It might not be necessary for all law's content to express perfectly its immanent form all of the time, but there must be a point at which the discrepancy between form and content is so large that the form must begin to change, if it is not to lose contact with its content. In Weinrib's terms, this means that at a certain point, "error" will become insight and "ignorance" will become knowledge. Consequently, Weinrib's announcement that "the only function of private law is simply to be private law" remains meaningful only if it is read as "the only function of private law is simply to be the private law that best substantiates Weinrib's idea of corrective justice." In other words, the common law only works itself pure when it draws its inspiration from the Weinribian fountain of justice.[48]

Of Wooden Heads and Human Minds

The common law is not a rock. Rather than being a found object in the world, it is the dynamic product of human imagination and ingenuity. While there exists a historical residue of cases and materials, the law is essentially a purposive activity through which society seeks to regulate itself. Weinrib has no difficulty with this understanding. However, it is surely the case, as Hart stressed, that any credible description of a social practice, such as law, must account for the beliefs of participants as to what they are doing or think they are doing. Accordingly, while legal theorists need not share or endorse the beliefs of participants in the legal community, they must offer an explanation of the participants' behavior as it is understood by those participants.[49] Weinrib respects that requirement or at least pays lip service to it. He notes early on in *The Idea of Private Law* that "the very presence in the common law of reasons for judgment is an invitation to take those reasons seriously *as* reasons," and later concludes with the reminder to take "seriously the discourse through which a sophisticated system of private law aspires to express its rationality." However, in the two-hundred-page bulk of the book bracketed by these two statements he manages to ignore and contravene this sound advice.[50] Of course, I do not mean to suggest that people are always the best judges of their own actions or that motivations are always conscious, transparent, or simple. However, insofar as Weinrib is offering a rational account of lawyering, as opposed to a psychoanalytic one, judges' reflective and stated self-understandings of what they are doing must be incorporated into any cogent theory of law's workings.

While Weinrib views private law as an essentially purposive endeavor, he is adamant that its operation "is intelligible without external referent as a harmony of parts making up a coherent whole" and, insofar as it is has any purpose, that "the purpose of private law is simply to be private law." This of course means that private law's personnel are, with varying degrees of success, single-mindedly devoted to and energized by one purpose—to perfect private law as the embodiment of corrective justice. Although Weinrib is entitled to state that "corrective justice and Kantian right are not themselves on the lips of judges," he surely cannot claim that "they are implicit in [the discourse of private law] as a coherent justificatory enterprise" when the empirical weight of historical evidence is to the contrary. This stands at sharp odds with the explicit self-understanding of many of those judges and officials who experience themselves as being involved in anything but such an internalist project. As the bulk of judgments remain silent on these larger issues, it is obvious that they are not consciously driven by any such jurisprudential imperative. Moreover, insofar as judges do explicitly reflect upon their jurisprudential modus operandi, there are many who articulate a very different justification for their decisions, and there are some who expressly deny that they are involved in the internalist elaboration of private law's commitment to corrective justice. For instance, although Weinrib can dismiss Posner's efforts *as an academic* to explain tort law as an exercise in economic rationalization, it is entirely another matter to ignore Posner's attempts *as a judge* to develop tort law in line with such an instrumentalist dynamic.[51]

Mindful of the fact that the historical evidence of articulated judicial purpose does not support his theoretical conclusions, Weinrib claims that although judges have not acted deliberately or in concert, the common law is seen to have a self-perfecting spirit that works toward its practical realization and institutional consummation as "an act of intelligence rather than a set of observed regularities." For Weinrib, therefore, intelligibility is an attribute of the system, not its individual participants. Although law is not "a super-intellect distinct from the intellect of individual human beings," judges and jurists are self-effacing participants rather than "freelancing intellectual adventurers." However, apart from the fact that many of his statements fit uneasily together (if at all), Weinrib has managed to impale himself on the horns of a painful dilemma. One possibility is that the expressed self-understandings of judges about what they are doing are unimportant (i.e., they are not part of law), in which case the law must be seen as developing coherently in spite of its judicial creators and in accordance with some superhuman intelligence. The second possibility is that the expressed self-understandings of judges about what they are doing are important (i.e., they are part of law), in which case Weinrib's formal methodology is substantively incomplete, and his idiosyncratic preference for "corrective justice" is externally imposed rather than internally generated. Whereas the former view speaks in mystical terms of a "legal super-intellect" and ignores the inescapably human dimensions of law, the latter reveals the all-too-human aristocratic accent of many judges and jurists.[52]

Weinrib not only concedes that law is more than an empirical phenomenon but also insists that law must be understood as "an act of intelligence rather than a set of observed regularities": it is about the justificatory ideas of willing agents as much as it is about the doctrinal artifacts of their intellect and imagination. For Weinrib, of course, the law's purpose is contained and exhausted by efforts to elaborate the noninstrumental and normative notion of corrective justice as "the abstract equality of free purposive beings under the Kantian concept of right." In defending this project, he underlines that "without the concept of right, law would be a merely empirical phenomenon: like a wooden head, beautiful, but brainless, it would lack inner intelligibility." However, it can also be said that with such an attenuated concept of purpose, that head would live a beautiful but wooden existence. Law would lead a life of pure fantasy, entirely internal to itself and with no contact with reality. In short, law would be autistic: it would spend every day in morbid self-absorption and self-contemplation. In stark contrast to almost all participants' perceptions, the common law would act and evolve with total indifference to its social and historical context; judging would be reduced to the arid pursuit of abstract refinement and logical coherence. For Weinrib, there is no source of change other than law's impersonal and intellectual perfection of itself.[53]

Indeed, despite his protestations to the contrary, Weinrib discloses law as a game without any players: it is a self-perpetuating project that *works itself pure*. In his hands, law becomes an artifact or series of performances that takes on the shape, shading, and meaning that it does regardless of the designs or diligence of its artisans or players. For instance, imagine if a jurist postulated that the development and formation of private law doctrines were explainable in terms of the thesis that judging was a branch of L. Ron Hubbard's Scientology and was directed by its implicit logic—that its locus is a synthetic consensual belief system; that it is a complex, costly, and hierarchical structure; and that it is centered on the correction of negative patterns of individual behavior by the intervention of adepts practicing something that is not quite science and not quite art. Such a bizarre thesis would not persuade no matter how well crafted the fit between theoretical essence and experiential data or how coherent the explanation.[54] Judges are not laboratory rats; their sense of what they are or are not engaged in doing is an important factor in any justificatory explanation of their behavior. In the same manner, to argue that the judicial development of the common law is about the elaboration of an Aristotelian metric makes little sense. If, as Weinrib seems to claim, truth is knowledge of the world that accounts to nothing but itself, and the aspiration to truth amounts to the only true purpose of philosophical study, he has failed to be true to himself. In reaching for the stars, he has managed to grasp only the void.

Not surprisingly, Weinrib does not claim that adjudication can operate at a perfect pitch of operational efficacy. However, he does insist, predictably, that judges act legitimately when they strive to act in accordance with *justice ensouled* by specifying "how corrective justice manifests itself in a particular set of dealings." This authoritative exercise can and must be handled through resort to the internal bidings of the law itself and without reference to political externalities. As such, adjudication consists of an exercise in justification that represents an internal mediation of the formal relation between law's universal generalities and its contingent particularities. In an important way, the law's forms of justice determine the ambit of juridical intelligibility and mark off the boundaries of the legal and the political. The fact that legal doctrine cannot predetermine every case is not fatal since the law's autonomy is found in the justificatory attempt to work through law as a normatively immanent and coherent enterprise. Although judges are always obliged to negotiate indeterminacy by giving particular meaning to general concepts through contextual acts of judgment, that exercise of judgment is legal rather than political as long as the resources it draws on—doctrinal materials, professional training, institutional integrity, and casuistic argument—are internal to the legal enterprise. As Weinrib himself sums up:

> The very notion of determinacy relates in different ways to the generality of the forms and to the particularity of external interaction. Formalism comprehends both these ways in their interrelation. The forms of justice are both determinate and indeterminate. They are indeterminate in that they do not predetermine exhaustively the particular results they govern. They are determinate in that they establish the bounds of coherence for the particulars that fall under them. In determining the character, kind, and unity of juridical relationships, the forms of justice determine all that they need to, or can, determine as forms.[55]

Pitched at this level of abstract generality, Weinrib's approach to indeterminacy seems sensitive and instructive. But once brought down to a more concrete level, it has to be reported that Weinrib has made no more headway than his lapsed colleagues. By way of illustration, Weinrib chooses to focus on the application of "reasonable foreseeability" (or proximate cause) in the controversial English case of *Lamb*.[56] The facts were that the negligence of the municipality's subcontractors in repairing a sewer pipe in the adjoining street had caused the plaintiff's house to subside. The issue was whether the municipality should be liable to the plaintiff for damage caused by squatters who occupied the house when the plaintiff was obliged to move out. For Weinrib, the contrasting judgments of an internalist Watkins and an instrumentalist Denning highlight the differences between a juridical (and, therefore, legitimate) approach and a political (and, therefore, illegitimate) approach to adjudication. Whereas the latter ruled against liability because of his political preference for utilizing tort law to effect a loss-spreading policy through insurance cover, the former eschewed such external considerations in reaching the same result. After exploring "the nature of the event or act, the time it occurred, the place where it occurred, the identity of the perpetrator and his intentions, and responsibility, if any, for taking measures to avoid the occurrence *and matters of public policy*," Watkins relied upon his "instinctive feeling" about how best to resolve this doctrinal matter "of very considerable obscurity and difficulty."[57]

After predictably dismissing Denning's judgment as a valid legal performance, Weinrib holds up Watkins's judgment as an exemplary illustration of what should be done by a foundationalist judge "whose job it is to exercise a judgment that relates particulars to the relevant concept . . . [and], if undertaken in good faith, these exercises of judgment are as nonpolitical as the concepts that inform them." Whereas Denning engaged in an instrumentalist exercise for which he "is neither positioned to canvass the range of possible collective goals nor accountable to the community for the particular goal chosen," Watkins restricted himself to an appropriate deliberation on the best way to understand a particular interaction in terms of corrective justice. In short, rather than "use proximate cause as the occasion for a political operation," Watkins struggles to specify "that concept's meaning in the context of the particular transaction he is judging." However, as with all those other foundationalists whom Weinrib chastises, his proffered way of proceeding is so open ended and so capacious that it turns law and adjudication into a formal exercise in the most pejorative sense. Indeed, to isolate Watkins's judgment in *Lamb* as the epitome of *justice ensouled* is perverse: it is a judgment that testifies as much to the bankruptcy (intellectual and moral) of the common law's tradition as to its celebration.[58]

According to Weinrib, judges can decide as they wish provided that they can justify and express their decisions through the law's "accumulated meaning" and "culture of reasoning." For instance, Learned Hand's cost-benefit formulation of "reasonable care" is not so much erroneous as improperly justified; it must not be understood as an instrumental tool but as an internal substantiation of law's internal form. In this way, like the more contemporary foundationalists, Weinrib depicts judicial craft as only being grounded in the limits of the judges' imagination and technical dexterity. As with the good game player, it is the way that judges play that matters, not what the outcome or result is. However, while the constraints of professional integrity, systemic coherence, and casuistic reasoning are not illusory or meaningless, they are never sufficiently determinate or fixed to provide any real constraints on the adventurous judge. Of course, the willingness to "use legal discourse as a cover for political decisions" is illegitimate and can be righteously deplored. Although Weinrib is mistaken to set "legal discourse" against "political decisions," his insistence on a good faith attempt to play the adjudicative game (as presently constituted) is entirely appropriate; using legal discourse as *only* "a cover" does not satisfy that requirement.[59] Nevertheless, and again, this condition speaks more to individual judges' personal talents than to any external constraints that doctrinal materials or legal reasoning impose. At some point, if Denning's style of judgment in *Lamb* becomes the norm, Weinrib is left in a familiar foundationalist bind—he must argue that whatever Denning and his followers are doing, they are not engaged in adjudication (which seems a peculiar and perverse assessment) or that the nature of legal adjudication has changed (in which case Weinrib's universal truths about law and adjudication cannot be sustained). What counts as good judging will itself always be a contingent feature of law and politics, not a universal characteristic of legal reasoning; whether Denning's or Watkins's style of judging is treated as worthy of praise or emulation is a matter of rhetorical exchange, not philosophical insight.

Of course, in rejecting Weinrib's account, I am not suggesting that private law is irrational or chaotic, but I am insisting that philosophical *necessity* is not the mother of legal invention. I resist his foundationalist contention that "one must accede to the possibility that law can be understood through itself or deny the possibility that law can be understood at all." Instead, I maintain that law and adjudication are understandable without subscribing to Weinrib's internalist, totalizing criteria of intelligibility and rationality. Being the product of human beings, law is untidy, diverse, complex, and contingent; it is a flawed enterprise, noble and ignoble in proportion to its judicial expositors. It is only by abstracting the human element and therefore misrepresenting law that Weinrib is able to claim any legitimacy or cogency for his account. Any theory that attempts to shoehorn the whirligig of lawmaking into one simplistic formula and smooth down its rough edges robs law of its rich and distinguishing character as a human process. Invention finds its source in a contingent and shifting mix of the essential and the accidental; there is always room in law's structure for judicial ingenuity or institutional fortuity. Law is a site at which judges work through and against law.

Consequently, a nonfoundationalist dismissal of Weinrib's philosophical project does not commit me to an irrationalist or antifoundationalist stance from which all efforts to understand law as "a declaration of principles and standards" are abandoned and from which law is viewed as a mere hotchpotch of whimsy, caprice, or perversity. Nor is the alternative to Weinrib's perfectly rational scheme a paranoid account of law as a Machiavellian conspiracy of gigantic proportions in which "adjudication involves the achievement of a collective goal through subterfuge or manipulation."[60] Rather than commune with Weinrib and other foundationalists about the common law *working itself pure*, it is more instructive to think about judges, through their own efforts and imagination, working the law to meet the changing demands of justice. There are patterns, trends, and threads that can be traced, but they often end as abruptly as they began: continuity and discontinuity, historical and theoretical, are twin features of the common law. As such, the history and development of private law is as much "the wake of a mobile mind falling in and out of love with the things it detaches by its attachment" as it is a necessary elaboration of law's internal dynamic.[61] In other words, law's adjudicative game develops and changes less in line with some subtle philosophical logic than in response to the political intimations of its judicial players as they shift from one playing context to another.

Conclusion

The ambition of this chapter has been to demonstrate how naturalist efforts to justify the exercise of judicial power as objectively bounded and morally just are ill advised and unsuccessful. In particular, I have sought to show how Dworkin's theory of law-as-integrity and Weinrib's law-as-justice-ensouled fail to ground themselves in terms of descriptive accuracy or prescriptive merit. While their accounts are an important and valuable improvement on positivist accounts of law and adjudication in their insistence that law is always about political and moral values, they are unable to defend their own claims that resort to such values can be made by judges in a way that is neither personal nor partisan. It is my contention that Dworkin's and Weinrib's accounts succeed in establishing quite the opposite—that legal doctrine is riddled with indeterminacy and that adjudication is an inevitably partisan and inescapably political process of value choices. By attempting to mask this fact with increasingly sophisticated and abstract theories, Dworkin and Weinrib join a long and established lineage of natural lawyers who have acted as apologists for the inherent justness of law and "who, attributing universality and cosmic rightness to their own views, put them forward as the teaching of Science, History or The Law."[62]

In contrast to the foundationalists' conceit, I contend that it is unhelpful to treat law as a game that *works itself pure* by dint of its naturalist performance. While I agree with the naturalists (as against the positivists) that law is about political morality, I agree with the positivists (as against the naturalists) that the substantive goodness or badness of law is separate from its formal validity: the difference between "good" and "bad" moves is game-specific and must be evaluated within the game, even as the rules are being reinterpreted. There is no Objective Truth or Coherence that inheres and endures in the efforts of judges and jurists across space and time and from context to context. Law and adjudication are thoroughly human and, therefore, flawed activities whose practices and performances earn as much legitimacy as they are able to achieve through their rhetorical play. Indeed, it is to the nonfoundationalist idea and practice of "play" that I now turn.

6 At Play in the Fields of Law: The Reasoning Game

......

We cannot ask reason to take us across the gulfs of the absurd. Only the imagination can get us out of the eternal present.

—Ursula Le Guin, *Dancing at the Edge of the World*

It seems like whole libraries or, at least, large tracts of them have been written about the mysterious concept and practice of *legal reasoning*. Although there has been much to-ing and fro-ing around the matter, the common wisdom still prevails that, as Chief Justice Coke put it in the seventeenth century, there is an "artificial Reason and Judgment of Law which requires long Study and Experience before a Man can attain to the Cognizance of it." By this, it is meant that law has its own special form of reasoning that distinguishes it in some important way from other disciplines and other forms of reasoning (economic, scientific, logical, political, sociological, etc.). However, like all reasoning, legal reasoning is a process of argumentation by which it is possible to infer or move from one already accepted proposition to another that has yet to be accepted. Nonetheless, as central as it is to the legal enterprise, the precise identity or nature of legal reasoning still remains elusive; it defies simple classification or easy analysis. While foundationalists continue to insist that "legal reasoning has a logic of its own . . . [whose] structure fits it to give meaning to ambiguity,"[1] I maintain that, shorn of its legal nomenclature and doctrinal dressing, it is simply a general and nonspecific style of reasoning that lawyers have colonized and at which judges have become particularly adept.

Of course, everyone agrees that legal reasoning is distinctive to the extent that it works upon a particular set of materials (cases and statutes), is framed in a professional jargon (e.g., stare decisis and obiter dicta), and is engaged in by a restricted community of professionals (lawyers and judges). However, that is as far as it goes. Legal reasoning is not the elusive grounding that jurists have sought for the legal enterprise. The claim that legal reasoning is special not only in its formal attributes but also in its ability to arrive at substantively better and worse answers cannot be sustained. As Duncan

Kennedy concludes, "Teachers teach nonsense when they persuade students that legal reasoning is distinct, *as a method of reaching correct results*, from ethical and political discourse in general."[2] As a normative exercise, it is not an empirical matter of truth or falsity: it is about persuasion and being convinced about the validity of any such reasoning maneuver. Accordingly, reasoning is less a demonstration of logical necessity and more a practice of human justification.

In this chapter, therefore, I want to explore further what it means to take seriously the idea and practice of law and adjudication as a playful and rhetorical activity. I begin by introducing a particular style of argumentation —analogical reasoning—that has held an enduring fascination for judges and jurists alike. By reference to the pragmatic work of Cass Sunstein, I disclose how this refocusing on law and adjudication as a practical activity flatters, but only to disappoint: the nonfoundationalist packaging belies the foundationalist commitment. By contrast, I offer a different understanding of legal reasoning that relies on what a deconstructive critique is (and, most important, is not) from a nonfoundationalist perspective. In particular, my discussion works to resist the tendency to transcendentalize or divinize notions like "play" or "*différance*" by turning them into metaphysical entities rather than treating them as pragmatic moves. Next, by resort to a well-known case, I offer a practical example of deconstruction at work in the service of a nonfoundationalist critique. From there, I demonstrate how a deconstructive notion of play can be deployed to understand the general practice of legal reasoning at large. In an appendix, I describe the argumentative maneuvers that presently (and only presently) comprise the organic rules of the adjudicative game, along with a short example that runs through a playful performance of that game. In short, I want to insist that in law's language game, there is nothing to ground play but more play: there is no final or privileged game that explains and grounds all others that is not itself a game.

Making Moves

Eschewing the hubristic aspirations of natural lawyers and other foundationalists, a new breed of pragmatists have sought to revalorize law and adjudication as a professional practice in which practical people pursue practical ends through practical means.[3] As a "back to basics" movement, legal pragmatism is not so much a philosophy or methodology as it is a way of professional life: it nurtures an existential ethic of inquiry rather than inculcates a catechism of substantive outcomes. By treating truth and correctness as experiential and experimental rather than apodictic and apocalyptic, adjudication comes to be understood as involving nurtured prudence, not revealed knowledge. While law remains a noble calling under such a perspective, its practitioners are more artisans than artists and more technicians than grand theorists; Cardozo, Holmes, Learned Hand, and Llewellyn are their heroes. Extolling the practical virtues of intellectual self-discipline and traditional craft, legal pragmatists conceive of law as being much more playful and practice-based than other contemporary jurists. However, while appreciating that adjudication is a kind of game, they do not have the confidence of their convictions in pushing through on the subversive implications of their insight that legal reasoning is all about "making moves" in a finite game of infinite possibilities.

Cass Sunstein is at the forefront of this pragmatist revival: his professed ambition is to restore the fading but vital faith in the worth and viability of the legal craft. While legal reasoning is a rule-based practice, law is not exhausted by the existence or application of rules; rules are an important resource, but they do not themselves fix the distinguishing characteristic of legal thinking, because "ideal justice outstrips rules; it adapts the account to the particulars of the case." More fundamentally, law is about reason giving as much as it is about decision making or rule application. According to Sunstein, law develops by self-conscious attention to its argumentative structure as much as by a formal consistency with substantive outcomes. Nevertheless, rules are important because they "sharply discipline the territory over which argument can occur."[4] For Sunstein, the life of the law is the (ana)logic of its own experience; there is method in the seeming madness of legal reasoning that is peculiarly and especially its own. Lawyers should not be embarrassed by their instinctive habits of mind or argumentative routines but should recognize and celebrate their pragmatic force and dispositive power. While he treasures coherence, Sunstein believes its demands are satisfied by much less than a snug fit between the almost infinite range of concrete propositions and their controlling abstract principles: law is neither wholly reducible to unadulterated politics nor wholly inflatable into pure integrity. Under this pragmatic calling, the judge is bound by an official tradition of legal reasoning but has room to experiment within its confines. While politics are always involved in legal disputations, the judge can remain agnostic and act in a uniquely and proudly legal way: law might be political, but it is not *merely* political. For Sunstein, therefore, the special method of the law is to be found in its traditional reliance on analogical reasoning. While analogical reasoning is pervasive in law and everyday life, "analogical reasoning is the key to legal casuistry" and "lies at the heart of legal thinking and for good reason"; it has a distinctive structure and faces distinctive constraints. Because analogical reasoning imposes a certain discipline, there is less need for a widespread moral or political consensus. Indeed, Sunstein's reliance on incompletely theorized agreements seems to have virtually eliminated the need for *any* agreement on such issues. As the most familiar means of legal reasoning, analogical reasoning runs neither inductively from particulars to generalities nor deductively from generalities to particulars but rather moves from particulars to particulars: analogical reasoning is not syllogistic and scientific in form and function but is practical and probabilistic. The beauty of legal reasoning is that it allows lawyers and judges to engage with political and moral values without reducing law to an open-ended ideological debate and without collapsing it into some other field of knowledge, like politics or economics. Large-scale debate about controversial issues is avoided by the fact that legal reasoning functions by relying on "a set of practices, conventions, and outcomes . . . [that] makes legal interpretation possible . . . and sharply constrains legal judgment." This legal culture of syntactic and substantive principles places off limits certain deep conflicts over the right and good as being too ideological and unsuited to legal resolution; "the lawyer's questions have everything to do with constraints of competence and role," and "there can be a real difference between the legally correct outcome and the morally correct outcome."[5]

Sunstein's account of how analogical reasoning works is fairly uncontroversial, but the claims that he makes for its operation are decidedly controversial in character. He highlights four steps in the analogical process: (1) fact pattern X has certain characteristics A, B, and C; (2) fact pattern Y differs from X in some respects but shares certain other characteristics A, B, and C; (3) the law treats X in a certain way; and (4) because fact pattern Y shares certain characteristics with fact pattern X, the law should treat fact pattern Y in the same way. Obviously, the application of such an analogical process involves normative judgments about relevance and valence in terms of the similarities and differences between fact patterns. However, according to Sunstein, the legitimacy and genius of analogical reasoning as a legal practice is that it "will impose a certain discipline . . . [such that] there can be a real difference between the legally correct outcome and the morally correct outcome; the difference lies in the fact that analogies will operate as entirely 'fixed points' in legal reasoning, whereas many of these are revisable in morality." Moreover, in understanding analogical reasoning in this way as the key maneuver in the judicial repertoire of legal moves, judges "need not, much of the time, attempt to say much about large-scale social controversies." In this important sense, therefore, analogical reasoning is different from and preferable to other forms of legal argumentation, such as resort to abstract theories of "wealth maximization" or "natural rights," because it operates at a much more concrete and modest level and in a much less theoretical and piecemeal way; it does not need to take a stand on such ideological and controversial matters. As such, analogical reasoning is the most effective, legitimate, and just form of legal argumentation in that it achieves "principled consistency, a focus on particulars, incompletely theorized judgments, and principles operating at a low or intermediate level of abstraction."[6]

However, despite the obvious appeal of this pragmatic and relatively playful approach to the nonfoundationalist sensibility, the new pragmatism tends to be pragmatic in the most unpragmatic and, at times, almost antipragmatic way. Although paying lip service to the decidedly pragmatic qualities of contextual sensitivity and prudential judgment, Sunstein is far too concerned with discovering and defining The Way Things Really Are; his pragmatism is a foundationalist theory in nonfoundationalist clothing. By demonstrating that "analogical reasoning is the key to legal casuistry,"[7] he enlists pragmatism to complete the foundationalist campaign of demonstrating that law is a self-sufficient system that can produce correct, determinate, predictable, and distinctly legal outcomes. This is a flat denial of the pragmatist's belief that legal reasoning is not really about anything unique or special at all. Indeed, from a rigorous nonfoundationalist perspective, legal reasoning is what it is and what it is is historically contingent and socially revisable. Lawyering is nothing more (and nothing less) than what particular lawyers do at particular times, and legal reasoning is how particular lawyers reason at particular times. While some modes of legal reasoning lend themselves better to some tasks than others, this conclusion entails a contingent evaluation of their practical utility in particular situations. It does not involve fixing "the nature of legal reasoning," because it has none in any foundational or lasting sense: there is no neutral or reliable algorithm for legal or any other kind of decision making.

While it is true that the law is much more pragmatic and less analytical than most contemporary theorists pretend or allow, it strains the bounds of credibility to promote analogical reasoning as the underwriter of correct, determinate, and distinctly legal operations and outcomes. On the contrary, although analogical reasoning plays an important and frequent role in law's reasoning game, it is thoroughly indeterminate in practice and consequence. Most typically, this indeterminacy will manifest itself where fact pattern Y has more or less similarities with and differences from fact pattern X. As no two cases are ever entirely the same or different, this will occur almost all the time. For example, fact pattern X might be comprised of characteristics A, B, C, D, and E, but fact pattern Y might possess either A, B, C, and D or A, B, C, D, E, and F. In either case, there is nothing internal to the process of analogical reasoning that can determine whether the existence of one more, less, or different characteristic is sufficient to warrant treating fact pattern Y like fact pattern X or not. Indeed, the addition or subtraction of one characteristic might alter the collective meaning of the other characteristics: without C, the remaining characteristics A, B, D, and E might take on a very different significance, and with F, the characteristics A, B, C, D, and E might amount to a very different whole. Also, it might happen that in fact pattern X, a reappraisal might suggest that its relevant characteristics were not A, B, C, D, and E but really A, B, C, and D or A, B, C, D, E, and F. For instance, once it is decided that a car is a "vehicle" in terms of the rule that there are to be "no vehicles in the park," whether a person on roller blades is a "vehicle" will depend on the presumed or postulated purpose of such a rule—is it intended to reduce noise, cut down on traffic, protect the safety of pedestrians, or something else?

In almost all circumstances, there will be a pragmatic embarrassment of analogical riches. If good arguments are the touchstone of law and its legitimate functioning, there are simply too many good arguments for the pragmatists' peace of mind. In this situation, while fact pattern Y has characteristics A, B, C, D, and E, there are two earlier fact patterns W and X that were disposed of in entirely opposite ways; fact pattern W has characteristics A, B, and C, and fact pattern X has characteristics C, D, and E. There is no way to compare the relative cogency of the two competing analogical options without resort to some values or principles that are extraneous to the process of analogical reasoning itself.[8] Analogical reasoning does not determine the result; it is only a testing device for the more important political determinations that are made prior to and after analogical testing occurs. At every stage, the judge is obliged to make resort to the values and principles that analogical reasoning is intended to finesse. Analogical reasoning is thereby debilitated by the same weaknesses that afflict a rule-based account of law. In the same way that it is never possible to simply "follow the rules," because the question of the relevant and precise rule—and what following it entails—remains irresolvably contestable, it is also not possible to simply engage in analogical reasoning, because the question of the relevant and precise analogy—and what following it entails—remains irresolvably contestable. Accordingly, analogical reasoning hides rather than does away with the historical values and social ideas that energize the law's operation.

For analogical reasoning to be cogent and compelling, there must be sufficient justification to warrant the inference that because property X is present in one instance, it is present in another. But there is no way to identify or confirm through the logic of analogical argument itself that certain characteristics are present or that any inferences are warrantable. This is a matter of imputation, not demonstration. Indeed, analogical reasoning must be complemented and supplemented by resort to what Sunstein is most at pains to avoid—what he describes as "large-scale social controversies"—if it is to make any sense at all. Conversely, with recourse to such external values, foundationalist-style claims about the "real difference between the legally correct outcome and the morally correct outcome" ring hollow. Moreover, because pragmatism is more ad hoc than a priori, any juristic attempt to effect a more programmatic or systematic appeal to political or social values ceases to be pragmatic. Like his pragmatic predecessors, Sunstein fails to provide any guide as to how to distinguish good from bad analogical reasoning. On this crucial question, he concludes that "the determination of similarity and difference is the function of each judge" and that "legal reasoning tests constantly whether society has come to see new differences or similarities."[9] While this strikes an agreeable note within a nonfoundationalist approach, it is cold comfort to Sunstein's foundationalist commitments. In short, while analogical reasoning is an important dimension of legal reasoning, it cannot provide the vital grounding that the new pragmatists suggest.

Unclear about whether analogical reasoning acts as a constraint on law or whether law acts as a constraint on analogical reasoning, Sunstein and other pragmatists are unable to overcome the criticism that the analytical validity of the substantive outcome is not warranted by the analogical form of the legal argument. It is not the force of Reason, analogical or otherwise, that determines what is important and relevant in legal decision making but what is substantively reasonable and contingently acceptable as a matter of practical reason. As such, the determinacy or correctness of legal reasoning is not closed but open and, therefore, is as much political as it is legal. While there are constraints that exist and are experienced by lawyers and judges, these constraints are less determinate and more revisable than is conceded. Constraints are as reinterpretable as the reasoning that they are intended to constrain. Of course, it is not that there are not better or worse answers or even correct ones but that "there is never any 'correct legal solution' that is other than the correct ethical and political solution to that legal problem."[10] Again, "correct" in the contingent and contextual sense that certain people for certain purposes at a certain time and place are persuaded that it is correct. A nonfoundationalist account does not deny the existence of such a standard but destabilizes its status and grounding.

If Sunstein is to make good on this deficiency, his primary responsibility must be to establish a distinctly legal standard against which to measure the weighting of the various similarities and differences. He maintains that as judges' convictions about the meaning and importance of certain decisions will warrant a certain priority in constraining the potentially open-ended operation of analogical reasoning, there are certain defining moments or "fixed points" of legal precedent that require judges "to square current judicial decisions with previous judicial decisions that have stood the test of time." For example, the fact that all judges accept that certain cases, such as *Brown* and *Roe*,[11] must be incorporated into any proposed theory about the United States Constitution emboldens Sunstein to maintain that "legal reasoning has a distinctive structure and faces distinctive constraints." However, while it might be possible to agree on a handful of fixed precedential points, they would be so limited as to be of little practical use: any attempts to enlarge this crucial category sufficiently for it to become practically operative would meet sharp and sectarian political disagreement. Moreover, even though Sunstein acknowledges that such fixed points "do not speak for themselves, and judgments about their meanings have large creative dimensions,"[12] it is difficult to understand how *Brown* or *Roe* could be seen as having a settled and shared interpretation capable of providing the necessary direction and force to get analogical reasoning up and running. Both *Brown* and *Roe* have been subjected to intense public attempts at interested interpretation and represent a site for the manufacture of meaning as much as an adequate grounding for the resolution of such contestation. Moreover, as *Brown* and *Roe* aptly illustrate, the genesis of these fixed precedential points is to be found in strikingly creative and nonanalogical judicial acts that break with existing legal traditions and reorient the legal enterprise.

For all his pragmatic protestations, Sunstein's account and defense of analogical reasoning remain profoundly abstruse and rationalistic in the sense that they are unsituated in the material circumstances of history and are inured to their political dynamics: "abstract universality" is ditched but only to be replaced by "abstract particularity." For a pragmatic approach that is supposed to valorize experience and contextuality, there is little appreciation that legal reasoning operates in the real world of historical struggle or of how law does (and does not) change. For Sunstein, the only experience and context that matter are the legal ones: the experience of the law is the life of its own logic. He makes no attempt to place *Roe* or *Brown* in their larger social setting so that it might be possible to appreciate the political dynamics of feminism and protest or the struggle for racial justice that impinged upon the legal process. On his terms, legal change is nothing more than the playing out of a legalistic game of analogical reasoning, with victory going to the analogically fleet and agile of mind. The pernicious effect of such a formulation is that legal change is not thought of as part of a sociopolitical process nor even as a pragmatic response to changing historical conditions. Instead, it is viewed solely as the culmination of the internal and irresistible force of legal reasoning. Notwithstanding many foundationalists' opinions to the contrary, it is surely unpardonable for lawyers and law professors to present themselves as the exclusive architects of legal and social change. To portray the development of legal doctrine as being brought about largely by dint of analogical reasoning is both dangerous and self-serving—dangerous because it trivializes the vital role of popular struggle and self-serving because it conveniently portrays academics as the saviors of social justice. On the contrary, analogical reasoning is mere prelude or postscript to a political letter.

Legal change is as much about political action as it is about making good legal arguments. Decisions like *Brown* and *Roe* become "fixed points" in the shifting constitutional universe not because they are legally correct or analytically sound but because they are considered politically valid and socially acceptable. The difference between *Plessy* v. *Ferguson* and *Brown* has nothing to do with interpretive cogency or hermeneutical integrity in constitutional doctrine;[13] analogical reasoning was not a decisive factor. It has everything to do with changing currents and concerns in the political context that frame and condition such germinal and disruptive judicial decisions. *Plessy* ceased to be a fixed point on the constitutional compass because it no longer enjoyed sufficient political confidence and public support; its perception as having an analytically weak or analogically suspect status was beside the historical point. Rightness was a matter of social policy and political persuasion, not constitutional law. Indeed, without abandoning his cherished attachment to analogical reasoning and the discredited doctrine of stare decisis, Sunstein would have been hard pressed to recognize *Brown* as a sound or correct legal decision in the summer of 1954. Like many other jurists, he would be thrown on the painful horns of the perennial foundationalist dilemma—either he would have to renounce his legal faith if he was to maintain his political beliefs or he could hold fast to his legal faith and accept the law's reactionary and, in that case, racist ethos.

While it might well be the case that "to argue from one factual situation to another and to decide by analogy is a natural tendency of the human and legal mind,"[14] it is not the be-all and end-all of law, and it most certainly is not the hallmark of legal practice that distinguishes it from moral, political, or ideological contestation. Indeed, it is only one part of law's repertoire of argumentative moves. Moreover, far from being insulated from large-scale moral controversies, analogical reasoning gains its intellectual purchase and practical efficacy by virtue of its resort to social and political values. Sunstein reluctantly concedes this but insists that incompletely theorized agreements function as "foundations for both rules and analogies." Such agreements allow judges to ground particular outcomes in something more substantial than their own legal instincts but less demanding than a fully thought-out theory or consensus for their political convictions: "While people diverge on some relatively high-level proposition, they might be able to agree when they lower the level of abstraction." By reference to such mid-level artifacts, he defends his claim that the legal arena does and should stand separately from any political involvement. Accordingly, as well as being pragmatically useful, incompletely theorized agreements allow judges to get on with their task without having to take a definitive or Herculean stand on deep political or moral values. In this way, Sunstein's championing of incompletely theorized agreements not only serves to explain how judges reach particular outcomes but also illuminates the hallmark of a well-functioning legal system because they are "an important source of social stability and . . . enable people to live together to permit them to show each other a measure of reciprocity and mutual respect."[15]

Sunstein is quick to admit that, on occasion, disagreements can be desirable. He concedes that incompletely theorized agreements can run the risk of reaching an outcome that is "mistaken" in situations where there may be widespread agreement about general value judgments but the agreement is nevertheless incompletely theorized. This, of course, prompts the query of why this outcome must be considered "mistaken" and on what basis it might be possible for judges to subject incompletely theorized agreements to "scrutiny and critique." Sunstein acknowledges that it would be foolish to deny that some general theories sometimes get it right, and even more foolish to suggest that incompletely theorized agreements warrant respect whatever their content: "Except in unusual situations and for multiple reasons, general theories are an unlikely foundation for judge-made law, and caution and humility about general theory are appropriate for courts, at least when multiple theories can lead in the same direction." While this could be interpreted as meaning that Sunstein is doing away with any foundation to legal reasoning at all, it is more reasonable to assume that he is merely replacing one foundation with another. Besides being the stuff of what good legal decisions comprise, incompletely theorized agreements are positioned to become Sunstein's contribution to the foundationalist task of determining "the crucial part of the lawyer's distinctive solution to social pluralism."[16]

For Sunstein, the need to make the system work on a daily basis is of paramount importance; efficacy is treasured more than consistency or candor. Indeed, he makes the telling suggestion that where judges have conflicting political frameworks, what is left unsaid can be as important as what is said, and that judges should keep silent so as to facilitate agreement on outcome in particular cases: "Silence—on something that may prove false, obtuse, or excessively contentious—can help minimize conflict, allow the present to learn from the future, and save a great deal of time and expense."

On the other hand, Sunstein also maintains that "if judges . . . have actually agreed on a general theory, and if they are really committed to it, they should say so." One could be forgiven for asking how judges could ever know they had reached agreement on such general theories in the first place, if they took Sunstein's vow of silence. Perhaps Sunstein also wondered about this when he later concluded that "in law, as in politics, disagreement can be a productive and creative force, revealing error, showing gaps, moving discussion and results in good directions." While this assessment seems to the jurisprudential point, it is an odd statement for someone who is committed to demonstrating that judges can resolve "large, contested issues of social life" in a distinctly legal way rather than "only on . . . a sectarian basis."[17]

Even if one accepts Sunstein's claim that incompletely theorized agreements can come to the rescue of analogical reasoning, he is still left with severe problems to overcome. For instance, in Sunstein's world, two judges may appeal to the same or different principles in order to energize analogical reasoning, but so long as they both lead to the same outcome, there is no cause for concern. It does not matters why fact pattern X and Y are deemed analogous; all that matters is that the dispute is resolved. Indeed, Sunstein worries that any attempt to explain what general theory was decisive might jeopardize the result. However, in this case, incompletely theorized agreements work less to facilitate adjudication than to conceal the actual basis of each judge's decision. While one judge may view A as the relevant characteristic, another may hold B to be it. If, however, the justification for why X and Y are held to be analogous is ignored, there is no possibility for predicting whether L or M may also be analogous. Stare decisis seems to have become so much unnecessary baggage in the pragmatic enterprise. Furthermore, a more serious problem would arise when there is no agreement at this more general level. Incompletely theorized agreements can only be possible or viable if both parties have at least some reason for accepting the result in question. If there is none, the judges are thrown back on their own political instincts. In such circumstances, it seems hopelessly inadequate to rely upon incompletely theorized agreements as "foundations for both rules and analogies."[18] As is so often the case, formalist theories run out at the very point where they are most needed.

In many ways, I do not disagree with Sunstein's claim that judges are able to make doctrinal progress by developing incompletely theorized agreements on controversial issues; it is a plausible and sensible account of judicial practice. However, when it is appreciated that Sunstein and I are engaged in very different jurisprudential projects, it is difficult to understand how such an account can advance Sunstein's ambitions. Whereas Sunstein is intent upon arguing that law is a self-sufficient practice that is significantly more constrained than political or moral argument and that can generate determinate and legitimate results, I want to offer a more critical account in which adjudication is one more site to play politics. Consequently, it is only when analogical reasoning is placed within a much broader and more expansive nonfoundationalist account of legal adjudication that the operation of legal reasoning as a practical exercise in decision making can be fully grasped and appreciated. Accordingly, it is to such an explanation of the playful performance of adjudication in law's language game that I now turn.

A Deconstructive Stretch

Efforts to utilize notions of "game" and "play" as devices for understanding various aspects of human thought and behavior have a long and distinguished philosophical lineage. However, despite general agreement over the relevance and utility of such notions, there has been little agreement on the role and status that games play in illuminating the human predicament and in advancing its critical analysis.[19] In entering this long-playing contest, I want to take a very particular strategy and side. The traditional stance toward games and play that passes from Plato through Kant and Schiller to Huizinga and Caillois apprehends them as activities that occur outside and in contrast to reason; they are undisciplined and represent an arbitrary, unmediated, exuberant, spontaneous, instinctual, chaotic, and unbounded outpouring of emotion. Play is a feature of the irrational side of life in which chance is opposed to necessity and is beyond the ken of analytical knowledge. In contrast to this tradition, I want to take my lead from the more subversive work of Saussure and Derrida. For a nonfoundationalist, this should come as no surprise. Rather than treat play as something that is to be set against or distinguished from reason or work, I want to defend an understanding of game playing that combines both free play and structure in a dynamic appreciation of the judicial performance in law's continuing game.

In particular, I want to argue that as far as the games of law and adjudication are concerned, it is always the case that play and reason, rules and discretion, and freedom and constraint go hand in hand; these are not so much polar opposites or dichotomies as interdependent parts or forces that both energize and destabilize the adjudicative challenge. In this deconstructive approach, play is treated less as irrational than as part of what it means to be rational: there is no Reason for settling arguments about reason that are not themselves part of the game of reasoning. This nonfoundationalist perspective is not so much a matter of either/or as one of both/and. While this broadly deconstructive approach to life, games, and law holds considerable promise, it must be emphasized that in depicting law as being constituted by the tension between structure and play, the ambition is not to privilege play at the expense of structure. Those who simply want to invert the relation and privilege play over structure remain trapped within the very system they claim to subvert and reject: a studied "anything goes" that pits Dionysian free play against Apollonian ruledness is simply the flip side and, therefore, the continuation of the traditionalist stance.[20] Instead, emphatically rejecting an antifoundationalist stance, I want to show how a more plausible and provocative nonfoundationalist account of the idea and practice of adjudication incorporates structure and play as both the condition for and contradiction of the other.

Although it has come to be used as a general catchall for any unconventional criticism of law and legal theory, deconstruction is a very specialized and subversive form of philosophical critique. It is not so much a philosophy as a theoretical strategy for disrupting traditional philosophy, especially its insistence upon the existence of a stable and universal foundation for Truth and Reason. A deconstructive critique does not, as is sometimes suggested, make the ridiculous claim that knowledge and meaning are unobtainable or nonexistent: it problematizes them to such an extent that their traditional status and stability are severely compromised. Deconstruction is not about the destruction of meaning or the random imposition of arbitrary meaning but rather the effort to de-construct meaning by showing how meaning is constructed through the oppositional forces of signification in the text itself. If anything is destructed, it is the foundationalist claim to have settled on a certain and fixed meaning. Meaning is found in the ungrounded and multiple "play of differences" between the opposites.[21] It foils any orderly attempt to progress to a final knowledge or recover a fixed meaning by denying that there can ever be philosophical closure to the vertiginous attempts at historical appropriation. Nonetheless, deconstructive critique is not random or wanton in its approach or ambition. It takes the object of its critique and, working to collapse it from within, de-constructs the constructs of philosophy to better reveal their constructedness; all understanding is interpretive and, therefore, corrigible, contingent, and partial—there is no neutral or disinterested apprehension of objective authority.

To understand and control the world, traditional thinking employs a set of enabling distinctions that are treated as natural and obvious, such as objective/subjective, reason/emotion, or mind/body. This means that any coherent and cogent account of fixed meaning and grounded knowledge must not only explain the precise and stable relation between these oppositions but also find a way of talking about them that is itself precise and stable. It claims to do this by privileging one over the other and granting epistemological authority to it. In contrast, deconstructive critique goes behind these hierarchical dichotomies and shows that they have a history and are far from natural or obvious. Operating from inside the traditional paradigm, the deconstructive task is to unravel and lay bare the contradictory, inescapable, and warring forces that both constitute and confound the commonsense meaning of words and texts. Moreover, these duplicitous dualities of consciousness cannot be sustained. The unprivileged "other" disrupts and undermines its privileged partner. While it is a necessary contrast to it, it is also a contradiction of it. So interrelated are they that the one not only makes the other possible but contributes to its negation: each side of the dichotomy is the "dangerous supplement" of the other, which is both a "terrifying menace and surest protection against that very menace."[22] The drawing of lines is both a necessity and an impossibility—necessary as a historical and existential act but impossible as an ahistorical and universal project; each is dependent on the other as it claims to negate it. In short, what is excluded is implicated in and dependent on what is included: philosophy depends on the very history that it is at pains to deny. However, the deconstructive technique is not intended simply to reverse the hierarchical order by placing, for instance, subjective over objective or emotion over reason in terms of epistemological authority. It is to be understood as rejecting entirely the dichotomous and passive mode of thinking about the world in favor of a more engaged and active way of truth making.

In a seminal essay, Derrida places the notion of play at the heart of the deconstructive critique and the subversive claim that "language bears within itself the necessity of its own critique."[23] He explains how the Western philosophical tradition has driven itself to metaphysical distraction by its insistence on compressing its thinking about the world into the straitjacket of dichotomous opposites—chance and necessity, reason and desire, mind and body, and so on. In particular, he concentrates on the ill-fated effort in discursive studies to ground the distinction between structure and free play in "a fundamental immobility and reassuring certitude . . . beyond the reach of freeplay." However, in rejecting the possibility of a structured foundation that is privileged over and controls play, Derrida is not suggesting that there is somehow a free play that happens outside of structure and that itself controls structure. Derrida insists that in matters of human discourse, there is no question of choosing between, on the one hand, a foundationalist interpretation—the "dreams of deciphering a truth or an origin which is free from freeplay"—and, on the other hand, an antifoundationalist interpretation—the affirmation of a free play that tries to pass beyond the dream "of full presence, the reassuring foundation, the origin and the end of the game." Instead, what must be done is "to conceive of the common ground and the *différance* of this irreducible difference." In other words, the apparent full presence of totalizing structure is only made viable and given force by the threatening absence of a disruptive free play, in the same way that the apparent full presence of free play is only rendered threatening by the pervasive absence of a stultifying structure. As Derrida states:

> If totalization no longer has any meaning, it is not because the infinity of a field cannot be covered by a finite glance or a finite discourse, but because the nature of the field—that is, language and a finite language—excludes totalization. This field is in fact that of a game, that is to say, a field of infinite substitutions in the closure of a finite ensemble. This field permits these infinite substitutions only because it is finite, that is to say, because instead of being an inexhaustible field . . . , instead of being too large, there is something missing from it: a centre which arrests and founds the freeplay of substitutions.[24]

In terms of jurisprudence, this deconstructive stance can be put to great and unsettling effect in the nonfoundationalist project. In the adjudicative performance, the structure of rules and the play of discretion interact and feed off each other in the game of legal interpretation: play is the element of the game that disrupts and destabilizes the structured rules that constitute the game. There is always a tension between order and disorder, freedom and constraint, and determinacy and indeterminacy that cannot be resolved by a totalizing account or performance. For example, it is not possible to think of or understand determinacy without indeterminacy: each plays off the other in the relentless encounter that both makes meaning possible and prevents its ultimate grounding. In this way, determinacy and indeterminacy in legal interpretation can be understood as locked in a relentless historical struggle for dominance that allows only temporary respites but no final resolution or ultimate balance. Determinacy is only realizable against an informing background of indeterminacy, and it is the possibility of determinacy that gives the threat of indeterminacy any bite. Accordingly, legal meaning is a simultaneous mix of the determinate and indeterminate. In Hartian terms, this translates into the acknowledgment that rules will be experienced as having a core of accepted meaning and a penumbra of uncertainty, but the identity of each will shift and change; what was once thought to be at the core will become penumbral and vice versa. The relation between core and penumbra cannot be described once and for all: it is a sociohistorical artifact and cannot be reduced to a simple formula or overarching narrative.[25] Whether particular interpretations of a rule are or are not compatible is not the point. It is the fact that the question of their compatibility is always open and contestable.

Both foundationalists and antifoundationalists overlook the crucial insight that meaning is found in the social interaction of freedom and constraint, not in the privileging of one over the other. Whereas foundationalists emphasize the stability and predominance of structured determinacy over the marginalized threat of a disruptive indeterminacy, antifoundationalists stress the unbounded play of an anarchic indeterminacy over the stabilizing force of an orderly determinacy. Both are mistaken. In contrast to foundationalist claims, law's game of adjudication has no greater (or lesser) legitimacy than that which its participants earn for themselves in their performance and play. As practiced by its mainstream operatives, legal theory exists as a kind of a grand narrative or metadiscourse that is produced by the discourse of law to validate its own status as a scientific discourse in the sense that it possesses an objectivity and foundation that lies outside itself and whose evaluative standards are adequacy, accuracy, and Truth itself. In short, jurisprudence exists to legitimate the rules of its own game. However, there is no metalanguage or one way of playing the game that is intrinsically or extrinsically capable of grounding and validating the conclusions reached or the justifications used.[26] Legitimacy and, therefore, justice is not achieved by judicial conformity to a set way of proceeding but is something that can only arise from within the adjudicative game itself and be generated by the participants' own discursive practices and institutional interactions. The correctness of any particular move is established through persuasion and argument, not proof and demonstration; the difference between "good" and "bad" moves is game-specific and must be judged within the game, even as the rules are being reinterpreted. Legitimacy, therefore, is not something that precedes or grounds any judgment given but rather something that follows or flows from the rhetorical force of the judgment made.

Whereas foundationalist jurisprudence seeks closure and legitimacy by privileging the passing as the permanent, antifoundationalist efforts are too ready to dismiss the fact that the adjudicative performance can only be made sense of as an exercise in rule application rather than as an unbounded exercise in judicial free play. Nevertheless, this concession does not undermine the nonfoundationalist claim that the adjudicative performance is an entirely fluid and contingent game in which "anything might go." While law is a game that is defined by and through its enabling rules, it is a game in which everything is always a move in the game. As a judicial player, there is no way to make a move that can itself not become a move in the game. As an activity that is always beyond absolute determination and never fully finished, adjudication not only passively allows but also actively encourages transformative and disruptive acts, because, without them, the game risks paralysis and irrelevance: "The novelty of the unexpected 'move' . . . can supply the system with that increased performativity it forever demands and consumes."[27] In this way, the adjudicative game is played both within and with the rules that constitute it as a game; the limits of the game and the validity of acceptable moves within any particular performance of the game are not established once and for all but are provisional markers that are constantly being negotiated and renegotiated as the game plays on. What counts as a move within the game is a part of the game, not apart from it.

A Cricketing Life

Most North American lawyers and legal theorists will have been introduced to the game of cricket and the passions that it arouses through the nuisance case of *Miller* v. *Jackson*. In a quintessentially typical judgment, Lord Denning introduces the quiet village of Lintz, where "in summer time village cricket is the delight of everyone,"[28] and the raging dispute between its cricket lovers and those in favor of less intrusive weekend afternoons. As even the most uninitiated readers soon realize, there is much more at stake here than the lofting of occasional cricket balls into neighboring gardens. It is nothing less than a battle over the lost soul of English country life, a titanic struggle between the cultural forces of dark and light. On one side are the public-spirited custodians of cricketing tradition; on the other side are the upstart killjoys of private interest. Although, like most games, cricket is basically a banal and silly exercise—grown people in fancy dress trying to hit a piece of leather-bound cork while defending three sticks in the ground and surrounded by other people trying to stop or catch the ball—it is clearly no mere idle pastime. From the Lintz square to Lord's and on to the Sydney Hill and Sabena Park, the game of cricket is a social drama of enormous human proportions and social significance whose performance and outcomes affect the fate of countries and individual lives daily. To repeat the Duke of Dorset's wry comment, "What is human life but a game of cricket?"

The Millers lived on a new housing estate next to a cricket ground where cricket had been played for about seventy years. As a result of the Millers' complaints, the club erected a high fence to prevent balls invading their garden. This proved to be no real deterrent, and, according to the Millers, the situation became so intolerable that they felt obliged to vacate their home whenever a game was played. In desperation, they applied to the court for an injunction to restrain the playing of cricket. The club conceded that as long as cricket continued to be played, there was no foolproof way of stopping cricket balls going into the Millers' garden. However, in the language of the relevant legal doctrine, the club denied that its activities amounted to an unreasonable interference with the Millers' enjoyment of their property.

Moreover, it insisted that it had taken all reasonable measures to protect the Millers and their property from harm. Although the Millers were successful at first instance, the Court of Appeal upheld their claim for damages but refused to grant an injunction against the playing of cricket. Lord Denning M.R. concluded that there was no negligence and no nuisance. As the club had offered to pay eight hundred dollars for past and future damages, he ordered the payment to the Millers of that amount. At the other extreme, Geoffrey Lane L.J. held that there was both negligence and nuisance and that an injunction should be granted. As a consoling gesture to the club, he postponed its issuance for twelve months in order to allow for the location of a new ground. Finally, Cumming-Bruce L.J. occupied a middle position and determined that there was both negligence and nuisance. However, he refused to grant an injunction and awarded damages of eight hundred dollars. Accordingly, while the Millers won their action and recovered eight hundred dollars in damages, cricket was still played and balls continued to pepper their garden.

In reaching their decisions, the judges' reasoning was a tour de force of adjudicative playmaking; they placed a whole range of judicial maneuvers into play and put them through their doctrinal paces. The simple fact that the judges' reasoning and conclusions were so evidently at odds with one another confirms little. However, their judgments do offer a rich set of textual materials with which to work. While some might want to criticize a particular judgment on the basis that it is unsound, unpersuasive, ill crafted, or impolitic, it is difficult to contend with any confidence that any of the three judgments does not amount to legal reasoning or cannot be justified in terms of the existing doctrinal materials. Accordingly, legitimacy or validity does not seem to be the issue; the more pressing question is one of rhetoric and cogency. Yet because each judgment can claim to be a plausible performance of the judicial craft, the foundationalist assertion that law is a constrained mode of decision making rings somewhat hollow: each judge stayed within the rules but put them to very different effect. Moreover, the antifoundationalist claim that the judges failed to take seriously the doctrinal rules that were in play and simply used them as ex post legal rationalizations of their ex ante political preferences is difficult to sustain: all of the judges grappled with the rules as they sought to bend them to their own purposes.[29]

The three judgments in *Miller* offer a fitting and fascinating occasion to showcase adjudication as a special kind of language game. In particular, Denning's judgment is an opportunity par excellence to illustrate and confirm the force of a nonfoundationalist deconstructive critique. Mindful that the nonfoundationalist challenge is neither to prescribe the correct way to engage in legal reasoning nor to unravel legal texts into a meaningless nothing, a deconstructive critique seeks to lay bare contradiction's insidious existence at the heart of doctrinal being. It illuminates the process by which a text's warring factions both allow meaning to occur and, at the same time, defer its ultimate grounding in anything but its own provisional and persuasive force. In many ways, Denning's judgment is a textbook example of the flipability of supposedly opposite categorizations and the arbitrary prioritization of one term over the other; the deconstructive task is to describe the way in which this game plays itself out and to note the interests that are likely served in its particular performance. Denning's efforts to negotiate the public/private distinction set the stage perfectly for such a description:

> It is our task to balance the right of the cricket club to continue playing cricket . . . as against the right of the householder not to be interfered with. . . . There is a contest here between the interest of the public at large and the interest of a private individual. The *public* interest lies in protecting the environment by preserving our playing fields in the face of mounting development, and by enabling our youth to enjoy all the benefits of outdoor games, such as cricket and football. The *private* interest lies in securing the privacy of his home and garden without intrusion or interference by anyone. . . . As between their conflicting interests, I am of the opinion that the public interest should prevail over the private interest.[30]

It takes little imagination to realize that Denning's formulation and resolution of the public and private interests that are at stake can be reworked in a very different way. In the same way that the playing of cricket can be as "private" a matter as sitting out in the sun, the security of people's homes can be as "public" a matter as the preservation of playing fields. Although the flipability of Denning's characterization is plain and simple in *Miller*, it is possible to make such a destabilizing switch in all situations. What counts as public or private does not regulate or constrain the practice of legal reasoning but rather forms part of the play within law's language game. In short, the raw materials of life do not present themselves to policymakers as always and already divided into natural categories of social interest. The world is not given but is constantly being made and remade; seeds of fact reap a rich harvest of values because they are always already cultivated in ideological soil. Denning's depiction of the contestants is a prescriptive act of creation rather than a descriptive report of detachment.

Having established the competing interests and assigned the litigants to their respective sides of the balancing scales, Denning proceeds to place his thumb on the side of public interest. In such contests, he seems to assume that it is axiomatic that "the public interest should prevail over the private interest." The whole judgment is given over to establishing a rhetorical climate in which the prevalence of the public interest seems obvious and natural. Yet Denning offers no argument as to why this conclusion should be treated as self-evident. Indeed, he begs the very question that his analysis is supposedly directed toward answering: when and why does the public interest prevail over private interest? When it comes to the decisional crunch, the Master of the Rolls hides behind declaratory platitudes, like "on taking the balance, I would . . ." and "as between their conflicting interests, I am of the opinion that . . ."[31] He elides any further explanation or support for his conclusion because there are none that can offer the kind of final or grounded justification that foundationalists crave; persuasion, not demonstration, is the name of the game. Denning's judgment draws what appeal and cogency it has from the only source that is available—not from the logical force of its doctrinal analysis but from his rhetorical efforts to tap the political sensibilities and sympathies of his intended audience.

The style and phrasing of Denning's offering is structured by the contradictory impulses of "progress" and "tradition." Although his judgment is voiced predominantly in the accent of a progressive preference for calculations of public interest in matters of competing land use, there is a more subtle idiom of traditional rhetoric that runs alongside and is often intertwined with the more dominant tone. At the same time that he refuses "to approach this case with the eyes of the judges of the nineteenth century" and insists that "it should be approached on principles applicable to modern conditions," he is adamant that temporal priority is deserving of legal precedence. He frequently and pejoratively contrasts the cricket club's long-standing contribution to the community with the Millers' status as "newcomers." In this consummate exercise in judicial craft, Denning manages to couch a defense of vested property rights in the language of social progress. For all his rhetorical support for progress and public interest, the driving force of the decision is the conservative desire to preserve the status quo: "I would agree [with Lord Reid's dictum that 'if cricket cannot be played on a ground without creating a substantial risk, then it should not be played there at all'] if the houses or road was there first and the cricket ground came there second."[32] Of course, to reach the same result, Denning could have run a more straightforward traditional defense of vested interests, but this would have robbed the decision of much of its success as a rhetorical exemplar.

Although Cumming-Bruce and Geoffrey Lane take a tack that is different from Denning's, their judgments are marked by the same general tension that arises from their efforts to negotiate the push-and-pull of contradictory impulses, even though the particular pairings in play are different. The specific dilemma that they perceive and from which they seek to escape is that between precedent and equity or, in grander terms, between positive law and natural law: it is a manifestation of the self-sustaining supplementarity between the desire for stability and certainty and the simultaneous urge for flexibility and maneuverability. Both Cumming-Bruce and Geoffrey Lane struggle to locate a neutral and workable equilibrium that will both provide a reassuring general grounding for the relevant legal doctrine and, at the same time, permit a degree of free play in the application of that structure to the particular situation: "The rules transcend the case as immediately experienced, the insight is immanent in it."[33] At the heart of this dilemma is the acceptance that justice demands, as an institutional and substantive matter, both the general embrace of rule-driven adjudication and the occasional departure from it. The challenge for judges is to decide in which particular circumstances the general rules are to be observed and in which they are to be overlooked. The traditional response by which to contain and mediate this contradiction has been the regular but unconvincing invocation of a kind of "rule-recognized discretion." The resort to this device is tantamount to a resignation by mainstream judges and juries of the traditional foundationalist project. However, while a "rule-recognized discretion" is almost oxymoronic in the foundationalist (and antifoundationalist) vocabulary, it captures neatly the both/and of Derrida's deconstructive *différance*; it underlines the nonfoundationalist insight that structure and play or rule and discretion are not so much negating opposites as mutually reinforcing relations.

Both Cumming-Bruce and Geoffrey Lane's personal sympathies clearly lay with the cricket club. As indicated by the not-so-subtle rhetoric of gender difference, whereas they found the male officials of the cricket club to be "candid and forthright" in their actions, they were less impressed with Mrs. Miller, whose behavior they thought verged on the "neurotic" and "obsessive." However, they both also agreed that a straightforward application of the existing doctrinal rules seemed to mandate a result in the Millers' favor. This meant that, at least in their own minds, Cumming-Bruce and Geoffrey Lane had to confront and resolve the classic contest between the pull of precedent and the lure of justice. For Geoffrey Lane's part, he opted to follow the rules laid down. But in doing this, he does not act against justice but in the name of justice. He collapses the distinction between law and equity by assuming that justice requires strict obedience to the results of rule application:

> Precedent apart, justice would seem to demand that the plaintiffs should be left to make the most of the site they have elected to occupy with all its obvious advantages and equally obvious disadvantages. . . . If

> the matter were *res integra*, I confess I should be inclined to find for the defendants. . . . Unfortunately, however, the question is not open. . . . It may be that [the rule in *Sturges* v. *Bridgman*] works injustice, it may be that one would decide the matter differently in the absence of authority. But we are bound by [that] decision . . . and it is not for this court as I see it to alter a rule which has stood for so long.[34]

Whereas Geoffrey Lane arbitrarily, conveniently, and effectively conflates law and equity, Cumming-Bruce manages to separate them in (and this is most important) an equally convenient and effective way. He seeks to demonstrate that discretion can be used to temper the rule without swallowing the rule; it is a matter of equity being ordered by the law and discretion being required by the rules. While justice requires that rules are followed, Cumming-Bruce insists that the rules themselves sanction the resort to discretion. In taking this line, he appears to be making an implicit attempt to instruct Geoffrey Lane in the possibilities of legal doctrine and judicial craft; it is, among other things, a good example of the way in which judges speak to other judges as much as to the litigants or public in crafting their judgments as exercises in rhetorical persuasion. Agreeing with Geoffrey Lane on "his reasoning and conclusion upon the liability of the defendants," Cumming-Bruce relies upon the distinction between liability and remedy to finesse the judicial dilemma of doctrinal contradiction:

> There is authority that, in considering whether to exercise a judicial discretion to grant an injunction, the court is under a duty to consider the interests of the public. . . . So on the facts of this case a court of equity must seek to strike a fair balance between the right of the plaintiffs to have quiet enjoyment of their house . . . and the opportunity of the inhabitants of the village . . . to enjoy . . . a summer recreation. . . . It is a relevant circumstance which a court of equity should take into account that the plaintiffs decided to buy a house which . . . was obviously on the boundary of a quite small cricket ground. . . . There are here special circumstances which should inhibit a court of equity from granting the injunction claimed.[35]

This deconstructive reading of *Miller* has hopefully shown that adjudication is very much a special language game in which the rules of legal doctrine are very much in play as both the contents and constraints of the game being played; it is not that the rules dominate, as foundationalists would have it understood, nor that rules are mere playthings, as antifoundationalists would suggest, but that they are the object of play as they frame that play. At the adjudicative sites of contestation, intelligible and legitimate legal judgment is not the product of a slavish adherence to the rules of the game or "the deliverance of a Reason so immanent that its own name is the only explanatory word it can utter."[36] Instead, it is very much a situated act of rhetorical argument that constructs the provisional grounds of its reasonableness and legitimacy as it proceeds. With varying degrees of sophistication, the three judges in *Miller* engage in a stylized exercise that, although intended to persuade people (and themselves) that law is insulated from the open-ended encounters of overt political confrontation, actually reveals the extent to which law and adjudication are inextricably implicated in such issues. In reading cases and judges, an important task of the deconstructive critic, as well as unraveling the contradictory threads that are weaved into a hermeneutical garment of meaning, is to counteract traditional attempts to depoliticize and dehistoricize the judicial game of doctrinal development. By re-surfacing the politics and history presently submerged in the legal enterprise, it becomes possible to grasp that the determination of legal meaning is not only contingent and conditional but also involves an inevitable taking of sides. Law and adjudication are crucial sites in which the infinite game to establish and reestablish the terms and arrangements of social life is played out.

The Reasoning Game

There are two aspects to deconstructive play—indeterminacy and decision. Like games, law's language game is a vast practice of almost infinitely possible moves in which each player must come to a decision as to which move to make. The moment and nature of the decision made cannot be grounded in anything outside itself; there is no possibility of an acontextual metric for closure. As Derrida puts it: "The moment of decision, as such, must be the consequence or effect of this theoretical or historical moment, of this reflection or this deliberation, since it always marks the interruption of the juridico- or ethico- or politico-cognitive deliberation that precedes it, that must precede it."[37] In simple jurisprudential terms, the decision is never entirely explainable by or reducible to the rule(s) of which it claims to be an application. A particular performance or move cannot be detached from the general game itself—each can only be fully appreciated in the context of the other. It is the subject or player that both occupies and fills the gap between the game's indeterminate possibilities and the determinate decision made. As such, judges do not stand astride the game but are altered and shaped by the game's limits as they play to reconstruct those limits; they are influenced by the present contours of the game as they influence the game's continuing performance and possibilities. In foundationalist terms, there is no final or enduring span between the game's general indeterminacy and particular decisions that is not destabilized by the constituted and constituting identity of the different players: indeterminacy "is not simply a moment to be overcome by the occurrence of the decision, . . . [but] continues the decision and the latter does not close itself off from the former."[38] Politics is always present and irrepressible because general indeterminacy both gives rise to and continues to permeate the particular decision made.

By understanding the move from general indeterminacy in this way, it should be clear why my approach is nonfoundational as opposed to antifoundational. It resists the conclusion that any decision is valid simply because it is a decision; the idea that there is complete freedom to decide makes no sense at all, because it is only within a structure of constraints, albeit thoroughly contingent and revisable in content and direction, that decision making can be comprehended as decision making. Without some formative structure or informing context, there would be no game as a process of human engagement and reflection but only a random collision of thought-less movements. Indeed, the very notion of choice implies a constrained context that identifies what is and is not being chosen between. At the very least, a decision has to possess an important element of cognition, even if the ultimate decision is to make an arbitrary choice. Moreover, the choice is not, as antifoundationalists suppose it to be, between an ultimate rational grounding or a free-floating irrational grunt: this is only to reinstall the idea of universal Reason and another false dichotomy between reason and nonreason. There are grounds of and for decisions, but they are contingent and unstable: reasons can be given as to why one decision is better than another, but these arguments are never themselves guaranteed or vouchsafed outside the context of argument. Consequently, legal reasoning is about the moves that are presently in play and that structure law's reasoning game in such a way as to enable choices between competing definitions of particular rules in light of their general indeterminacy. However, while providing an argumentative context for reasoning and definition, these moves are themselves being contingently reworked. As such, the rules of the reasoning game do not so much constrain or cabin judges' room for maneuver as make it possible and operational.

Accordingly, in understanding adjudication as a game of playful activity, it is important to recognize that there are two sets or structures of rules in play.[39] There are those rules that are the object and substance of the game. These are comparable to the equipment in cricket or the pieces in chess; they are what you play the game with. In law, their equivalent are the constitutional, common law, and statutory rules that comprise the body of the legal system's substantive norms. However, there is also a second set of rules. As far as jurisprudence is concerned, these are the rules of the adjudicative game—they comprise those often implicit and occasionally explicit rules that stipulate how the game of "playing with the rules" is to be played. These rules are interpretive in nature and provide judges with the basic maneuvers that they are allowed to make in deploying and applying the substantive legal rules; they include directions about precedential analysis and policy arguments. Of course, these interpretive rules are themselves open to constant reinterpretation and revision; they are never fixed or static in number or meaning. Indeed, the acceptance and weight given to these "adjudicative rules" vary from jurisdiction to jurisdiction and from time to time. As such, legal reasoning comprises a repertoire of arguments that combine to sustain a culture of legal reasoning.[40]

Legal reasoning, therefore, is primarily a practical activity, not an abstract and arcane meditation on legal intelligence. Like most practical skills, it is acquired by the experience of doing it and handed down from practitioner to practitioner: it is about "knowing the ropes." Legal reasoning is not a series of formulaic applications in an abstract space but a functional engagement in real time; it is not a philosophical reflection but a practical activity; it is not a logical operation but an exercise in operational logic. However, although it is primarily an activity, it does not mean that it does not have a basic structure, nor that there are no basic guidelines to follow. Although they refer to constitutional cases, Brian Slattery's comments are equally applicable to legal reasoning generally:

> Deciding constitutional cases is a practical art, just like playing baseball, raising children, writing short stories, cooking a good meal, diagnosing an illness or governing your country. Good constitutional decisions are made, not by logical deductions from explicit constitutional standards, but by tapping one's tacit knowledge of the practical workings of the constitutional system and its implicit values and principles, which the explicit standards only partially and palely reflect. To attempt to use these standards as the sole basis of decision will be like trying to learn driving from the provisions of the *Highway Traffic Act*. . . . The indeterminacy of general constitutional standards is a reflection of the fact that constitutional decision-making is a highly concrete and contextual art that requires experience and skill and more than a little wisdom.[41]

Legal reasoning, therefore, refers as much to an attitude or style of argument as to the techniques of argument themselves. As a particular form of rhetoric, it ought not to be thought of, like links in a chain or chapters in a novel, as part of a linear and one-dimensional process that proceeds in any simple or direct way from argument to decision. Instead, as the philosopher John Wisdom observes, the work of reasoning more resembles the legs of a chair in which reasoning is related to the ultimate decision as a pragmatic support rather than a causal sine qua non that connects premise to conclusion.[42] A good legal argument or exercise in reasoning has no essential hallmark that fixes it as "good" outside of the particular context in which it is made or received. This explains why a good legal decision one day might be considered unconvincing at a later time. This fact, of course, means that the "soundness" of any particular episode of legal reasoning is to be adjudged in terms of its capacity to persuade other judges and lawyers in a particular community at a particular time rather than its analytical approximation to some logical ideal of argument; the fact that *Brown* is treated as a better legal decision than *Plessy* is about its political value and acceptability, not its inherent argumentative force and cogency. As in game playing, so in legal reasoning—form follows function. In the same way that the style of the maneuver does not guarantee the success of the move, the formal validity of the legal argument does not guarantee the substantive correctness of the decision.

Viewed in this way, law is confirmed as a rhetorical activity; the different techniques of legal reasoning are to be treated less as "rules" than as moves in a game in which its defining rules are always in play. In this vibrant and ever-changing game, there are a limited number of formal moves that can be made. However, as with all games, these moves can be put into practice in a bewildering combination and to unexpected effect; the specifics of the particular context, the techniques, the vision, and the timing of the judicial players will be crucial in determining the right move to make and its subsequent success. For every argument that can be made, there is a counterargument or counterthrust: they are not so much solutions to problems as probes into formulating a solution. Legal reasoning is about justification, not demonstration—a winning move is one where the cumulative effect of several different and often inconclusive strategies is enough, relative to a particular context and any other countermoves made, to convince someone to prefer one result or line of justification to another. In this way, law and legal reasoning, rather than being treated as tools or data banks, comprise performative activities in the game of adjudicative interpretation. Within such a nonfoundational account of the reasoning game in law, it should be clear that everything is a matter of strategy and risk. As Derrida puts it:

> It is a question of strategy because no transcendent truth outside the sphere of writing can theologically command the totality of this field. It is hazardous because this strategy is not simple in the sense that we say

> that strategy orients the tactics according to final aim, a telos or the theme of a domination, a mastery or an ultimate appropriation of movement and field. In the end, it is strategy without finality. We might call it blind tactics.[43]

Nevertheless, despite the apocalyptic predictions and dire warnings of traditional scholars, there is nothing about this approach that will *necessarily* change how judges actually apply rules. A different appreciation of what it is to apply a rule has no necessary impact on the practice of rule application: theory does not alter practice in and of itself. Judges and lawyers will still go on interpreting particular rules in particular ways—whether a person on roller blades is a "vehicle" in terms of the rule that there are to be "no vehicles in the park" will still depend on a commitment to the presumed or postulated purpose(s) that the judge decides that the rule is intended to advance. But what *might* change is the cogency and bindingness of particular applications in particular circumstances in light of the altered reflective appreciation of what it means to apply a rule: "Once we admit the rules are mutable and inextricable from material social practice, we will at least experience a psychological change in the way we perceive our roles as legal actors."[44] There will still be general agreement on what particular rules mean, and individual judges will still experience exactly the same degree of (in)determinacy, but the vital justification for that result will be subverted and the question of authority will be challenged. Judges will no longer be able to claim that "the rule made me do it," but instead will have to take greater responsibility for judicial decisions and their social consequences. If judges believe that they should follow rules for the simple reason that they are rules, they will be lost when the rules are ambiguous or run out. The life of the law will not be logic but rather the experience of what it is to recognize a logic that is being reconstructed at the same time as it is being followed.

In pursuing a deconstructive critique, therefore, it must not be forgotten that it does not offer itself as an alternative game but as a different way of understanding and playing the existing games of law and adjudication: it is not a method and much less a manifesto for establishing and adding a new game to the jurisprudential compendium. Moreover, it is a strategic intervention that is not offered as the best or only way to play the legal game in the service of some remote philosophical method or political ideal. On the contrary, it is merely intended to underline the extent to which adjudication is not a retreat or relief from the struggle over meaning and value in people's collective and individual lives; it is simply another institutional venue where the competing forces that comprise that struggle can be addressed and accommodated in tentative, temporary, and revisable ways. However, a deconstructive mode of legal critique does insist that while the play of the judicial game is not reducible to a simple or totalizing political logic, any particular performance involves a historical taking of political sides and is "open to interested appropriation."[45] It is the task of nonfoundational criticism to note the meaning actually ascribed to texts, to identify the historical determinants of the meaning-giving exercise, to draw out the social practices that the judicial performance reflects and re-works, and to uncover the relations of power that produce and benefit from this legal knowledge. In short, although its connection will always be itself revisable and provisional, the judicial game must be placed within its historical context so as to re-establish its affiliations with institutions, classes, professionals, and the like.

Conclusion

In this chapter, therefore, I have sought to show that it is time to abandon Chief Justice Coke's claim that there is an "artificial Reason and Judgment of Law which requires long Study and Experience before a Man can attain to the Cognizance of it." This is a self-serving myth of lawyers, judges, and jurists that cannot be sustained as a descriptive truth or a prescriptive claim. While it is true that proficiency in legal reasoning, as with all other kinds of reasoning, is something that is attained through "long study and experience," legal reasoning is not something that stands outside that practice, that disciplines that practice, or that has an independent existence from it. There is nothing more (or less) to legal reasoning than the practice of doing it. Again, like other kinds of reasoning, it is only "artificial" in that it is not given but is produced by the craft of its practitioners; it is elaborated, constituted, and changed through its contingent performance. Accordingly, the point of my inquiry has not been to pin down some essential truths about legal argument but to understand better the playful practice of adjudication as its own political practice and not as a reflection or embodiment of something else. I maintain that this can be done by treating law's language as a deconstructive game of philosophical improvisation that captures "change, movement, action, continuance, unlimited and unending possibility."[46]

The beauty of a nonfoundationalist approach is that it can both recognize the way in which the game of adjudication is presently constituted by these particular maneuvers and, at the same time, accept that the game of adjudication might come to be constituted by a transformed or entirely different set of maneuvers. The central claim, therefore, is not that law and adjudication are reducible to this or any other set of game-defining rules but that some set of game-defining rules are in play that, however contingently and temporarily, ensure that the judicial player is both bound and free at one and the same time. As Duncan Kennedy concludes, "There are no killer arguments outside a particular context."[47] And by that I take him to be saying at least two important things—not only that there is no argument that brings debate and disagreement to an end by sheer force of its own universal force but that there are no arguments whatsoever that do not owe their existence and force to a particular context. What it means to get something "right" is nothing more (and nothing less) than that an argument manages to persuade certain people for certain purposes at a certain time and place. In law, as in so much else, *play* is the thing.

7 Playing by the Rules: A Good Faith Approach

......

> And now what shall become of us without any barbarians?
>
> Those people were a kind of solution.
>
> —Constantine Cavafy, "Expecting the Barbarians"

In defending and elaborating a nonfoundationalist account of law and adjudication, my primary concern up to this point has been to criticize foundationalist theories. This has been for the good reason that foundationalist accounts tend to dominate contemporary jurisprudential literature. However, in touting the advantages of a nonfoundationalist account over a foundationalist approach, I have tried to distinguish my ideas and observations from an antifoundationalist understanding of law and adjudication. This so-called nihilist strand in critical theorizing presents itself as being tied to the understanding that "anything goes" at any time when it comes to adjudication in law. Judges are unconstrained in their freedom to do whatever their ideological commitments prompt or require: adjudication is a series of arbitrary encounters in which justice will "be left to the unguided, even if experienced, sage sitting under the spreading oak tree."[1] Offering this view as a critical assault upon the actual practice of law and adjudication, its protagonists insist that "law is politics" in all its stylistic and substantive manifestations. Although this line of critique has much to recommend it as an uncompromising challenge to the complacent claims of much foundationalist literature, its critical zeal has got the better of its intellectual rigor. Consequently, mindful of the old adage that the enemy of one's enemy is not necessarily one's friend, I have sought in this chapter to distinguish further my own nonfoundationalist claims from those of the antifoundationalists so that there is no confusion about their important differences.

Rather than reject the critical claim that "law is politics," a nonfoundationalist account works to elaborate and defend this claim to more compelling effect. Taking a more nuanced and sophisticated approach than the antifoundationalists, I want to argue that a loss of faith in foundationalist metanarratives does not commit jurists to an antifoundationalist position in which law is reduced to raw power and adjudication is viewed as nothing more than a faux exercise in ideological rationalization. Not only is this gloomy depiction merely the flip side of a foundationalist faith, but it also undercuts the political force of any critique of the foundationalist project. From a nonfoundationalist perspective, there remains the insistence that there are legitimate and illegitimate ways to act, but there is also an acknowledgment that "legitimation can only spring from [judges'] own linguistic practice and communicational interaction."[2] A nonfoundationalist account of adjudication is able to take seriously the foundationalist claim that adjudication is a sincere effort to engage with legal materials and, at the same time, hold on to the antifoundationalist claim that law is an exercise in political choice. By understanding adjudication as a playful performance in law's language game, it is possible to grasp that judges are both constrained and free in reaching decisions. Indeed, I contend that freedom and constraint are not simply competing pulls on the judicial mind but comprise the joint and mutual conditions for any act of interpretive decision making; meaning is found in the social interaction of freedom and constraint, not in the privileging of one over the other.

In this chapter, therefore, I intend to explain more clearly the different and important ways in which a nonfoundationalist account of law and adjudication must be distinguished from an antifoundationalist critique. I begin by taking stock of the main features of a nonfoundational critique when juxtaposed to an antifoundationalist account. In order to join issue with the antifoundationalist critics, I will concentrate on the neglected issue of what it means for a judge to act in good faith and revisit the related problem of whether and what kind of bias is sufficient to render the adjudicative performance illegitimate. As a way to give some practical substance to these abstract claims, I offer a critical exegesis of a recent and controversial South African case in which the Constitutional Court's judgments engaged as much over the appropriate way to go about judging as they did about the appropriate result to be reached in the problem at hand. Finally, I use the last section as a convenient occasion to pull together some of the different nonfoundational themes that I have developed throughout the book. Throughout the chapter, I will emphasize that it is not that "anything goes" but that "anything might go"—everything is always a move in the game; there is no game without some set of rules; and the rules are always part of the game being played.

Resisting Nihilism

In a high-profile spat, Laurence Tribe took Bruce Ackerman to task for his casual and free-form approach to constitutional interpretation. Defending a more traditional and rigorous mode of constitutional analysis, Tribe insisted that there are certain conventions and constraints that a constitutional argument must observe and respect if it is to be taken seriously as a legal interpretation. While there are many ways to read the Constitution, what makes constitutional interpretation "truly a *legal* enterprise" is that it is "genuinely disciplined by widely shared canons of the interpretive arts and by stubborn truths of text, structure, and history." In short, Tribe makes the extreme and ultimately devastating criticism that, whatever merits some arguments have as moral or political claims, there are some arguments that simply do not count as legal arguments; it is not that the kind of "free-form" and "disturbingly loose" arguments in which Ackerman indulges are wrong but that they rest "on something other than genuine interpretation." Indeed, Tribe's most damning indictment of jurists like Ackerman is that they are not serious in the sense that, for them, legal interpretation becomes "merely a language for pressing one's preferences," for replacing established understandings "with their own legal conceits," and "is barely recognizable as an interpretive undertaking at all."[3]

In this chapter, I do not intend to defend or denounce Ackerman's approach. Nor do I want to focus on the validity or cogency of Tribe's preferred mode of constitutional interpretation. Instead, I concentrate on the more enduring and deeper aspect of their disagreement over "what is required if one is to engage in genuine conversation about what a legal text means." Indeed, the question of what does and does not count as genuine legal interpretation goes to the heart of contemporary jurisprudential debate. Unfortunately, as Tribe and Ackerman's exchange attests, that debate has become polarized. The dominant strain in jurisprudence is devoted to formulating a method that can isolate and stamp particular interpretations with the imprimatur of interpretive correctness and legal validity. Although the foundationalist project seems to exist in a permanent state of terminal crisis, it would appear that its mainstream practitioners remain united and sustained in their ambitions by the paralyzing fear that without a plausible theory and realizable practice of bounded rule application, law will become indistinguishable from open-ended political wrangling. However, no matter how heated the debate among foundationalists, the real fire is reserved for those critics who deny the worth or legitimacy of this formalist project. Whether their interpretive proposals are efficacious, consistent with democratic theory, or legitimate in some popular or moral sense, those scholars are almost denied the status of jurists on the basis that their hermeneutical approach "just doesn't cut much ice when the question before us is whether that practice is *constitutional*."[4] Notwithstanding the extreme claims by a handful of antifoundationalists, this threat of nihilistic hordes who are poised to ransack the juridical citadel of principled decision making is, like most specters, as much a figment of a fevered jurisprudential imagination as anything else. Indeed, it says more about the insecurities of the legal establishment than it does about the aspirations of most juristic critics: established jurists seem to require such a disruptive threat from outside the foundationalist gates to keep the faithful in check.

At their most uncompromising, foundationalists maintain that any jurisprudential account of law and adjudication that rejects their common project is decidedly nihilist in ambition and scope—all is mere pretense and decision making is an indulgent will to power. They routinely suggest that a nonfoundational approach to rules denies the existence of rules and, therefore, undercuts the possibility of anything that might be reasonably recognized as judging. The common allegation is that a nonfoundationalist critique takes the view that rules do not operate as prior constraints upon or sources for judgment but simply serve as convenient tools by which to legitimate after-the-fact decisions that were reached without any regard to the rules. Acting in an entirely cavalier and irresponsible way, judges treat law as if it were nothing more than a hotchpotch of the whimsical, capricious, and perverse that has accumulated over time. For example, in an otherwise sophisticated and restrained monograph, Wil Waluchow accuses critical legal scholars generally of adopting a jurisprudential perspective "according to which there are in actual fact no binding rules at all and judges simply decide cases on grounds of their own choosing. These grounds might be political, moral or personal. Judges only pretend to be following rules when what they are in fact doing is rationalizing their blatant, and often abusive and reactionary exercise of political power."[5] The suggestion seems to be that critics know and accept that it would be possible to follow the rules in some foundationalist sense, but they simply choose to ignore this course of action. Not even making the effort to work with the rules, they proceed to make decisions in spite of the rules. As such, the foundationalist charge is that such critics are not only intellectually mistaken but morally bankrupt.

This is the stuff of rank caricature. It suggests in no uncertain terms that those jurists who reject the foundationalist project are willfully blind and that they trade in deception and other immoral practices. Indeed, one commentator has gone so far as to contend that "in an honest effort to proclaim a need for revolution, nihilist teachers are more likely to train crooks than radicals."[6] Although certain critics of a foundationalist jurisprudence might have given unfortunate credibility to such assessments in their more polemical and outrageous moments, this dystopian vision of a nonfoundationalist account of the theory and practice of law and adjudication is neither warranted nor justified. While some judges and academics might well engage in the occasional cynical manipulation of rules and ought to be held to institutional account for such intellectual or political disingenuity, it is far from my nonfoundationalist claim that rules cannot or ought not to be taken seriously. In this sense, I agree with Tribe that belief in such an antifoundationalist approach is tantamount to declaring that "the text of the Constitution can be read to justify just about any decision—and so can safely be ignored."[7] As I have tried to make clear, what more often occurs in adjudication is the good faith attempt to interpret and apply a rule so as to produce a satisfactory result. Judges do follow and apply rules, but what is the relevant rule and what it means to follow or apply it are always up for grabs. Consequently, for nonfoundationalists, law remains primarily a system of rules, provided that its existence and operation are understood in an appropriately nonfoundationalist sense. This approach provides not only an intellectually compelling understanding of adjudication, but it places the moral responsibility of judges and jurists at its normative heart. Accordingly, it is extremely important to distinguish my nonfoundationalist account from the antifoundationalist critique and the nihilist claims that are made in its name.

One critic who does seem to adopt an unmitigated antifoundationalist line is David Kairys. In a crisp account of critical legal theory and practice, he begins well when he declares that "legal reasoning is not a method or process that leads reasonable, competent and fair-minded people to particular results in particular cases" and that "the ultimate basis for a decision is a social and political judgment." This kind of skepticism is exactly what a nonfoundationalist critique recommends and adopts (provided, of course, that "the ultimate basis . . . [of] social and political judgment" is itself understood in a suitably nonfoundationalist way). However, Kairys begins to go astray when he projects law as "a variety of rationalisations that a judge may freely chose from" and concludes that "the decision is not based on, or determined by, legal reasoning."[8] While it is no doubt accurate that some judges do use legal reasoning as only a rationalization for an existing prejudice, this characterization of the judicial performance fails to incorporate the fact that most judges do base their decisions on legal reasoning in that they make a good faith effort to interpret and deploy legal rules as the argumentative resources and occasions for their decision. Furthermore, this antifoundationalist stance seems to commit Kairys to the untenable proposition that all judges are engaged in a giant and unavoidable hoax when they claim that their decisions and judgments are based on and restrained by the rules of legal doctrine. It is not so much that judges ignore the rules as that they could not follow the rules even if they were minded to do so—the availability of rules as heuristic directives for decision making is simply denied by the antifoundationalist critic.

In rejecting Kairy's assertions, I do not deny or resist his observation that "the ultimate basis for a decision is a social and political judgment," but only that this claim is not incompatible with both judges' experienced sense of felt boundedness by the rules and the nonfoundationalist assertion that law is a matter of rule application rather than simply ex post rationalization. Indeed, from a nonfoundationalist perspective, it is important to draw a distinction between two kinds of justification—one that is a mode of *reasoning* and another that is a style of *rationalization*. Each of them is concerned with the result or decision, but they have different understandings about the role and significance of rules and reasoning in justifying that result or decision. Whereas reasoning involves a good faith attempt to work with and within the law's rules and argumentative resources, rationalization makes no such attempt. While the difference between the two is, as it should be from a nonfoundationalist perspective, far from clear-cut, its importance is critical and distinguishes a nonfoundational approach from an antifoundationalist one. Beginning the reasoning process with a more or less definite conclusion in mind is not the problem: most judges start with some more or less vague notion of where they think that their judgment should go or come out. The key issue is how they relate or connect that conclusion to the legal materials. While reasoning asks that they make some genuine effort to support that conclusion by reference to the rules, rationalization places no such burden on them. Whereas the nonfoundationalist judge or jurist takes the adjudicative task seriously, the antifoundationalist critic does not even bother. An antifoundationalist critique, therefore, is not so much a way of playing law's adjudicative game as it is a denial that there is any game worth playing or even the possibility of there being one. As such, rationalization is less a rhetorical mode of reasoning than a crude exercise of arbitrary power: those antifoundationalists who engage in it are no better than the illegitimate "judicial tyrants" whom they purport to condemn.

For judges who make a good faith attempt to engage with the available legal resources, a number of possibilities might arise. They might be persuaded that their initial conclusion was mistaken in the sense of being no longer the best substantive response to the matter at hand; the wisdom of earlier judgments might have an educative effect on them. Alternatively, they might not be able to find sufficient support from the legal resources that persuades them that there is a close enough fit between those materials and their desired outcome. If this occurs, judges "will, unless [they are] arbitrary or mad, reject the conclusion and . . . consider more acutely whether [their] tentative conclusion is wise, both with respect to the case before [them] and with respect to possible implications for future cases."[9] Further, they might be able to come out where they want with little effort or imagination; their engagement with legal rules and arguments might confirm and reinforce their initial conclusion as to the best solution. In each of these situations, it will not be the materials that recommend or resist a particular reading or use; the constraints on judges are as much in the limits of their technical skills and legal imagination as in the claimed bruteness of the legal facts. What counts as "a close enough fit between those materials and their desired outcome" is not amenable to final or fixed definition. It is for each judge to arrive at some decision in the particular context as to whether they have done enough to persuade themselves that such a justification is warranted. On a nonfoundationalist account, nothing more (or less) can be expected or demanded.

Foundationalist jurists are mistaken, therefore, when they assert that their critics "reject reason-giving altogether, putting in its place power, or play, or conventions."[10] The stark contrast between a reluctant attachment to a foundationalist account of law and adjudication, with its promise of coherent, determinate, and correct answers, and the capitulation to a faithless world in which arbitrary power and ideologues run amok is contrived. As I have tried to demonstrate, a nonfoundationalist critique does not deny the possibility of reason giving or shared understanding. While reason and power are inseparable, they are not identical or entirely collapsible into each other. In the same way that reason cannot detach itself completely from power and determine the terms of its own cogency, power does not consume all of reason and reduce politics to only arbitrary and random power plays. While a nonfoundationalist approach does undermine the practice of legal reasoning as a complete and grounded craft, it does not depict judging and decision making generally as only the quirky or idiosyncratic performance of the Nietzschean will to power: Zarathustra is not the nonfoundationalist judicial alter ego. As a Dionysiac monster, Zarathustra converts all interpretation and, therefore, knowledge and truth into nothing more than a stylized power play and, as such, privileges only one side of the deconstructive equation of structure and play.[11] In contrast, while a nonfoundationalist account refuses to understand adjudication as separate from politics, it does not subscribe to an "anything goes" ethic. In so doing, it maintains that meaning giving, rather than being simply subjective and narcissistic, is constrained in the same way that all individuals are constrained and constituted by the context of relations and conventions within which they find themselves. A nonfoundationalist critique is not beholden to an account of adjudication that comprehends it either as a foundationalist act of commitment to an abiding Reason or as an antifoundationalist surrender to a capricious irrationality: adjudication is based on reason insofar as it is constructed in and through the very judicial arguments that it is intended to guide.

Consequently, the nonfoundationalist claim that I am actually making is that judges do not stand outside the rules, but they inhabit the rules in a particular way. Judges (and jurists) are always situated within a context of freedom and restraint; they are neither never fully restrained nor ever entirely free. Judges give meaning to rules and their own lives in the constant struggle to negotiate the forces of freedom and constraint that constitute the rules and their own lives; they are freely restrained and restrainedly free. Indeed, freedom and constraint can only be made sense of reciprocally. The rule-engaged judge is neither context-dependent nor context-transcendent; the rules and the rule user are enmeshed in a mutually affecting relationship. While there will be occasions of Machiavellian manipulation, it is as mistaken to suggest that the judge has complete interpretive freedom as it is to claim that the law exerts complete interpretive control. In the same way that people (re)constitute themselves in their lived relations with others, so judges (re)constitute themselves in their participation in law's language game. While there is nothing fixed or determinate about this dynamic interaction, judges will continue to change as they engage in the play of difference that constitutes the adjudicative practice. Indeed, the claim to have moved beyond the play of power or to have got "outside" it is the "most insidious ruse of power."[12] Thus, a nonfoundational account of adjudication takes seriously both the restrictive pull of rules and the liberating push of interpretation. It is not possible to dispense with rules nor with the need to interpret them; each is what makes the other tick. Within a nonfoundationalist account, not only is there no set of rules that stands apart from interpretive attempts at its hermeneutical appropriation, but there is no literal interpretation—one that claims to be transparently representational rather than opaquely constitutive—against which other interpretations can be contrasted.

In order to distinguish between a nonformalist and antiformalist approach, further resort to a distinction by Hart is useful. In his critical account of the skeptics' claim that "the law is what the judges say it is," Hart makes a crucial distinction between two understandings of this assertion. In doing so, he draws directly on the game analogy. On one reading, the skeptical claim can be interpreted as meaning that law is literally nothing more than what the judges say it is and that there are no rules that bind or constrain the judges in the exercise of their authority. It is like a game of scorer's discretion in which "there was no rule for scoring save what the scorer in his discretion chose to apply." I agree with Hart's conclusion that while scorer's discretion might qualify as a game, this is an unconvincing explanation of adjudication in law because it ignores the fact that judges are at least required to make the effort to apply the extant rules of the legal system. As Hart puts it, there is "a distinction between a constitution which, after setting up a system of courts, provides that the law shall be whatever the supreme court thinks fit, and the actual . . . constitution of any modern State."[13] The antiformalist critique runs extremely close to positing adjudication as little more than a legal game of scorer's discretion in which judges can do whatever they wish and for whatever reason, no matter how capricious or perverse. The proponents of such a minimalist account are not only committed to the untenable view that "anything goes" but also to the view that legal doctrine is nothing more than a miscellany of previous exercises of that discretion, which have no bearing on or relevance to future adjudicative performances: all references to such rules are simply a ploy in a game of chance.

On another reading, the skeptical claim that "the law is what the judges say it is" is taken by Hart to mean that while judges have the final authority to determine law's scope and application, there are nevertheless rules that "are regarded by the courts as something which they are not free to disregard." As with most games, the scorer is both empowered and constrained by those rules that define the point and purpose of the game being played. This is the nonformalist way of understanding the skeptical claim. In contrast to the game of scorer's discretion or the antifoundational critique, it is not simply a matter of recording the judge's ruling with no opportunity for comment or criticism on the basis that what scorers or judges do is right and unchallengeably so. From a nonformalist perspective, there are standards by which the judicial performance can be assessed or criticized; law is a rhetorical performance that can be played in better or worse ways. However, unlike Hart, I do not insist that "we are able to distinguish a normal game from the game of scorer's discretion simply because the scoring rule . . . has a core of settled meaning . . . which the scorer is not free to depart from and which . . . constitutes the standard of correct and incorrect scoring."[14] As I have been at pains to establish, while judges are bound by the rules, the rules are always in play; the core of settled meaning is no less contingent than any other meaning and the standards for correct decision making are no more fixed than any other decision. Accordingly, the skeptical claim that "the law is what the judges say it is" is an accurate and compelling description, provided that it is understood in a thoroughly nonformalist way; adjudication is a rule-bound game about legal rules in which both sets of rules are always creatively in play.

As Hart stressed, any credible description of rule application must be able to account for the beliefs of participants as to what they are doing or think they are doing. While legal theorists need not share or endorse the beliefs of participants in the legal community, they must offer an explanation of that behavior as it is understood by its participants. Consequently, the fact that judges experience themselves applying and being morally bound by rules is a vital factor that cannot be ignored, even if it need not be endorsed or shared: "Description may still be description, even when what is described is an evaluation."[15] Nothing that I have said contravenes this injunction. My account of what it is to take rules seriously accepts completely that a rule's existence will be relevant to the question of what judges do and should do. However, the need to incorporate judges' feeling of bindingness leaves open the key issue of how to fix what it is that this bindingness applies to—namely, the rule's meaning. Notwithstanding Hart's emphasis on the beliefs of insiders, he posits a false tension between those who "accept and voluntarily co-operate in maintaining the rules" and those who "reject the rules and attend to them only . . . as a possible sign of punishment."[16] Insofar as this division is intended to undercut the nonfoundationalist claims about rules, it only bites if there is some largely objective, determinate, and uncontroversial way to ascertain the meaning of rules. Because there is no such method, it is a toothless distinction. Accordingly, the judge both "accepts" rather than "rejects" the rules and, at the same time, "maintains" them as only "a possible sign of punishment."

Acting in Good Faith

In this defense of a nonfoundationalist account, I have made much of the requirement that judges must act in *good faith* when they are applying or interpreting rules. It is a critically important and controversial idea that demands further elaboration and defense. Even from the most foundationalist of perspectives, it is clearly not enough to declare that good faith adjudication is satisfied by adhering to the injunction that a judge must "follow the rules," because it is never obvious or uncontroversial what the rules are or what it would mean to follow them. There must be some other operating standard or criterion in play. In constructing such a yardstick, care must be taken to ensure that it is nonfoundational in both origin and operation; the idea and practice of good faith will itself be part of the game that it is intended to influence. Moreover, a distinction must be maintained between a judicial maneuver or judgment that is simply badly crafted or unpersuasive and one that is done in bad faith; it may be that a judgment that is not produced in good faith is both well crafted and persuasive or that a judgment made in good faith is badly crafted and unpersuasive. As with any game, there needs to be a (nonfoundationalist) way of differentiating instances of bad play from outright cheating. Furthermore, in order to be considered to be judging in good faith, something more needs to be required of judges than simply producing a judgment that looks like and reads like a typical judicial opinion. If there was nothing more to good faith judging than that, pure rationalization would be as acceptable as anything else: the dice-rolling Judge Bridlegoose would be qualified to take his place in the pantheon of great judges.[17]

The requirement of *good faith* is not unique to adjudicative practice: it arises in all matters of decision and justification. Whether it is referred to as good faith, integrity, or by similar terms, the basic thrust is that persons are expected to behave in such a way that they reflect on what is right and wrong, act consistently with that decision (even at personal cost), and then take responsibility for their action. While this demands honesty and sincerity in one's actions, these qualities amount to only part of the requirement. To accept that one must act in good faith is to recognize that the end does not always justify the means and that sometimes things might not always go. Of course, there is no reason to assume that two people who act with integrity will agree on what is right and wrong or on a common course of action: to maintain otherwise is a foundationalist conceit. Good faith cannot in itself tell people what to do in situations of uncertainty and doubt; it can only give them the courage to act on their own convictions in a way that takes seriously the responsibility to act fairly.[18] Moreover, it does not insist upon a stubborn consistency; people act with integrity when they are neither dogmatic nor unprincipled but are open to engagement and, therefore, change. This is particularly so where, in situations like law, people are expected to play a professional or rule-defined role that places a premium on acting in accordance with extant practices. Indeed, a commitment to adjudicate in good faith demands that the desire to win or to decide a case in a particular way is tempered by the willingness to lose or to decide in a less than ideal way. In short, the requirement to act in good faith is the difference between an attachment to the ill-considered claim that "anything goes" and to the more cogent commitment that "anything might (but also might not) go."

Accordingly, good faith can be thought of as acting in line with the spirit of the enterprise in which one is engaged and respecting other people's expectations about what is supposed to happen. It demands, at a minimum, that this should be done without furtively or opportunistically imposing one's own view of what should happen; it implies more than avoiding outright cheating and deception. While this standard is open and indeterminate, it imposes a constraint on action, even if there are no objective or uncontroversial norms for compliance and even if the constraint of good faith is always in play. In this nonformalist sense, the good faith requirement is about "playing fair."[19] Of course, when understood in a nonformalist sense, this injunction is not as restrictive or as limiting as it might seem. In particular, this obligation does not mean that judges cannot work to change what it means to *play the game* but only that they must do so from within the presently constituted game. In a nonformalist account, therefore, while there is a difference between those who do and do not adjudicate in good faith, there is none between those who play by the existing rules of the game and those who play to change them. All of the judges are engaged in the political practice of adjudication; it is simply that they are making different choices about particular rules and their application in particular contexts. For instance, in matters of constitutional or statutory interpretation, there is a significant difference between judges who are trying to make sense of a particular text, even if that process does generate multiple and contradictory meanings, and judges who are not making that effort at all. This is particularly the case in circumstances where a judge has made the effort to engage the text or rule but chooses to ignore the results and, instead, deliberately grafts an extraneous and different meaning onto a particular text.[20] Accordingly, this constraint of good faith does not in itself limit or restrict the kind or range of meanings that can be attributed to different rules. The judge is still empowered to construct meaning within the enabling and constraining context of the rules: good faith goes less to the actual substance of judgment than to its rhetorical performance.

What the requirement of good faith does demand, however, is that whatever interpretation is offered or whatever application is suggested, it must result from a genuine effort to make sense of the rule in hand or to deploy law's argumentative resources in a conscientious way. Understood in this way, the requirement of good faith is more an issue of moral integrity than a matter of analytical accuracy; it is less about legal rightness than it is about political reasonableness. Whether a particular judicial performance is accepted or rejected by others will not be because it is somehow validated by reference to a foundationalist algorithm as a correct or true interpretation of the rule. A judgment will gain acceptance or rejection because the judge is able to persuade others that it is a reasonable interpretation and that it has earned its legitimacy through the persuasive force of its supporting arguments. Of course, "reasonableness" will itself be a topic for debate in the continuing round of adjudicative performances rather than an external standard for its evaluation or review; what it means to act in good faith has no essential meaning that is not situated and contextual. For example, the question of whether coin tossing and conflict of interest invalidate a particular judicial performance is not resolvable by stipulation; it is grounded in nothing more (and nothing less) than the contingent and changing practices of the legal community. Like the meaning of "vehicles," the definition and application of good faith and validity will take on different meanings in different contexts. To argue that only good renditions of particular performances can count as valid performances would mean that a "poor" performance would have to be treated as oxymoronic. Within conventional practice, it is quite sensible to insist that a bad performance or even parody of an artistic work is no less a performance of that work.[21] As such, a nonfoundational test of good faith judging is appropriately playful in the sense of being itself always part of law's language game.

An instructive discussion of the good faith requirement takes places around the issue of frivolity in pleadings. In a provision that is typical of many jurisdictions, Rule 11(b), (2) of the U.S. Federal Rules of Civil Procedure obliges lawyers to certify that any legal claims made in their pleadings are, among other things, "warranted by existing law or by a nonfrivolous argument for [its] extension, modification or reversal . . . after an inquiry reasonable under the circumstances." While there is considerable agreement about the need to discipline lawyers who burden the courts and other litigants with unrealistic claims, it has been notoriously difficult to agree on what frivolity or good faith means. Ultimately, mindful that all lawyers have a penchant for persuading themselves of the viability of the most outlandish argument if it benefits their case, courts have been able to do no more than call in aid community standards. Bad faith or frivolity has only been found where there is clear evidence that no reasonable attorney could have concluded that such a claim *might* be established and also that it was made for improper purposes; the individual lawyer's belief as to reasonableness of claim is key.[22] This kind of approach fits well with the nonfoundationalist approach that I have been suggesting for judicial decision making. Like all questions of legal interpretation, the issue of whether a particular argument is frivolous or made in bad faith is not an external constraint placed upon the reasoning practices of lawyers or judges but is rather a constraint that is itself internal to the practice; what counts as a serious move in the game is itself part of law's language game. As one civil proceduralist has commented, "Today's frivolity may be tomorrow's law, and the law often grows by an organic process in which a concept is conceived, then derided as absurd (and clearly not the law), then recognised as theoretically tenable (though not the law), then accepted as the law."[23] With its emphasis on imagination and persuasion, this is exactly the dynamic process of legal development that a nonfoundationalist approach seeks to capture.

In a similar fashion, the Canadian courts have developed an interpretive doctrine that is suggestive of my nonfoundationalist stance. Although the courts' approach is intended to be applied only to decide when courts should interfere with an administrative agency's exercise of discretion, its informing rationale can be used to nonfoundational effect in contested matters of judicial discretion. In deciding the acceptability of an administrative tribunal's interpretation of a governing statute, the Supreme Court of Canada has held that the reviewing court should defer to the tribunal's interpretation unless it is "so patently unreasonable that its construction cannot be rationally supported by the relevant legislation."[24] Recognizing that there is hardly ever only one plausible interpretation of a statutory provision, the courts have shifted the terms of the legal debate from whether the initial interpretation was correct to whether it is reasonable. This, of course, will not bring an end to debate and judges will not cease to argue vigorously over what is and is not reasonable. However, such a "patently unreasonable" threshold does at least place the emphasis where it should be—on the rhetorical force and political acceptability of the decision, not on its philosophical validity or interpretive correctness. The important question to be asked is not whether one would have made the same decision or interpretation but whether that decision or interpretation is reasonable. Debate will continue over whether particular interpretations are more or less reasonable and whether such curial deference is desirable, but the focus of that debate will be less on the particular wording of the rules and more on the wisdom of its suggested interpretation. By switching the hermeneutic focus from rightness to reasonableness, the courts are indicating their disenchantment with a foundationalist approach to legal interpretation.

Moreover, as the courts become increasingly frustrated with traditional jurisprudential advice, they are beginning to incorporate more directly the nonfoundationalist insight that the meaning of particular words or phrases will vary from one context to another; judges seem to be conceding that there is no fixed or enduring interpretation that can be relied upon to ground the adjudicative task. Indeed, when this contextual approach is combined with the deferential standard of "patent unreasonableness," it begins to confirm that a nonfoundationalist account is not so far removed from the present practice of adjudicative interpretation as might initially be thought. For example, a recent challenge for judges has been to determine what constitutes "family" and, in particular, whether it encompasses same-sex relationships. In one Canadian case, the courts were faced with the task of deciding whether a refusal to grant "family" bereavement leave to a gay complainant on the death of his partner's father offended the legislative prohibition against discrimination on the basis of "family status." Although the judges disagreed over the particular meaning to be ascribed to it in the particular context of the facts and the legislative history, there was almost complete agreement that each statute was to be determined in its own context. As one judge put it, her discussion of what "family status" should be taken to mean "is not intended to be an authoritative definition of what constitutes the family, but is rather to illustrate that a purposive approach to the term 'family status' can result in an interpretation that can vary depending on the specific context."[25] Again, the courts are recognizing that it is not hermeneutic accuracy that determines the validity of interpretation but rather its political and contextual merit. The words and language of the law help to define and delimit the adjudicative performance, but they are also always in its productive and contingent play. It is not so much that "anything goes" or that words have no (and, therefore, any) meaning but instead that "anything might go."

In helping to understand the contested role of the good faith requirement and to illuminate the jurisprudential conflict, reference to a parallel and instructive debate in sport and other competitive activities over the use of "performance-enhancing" substances or procedures is helpful. Indeed, the main positions that have been staked out bear considerable resemblance to those of the legal foundationalists and their critics. Among other reasons for banning performance-enhancing substances or procedures (i.e., health reasons, coercion, role model, etc.), the main concern seems to be that their use is unnatural and will give their users an unfair advantage over other competitors; there is something that is not sporting about such practices because they offend the ideal of what it means to *play the game*. However, there are others who argue that while performance-enhancing substances are not to be encouraged, there is considerable confusion and inconsistency in the case for their prohibition. Apart from the difficulty of determining what generally counts as a drug (i.e., does it include coffee, Gatorade, or even water?), there is the problem of distinguishing performance-enhancing drugs from those of a restorative or medicinal kind. Also, insofar as prohibitions are intended to protect performers' health or well-being, it is widely accepted that many drugs are much less harmful to people's health than the sporting performances actually played and that many drugs (e.g., steroids) have a vital role to play outside of sporting competitions. Furthermore, in terms of fairness or equal (dis)advantage, it is contended that if the fact that some people train longer or have better equipment than others is not considered unfair, it is unclear why the use of other performance-enhancing activities should be curtailed—if some students use sleep inhibitors to study longer the night before an exam, are they cheating? Indeed, in earlier days, even training was considered unnatural and, therefore, to be discouraged or frowned upon—if some students are able to afford private tutors to improve their performance, are they cheating?[26]

The point of this digression is not to take one side of the debate over another but to emphasize that the distinction between legitimate and illegitimate behavior is not a bright line but a spectrum of options and choices—the ideal of natural or fair play is itself part of the argumentative contest over what it means to *play the game*. It is not possible to withdraw to some grounded position outside the contested area to validate or vouchsafe objective standards for evaluation or criticism: there is no escape from the responsibility of choosing among competing values. As with all such discussions, whether in sport or law, the context and timing of the argumentative contest will influence the problem and its resolution—what counts as cheating is no less (or more) contingent than what counts as good play. There are situations in which adherence to the so-called letter of the rules can be taken to violate the spirit of the game. For example, it might be thought that while an ambulance is usually treated as a vehicle, it would be unjust to prosecute ambulance drivers for breaches of the rule that there are to be "no vehicles in the park" when they enter the park to aid an injured person. Whether this is considered good or bad judging will not be determined by resort to something outside the game but will be played out as a different phase or part of the game itself. What it all comes down to is that to adjudicate in good faith is not about following a set of fixed guidelines or code of conduct. It is more an attitude or spirit that asks that judges "do the right thing" in the nonfoundational sense of playing the adjudicative game in the best way that they can at that particular time.[27] To ask more is to flirt with the seductive appeal of a foundationalist approach, but to ask less is to succumb to the false allure of an antifoundationalist critique.

On the Bias

This whole area of disagreement and discussion can best be appreciated in terms of the meaning and salience of *bias* in any evaluation of actual or ideal performances of the judicial craft. Of course, the issue of bias is more complex than many commentators are prepared to concede. This is because what counts as bias has implications for the entire practice and legitimacy of adjudication. Any sophisticated account of law and adjudication must be concerned to identify what counts as impermissible bias rather than invalidate or condemn bias generally. From a nonfoundationalist perspective, of course, this means that whether judicial bias exists will depend less on drawing formal lines than on making contextual judgments. Consequently, bias is not something that stands in categoric opposition to objectivity but rather comprises a spectrum of issues and influences whose particular valence and illegitimacy will vary from context to context. From an archfoundationalist viewpoint, bias is something that will compromise (or be seen to compromise) the judge's capacity to decide the case objectively. However, once the notion of objectivity is understood in a nonfoundationalist way, the status and influence of bias are made more problematic. Contrary to the foundationalist claim, I have insisted that political values are always in play during any performance of the adjudicative game; judges are never in a position where they can apply the rules to the facts in an uncontroversial or value-free way. Even from a foundational perspective, if the claim that judges must be unbiased is taken too seriously, all judges will be disqualified from law's adjudicative game; judges must call on some set of normative predispositions in order to give any decision at all. Without such political convictions, the faculty and exercise of judgment would be impossible. Accordingly, the difference between expertise and bias must be understood as one of degree, not kind.

One familiar foundationalist refrain about *good faith* in adjudication is put forward by Steven Burton. In a book-length study, he seeks to demonstrate that the law constrains judges in the kind of reasons that they can employ, but it does not entail one particular result. To operationalize this theoretical claim, Burton maintains that judges must consider themselves to be under a legal obligation to uphold conventional law, even when they have discretion. However, when exercising this discretion, he advises judges that they can only do this legitimately by acting on reasons warranted by that law as grounds for judicial decision and by not acting out of bias. By this, he means that judges will be restrained and influenced by legal considerations and not those considerations of an excluded and nonlegal nature, such as "the judge's own prior political convictions, . . . his fear of criticisms by his friends and enemies, his instincts to husband and enhance his personal power, and his intellectual curiosity."[28] While I do not really disagree too much with his claim that judges must "uphold conventional law" if they are to act in good faith, the fact is that nothing practical follows from it, except the trivial and insufficient mandate for judges to situate their reasoning within the extant context of legal materials. Even the antifoundationalist would have no difficulty conceding this. However, the instruction "to uphold conventional law" begs the central question for foundationalists of whether the law actually places constraints on judges in concrete cases. I, of course, insist that it both does and does not; the constraints (and the judicial obligation to work within them) are themselves always part and parcel of the interpretive play in the adjudicative game. Nevertheless, in forbidding judges from acting out of bias, Burton is far too blunt in his admonitions. It is not that a nonfoundationalist account ignores or dismisses the problem of bias; it is that it takes a much more nuanced and sophisticated approach to the definition of bias's scope and substance. Burton insists that when judges act out of bias, they have failed in their legal obligation and are judging in bad faith. However, this conclusion is far from compelling so long as he lumps together judicial performances that incorporate "prior political convictions" and those that are motivated by judges' "instincts to husband and enhance [their] personal power"; bribed or nepotistic judges are surely a different kettle of fish than judges who make a serious effort to square their political views with those of the law. From a nonfoundationalist perspective, it is never possible not to be "acting out of bias," if by that it is meant that judges bring values to the adjudicative task; the judicial application of rules is always about the choice between and among values. In terms of legal correctness, there is no difference between the racist judge and the antiracist judge; the only relevant difference is political and, of course, one—whether one is a racist or what is racist?—that is itself not outside of debate or context. Accordingly, while Burton's and other foundationalists' desire for an objective touchstone of judicial legitimacy and *good faith* is understandable, it is not something that can be appealed to or grounded in something that is external to the legal arguments made. All standards to evaluate judicial performance, including the scope and import of good faith, have to be established within the law itself when understood as a language game of playful proportions and rhetorical performance.

In dealing with the definition and consequences of judicial bias, the courts have been far from consistent in holding in what circumstances judges become so involved or connected to the outcome of a case that their continued participation in the case becomes suspect. The relevant doctrine concentrates on the perception of bias, not its actual existence. Rather than engage in fruitless or impracticable inquiries into a judge's state of mind, the courts have tended to concentrate on whether the surrounding circumstances give rise to the appearance of bias—"Justice should not only be done, but should manifestly and undoubtedly be seen to be done."[29] Indeed, the courts have begun to concede that complete impartiality cannot be expected or sustained. Rather than demand that adjudicators approach their exercise of discretion with an empty mind, the judges accept that there will be a lack of bias when judges' minds are "kept ajar."[30] Moreover, while pecuniary interest in the outcome of a case, whether direct or by way of bribe, has always been sufficient to disqualify a judge's participation or to invalidate any decision made, there remains debate over the precise meaning and extent of "pecuniary interest": there is a difference between a judge who is pro-business in orientation and one who holds shares in a litigant's company.[31] Again, the resolution of that debate will not be outside the practice of legal adjudication. Nor will it be concluded in any final and ahistorical manner: any resolution achieved will be as provisional and reconfigurable as all interpretations and applications of other legal rules and practices.

None of this is to be taken as suggesting that judges are free to indulge their biases or political convictions. As I have tried to explain, a nonfoundationalist account of good faith adjudication incorporates the requirement that judges have a serious and sincere commitment to play the adjudicative game as constituted by its extant operating rules. However, it must also be emphasized that the necessary reliance on some political preferences in the judicial performance must also not be understood as an escape to a fixed set of grounded values; judges are influenced by the adjudicative game at the same time that they are influencing it. No less than the adjudicative game itself, individual judges' political values are themselves never completely immune to change; they are as open to transformation as the judicial playmaking that they inform. While deeply held convictions may change only slow and imperceptibly, their strength and application to concrete situations will not remain constant. Accordingly, in the same way that a nonfoundationalist account does not expect judges to check in their values at the courtroom door, it does not allow them to indulge those values freely. What it does expect is that judges work hard to bring those biases and convictions to articulate consciousness so that they can be better understood and interrogated. In this way, it can be appreciated that a nonfoundationalist judge is someone who knows that there are no easy answers to be discovered, but only difficult choices to be made. In scrutinizing their own views in light of the problem or dispute to be decided, judges ought to be prepared to take full responsibility for their decisions and their consequences: they will not hide behind the impersonal authority and assumed obligation of the law, because there is none.

Within this nonfoundational account of good faith adjudication, it might well be possible for someone somewhere at sometime to formulate rules or apply familiar rules in what presently appear to be bizarre or perverse ways. However, in order to count as a good faith act of legal judgment, all that must be demonstrated is that such a judge holds a practical and actual belief that the rules do permit such a course of action. If there is such a felt sense of what a rule or rules might plausibly be interpreted to mean, the debate over meaning will be joined as one about substantive wisdom as opposed to interpretive correctness. Such judges might be persuaded that there are better or more compelling ways to apply a particular rule, but that debate will be a rhetorical engagement over substantive reasonableness, not a philosophical reflection over formal truth. If such judges are not persuaded by the arguments of their colleagues or commentators, the upshot will be that their ensuing judgment will simply fall by the doctrinal wayside as one more failed effort to convince the legal community of the judgment's political merit or good sense; it ought not to be that such judges are condemned as having failed to play the judicial game properly or that their judgments are rejected as not amounting to valid judgments. The legal game of adjudication not only allows for and accommodates bad performances, but it also actively encourages adventurous performances that are intended to transform its operating rules and that will risk failure.

The broader jurisprudential implication of insisting upon this threshold condition and taking this stance is that a nonfoundational account puts as much weight on *how* something is decided as on *what* is decided. Not only does the requirement of good faith distinguish my nonfoundational account from an antifoundationalist critique, but it points to an important difference between my nonfoundational account and the mainstream foundationalist theories of a Hart or a Dworkin. Their jurisprudential accounts seem committed to the idea that some legal decisions are plainly wrong as a matter of legal rightness as well as political wisdom. To join issue in more practical terms, imagine two concrete and challenging scenarios—a good faith judge who reaches a "crazy" decision (i.e., one that is outside the prevailing bounds of professional consensus) and a bad faith judge who reaches a "sensible" decision (i.e., one that is squarely inside the prevailing bounds of professional consensus). In these situations, what would it mean to say that the judges got it wrong or right? Or that the decision was illegitimate or legitimate? If they remain consistent with their theoretical commitments, traditional foundationalist theorists, like Dworkin and Sunstein, would likely be more troubled by the good faith and crazy decision than they would by the bad faith and sensible decision: the capability of the decision to fit into and with the canon of leading decisions is what a foundationalist account considers to be its most important quality.[32] However, from a nonfoundationalist perspective, I maintain that their concern is misplaced and that the latter situation is more troubling than the former—a sensible decision by a judge acting in bad faith is more jurisprudentially disturbing (even if it is not so for the parties involved) than a bizarre decision made in good faith.

If one takes a few steps back and assesses these nonfoundationalist claims in light of the actual historical sweep of common law adjudication, they become less startling and more reasonable. Some of what are now considered the most renowned and "great" decisions of yesteryear often began their doctrinal life with a barrage of condemnation. Judgments like those of *Brown* in the United States, *Morgentaler* in Canada, and *Donoghue* v. *Stevenson* in the United Kingdom were the subject of all kinds of criticism.[33] This negative response not only fixed on their political (un)desirability but also made much of their doctrinal infirmities and often complained that, whatever else they were, they were legally wrong. However, the ensuing history of these decisions shows that criticisms made in terms of legal accuracy or validity were beside the point. What established them in the firmament of leading legal decisions is that, through a combination of timeliness, insight, and argumentation, the judgments and decisions managed to persuade people that their applications or interpretations were both formally legitimate and substantively desirable. Similarly, the host of cases that began as potential candidates for doctrinal greatness and fell short of acquiring that revered status did so, not because the judicial arguments were wrong in some strictly legal sense but because they failed to carry the rhetorical day; the individual sensibilities and supporting justifications did not register in the larger legal (and public) consciousness and conscience. Accordingly, the difference between "great" and "crazy" decisions is political and rhetorical, not legal and logical. Competing strategies of adjudication are rhetorical resources in a continuing struggle for the hermeneutical soul of law; their impact and success will vary with context and audience. Any meaning that gels is a rhetorical function of a temporary and provisional agreement between contending parties, not a lasting or conclusive recognition of a preexisting ground for interpretive Truth or legal Reason.

Finally, the cogency of the nonfoundationalist position on the good faith requirement can be usefully reinforced by contrasting it with the critical recommendations of antifoundationalists. For instance, Mark Tushnet once contended that if he were appointed to the bench, he would adopt a "currently fashionable theory" of adjudication and then use it to advance the cause of socialism or whatever.[34] This strategy might be good or bad from a nonfoundationalist perspective, depending upon its particular modus operandi. If he engages in good faith with the available legal resources and is able to make a plausible argument to support his desired conclusion, he will have acted in a way that meets the threshold requirement of good legal reasoning. In making this assessment, it will be important to inquire into whether he accepted the possibility that, at least in theory, he might not be able to pull it off; there might be a situation in which his rhetorical skills and technical vision could not do the job to his own minimal standards of rhetorical satisfaction. In which case, he would be required to admit temporary defeat until he was able to construct a sufficiently plausible argument. On the other hand, if he made no attempt to engage in such a way with the law's materials and resources, he would be involved in an act of rationalization, not reasoning. This would mean that while he would still be acting as a judge, he would be acting in bad faith. Whatever game he was playing, his performance would not be taken seriously as an example of what it means to *play the game* of law and adjudication, at least as currently conceived and practiced. It would, of course, be open to Tushnet (or anyone else) to persuade judges and lawyers that such a style of performance was a possible and acceptable way to play the game, because, as a nonfoundationalist account insists, what it means to *play the game* is itself always a part of the game.

Accordingly, a nonfoundationalist approach resists the traditional insistence that whenever judges attend to the consequences of applying a rule, they are no longer applying the rule in any serious sense. It is willingly acknowledged that, whatever else they might be doing, judges are not engaged in rule application when they deliberately use rules as after-the-fact justifications for decisions. However, I do maintain that some resort to the likely consequences of a decision is not only an acceptable feature of rule application but also an unavoidably practical dimension of rule application, if "resort to consequences" is used as a cryptic reference to certain aspects of the rules' informing context and normative framework. Without reference to something beyond the verbal formulation of the rule itself, it is nonsensical to talk about rule application at all. As I have been at pains to demonstrate, rule application only makes sense as a dynamic exercise in normative judgment, not as a passive act of unreflective conformity.[35] Consequently, a nonfoundationalist account is only troubled when judges attend to consequences *and nothing else*—that is, when they forgo or ignore their own good faith attempts at interpretation of the rules. The fact that judges arrive at different or even contradictory applications of particular rules is less of a concern than the failure of judges to take the body of rules as a whole seriously. While judges are obligated to apply rules, this does not oblige them to reach certain decisions. Of course, to concede that there may be several applications of a rule that count as valid or legitimate is to confirm that law is rife with indeterminacy and that adjudication is inescapably permeated with choices. As such, traditional jurists need not so much fear that "anything goes" as a matter of judicial decision—that judges might decide cases on the basis of a coin toss, the litigants' hair color, astrological charts, or the like—as that, as a matter of rule application and through a process of rational disagreement, judges might justify almost any outcome. Again, a nonfoundational account does not reduce adjudication to brute preference nor dispense with the possibility of rational debate. It simply insists that the idea of rational debate be understood in a playful way that recognizes that "rational debate" is part of the game and not a grounding for its continuing performance or critique.

A Pending Affair

The requirement that judges act in good faith is the hallmark feature of a nonfoundationalist account of law and adjudication; it is what distinguishes it from an antifoundationalist critique. When it is demanded that judges make a serious effort to engage the relevant materials rather than treat them in a cavalier or dismissive way, it serves to confirm that there will be a vital, albeit shifting and contextualized, difference between reasoning and rationalization. However, as important as this good faith requirement is, it is a difficult idea and practice to explore or illustrate in decided cases. Reading a judgment will reveal little about the intention or state of mind of its perpetrator. A judgment reached in good faith and one delivered in bad faith will betray very little, if anything, about whether the judge acted properly or out of unacceptable bias. Nevertheless, it is possible to make some telling points about the antifoundationalist critique (and the foundationalist project as well) by working through one particular kind of case. The objective of my discussion is not to argue that the case was decided rightly or wrongly; that would miss the point of any nonfoundationalist analysis. Instead, I will canvass the court's various judgments and attempt to articulate how they support the nonfoundationalist claims about good faith. In particular, I will give particular attention to the argument that while judges should and most often do tend to act in good faith, this requirement will not in itself crimp their judicial style or limit the results that they can achieve. To carry out this undertaking, I have quoted generously from the court's judgments because it is as important to capture the individual judges' different approaches to their interpretive responsibilities as it is to appreciate the substantive arguments made on the particular interpretive issue.

In *Mhlungu*, the Constitutional Court of South Africa had to determine when a criminal proceeding is considered to be pending.[36] Although the legal issue to be decided appeared quite straightforward and run-of-the-mill, the surrounding institutional and political context ensured that the case was destined to be important and troublesome. With the overthrow of the apartheid regime, an interim constitution was introduced in 1993 and came into effect on 27 April 1994. A legal document of momentous historical significance, the constitution entrenched a set of criminal protections and civil benefits that had previously been denied to black South Africans. In one of its first decisions, the new Constitutional Court had to decide the meaning and extent of an accused person's entitlement to a fair trial. Under the old apartheid Criminal Code, the onus was on the accused to prove that a confession had not been freely and voluntarily made. In a unanimous judgment in *Zuma*, the eleven-judge Constitutional Court held that such provisions offended the interim constitution's guarantee of a fair trial; the relevant section of the Criminal Code was invalidated and the onus was put on the state to prove that the accused's confession was freely and voluntarily made.[37] This decision was delivered on 5 April 1995, and, as well as its substantive holding, its precise timing came to be significant.

In April 1993, Mhlungu and four others were allegedly involved in a murder. An indictment in Afrikaans was served on them on 11 March 1994 and re-served in English on 4 May 1994. The trial commenced on 18 May

1994 and the accuseds pleaded not guilty. The prosecution tendered evidence of confessions made by the accuseds, and, in accordance with the Criminal Code (as yet not invalidated), it was for the accuseds to prove that the confessions were illegally obtained. Mhlungu's counsel informed the court that he intended to challenge the constitutionality of the Criminal Code's provisions on the admissibility of confessions. The threshold issue for the trial judge was whether the protections contained in the interim constitution, whatever they were interpreted to demand, were available to Mhlungu. The relevant provision was s.241(8):

> All proceedings which immediately before the commencement of this Constitution were pending before any court of law, including any tribunal or reviewing authority established by or under law, exercising jurisdiction in accordance with the law then in force, shall be dealt with as if this Constitution had not been passed: Provided that if an appeal in such proceedings is noted or review proceedings with regard thereto are instituted after such commencement such proceedings shall be brought before the court having jurisdiction under this Constitution.

The crucial question, therefore, was whether the proceedings against Mhlungu were "pending" on 27 April 1994, the date that the constitution came into effect—if they were, he would not be entitled to any potential benefits under the constitution; if they were not, he would be able to take advantage of its possible protections.

The trial judge made no finding on either the constitutionality of the Criminal Code provisions or whether the constitution was in force. Instead, Page J. referred the matter directly to the Constitutional Court. The decision was heard by that court in February 1995, and its decision was handed down on 8 June 1995. During this time, of course, the court had delivered its decision in *Zuma*, holding that the contested provisions of the Criminal Code were unconstitutional. Although the court held, in *Mhlungu*, that a referral was inappropriate in such circumstances (as the trial judge had jurisdiction to make an initial decision on the matters himself), it went on to decide that Mhlungu's proceedings were not pending and that he should receive the benefits of the constitutional right to a fair trial. The decision was reached by a majority of 7 to 4. Four judgments were given: one by Kentridge for the minority; one by Mahomed for five of the majority; and one each by Kriegler and Sachs in concurrence with Mahomed's disposition, although for slightly different reasons. All in all, the judgments cover the gamut of jurisprudential positions and problems—the positivist focus on language and institutional competence; the naturalist resort to political values; the pragmatic concern with context and purpose; and the formalist emphasis on coherence and harmony. As I will show, no judgment is either right or wrong: they are all best read as rhetorical probes in the continuing performance of law's language game.

From my particular line of nonfoundational inquiry, the major tension in the judgments is not so much over whether, as a matter of political morality, Mhlungu should be obliged to prove the voluntariness of his alleged confession (as the *Zuma* decision indicated, all the judges of the Constitutional Court agreed that he should not), but whether the wording of the interim constitution enabled such a conclusion to be reached. Even the majority, while critical of the minority's "literal" approach, maintained that the most politically desirable result is only possible "if the language and context of the relevant provision, interpreted with regard to the objectives of the Constitution, permits such a course": an antifoundationalist rationalization was to be studiously avoided. Indeed, all the judges agreed that it was imperative that the court approach its constitutional responsibility with a liberal sense of the larger political context and that a purposive approach to such interpretive matters was required. Nevertheless, as Kentridge put it, "There are limits to the principle that a Constitution should be construed generously . . . and those limits are to be found in the language of the Constitution itself." The judges shared the opinion, therefore, that even though (or especially because) it was a *constitution* that they were dealing with, they must take their judicial responsibilities seriously. For them, this demands that they adjudicate rather than engage in a freewheeling ideological exercise of critical revision. Accordingly, all the judges begin from a common task and shared sense of adjudicative purpose—to interpret the legal document as it exists rather than to ignore it in favor of their own preferred values. Reiterating the judgment of the court in *Zuma*, they concur that in avoiding "the austerity of a tabulated legalism," they must be solicitous not to make "a general resort to 'values' [such that] the result is not interpretation but divination."[38]

Kentridge stakes out the hermeneutical territory on which the other judges meet and join issue. For him, the crucial issue is to determine the meaning of "pending" in s.241(8) and, in particular, whether proceedings against Mhlungu began before or after 27 April 1994.[39] Mindful that lower courts had disagreed over whether s.241(8) referred to curial, procedural, or substantive matters, Kentridge confirms his commitment to a purposive approach in which the constitution is to be given a generous and nontechnical interpretation. However, he insists that "a purposive construction requires one to search for the specific purpose of section 241(8) within its context in the Constitution." He finds this purpose to be twofold—to preserve the jurisdiction of courts established under the old constitutional order to hear cases under the new constitution and, also, to ensure an orderly transition from the old to new legal regime. In line with this purpose, Kentridge holds that no "other meaning can reasonably be given to the language used" than that all pending cases be dealt with as if the constitution had not been passed. Finding against Mhlungu, therefore, he concludes:

> I am fully aware that it is a Constitution and not an ordinary statute that we are expounding. One of the distinctions between them is that a constitution is drafted with an eye to the future. Another is that a constitutional bill of rights should as far as possible be read as protecting individual rights, if necessary against the public interest. I thus agree with the [liberal and purposive] approach to constitutional interpretation, and find the narrow approach to the language of a constitution unacceptable. Nonetheless, there are some provisions, even in a constitution, where the language used, read in its context, is too clear to be capable of sensible qualification. It is the duty of all courts, in terms of section 35, to promote the values which underlie a democratic society based on freedom and equality. In the long run, I respectfully suggest, those values are not promoted by doing violence to the language of the Constitution in order to remedy what may seem to be hard cases.[40]

In arriving at this decision, Kentridge opts for a jurisprudential approach that resembles something of a mix between that of Hart and Dworkin. He defines his task as being largely about deciphering the language of the relevant legal rule. While he make references to its purposes and to appropriate interpretive presumptions, his primary focus is upon the actual language used: "There are limits to the principle that a Constitution should be construed generously . . . and those limits are to be found in the language of the Constitution itself." However, he does not insist that words have a fixed or single meaning. Instead, he recognizes that judges will disagree about what that meaning is and so concedes that a judicial interpretation will be valid if a particular meaning "can reasonably be given to the language used." In this way, he stakes out a position that acknowledges that judges' values will influence textual interpretation, but he maintains that they will be constrained by the legal rules themselves. Nevertheless, Kentridge is adamant that "when the language is clear, it must be given effect." Consequently, he rejects as "unreasonable" any meaning attributed to s.241(8) that is different to his own, including those of the majority of his colleagues on the court. This, of course, means that the bottom line of his judgment is not so much the language of the rule but his assessment of what is a "reasonable" interpretation of that language.[41]

Mahomed's (leading?) judgment responds directly to Kentridge's "literal approach." Although Mahomed's criticism is framed in strongly adversarial terms, there is less jurisprudential difference between them than meets the legal eye: he remains more the Hartian than the Dworkinian judge. Mahomed believes passionately that to deny accused persons the benefit of constitutional protections on the basis of such a vague and minor provision in the constitution would lead to the "plainly outrageous consequence" of depriving thousands of constitutional protection merely by virtue of the fortuitous fact that they were involved in proceedings that had commenced before 27 April 1994. He is acutely aware of the inequality and suffering that South Africa's black population has experienced. Consequently, he emphasizes that the only way to respect the constitution's noble ambitions and to expiate South Africa's ignoble past is to give the constitution "a purposive and generous focus." However, he does not ignore the actual wording of the constitution generally or the disputed section in particular. Indeed, he goes so far as to state that injustice should "be avoided if the language and context of the relevant sections reasonably permit such a course." Taking Kentridge seriously on his own "literal" terms, Mahomed argues forcefully that when s.241(8) is placed within "the larger context of the Constitution regarded as a holistic and integrated document with critical and important objectives, . . . an alternative construction is reasonably available." Reaching a decision in favor of Mhlungu, Mahomed holds:

> The language of section 241(8) is not, in the circumstances, cogently supportive of the suggestion that it had two purposes. The proposition that its only purpose was to preserve the authority of pre-Constitution Courts to continue to function as Courts for the purposes of adjudication in pending cases, appeals to me as a more persuasive interpretation of the section. At the very least it seems to me to be an interpretation of the section which is reasonable and the fact that it is more effective in securing the equal protection of the Constitution for all persons makes it significantly more attractive and defensible.[42]

Again, Mahomed does not treat the language in a cavalier manner but makes a good faith effort to engage in constitutional interpretation in such a way that there is a plausible connection between the relevant constitutional provision and the desired substantive outcome. He does not claim that his is the only possible interpretation or that it "is not free from difficulties." He simply asserts that it is, for him, "a more persuasive interpretation" in that "it gives force and effect to the fundamental objectives and aspirations of the Constitution, because it is less arbitrary in its consequences and because it is more naturally in harmony with the context of section 241(8) itself and the Constitution as a whole."[43] In adopting this more naturalist view of the adjudicative task, Mahomed does not reach the conclusion that Kentridge's interpretation is "unreasonable," although he comes extremely close to doing so. Instead, he takes the more modest position that, out of all the competing and plausible interpretations, his own judgment is plausible as a matter of legal interpretation and preferable as an issue of political morality.

Although Kriegler and Sachs each support Mahomed's conclusion, they arrive there by a slightly different hermeneutical route. Kriegler's judgment is full of Dworkinian motifs. In his short judgment, he expresses amazement at the suggestion that the historic rights attained by all South Africans should be rendered illusory by "the vague wording of an obscure subsection of a prosaic transitional provision." When placed in the larger context of the whole section and the overall scheme of the constitution, he maintains that "despite the equivocal nature of its wording, it has nothing to do with the substantive law to be applied by courts." Indeed, not content simply to offer his interpretation as reasonable or more persuasive, he goes so far as to declare that his interpretation "simply and only means" what he concludes. In Kriegler's approach to judging, it is important that whereas some rules are given a generous and purposive interpretation, other rules are best suited to a narrow, technical, and close reading.[44] Unfortunately, he offers few clues on how such a distinction is to be made; he is content simply to insist upon the importance and relevance of such a distinction.

In the final judgment, Sachs adopts a line of reasoning that challenges the interpretive frameworks of both Kentridge and Mahomed; it is a subtle combination of positivist common sense and naturalist aspiration. Whereas Kentridge "gives far too little weight to the overall design and purpose of the Constitution," Mahomed "unnecessarily strips s.241(8) of its more obvious meaning." Insisting that there is a "need to distinguish between grammatical exegesis and constitutional analysis," Sachs maintains that "the issue is how to reconcile the two sets of provisions when they collide with each other, not how to interpret each on its own." In balancing the technical provisions of the "puny" s.241(8) against the "powerful" provisions that entrench fundamental freedoms, he chooses to read back the former in light of the latter. Throughout his judgment, Sachs is at pains to stress that his judgment "is not a case of making the Constitution mean what we like, but of making it mean what the framers wanted it to mean; we gather their intention not from our subjective wishes, but from looking at the document as a whole." By way of conclusion, the former law professor Sachs reflects on his jurisprudential stance:

> I regard the question of interpretation to be one to which there can never be an absolute and definitive answer and that, in particular, the search of where to locate ourselves on the literal/purposive continuum

or how to balance out competing provisions, will always take the form of a principled judicial dialogue, in the first place between members of this court, then between our court and other courts, the legal profession, law schools, Parliament, and, indirectly, with the public at large. ... The objective of my approach is to preserve the essential functional core of section 241(8), while causing the minimum disturbance to the fundamental rights entrenched in Chapter 3. In other words, instead of mechanically applying section 241(8) and then lamenting, ignoring or minimizing the injustices which follow, the court gives effect to the gravamen of the section, but construes it in such a way as best to harmonize with [the fundamental freedoms] and so avoid needless incongruity and eliminate unnecessary postponement of enjoyment of fundamental rights.[45]

A Nonfoundational Review

As I hope will be clear, my critical exegesis of *Mhlungu* is intended to confirm the relevance and cogency of a nonfoundationalist account of law and adjudication. It was not intended to demonstrate that the decision made was right or wrong, nor that any particular judicial approach was right or wrong; the merits of any decision or approach are more appropriately assessed in terms of them being more or less persuasive and more or less useful (as long as "persuasive" or "useful" are understood in nonfoundational terms as ungrounded and contextual). However, most important, I have sought to emphasize, in contrast to an antifoundationalist critique, how and why a nonfoundationalist account insists that while "anything might go" in the legal performance of the adjudicative task, it is not the case that "anything goes." As Derrida puts it, interpretation cannot be executed "however one wishes," as to do so would mean that nonfoundationalist intervention "would risk developing in any direction at all and authorize itself to say almost anything."[46] Outside a particular context, "anything goes" is an absurd and indefensible claim. The force and appeal of a nonfoundationalist perspective is that, unlike either a foundationalist or antifoundationalist approach, it can account for the fact that judicial decision making is both always situated within the rules and never compelled by any interpretation of them.

Accordingly, while continuing to draw on the fecund judgments in *Mhlungu*, this closing section of the chapter will serve as a convenient occasion to pull together some of the more misunderstood and contested nonfoundational themes that I have developed throughout this chapter and the book generally—the requirement of good faith; the idea of law as an activity;

the difference between reason and rationalization; the source of legitimacy; the connection between method and result; the role of intention; the influence of identity; and the importance of reasonableness. By summarizing and focusing on them in this way, it might be possible to gain a more subtle and sustained fix on the detailed implications of a nonfoundationalist position. The following themes have been compiled to include those that arose in the judgments in *Mhlungu*.

—All the judges maintain that they are interpreting the words of the constitutional text, not gratuitously grafting on an extraneous meaning. It is a constant theme of their judgments that they want their audience to understand and accept that they appreciate that their legitimate task is one of legal interpretation, not ideological prognostication. Of course, there is no way of demonstrating that this in fact is what they are actually doing. Like any other group of judges, they could either jointly or severally be involved in a huge scam or sham. Their judgments might be nothing more than a crude and calculated rationalization of their initial ideological leanings; no genuine effort might have been made to engage the legal materials, and the ensuing judgments might be all show and no substance. This antifoundationalist assault not only denies that judges experience any sense of "felt boundedness" but argues that if judges have any felt sense at all, it is the experience of being willing to act in bad faith to achieve the results that they desire. However, such a cynical line of critique, while incapable of any final or irresistible refutation, is committed to the extreme position that some judges (and presumably all at some time or other) are actively deceiving not only themselves but the legal (and general) community. This is a paranoid and unconvincing account of law and adjudication.

—However, a dismissal of foundationalist jurisprudence does not commit the critic to such a bleak antifoundationalist stance in which adjudication is reduced to a conniving or insincere exercise in ideological manipulation. This dystopian depiction of judging is merely the flip side of an uncompromising foundationalist approach and, to have any theoretical or practical bite, depends upon the discredited validity of an objectivist epistemology in which there is only a choice between the embrace of a legal Reason, with its promise of coherent, determinate, and correct answers, and a capitulation to a faithless world in which arbitrary power and ideologues run amok. However, if one rejects entirely this epistemological paradigm, there is no longer any need to choose between a foundationalist account and its antifoundationalist critique. As *Mhlungu* illustrates, adjudication is no more about the inevitable articulation of objective truths than it is about the direct imposition of ideological preference. Taking a reasonable look at the judgments that is neither jaundiced nor roseate, the judges can be seen as being involved in a sincere effort to engage with legal materials that is neither completely free from their political convictions nor only reducible to them. Like most players in a game, they are struggling to do the best that they can with the skills that they have and with the context in which they find themselves. While some of the judicial performances are more convincing than others, each judge seems to be engaged in a good faith attempt to play law's language game.

—In committing to a good faith approach to their adjudicative task, none of the judges is precluded from reaching any particular decision. With insight and imagination, they demonstrate that there is a real sense in which "anything might go." Their judgments presumably did not simply take shape and substance without sustained and serious engagement with a whole host of competing factors—the facts, the legal rules, the political context, the constitutional structure, institutional values, their own experience, and so on. In an important sense, the published judgments lend a false appearance of inevitability and cohesion to the adjudicative process: judgments are the polished product of a much grubbier process of argument and counterargument. In working through this task, the judges grapple with themselves as well as the complex of legal materials and considerations. The subtle exchanges between the judges over the worth of different general approaches and particular arguments reveals a glimpse of that engagement. Indeed, the judgments are a stylized record of the legal game. From the nonfoundationalist understanding that law is something that judges and lawyers do rather than something that results from what they do, the actual performance of law's language game can be found in the good faith struggle itself.

—As apparent as it is that all the judges takes seriously their obligation to engage with the legal materials (albeit defined in narrower or broader ways), it is also obvious that they are all heavily influenced by their political predispositions. Reading between the lines, it seems to be the case that none of the judges comes to *Mhlungu* without some sense of what would be a politically appropriate decision in the circumstances. Of course, each judge not only brings a different mix of values to the judicial task but also attaches a different weighting to those values. While each judge in *Mhlungu* seems to share a sense in which it would work an injustice to deny basic protections to these accused persons, each combines that value in different ways with other values. For instance, whereas Mahomed insists that the avoidance of such an injustice trumps other considerations, Kentridge maintains that while the avoidance of individual injustice is important, it must be balanced against broader institutional values, including the sanctity of the constitutional compact and the need to discourage future judicial manipulation for less noble objectives. It was less a question of whether politics played a part than a matter of which politics won the day. Consequently, adjudication in

Mhlungu might be said to have begun in politics and ended in politics but was played out in and through law's language game. In this way, law is politics.

—What ultimately divides the judges in *Mhlungu* is not their attachment to different judicial methodologies or understandings of the law. Indeed, there is considerable agreement over the proper role and parameters of judicial review in a constitutional democracy. What divides the judges is their disagreement over what is and is not a reasonable decision in the particular circumstances. Again, while the decision over reasonableness is not completely unfettered or absolute, neither is it grounded in any foundational way; judges work the rules and context to arrive at decisions that are based on the rules and context but not reducible to them in any simple or predictable way. Judges do not stand outside the rules but instead inhabit the rules in a particular way. Being neither context-dependent nor context-transcendent, judges (re-)constitute themselves in their playful participation in law's language game. While there is nothing fixed or determinate about this dynamic interaction, judges will continue to change as they engage in the play of difference that constitutes the adjudicative practice. There is no guaranteed politics that can provide a reliable or determinate guide to the concrete resolution of particular disputes. The meaning and application of reasonableness will vary both across judges and within individual judges.

—Large parts of each judgment in *Mhlungu* are devoted to the important task of trying to persuade the other judges not only about the legitimacy and desirability of the actual substantive decision in the case but also about the legitimacy and cogency of a particular methodology used to arrive at that decision. All the judges recognize that their particular judicial style and contribution to law's game of adjudication have no greater (or lesser) legitimacy than that which they are able to earn in their performance and play. Legitimacy and, therefore, justice are not achieved by judicial conformity to a set way of proceeding but can only arise from within the adjudicative game itself and be generated by the participants' own discursive practices and institutional interactions. The correctness of any particular move is established through persuasion and argument, not proof and demonstration; the difference between "good" and "bad" moves is game-specific and must be judged within the game, even as the rules are being reinterpreted. Legitimacy, therefore, is something that does not precede or ground any judgment given but rather follows or flows from the rhetorical force of the judgment made. There are grounds for decisions, but they are contingent and unstable: reasons can be given as to why one decision is better than another, but these arguments are never themselves guaranteed or vouchsafed outside the context of the game itself.

—As part of this nonfoundational understanding of adjudication as a rhetorical exercise, it is important to recognize that there is no metalanguage or one way of playing the game that is intrinsically or extrinsically capable of grounding and validating the conclusions reached or the justifications used. However, while providing an argumentative context for reasoning and definition, these moves are themselves being contingently reworked. As such, the rules of the reasoning game do not so much constrain or cabin judges' room for maneuver as they make it possible and operational. However, it needs to be appreciated that there is no necessary connection between the judicial approach adopted and the particular result reached. As the "purposive" judgments of Mahomed and Kentridge in *Mhlungu* show, it is possible to deploy any judicial approach to contradictory effect. While some approaches tend to make some kinds of decisions more easy to justify than others, they have no natural or determinate political allegiance. Depending on the particular context, a so-called literal approach to legal interpretation can be progressive or conservative. To think or argue otherwise would be to subscribe to a foundationalist assumption that I have been at pains to undermine. Consequently, no one approach to adjudicative method is right or wrong in any final way; different approaches are only more (and less) appealing or convincing in different contexts. In short, there is no one way to get it right.

—As part of their judicial commitment to perform their constitutional responsibilities, all the judges in *Mhlungu* accept that their task is to give effect to the intentions of the constitution's architects. Indeed, while they all claim to be deferring to the constitutional creators in interpreting the text's provisions, no judge makes a real effort to pursue a serious inquiry into the historical and documentary record. Of course, there could be many reasons for this, but the nonfoundational explanation—that such an inquiry would be fruitless and incomplete—seems as plausible as any other. As the judgments attest, the realization that there is no authorial source of ultimate authority does not lead to an irresistible slide into "the flux, the gossip, the muddle and the motley." Although no meaning is ever entirely reducible to intention, the judges appreciate that intention, no less than the textual provisions that it is supposed to clarify, is itself always open to interpretation. In a nonfoundational manner of speaking, it is interpretation all the way up and down. In struggling to give concrete and specific meaning to the drafters' abstract and general intent, the judges do not so much ignore or treat lightly that intent: they take it as seriously as they can by reconstructing it in the process of defining it. The existence of constitutional intent becomes part of the adjudicative game, not something to validate or instruct the play of judicial performances.

—As with any performance, it is vital to remember that what is not said or revealed might be as important as what is said or revealed: the identification of unstated assumptions or circumstances of the informing context can help to give aspects of the judicial performance a different meaning or resonance. While the broad details of recent South African history and politics are reasonably well known and frame the decision in *Mhlungu* and its symbolic importance, the (racial) identities of the eleven judges are left unstated—there are seven white judges and four black judges. In particular, it is perhaps worth noting that the four judges in the minority are white. I say "perhaps" because the salience of that fact to any understanding of the decision reached and the judgments rendered is not itself beyond debate or disagreement.[47] Nevertheless, it seems as strained to contend that the racial experiences of the judges are of no weight whatsoever in seeking to understand the dynamics and wellsprings of the judgments as it is to insist that those judgments are entirely reducible to such experiences. The effect that the judges' identity has on their judicial performance is as variable and contingent as the experience itself. Accordingly, whether the judgments in *Mhlungu*, singly or collectively, are explainable in some way by reference to the (racial) identities of the judges is always in play, to a greater or lesser extent, in the jurisprudential effort to fathom the adjudicative game and its constitutive performances.

—There are, of course, grave dangers in assessing the contributions of particular judges or the worth of particular judicial approaches by reference to only one case, no matter how rich and varied its judgments. While it is true that a broader sample of cases would help to assemble a fuller and more convincing argument, a focus on a single case, like *Mhlungu*, does not weaken or undermine my critical analysis. A common reason for extending the range of examples is that it can help to confirm the extent to which judges remain consistent in their hermeneutical or methodological approach. However, this finding is of no particular relevance or import from a nonfoundationalist point of view. If individual judges are not consistent in their approach, it might be for the simple reason that they appreciate the telling observation that adjudication is first and foremost a rhetorical performance in which different maneuvers work better in some circumstances and than others. Of course, one important factor that judges should consider in shifting between different judicial techniques is that such inconsistency might detract from the overall rhetorical force of their judicial work. Other than that, there is little to recommend consistency in the performance of the judicial craft. Indeed, with apologies to Emerson, it might be said that judicial consistency is the hobgoblin of small (foundationalist and antifoundationalist) minds. Consequently, the judgments in *Mhlungu* can reveal as much and as little about the process of judicial decision making as any other case or series of cases: the judgments and my critical analysis of them ought to be taken as a suggestive illustration, not a definitive summary.

Conclusion

In this chapter, I have sought to show the important way in which a nonfoundational account of law and adjudication differs from an antifoundationalist critique. Although I stand firm on the basic critical claim that "law is politics," I have offered a more sophisticated and nuanced explanation of what such a conclusion does and does not entail. At the heart of this elaboration is the insistence that a loss of faith in foundationalist metanarratives does not commit jurists to an antifoundationalist position in which law is reduced to raw power and adjudication is viewed as nothing more than a faux exercise in ideological rationalization. From a nonfoundational perspective, adjudication is a playful performance in law's language game that involves a serious engagement with legal materials and, at the same time, an inextinguishable exercise of political choice. In the same way that soccer is a sport but not all sports are soccer, so law is politics but not everything that passes for politics is law.

As regards the treasonous charges that foundationalists, like Tribe, lay against juristic critics, I have insisted that a rejection of the foundationalist project does not entail a commitment to an antifoundationalist or nihilistic position; there are more subtle characters in the jurisprudential drama than the stock figures that Tribe portrays. It is true that Tribe does not subscribe to a "petty formalism" in that he acknowledges that there is "considerable room for disagreement about method and result in constitutional interpretation." However, he overreaches himself when he concludes that "there are legal truths out there, or at least legal falsehoods, that simply cannot be wished away." Truths and falsehoods are not the stuff of legal hermeneutics. Although certain interpretations will be difficult to dislodge or avoid, they will be not so much "wished away" as worked through by serious attention to genuine efforts at legal reasoning. While Tribe is correct to insist that "legal discourse itself imposes serious constraints," there is no reason to maintain that this results from "interpretive canons that are as immune as we can make them from the pushes and pulls of our own policy predilections." As I have argued, those constraints and interpretive canons exist and have considerable influence on the performance and possibilities of legal discourse, but they are part of the pushes and pulls that comprise that discourse, not apart from it. Being always situated within a legal context of freedom and restraint, judges (and jurists) are never fully restrained nor ever entirely free. Consequently, it is not that a nonfoundationalist approach (whatever might be the case for an antiformalist critique) "just doesn't cut much ice when the question before us is whether that practice is *constitutional*."[48] On the contrary, not only does it cut the ice of constitutional interpretation, but it also helps in the important tasks of skating on thin ice and resculpting the ice to better effect.

However, the claim that "law is politics" is not exhausted by deflecting and disposing of the extravagant arguments of antifoundationalists. There is a whole group of juristic critics who insist that the best way to understand law and adjudication is as foundational exercises in ideological politics. While they accept that law is determinate in nature and that adjudication is predictable in practice, they deny that law and adjudication can be understood as enterprises that are explainable to themselves and in their own terms. On the contrary, such theorists insist that there is a deep logic to law and adjudication that reflects and instantiates the dominant forms of social organization and political control. It is to this externalist account of legal development and practice that I now turn.

8 Calling the Shots: The Development of Legal Doctrine

••••••

All generalizations are dangerous, even this one.

—attributed to Alexandre Dumas *fils*

Most jurists consider that law is primarily an intellectual practice. Efforts to explicate the internal structure of law and adjudication as the coherent elaboration of justificatory arguments for the exercise of official power dominate the contemporary jurisprudential scene. However, there is a jurisprudential strain that rejects that notion. Instead, some theorists insist that law is less an independent field of intellectual endeavor and more the stylized product of material forces. This attempt to comprehend doctrinal development in terms of a political dynamic that is external to law represents a longstanding, if marginal, tradition in jurisprudence. Although there is much diversity and disagreement among these scholars, the main focus and ambition of this (largely but not exclusively Marxist) tendency are to isolate the dominant dialectic of social relations and demonstrate how the pattern of legal development and change is directly caused or heavily determined by that dialectic; law is a structured and finite game whose patterns and proceedings conform, or are at least responsive, to the dictates of certain interests. While these externalist accounts have much to offer by way of correction and balance to the inward-looking preoccupations of mainstream jurisprudence, they share a methodology with their more traditional counterparts—they are equally foundationalist in that they maintain that law can be grounded in something more ordered and scientific than the changing routines of its own prosaic practices as a site of political engagement.

In line with its "incredulity to master-narratives,"[1] a nonfoundationalist approach rejects such efforts to place the history and performance of law and adjudication on simple, straightforward, and secure footings. Just as law does not satisfy the rigorous discipline of an inner coherence and intelligibility, so does it fail to conform to the dominant requirements of an external dialectic and standard. Both society in general and the legal process in particular are far too messy in their patterns and practices to be reduced to neat equations of cause and effect; their importance is as much in the small details as in the grand design. The historical interaction between one feature of society and another cannot be described once and for all. Indeed, by virtue of the fact that it is historical and, therefore, endlessly contingent, it is not possible or meaningful to cram the richness of social life into one simplistic formula or overarching narrative: the only outcome would be to impoverish both social life and any explanatory account that is forthcoming. History can never be the grounding for anything, because history is itself always in need of interpretation. In taking such a nonfoundationalist perspective, it is not a question of being for or against Marxism, feminism, or anything else. It is simply a matter of refusing to accept such totalizing accounts as all-encompassing theoretical statements about social and legal development. The connections between legal doctrines and their historical contexts are sporadic and specific rather than systemic and abstract: "The system as a whole has no single ideological imprint."[2] A nonfoundationalist response is much more pragmatic, piecemeal, and eclectic: what it might be considered to lose in theoretical elegance, it gains in historical pertinence and political salience.

In this chapter, therefore, I intend to canvass the claims of those foundationalist jurists who maintain that law and adjudication are best understood not as the argumentative workings-out of an immanent logic but as the instrumental effects of larger social causes. After introducing the central tenets of such deep-logic theories of law and society, I provide a critique that highlights their explanatory shortcomings. Using strong feminist accounts of legal development as a focal point, I concentrate on the difficulties in reducing social history and interaction to one simple or single dynamic; such totalizing accounts tends to depoliticize oppression and, therefore, reduce the possibilities for transformative action. On the other hand, in my discussion of Marxist theories, I focus on the enduring indeterminacy of any posited relation between law and society. In so doing, I do not mean to imply that the effort to understand the shifting nexus between law and society is wasted or that "anything goes" in charting this important relation. Throughout the chapter, the ambition will not be to junk entirely the important work of the deep-logic theories but to relieve them of their scientistic pretensions and, thereby, to improve the worth of their contribution to the study of law and adjudication. Like all histories, the development of legal doctrine is best understood as being "one damn thing after another."

Going Deep

Much of modern social theory strives to provide an account of how social structures and values relate to the material conditions of people's daily lives.

Without some plausible explanation of this relation, the validity of social knowledge is suspect and the status of social theorizing remains deeply problematic. The challenge for contemporary scholars has been to craft a convincing account of how large and local struggles over social structures and values—from efforts to combat widespread sexist and racist practices to attempts to overcome poor working conditions and abusive intimate relations—relate to the dynamic system of material conditions that are in place. As a branch of social theory, legal theory has understandably felt obliged to share in that explanatory task. Whether one believes that it is possible to ground law as a social practice that can be apprehended in its own terms, the challenge of providing a convincing account of how law and adjudication connect with the society of which they are a part seems a vital aspect of any serious jurisprudential enterprise. However, for those who believe that the traditional foundationalist project has failed, this task seems both more promising and more pressing. For some, this turn to something outside of law is a reassuring exercise in political and economic ethics; for others, it is a convenient occasion to expose the oppressive force of law and adjudication as ideological constructs. However, in both cases, there is a shared commitment to the foundationalist premise that law and adjudication can be understood as a coherent and rational, even if unjust, enterprise by reference to an extralegal source of insight.

In fathoming the relation between law and its larger social context, there are three possible outcomes to the traditional inquiry—that law is an autonomous discipline and practice that has no necessary connection with other social values and institutions; that law is entirely and exclusively determined by forces and influences that operate independently of law; and that law is related to a greater or lesser extent to social values and forces. In contemporary debate, there is almost complete agreement that law is neither fully beholden to socioeconomic circumstances, nor fully independent of them. That law and adjudication might not possess any autonomy or distinctiveness at all as an intellectual discipline and professional practice is no more taken seriously than the belief that law can be thought about as an entirely autonomous field of human activity. Rather than make a futile Kelsenian attempt "to free the science of law from alien elements," the predominant concern is to reveal the formal and substantive connections between law and these "alien elements."[3] Indeed, contemporary jurisprudence seems to find an otherwise elusive intellectual unity in the notion that legal doctrine is relatively autonomous from the political formation and social struggles of history. Unfortunately, this unity is more apparent than real. The notion of *relative autonomy* is so ample that it can accommodate almost all theorizing about law's relation to other social phenomena. There is a vast and intellectually significant difference between those scholars who maintain that law is primarily separate from society but is partly determined by it, and those who hold that law is primarily determined by society but is partly separate from it. The differences between these positions are more than matters of emphasis and degree; they go to the very heart of the jurisprudential challenge.

My main focus in this chapter is on the work of those jurists who hold that law is primarily determined by society but is partly separate from it. From a range of perspectives and with a variety of strategies, these scholars maintain that there is a deep logic to social behavior that can be understood by reference to the central distinction between routine instances—the prosaic details of regular activity—and the larger formative context—the framework of institutional arrangements.[4] It is claimed, in construing law and adjudication as routine activities, that they are shaped by the broader context of political forces and social factors. In seeking to identify the fundamental and primary social feature that comprehends and determines others, some isolate the economic relations of capitalist production; others single out the patriarchal basis of gender relations; others give priority to the racist dynamic of ethnic identities; and still others focus on the ennobling dictates of liberal democracy. In each case, the unifying premise is that the prevailing patterns of social behavior and, in particular, the relation between doctrinal development and the material conditions of social life are mediated through and constrained by a foundational category of social organization. Whatever is doing the shaping, law is being shaped; adjudication is a secondary or epiphenomenal site of social behavior.[5]

It is important to understand exactly what common claim is being made by the proponents of these otherwise disparate theories. The fact that there exists a substantial degree of descriptive congruence between the particular feature of social relations and the substantive decisions made by judges is almost beside the jurisprudential point. What distinguishes these deep-logic theories from less ambitious and more parochial ones is not that they posit a connection between a certain aspect of material conditions and law. It is their audacious claim about the nature of that connection—that there exists a causal relation that is largely necessary and sufficient in itself to explain the patterns and changes in doctrinal development. In their most extreme scientistic manifestations, such theorists insist that *all* social action and arrangements can be adequately explained in terms of the favored social relation, be it capitalist exploitation, patriarchal oppression, liberal democracy, or racist domination. As such, these are totalizing accounts par excellence that offer themselves as universal metanarratives through which law and most other sites of social practice can be rendered intelligible and coherent as schemes of institutional (in)justice. In this important sense, deep-logic theories of law and adjudication are as foundationalist as legal theory can be.

The most well known of these deep-logic foundationalist theories is

Marxism. Nevertheless, for all its notoriety, there is very little agreement as to what amounts to a Marxist critique generally, let alone a Marxist theory of law.[6] In offering an account of social justice and injustice as an internally coherent and systemic state of affairs that is constantly changing in inevitable ways, traditional Marxism analyzes society in dynamic rather than static terms; what began as accident gradually crystallizes and ossifies into a fixed system of social relations. It is primarily an account of society in which history is driven by the exploitative and antagonistic economic relations that exist between classes; this material struggle determines that the benefits of production are owned by employers, not workers. As a superstructural phenomenon, law is understood to be an institutional process that responds to and reflects the social base of prevailing economic structures and interests. In this way, law is not so much a neutral or independent site for the resolution of disputes as a social resource to maintain class inequalities and social domination: "The sum total of material relations of production constitutes the economic structure of society" and is "the real foundation on which rises a legal and political superstructure."[7] Law and adjudication are, in very large part, routinized and developed in accordance with the deep structure of these economic relations. While there are occasional anomalies and aberrations, the tune of legal doctrine is called by the piper of established interests.

However, a Marxist approach insists that while the legal process and its personnel function as a coercive weapon (the threat or imposition of criminal sanctions and civil damages), they also operate as an ideological medium (the manufacture of legitimating explanations to gloss over the contradictions and false necessity of the status quo); law is never only the tool of the ruling class, and adjudicative rationality is never only the reflective logic of structural capitalism. As members of the elite, judges hold values and make decisions that are beneficial or, at least, acceptable to that elite. For example, in his analysis of (American) tort law, Richard Abel claims that "contemporary tort law is intimately related to the rise of capitalism, as both cause and effect." In an uncompromising essay, Abel argues that capitalist tort law exploits and alienates accident victims in ways that parallel the exploitation of labor by the capitalist mode of production. Whereas, in the realm of production, those who produce are separated from the fruits of their labor, in tort the legal profession separates victims from the means of redressing their wrongs. Like labor and all other relations in a capitalist society, the victim's injuries and, therefore, victims themselves are reduced to a bare commodity that can be bought and sold for money in the market of personal injuries and insurance. In this way, according to Abel, tort law fulfills the same purpose and operates in the same way as any other social practice:

"A fraction of the dominant class mobilizes the power of the state in its own interests—to protect the property of the capitalist and the monopoly of expertise of the lawyer and physician."[8]

On a different tack but relying on the same deep-logic maneuver, Francis Fukuyama contends that there is an implicit directionality to Western history. Acting as the reactionary sheep of the Marxist flock, he offers "a Marxist interpretation of History that leads to a completely non-Marxist conclusion." Designating America of 1776 as history's first genuine sighting of stable democracy, Fukuyama projects the world beating a path to American liberal democracy on the unfolding carpet of a Universal History whose woof and warp comprise the motifs of political individualism and economic privatism. While it is incompletely implemented and capable of further refinement, the ideal of liberal democracy marks the final end of History: "The modern liberal democratic world . . . is free of contradictions" and "at the end of history, there are no serious ideological competitors left to liberal democracy." Moreover, Fukuyama insists that contemporary events have reinforced such a teleological historiography and warranted the conclusion that "there is a fundamental process at work that dictates a common evolutionary patent for *all* human societies—in short, something like a universal History of mankind in the direction of liberal democracy."[9] Within this scenario, the role of rights and law are treasured and adjudication becomes a privileged site for the elaboration and defense of those liberal entitlements. Fukuyama's liberal account is the lighter side of Marxism's and feminism's darker vision.

At the heart of these deep-logic renditions of foundationalist jurisprudence is the claim that it is possible to generate some reasonably precise, fixed, and workable definitions of its three essential components—the nature and contours of social relations; the shape and substance of legal doctrine; and the character and thread of the connection between them over time. Without some cogent and clear explanation of these three variables, any explanatory or predictive equation will be rendered empty and unhelpful. However, the possibility of settling on a viable set of definitions is remote: no theory will be able to achieve the appropriate mix of analytical generality and historical particularity. Despite efforts to revise their theories, deep-logic jurists will experience the same fate as their more traditional foundationalist counterparts. Just as it cannot be shown that legal doctrine conforms to any simple internal rationality or coherence, so cannot law be reduced to a straightforward function of external organizing principles. While there is clearly an inseparable and organic relation between law and social relations, there is no one account of that relation that is valid for all time, all societies, and all legal developments. Moreover, as soon as it is acknowledged that there is a significant, let alone pervasive, extent of indeterminacy, the posited close and causal relation between legal rules and particular social relations begins to unravel—the relations become more contingent than universal and more ad hoc than necessary. Any explanation becomes indeterminate itself; its character and implications will vary significantly with the historical and social context.

Before exploring the general indeterminacy of legal doctrine, social relations, and their connection, it is useful to dispense with two preliminary but important matters—the challenges of *actualization* and *constitutiveness*. The first deals with the problem of identifying the particular mechanism through which any causal relation between the organizing dynamic of social relations and legal doctrine is put into effect or actualized. As with more traditional foundationalists, like Weinrib, the deep-logic jurists have to explain why judges do what they do in making and changing legal doctrine, especially when judges often claim to be doing something entirely different from what deep-logic theorists claim that they are doing. While the deliberate promotion of class, race, or gender interests obviously occurs, it is sufficiently unusual for it to be done in so stark a way as to supply a convincing explanation for why judges make the particular decisions that they do. The answer, of course, has to do with "ideology" in the sense that law comprises a discourse of power that incorporates certain values and that judges treat as natural, neutral, or inevitable. However, the connection between such a very general and fluid ideological medium and the detailed patterns of legal doctrine is itself very general and fluid; there is a tilt toward certain very broad preferences but not the degree of partisanship that deep-logic theories would suggest.

Accordingly, some contemporary deep-logic theorists have moderated their more causal and scientific claims by arguing that it is not so much that law is determined by prevailing class, race, or gender interests but that adjudication is carried out "in tune with the main themes in the dominant ideology."[10] However, this concession that law is more loosely related to dominant interests is less a partial modification of deep-logic theory than a sustained rejection of it. Indeed, it sufficiently dilutes the deep-logic rationale that a rendition of "relative autonomy" becomes so wide and open-ended that it loses its distinctive character as a Marxist account. Because almost any legal decision or doctrinal development qualifies as causally related to some dominant interests on such an account, a revised and moderated deep-logic theory will have to abandon its hallmark claim of "necessary connection" or it will come up short as a comprehensive explanation of legal development. After all, even the deep logic of mainstream jurists holds that there is some connection between law and dominant interests.

The second problem of *constitutiveness* concerns the need for a deep-logic jurisprudence to posit a clear separation between law and social relations, if the society's basic dialectic is supposed to determine the development of legal doctrine. However, although economic relations are claimed to give rise to legal relations, the fact is that economic relations are always and already constituted by legal relations. In any organic understanding of history, economic relations are situated in a historical context that is itself defined by its social and legal form. For instance, if capitalism is defined as the private ownership of the means of production, it is difficult to understand how law is determined by such material conditions when "private" and "ownership" are legal constructs. Some theorists have responded by arguing that the point of the base/superstructure metaphor is not to make law irrelevant but to show that capitalist or sexist relations rely upon law to provide the necessary official validation and normative force for the exercise of physical force over the means of production or reproduction: "Bases need superstructures, and they get the superstructures they need because they need them."[11] However, once might is turned into right, it is difficult to sustain the claim that the social base and legal superstructure are separate: they will merge back into one another. It is surely more useful to contend that except in periods of upheaval and transition, law comes to constitute the base of class or gender relations through the domination of a particular ideology. Yet, again, this modification seems to deprive the deep-logic critique of its analytical bite as an account of the causal dynamic between social conditions and law. Indeed, it seems to lead to the distinctly undeep-logic conclusion that law and society are not so much separate as integrated in manifold and mutually generative ways. Of course, because law and politics are fully implicated in one another, it does not mean that they replicate each other in a simple or undistorted fashion. There is no form of social life "out there" independent of the law that constitutes and structures it. Nor is there any law "out there" independent of the society that generates and defines itself through that law.[12]

In responding to these critical queries, the obvious challenge for deep-logic theorists has been to revise their original explanatory schema so as to close the gap between theoretical simplicity and practical complexity. Yet, as should now be clear, the would-be revisionists are caught on the horns of a familiar dilemma—to fail to close the gap sufficiently and leave too many anomalies outstanding would risk irrelevance, since empirical validity would be sacrificed to explanatory elegance, but, at the same time, to close the gap entirely and accommodate uncritically all anomalies would also countenance irrelevance, since each anomaly contains the embryo of a competing world view that threatens the very survival of the original theory.

Accordingly, the foundationalist theorist of deep-logic explanation is committed to treading an impossibly thin line between dogmatism and disintegration. As the next sections seek to demonstrate, that revisionist effort in foundational theorizing is difficult enough in regard to the first two problems of actualization and constitutiveness, but it is doomed to failure in regard to the third problem of *indeterminacy* as regards both social relations, legal doctrine, and their interaction.

Not a Game of Snooker

The deep-logic tendency to reduce the complexity of social relations to one simple and single organizing dynamic is nowhere better illustrated than in the vastly influential feminist work of Catharine MacKinnon. Although her views are by no means accepted by all radical legal feminists, they do tend to set the terms of current debate and orthodoxy. Developing a thesis that stands as the most rigorous and uncompromising challenge to the patriarchal theories and practices of contemporary society, she has sought to demonstrate that sexism is a matter of political domination and material subordination, not sexual difference and moral error. She is unrelenting in her determination to unravel the patriarchal threads of the social fabric. When it comes to law, she gives a new and powerful twist to Holmes's famous apothegm that "the life of the law has not been logic, but the experience of men." For her, the law has assumed the male experience as its own and turned it into the natural or neutral account of human experience. In overt and clandestine ways, the law represents and validates men's experience. It does this both substantively and theoretically: not only is the content of the law male but its thinking and forms are male. Law's power and prestige derives from its success at achieving this objectification through a denial of its very happening—the male point of view has effected and effaced itself as no point of view at all. Moreover, the law's apparent defense of freedom has often facilitated rather than curbed the corrupting influence of economic (and, therefore, male) power. For MacKinnon, law is the domination of patriarchy writ official.

In MacKinnon's world of gender relations, relations between men and women are structured around a dynamic of sexual violence in which "women exist in a context of terror."[13] Domination is the inescapable order of the day, and sex is an unmitigated war in which violation is the defining characteristic. Sex and sexual abuse are treated as indistinguishable; it is a relation in which "men may dominate and women must submit."[14] Within this sordid reality, there is little to distinguish prostitution from marriage and violent assault from consensual sex; romance and rape walk hand in hand down history's boulevards. For MacKinnon, the social roles of men and women are fixed by this violent dynamic: sexuality is eroticized inequality and sexual pleasure is a perverse achievement that is inextricably caught in a demeaning spiral of male dominance and female submission. Heterosexual encounters are a one-dimensional terrain where men actualize their potential as irrepressible rapists and women await their realization as hapless victims. Indeed, in such a patriarchal world, women are not only abused in what passes for sex but lose their status as human beings.

As a thematic observation and general conclusion, MacKinnon's account is potent and pervasive. Her uncompromising work has changed profoundly the sexual cartography of the jurisprudential landscape. As depicted by MacKinnon, sexual relations are an infernal occurrence of Dantesque proportions; erotic pleasure is as elusive as sexual inequality is endemic. However, in seeking to drive home her argument, MacKinnon succumbs to the temptation to represent the discourse of patriarchy as much more hegemonic and totalizing than it actually is. MacKinnon is right that violence against women is not aberrational or pathological; it is a staple feature of contemporary gender relations. Moreover, it is reasonable to assume that all men, even those who decry it and desist from it, benefit from the prevalence of abuse because women become more vulnerable and acquiescent to male advances.[15] Nevertheless, although sexual violence is a significant dimension of contemporary society, the relations between men and women are not reducible in some essential or necessary way to such a simple and flat metanarrative. The experiences of pleasure and oppression are much more nuanced and much less tractable than MacKinnon reports—celibacy, masturbation, and rape are not the only alternatives. Women (and men) may be trapped creatures in the iron cage of patriarchy, but its socio-legal bars are not as secure nor as closed as MacKinnon would have us believe.

In MacKinnon's scenario, there are only banal Barbie and Ken stereotypes into which all the differences and diversity that mark women and men are shoehorned. There is no room in MacKinnon's world for heterosexual dominatrices, lesbian sadists, gay masochists, or the like. At best, these deviant characters are falsely conscious sexual actors who are acting out the obligatory two-role drama of heterosexual domination. Moreover, gender identity is the primary hallmark of people's lives. Although people's class, race, ethnicity, and other characteristics might influence and modulate sexual encounters, they are distinctly peripheral and secondary in their impact. Gender is the primary and primeval force at work in sex matters. Social life comprises the inevitable enactment of a vicious script in which men and women conform to the "deterministic divine will" of a patriarchal playwright.[16] For MacKinnon, the raper and the raped exist prior to any act and, therefore, all they do is to play out their scripted roles. There is no sense in which they can be in control of their own lives and fates: men cannot escape their performances as rapists, and women can only wait to be violated. Both seem to be fulfilled and confirmed in their humanity through such sexual violence.

Within MacKinnon's erotic taxonomy, there are only three kinds of women who can claim to experience sexual pleasure—the intimidated "Linda Lovelace," the deluded "Phyllis Schlafly," and the collaborationist "Nadine Strossen."[17] In each case, the experience of sexual pleasure is simulated or illusory because it is unauthenticated by the existence of male domination. While there exist many examples of each kind of woman, it is doubtful that the multiplicity of women's identity and sexual experience can be reduced to a tripartite schema in which all women are united in their status as victims of sexual violence and are only divided in the circumstances of their submission to it. It is surely problematic to assert that each woman's sexual experience with different men is essentially the same and can be meaningfully gathered under the rubric *rape*.[18] While the attainment of sexual pleasure is always precarious and problematic in a sexist society, it is surely exaggerated to suggest that such pleasure is never attainable and that what individual women experience as sexual pleasure is actually the sensation of being raped. The fact that present laws fail to do an effective job at distinguishing between consensual sex and rape is no reason to maintain that there is no important or viable difference between the two. Of course, many women are intimidated and brutalized into subordination by and for men. But any account of women's oppression that gains so much of its theoretical purchase from its depiction of women as duped or pusillanimous victims is to be resisted. Not only does MacKinnon's patronizing explanation deny the diversity of women's experience, but it impugns the courage and achievement of many women. Hemmed in by the deprivations of class and race, most women are not the dupes of a misogynist mind-set.

A focused example of MacKinnon's commitment to a simplistic and scientistic account of social relations can be found in her claims about the nature of the connection between pornography and rape. She is insistent that there is a direct and unmediated causal relation between men's consumption of pornography and their infliction of harm on women. In defending her claim that there is a clear and uncontestable connection between pornography and rape, she states:

> The evidence of harm of [pornographic] materials—from the testimony of witnesses . . . to laboratory studies in which variables and predisposed men are controlled for, to social studies in which social

reality is captured in all its messiness—shows that these materials change attitudes and impel behaviour in ways that are unique in their extent and devastating in their consequences. In human society, where no one does not live, the physical response to pornography is nearly a universal conditioned male reaction, whether they like or agree with what the materials say or not. There is a lot wider variation in men's conscious attitude toward pornography than there is in their sexual responses to it.[19]

The problem with MacKinnon's account is that it is much too reductionist and simplistic. The relation between one social practice and another is much more complex and contingent than MacKinnon is prepared to concede. As part of a dynamic historical process, social interaction cannot be described once and for all in terms of a universal social law.[20] To attempt to discover a crude Newtonian-like nexus between social patterns of events and occurrences is to engage in a philosophically futile and politically suspect search. Even as depicted in the scientific language of causation, the physical world is probabilistic and continuous, not unique and dichotomous. The unfathomable interaction of different causes prevents the isolation of particular causes for particular injuries: the best that can be achieved is a general correlation of acts and consequences in terms of their statistical aggregation so as to establish a rebuttable hypothesis of probabilistic generality. When it comes to the world of human living, society is in such constant flux that its operation cannot be reduced to one formulaic narrative. Moreover, for any theory of social causality to carry any explanatory clout, it must be able to account for the intentions and motivations of social actors: people are not billiard balls in a cosmic game of snooker.

On some occasions of violence against women, pornography will be a weighty factor; on other occasions, it will play no part. Indeed, it might be that, in some instances, pornography provides an outlet for some men that assuages their sexual desires and prevents further violence against women. This possibility, of course, speaks to the larger proposition that pornography might be a symptom of a sexist society rather than its major cause, as MacKinnon suggests. Pornography can be seen as mirroring the violence that goes on, both feeding it and feeding on it. Some societies that lack a pornography industry as such also have traditions and practices of violence against women. While pornography can exacerbate and partially legitimate those practices, it is doubtful that it generates and originates them. Other images contribute to a social milieu in which women are devalued and, therefore, vulnerable to unequal treatment; the stereotype of the "economic man" and its idealized feminine other is as detrimental as the tumescent "stud" and its nymphomaniac other.[21] Furthermore, MacKinnon's instrumentalist account demonstrates the same kind of fundamentalist assumptions that encourage some reactionaries to argue that the exposure to homosexual people and ideas is the cause of children becoming gays and lesbians.

Nevertheless, because MacKinnon's instrumental view of the relation between pornographic causes and violent effects is discredited, it does not mean that the explanation of any correlation between the two is not possible: to think that would be to imagine that the MacKinnon's billiard ball theory of cause and effect is the only useful or most meaningful one in play. The impact of pornography on women is better understood in more contextual and less absolutist terms.[22] Because pornography always stands in need of interpretation, its meaning is too contingent and contextual to underwrite any general causative description of its effect on particular acts of violence against women. Pornography and its effects have to be understood in the only way that they can be—as discursive practices that constitute and are constituted through reality. While neither determinate nor free-standing in its meanings, pornography is a social resource through which men and women assume and constitute their sexual identities and desires. Its effects and consequences will vary with its social setting and historical context in the same way that its causes and motivations will vary. As a discourse of violence, some kinds of pornography can inculcate a set of social constructs that project sexual pleasure and misogynist violence as mutually reinforcing.

While pornography can and does cause harm to women, the effect of pornography is not as universal in its extent or as uniform in its consequences as MacKinnon claims. The same pornographic material will have different effects at different times, in different places, and for different people. The dissemination of certain images and representations in certain situations might be productive of social styles and sexual identities that normalize violence against women: a steady diet of violent pornography to very young children would seem to be a very hazardous course of instruction about sex. While the effect of pornography is not rape, it does contribute to a social practice in which some men can be desensitized to the nature of abuse and the harm that it does.[23] It can be a formative influence in the kind of society that makes such acts more thinkable and realizable. Pornography will not be *the cause*—a sine qua non—but one that goes into the mix that cannot be isolated in its effect nor negatived as a possible cause. Pornography does not operate as a one-on-one individualized phenomenon that causes a particular man to rape a particular woman, but it can generate a social environment in which women are devalued as a group and sex is presented as eroticized violence through which men gratify themselves. Accordingly, pornography has no necessary or inherent meaning. Like anything and everything else, it stands in need of interpretation, and those interpretations will not be reducible to the kind of blanket condemnation that MacKinnon levels.

For instance, while MacKinnon sees nothing other than demeaning images and portrayals of violated women, other women contend that pornography can—although not in any necessary or inherent way—"validate a range of female sexuality that is wider and truer than that legitimated by the non-pornographic culture."[24] To resist this challenge to her essentialist and one-dimensional account of pornography and its effects, MacKinnon falls back again on the elite view that while she can speak truth to pornographic power, other women (and certainly men) cannot be trusted with its corrupting influence. However, it is in her claims about the effects that pornography has on men that MacKinnon is at her most essentialist and outrageous. For example, in explaining the "nearly universalised male reaction" to pornography, she makes the claim that "there is a lot wider variation in men's conscious attitudes toward pornography than there is in their sexual responses to it."[25] This is a truly sweeping claim about the uniformity of men's violent reaction to pornography. All men, regardless of age, education, physical ability, class, ethnicity, and especially sexual orientation, are captive to their nonconscious appetites. Indeed, the claim is so sweeping that it seems to almost exonerate men from any genuine responsibility for their actions. In MacKinnon's portrayal, all men are reduced to little more than Pavlov's dogs, sexual beasts who can neither resist nor reform their violent tendencies to all women. It is simply part of the biological urge that comes from being born with male genitalia. Yet this would reduce completely sex to biology and reject entirely the idea of the socially constructed nature of gender and sexuality.

To contend that MacKinnon's foundationalist account of pornography's causality is a caricature is not to deny that men are violent to women or that pornography is harmful. But it is to question MacKinnon's account as a way of understanding and, most important, of changing the situation in which violence against women is far too commonplace in contemporary society. Contrary to her intentions, MacKinnon manages to reify the patriarchal script of history and to make its continued performance almost inevitable. She casts reality as being outside discourse and, therefore, almost beyond people's control and transformation. Nothing necessarily follows from exposure to pornography. In the same way that reading "good books" is not guaranteed to make better people, watching pornography is not certain to make worse people.[26] In contrast to MacKinnon's essentialism, a nonfoundational approach insists on treating experience as contingent rather than metaphysical: it talks in terms of likelihoods, not certainties. By doing so, it ensures that experience is always within politics (and therefore open to reappropriation and revalorization by women) and not outside politics (and therefore closed to women's transformative action). Accordingly, because a clean break from extant practices is not possible, the nonfoundational challenge is to accept the political code and social systematization of patriarchy, not so as to comply with it but to disrupt and destabilize it.

Finally, an unanticipated consequence of MacKinnon's claim that patriarchal power is pervasive and that women's oppression is a wall-to-wall experience is that, if true, her own work would be severely compromised. In blunt terms, the central question has to be: How is MacKinnon able to know, in regard to prostitution, rape, or sex generally, what all other women do not know and what many actually deny to be the case? The fact is that MacKinnon's work does not permit her to make any consistent or cogent answer to that question. If she claims to know what other women cannot know, she has to concede that male domination is not as perfected as she argues that it is. However, if she insists that male domination is total, she undercuts the very epistemological ground from which she claims to write. The answer is that MacKinnon is both right and wrong. She is right in arguing that patriarchy is pervasive but wrong in arguing that it is perfected. However, she is wrong in arguing that she has a unique privilege or insight, but right in arguing that many women are not aware of their oppressed condition. In short, MacKinnon overstates the hegemony of patriarchy and runs perilously close to grounding her analysis of women's oppression in a notion of "essential womanhood." Her account is so flat, static, and all-embracing that there is no space or opening from which to launch any transformative action: she can only chronicle the sources and strategies of victimization rather than provide explanations that themselves can become forms and founts of resistance.[27] For MacKinnon, domination becomes a seamless web that is total in its intelligibility and, being bereft of complexity and contradiction, is exclusionary in its politics.

Coming Up Short

Accordingly, as far as social relations are concerned, there is too much messiness to sustain any precise definition of a single and primary category. Indeed, the concentration on one category of social relations is too restrictive; not only is each category itself internally confused, but it cannot claim any universal priority over other categories. For instance, in the late twentieth century, the intersection of economic, racial, military, technological, national, gender, and personal interests have added to the complexity of society such that it is impossible to demark the clear class lines that Marx relied upon so extensively. Capitalism no longer exists as a conceptual unity or historical entity. While society may be hegemonic, it is not monolithically or uniformly so. What Marx himself recognized (but what many of his followers have forgotten or chosen to ignore) is that society is never static or still; it is always in flux. Accordingly, the effort to fix on a workable definition of class interests is confounded and defeated by the inescapable historicity and messiness of social activity and change: "The different institutional features that defined the global conception of capitalism could be taken apart, recombined, and replaced in different ways and degrees . . . [such that] no general causal relationship seemed likely to apply to so haphazard a collection of traits."[28] Similarly, in the same way that the priority of "class" was rejected by feminists who insisted that it was unable to explain adequately the persistent patterns of patriarchy, feminism itself has been challenged by those who maintain that the category of "woman" is diverse and multiple; it is intersected by considerations of race, sexuality, and class and cannot be reduced to the political interests and social identities of the white, heterosexual, and middle-class woman. At the heart of these exchanges is the more general and debilitating critique that oppression takes place in all kinds of ways and in all kinds of places: any critical account of politics must resist the temptation to shoehorn the dynamic flux of society into one single and simple deep-logic theory of social explanation.

As far as law is concerned, the Marxists and other deep-logic jurists are obliged to take an equally determinate and unconvincing account of adjudication and the development of legal doctrine. They tend to be formalistic in the way that they construe and represent legal rules. An example is found in the work of Peter Gabel and Jay Feinman. Focusing more on the operation of law as a conditioning mode of consciousness, they trace "the relationship between the history of contract law and the development of capitalism over the last two hundred years." They argue that capitalism has progressed through three distinct stages over the past two centuries. Early-eighteenth-century economic life, premised on status and social responsibility, was hostile to commercial enterprise. These traditional patterns of social relations were burst asunder in the late eighteenth and early nineteenth centuries as society was split into capital-owning and nonowning classes; free-market capitalism achieved its fullest development. However, in the twentieth century, unbridled competition has been replaced by integration, coordination, and the dominance of monopoly. Feinman and Gabel claim that each period in economic history generated a set of "ideological or utopian imagery" that served to justify the underlying hierarchy and division in the social world—eighteenth-century rules were based on the implementation of customary religious and moral principles; nineteenth-century contract law emphasized the principle of freedom of choice and refused to police the fairness of bargains; and the dominant principle in twentieth-century contract law is the regulation of free competition by trade custom. These two jurists refuse to explain the congruence between socioeconomic reality and legal consciousness as the product of conspiratorial manipulation by lawyers and judges. Instead, they prefer the Gramscian explanation that lawyers and judges tend to identify with the structure of the economic order and thus become "imbued" with the "logic of the system." In arguing and deciding cases, they reach results that conform to that "logic" and thereby legitimize it.[29]

As evidenced by Gabel and Feinman, the work of deep-logic jurists are more resolutely foundationalist than almost any other jurists in their grounded claims about the status and meaning of legal rules. Marxists view the development and application of rules as proceeding in a determinate and fixed way with much less room for hermeneutical improvisation than is traditionally allowed; the game of law is played out within the clear confines of a relatively fixed set of rules.[30] However, as I have insisted throughout, legal rules do not have the extent or depth of interpretive determinacy that deep-logic jurisprudence projects and requires; legal doctrine is never simply there but always stands in need of interpretation. The meaning of legal rules does not exist before or outside the context of its apprehension and remains thoroughly provisional in status and strength. Indeterminacy is not a penumbral feature of legal doctrine but pervades its entire existence. Accordingly, legal doctrine is not a reflected embodiment of an external set of social relations that is sufficient to discipline law's textual imprecision: it is the formal site for the attempted but elusive blending and reconciliation of competing social forces and influences. The temporary accommodations made are as much a result of historical expediency and contingent circumstance as ideological purity or political logic.

The fact that the two entities to be connected—social relations and legal doctrine—are themselves indeterminate would likely be enough without more to scuttle any claims that there is some necessary and causal connection between the two. Notwithstanding this, the historical relation between law and particular formations of social relations is decidedly indeterminate. In a manner of speaking, the indeterminacy thesis is itself indeterminate. Law is indeterminate not in relation to a stable social context but because of the contingency of that social context. The socioeconomic context is itself largely indeterminate and requires no particular rule for its continued survival. While a shift in the entire regime of legal rules (e.g., contract and property) might well be significant, the existence or shading of large doctrinal areas (e.g., the postal rules, the finders' rules, and the change-of-name rules) would not be crucial to the preservation of particular class interests. In the same way that the socioeconomic context underdetermines law, that very same law overdetermines the possible outcomes to any legal dispute. There is a general and pervasive indeterminacy that plagues all attempts, not simply jurisprudential ones, to explain social events and to fix social knowledge in any strongly objective way. As such, a nonfoundationalist account of law resists the instrumentalist idea that it is possible to map with any certainty the correlation between, on the one hand, the forces that give rise to particular rules and doctrines and, on the other hand, the interests that those rules and doctrines serve. Except in specific contexts, history is too messy and mobile to pair causes and effects with any confidence, let alone devise general accounts of legal causality. All attempts to justify a foundational metanarrative of the past, either from a materialist right or left, that claims to maintain a distinction between essence and accident as a matter of universal necessity are invalid. Law is "neither a ruling-class game plan nor a repository of noble if perverted principles . . . , [but instead] a plastic medium of discourse that subtly conditions how we experience social life."[31]

None of this is to be taken as saying that historical or legal development is whimsical or serendipitous. On the contrary, what is being said is that there is no one monolithic and unified account of the past that stands in for history. In place of such totalizing metanarratives, the emphasis must be placed on the generation of alternative micro accounts of contextual history. However, the stricture to avoid totalistic, static, or vulgarly deep-logic analyses of society must not be met at the expense of divorcing social structures and values from the historical setting from which they take shape and on which, in turn, they react. For instance, a nonfoundationalist perspective does not require that analyses of law in terms of class, gender, or race be abandoned—far from it. Such detailed and focused accounts are a vital part of any comprehensive and compelling account of law and adjudication. For the nonfoundationalist, it is not the existence of such studies that is problematic but the generalized claims made for them.[32] Rich and episodic accounts of the formative relation between law and society can advance knowledge about both legal and social development, but their scholarly authors must resist the foundationalist temptation to extrapolate to universal claims about the general relation between law and society or to isolate the deep logic of social and legal change. Accordingly, law and adjudication are relatively autonomous from the social struggles of history at certain times and places, legal doctrine is primarily separate from society but is partly determined by it, and, at other time and places, legal doctrine is primarily determined by society but is partly separate from it. There is no one unsituated or once-and-for-all accounting of that interaction.

A good example of the kind of jurisprudential work that should be done and of the kind of claims that should not be made for such work are the historical writings of E. P. Thompson. In his justly famous monograph, Thompson examines how the barbarous Black Act of 1723 came into effect and ostensibly imposed a harsh code of prohibitions and punishments on poachers; it was the intended denouement in a class struggle over a coveted means of production—the plentiful bounty of England's rural forests. However, in carefully uncovering the local and varied implementation of the act, he demonstrates that its brutality was moderated by the mercy of its judicial guardians. Thompson makes it clear that while parts of his story support the thesis that law is the crude instrument of the ruling class, it also demonstrates the extent to which law can be "seen simply in terms of its own logic, rules, and procedures—that is, simply *as law*." For him, the two—legal logic and political expediency—go hand in hand; they are not separate entities but rather related ideas that conjoin in practice to greater and lesser extent:

> The essential precondition for the effectiveness of law, in its function as ideology, is that it shall display an independence from gross manipulation and shall seem to be just. It cannot seem to be so without upholding its own logic and criteria of equity; indeed, on occasion, by actually *being* just.

In developing this jurisprudential theme, Thompson is clear that the Rule of Law is not a complete sham, in that, without some semblance of just operation, law would be unable to perform its legitimating function. He maintains that the rulers in society become the prisoners of their own rhetoric: "They played the games of power according to the rules which suited them, but they could not break those rules or the whole game would be thrown away."[33]

Although many have taken Thompson to be making grand claims about the deep logic that governs the general connection of law and social relations, it is mistaken to extrapolate from those findings to more universalizable statements about law in general at different times and in different places. The relation between law and social conditions is indeterminate and indeterminately so. Like law and society themselves, the relationship is contingent, and its precise nature will vary with the context. In line with a nonfoundationalist perspective, "anything might go," but whether it actually does or does not go will depend on many things, including the political context, the individualized circumstances of each adjudicative incident, the personalities involved, and the perceived implications of different resolutions. For instance, in contrast to foundationalist scholars, like Abel and Gabel, who see capitalism as progressing through a defined series of stages with each economic period generating a recognizable body of legal doctrine informed by the deep structure of the prevailing mode of production, it might be more instructive to depict the evolution of legal doctrine as an endless conflict between opposing and unassimilable world views. Because each vision is a contradiction of the other rather than a mere contrast to it, neither vision is able to mold the legal materials precisely in its own image. Instead, contemporary legal doctrine must be understood as an endless series of ad hoc and fragile compromises between contradictory political impulses. Whereas Marxist foundationalists (even those of a more modest persuasion than Abel and Gabel) are committed to the idea of an ordered social world in which law is informed by the deep logic of that structure, a nonfoundationalist critique does not hedge on the corrosive implications of historical contingency and regards as futile the attempt to discover a derivative logic to the legal materials that operates across time, place, and different areas of law: "The outcomes of struggle are not preordained by any aspect of the social totality, and the outcomes within law have no *inherent logic*."[34] Such an approach does not deny that legal doctrine's task is to maintain the false distinction between law and politics or that established interests benefit from legal development. A nonfoundational critique simply claims that such a conclusion cannot be turned into scientific or universalizable theories.

In the next section, I will develop a particular understanding of the nonfoundational relation between law and social conditions. Although the informing insight will be the indeterminacy of that relation and any particular theoretical attempts to understand it, I will suggest that this does not mean that the ambition of theorizing in general is self-defeating or that "anything goes." In particular, I will respond implicitly to twin charges that are made about the difficulties with such an approach—either that the critique of legal doctrine is too instrumental and neglects law's partial intellectual autonomy and transformative possibilities or that the critique overstates the indeterminacy of legal doctrine and ignores its instrumental connections to larger political forces.[35] Accordingly, in light of such a double threat, I illustrate the politics of legal indeterminacy by tracking the modern development of the law of torts and its relation to other social structures, material conditions, and intellectual currents, with especial reference to the contorted relationship between contract and tort as exemplified in the perennial puzzle over the recoverability of so-called "pure economic loss"—can Mrs. Donoghue and her doctrinal descendants recover for the diminished value of their flawed or damaged products? Because of both the considerable doctrinal movement and political upheaval over the past few decades, there is more than the usual amount of judicial and scholarly introspection on the theoretical underpinnings of tort law, the nature of the judicial enterprise, and the motivation and causes of those doctrinal developments. Nevertheless, while the varying trajectory of tort law and the related shifts in contract law offer a vivid opportunity to assess the relation of legal doctrine to broad changes in the constitutive (and constituted) context of political culture and social relations, it would contradict a nonfoundational perspective to attempt to extrapolate too generally to each and every episode in legal and social change.

Snail Tales

The snail had known better days. And the unsuspecting May Donoghue was to know healthier times. But this unlikely encounter between a decomposing mollusk and a Scottish shop assistant in 1928 set the main stage for the evolving drama of the common law. When Mrs. Donoghue and her friend went to Paisley's Wellmeadow Cafe on a bright summer's evening, she could have had no inkling of the doctrinal mayhem that their innocent social outing was to wreak. Seeking only modest refreshment, she received a severe dose of gastroenteritis and a few days in Glasgow Royal Infirmary. Championed by the irrepressible Walter Leechman, she was able to obtain five years later from the estate of the late David Stevenson, the offending ginger beer's manufacturer, a settlement of four hundred dollars for her troubles. Nonetheless, it was the law and legal theory, at least as practiced by foundationalist scholars, that probably suffered the more lasting discomfort. Indeed, Thomas Minchella, the café's owner, served up a noisome concoction that the common law has still not managed to get out of its system and that continues to cause traditional jurists more than their fair share of doctrinal queasiness. However, courts and commentators have been slow to realize that the real challenge is not to purge the common law of this doctrinal contagion but to adapt themselves to this unsettled condition as law and adjudication's normal state of health. In legal terms, *Donoghue* v. *Stevenson* was the first major case to explore the fractious relation between contract and tort. Lord Atkin's pioneering judgment about "reasonable foreseeability" set the tone and standard for future doctrinal contributions to the law and politics of civil obligation. The ensuing six decades have witnessed the common law's efforts both to respond to the changing demands of economic life and to negotiate the competing pushes and pulls of Contract and Tort for doctrinal priority. Indeed, as well as establishing the basic substantive terms within which this doctrinal struggle would occur, Atkin also laid out the formal challenge for judges—to uncover "some general conception of relations giving rise to a duty of care, which the particular cases found in the books are but instances."[36] However, typical of the common law generally, the judicial history of this civil doctrine cannot be charted in line with an unfolding internal intelligibility or an insistent external logic; it progresses in fits and starts through a haphazard series of factual encounters (involving decomposed snails, peeling floors, diseased cattle, broken bridges, dead fish, and collapsing walls) in which the judges have little choice other than to work and rework a familiar but inconclusive series of argumentative maneuvers. In this judicial performance, the law is less working itself pure, as many traditionalists contend, than simply seeking to work itself through a set of ludic encounters in the best way that they can at the particular time and under the particular circumstances. Indeed, efforts to effect a suitable rapprochement between Contract and Tort reverberate to the echo of Lord Buckmaster's chilling chant of "If one step, why not fifty?"[37] It is a question that judges and jurists must always answer but that they can never resolve.

Contrary to common understanding, *Donoghue* did not release tort liability onto an unsuspecting legal world. While contract was the primary mode of civil obligation, there existed a patchwork quilt of statutory and judicial schemes of tort liability. *Donoghue* extended liability to some new areas but also reduced liability in other old areas from its existing strictness.[38] In his celebrated judgment, Atkin introduced the general notion that a civil obligation arises between "neighbours" to take care for each other's safety. Consequently, Mrs. Donoghue could recover damages for her sickness and, because they were a direct consequence, her lost wages. Nevertheless, while *Donoghue* extended the general provenance of negligence liability and remained silent on the issue of pure economic loss, it is clear that Mrs. Donoghue could not recover the diminished value of the ginger beer. No claim was made by Mrs. Donoghue for the reduced value of her ginger beer. Not only did she have more important and pressing concerns, but it is highly unlikely that she would have been successful in such a claim, whether it was a bottle of ginger beer or something much more substantial in importance and value. Since 1875, there had been a rule against the recovery of economic loss in tort: while plaintiffs could recover for damage to themselves and their property, they could not recover lost wages as a result of their place of employment being closed by the defendant's negligence.[39]

This situation prevailed until 1964 when the momentous decision in *Hedley Byrne* was reached. A defendant bank had negligently provided incorrect information about a customer's financial status to the plaintiff, who relied on it to its substantial cost. The House of Lords was prepared to lift the rule against the recovery of pure economic loss because the advice was given in a professional situation and the defendant knew that the plaintiff might act on it. However, the defendant avoided liability as there was a disclaimer clause attached to the information provided. Accordingly, while the case was framed in tort principles, the fact that the parties were in "a relationship equivalent to contract" was vitally important: the duty is more restrictive than in *Donoghue* because of the fear that liability for negligent misstatements would be more difficult to determine than negligent acts.[40] Moreover, *Hedley Byrne* left the law in a state of considerable confusion. Prior to the decision, there was no liability for negligent statements or pure economic loss. After the decision, there was recovery for negligent statements and, of necessity, for pure economic loss. Did this mean that pure economic loss was now generally recoverable?

In subsequent cases, the courts blew hot and cold in their responses. In some cases, they stuck with the requirement that there was to be no recovery for economic loss unless it was consequential upon physical or property damage. For instance, in *Spartan Steel*,[41] where the defendant struck an electrical wire that serviced the plaintiff's factory, the court held that while any property damaged and the consequential profit expected from that property could be recovered, the lost profits from further loss of production in the time that the factory was closed could not be recovered, as there had been no property damage during that period: it was a pure economic loss whose recovery was better governed by the rules for contractual liability. In other cases, the courts allowed recovery for pure economic loss where there had been no originating physical or property damage. For instance, in *Dutton*,[42] a municipality was held liable to a subsequent owner for the cost of repairing a house's defective foundations because the municipality had negligently inspected them and approved them as being in accordance with building regulations. While the court characterized this as physical damage resulting from a negligent statement, it is now generally agreed that the defendant's negligence was as much an act or omission as a statement and that the plaintiff's loss was purely economic in nature; there was no undamaged house that was later damaged by the defendant's negligence.

However, by 1978, the courts had begun to concede that some recovery for economic loss was possible. Although it was primarily concerned with the tort liability of municipalities, the House of Lord's decision in *Anns* accepted that where there had been a negligent failure to inspect properly the defective foundations of a housing block and structural damage had begun to appear, the plaintiff could recover the reduced market value of the property. In seeking to satisfy Atkin's aspiration to establish a single framework for analyzing the duty of care, Lord Wilberforce declared that it was no longer necessary to proceed by way of a case-by-case basis. Instead, courts should ask "whether there is a sufficient relationship of proximity or neighbourhood such that, in the reasonable contemplation of [the defendant], carelessness on his part may be likely to cause damage to [the plaintiff], in which case a prima facie duty of care arises." Once this is established, the court should then look to "any considerations which ought to negative, or to reduce or limit the scope of the duty or the class of person to whom it is owed or the damages to which a breach of it may give rise."[43] In laying down such a general two-step approach, the House of Lords made it almost inevitable that further exceptions would be established to the rule against recovery of economic loss. Indeed, a year later in 1979 in *Ross* v. *Caunters*, it was held that a frustrated beneficiary could succeed in recovering the value of a projected legacy from the defendant solicitor who had negligently failed to follow the deceased's testamentary wishes. In reaching his decision, Vice Chancellor Megarry stated that "the basis of the solicitor's liability to others is either an extension of *Hedley Bryne* or, more probably, a direct application of the principle of *Donoghue*."[44] It seemed only a matter of time, therefore, before some future case did away with the separate and exclusionary rule for economic loss entirely.

Junior Books Ltd. was that case. In short, it did away with the requirement of related damage to person or property and made the existence of defectively manufactured property sufficient to trigger tortious liability. As well as appearing to put recovery for economic loss on the same footing as other losses, the House of Lord effectively placed Tort ahead of Contract in the doctrinal hierarchy of civil obligations. The pertinent facts were that during the construction of a factory, a subcontractor negligently laid a defective floor; there was no contract between the subcontractor and the factory owner. Although the floor was not dangerous, the owner had the floor relaid at a cost of $100,000, with an extra $300,000 in expenses due to lost production, in order that the company's precision machinery would operate more efficiently. While the law lords held that the recovery of all $400,000 was appropriate, the precise basis on which they did this was not entirely clear. The parties were in a sufficiently close relationship to meet the requirements for an established duty (whether based upon neighborhood, special relationship, or proximity), but the substance and scope of such a duty needed to be established. While it could simply amount to a duty to perform a service in a nonnegligent manner, it might also entail a general duty to all neighbors to meet any reasonable (contractual) expectations. Whichever it was, such extensive recovery in tort would significantly undermine the significance of contiguous contractual relationships between parties: the plaintiff would be able to insist on compensation from the defendant even when the defendant might not have known that the plaintiff had special demands or that there was no risk of physical injury to the plaintiff. The nature of the challenge was clearly put by Lord Roskill. In responding to the argument that recovery for the diminished value of a defective product should only sound in contract, he stated:

> I seem to detect in that able argument reflections of the previous judicial approach to comparable problems before *Donoghue* was decided. That approach usually resulted in the conclusion that in principle the proper remedy lay in contract and not outside it. But that approach and its concomitant philosophy ended in 1932 and for my part I should be reluctant to countenance its re-emergence some fifty years later in the instant case. I think today the proper control lies not in asking whether the proper remedy should lie in contract or . . . tort, not in somewhat capricious judicial determination whether a particular case falls on one side of the line or the other, not in somewhat artificial distinctions between physical and economic or financial loss when the two sometimes go together and sometimes do not . . . , but in the first instance in establishing the relevant principles and then in deciding whether the particular case falls within or without those principles.[45]

Under such a legal regimen, it would no longer be taken for granted that contract was the primary mode of imposing civil obligations or that, without the existence of a contract, people had no legal obligation to safeguard the economic interests of others. Indeed, the upshot of *Junior Books* might well have been that a plaintiff in tort could be better off than a similar plaintiff with a relevant contract because warranties would run with the product: a subsequent purchaser could have a broader range of legal rights and remedies than the original purchaser. In effect, the role of contract would be to vary preexisting tort duties. In a neat inversion of history, contract would become the caulking of the gaps in tort's general scheme of civil obligations. Manufacturers' liability would no longer rest on the formalistic dictates of contractual privity but on the substantive demands of social justice. However, this doctrinal transformation did not take place. The response to *Junior Books* was decidedly swift and negative. In a series of cases, the courts managed to undermine and cabin the decision without actually overruling it. Abandoning Atkin's search for some golden thread that would make general sense of the law's particulars, the judges opted for a less doctrinaire and more pragmatic approach to tort law: there is "no precedent for the application of strict logic in treading the path leading from the general principle established in *Donoghue* towards the Pandora's Box of unbridled damages at the end of the path of foreseeability."[46]

Only three years after *Junior Books* in 1985, the sole *Junior Books* dissenter, Lord Brandon, had managed to persuade all his fellow judges to come over to his way of thinking. In that judgment, he had tapped into and articulated a distinctive vision of civil obligation that is as traditionally individualistic as Roskill's was progressively communitarian. After wrongly stating that negligence liability had been restricted to instances of physical damage to persons or their property, Brandon cut to the doctrinal chase and warned against the introduction of a "transmissible warrant of quality":

> The effect . . . would be, in substance, to create, as between two persons who are not in any contractual relation with each other, obligations on one of those two persons to the other which are only really appropriate as between persons who do have such a relationship between them. In the case of a manufacturer or distributor of goods, the position would be that [it] warranted to the ultimate user or consumer of such goods that they were as well designed, as merchantable and as fit for their contemplated purpose as the exercise of reasonable care could make them. . . . In my view, the imposition of warranties of this kind on one person in favour of another, when there is no contractual relationship between them, is contrary to any sound policy requirement.[47]

These doctrinal developments culminated in *Murphy*, in which a municipality was held to owe no duty to a subsequent owner when its building inspector failed to find defects in the faulty foundations of the plaintiff's home. It was held that the loss was purely economic and was more appropriately dealt with under contract, not tort. In overruling *Anns*, the rare septet of law lords in *Murphy* left no doubt that *Junior Books* was the high-water mark of civil obligation and that liability based on a "transmissible warrant of quality" was to be strenuously resisted. As Lord Keith put it, cases like *Anns* and *Junior Books* "introduced a new species of liability governed by a principle indeterminate in character but having the potentiality of covering a wide range of situations, involving chattels as well as property, in which it had never hitherto been thought that the law of negligence had any place."[48] Recovery for pure economic loss was thus restricted to situations of close party proximity that are tantamount to contract relationships. Accordingly, only a decade after *Junior Books*, the English courts seemed to have reverted to the more traditional rule of no recovery for economic loss. However, almost no sooner than the ink was dry on its decision, the House of Lords began to erode the general implications of *Murphy* for recovery of economic loss. Moreover, along with a growing tendency to carve out exceptions to the general exclusionary rule, it is very difficult to appreciate or rationalize such departures. For instance, whereas *Henderson* decided that the duty to take care to avoid economic loss was not excluded by the mere existence of a contractual arrangement and *Spring* held that lost job opportunities resulting from a negligently formulated reference could be recovered, *White* reaffirmed the liability of a negligent solicitor to a frustrated beneficiary.[49]

An Outside Look

Jurisprudential efforts to rationalize the development and contemporary state of the legal doctrine on recovery for economic loss are not in short supply. Nevertheless, the width and variety of such scholarly inventiveness should give considerable food for thought. The bulk of attempts are devoted to the more traditional exercise of unearthing a foundational logic or intelligibility that is internal to the law itself and that, although not claiming to account for every twist and turn in the judicial peregrinations, can present the resulting doctrine in rational, consistent, and coherent terms. In working out a doctrinal schema that allows recovery for economic loss in some contexts, while denying it in others, the challenge for the courts has been to map out a network of intersections and turnings that can be rationally defended and intellectually justified within the law's own frame of reference. In an occasion of rare agreement, tort scholars seem to concur in the opinion that the outcome of any case cannot be predicted with any confidence and that there is no one principle—whether it is compensation, deterrence, economic efficiency, retribution, or anything else—that is even "achieved imperfectly and inconsistently."[50] It is not that doctrine is without any logic or intelligibility at all but that any efforts to go beyond the most general or the most detailed account are confounded by the doctrinal and social facts; the explanations become either so abstract as to lack any practical predictive force or so elaborate as to capture only a particular historical moment in time. There are always competing rationales and too many plausible explanations to satisfy the foundationalist need for explanatory primacy or closure. In matters of economic loss, it would seem that the best-laid plans of judges and jurists are destined to fail.

To begin with, the claim that there is any definitive or decisive difference between "foreseeability" and "proximity" is entirely illusory. *Murphy* may have formulated a new test, but the test lacks determinate meaning unless the implicit values that have taken law from *Anns* to *Murphy* by way of *Junior Books* are made explicit. The law lords have marched to the top of the doctrinal hill and marched down again, but they have not really gone anywhere. The formal appearances of *Anns* and *Murphy* may look different, but their reasonable application does not demand any different substantive outcome. Proximity is, therefore, meaningless without discussion of the values and policy choices that energize these cases and operationalize their application. *Murphy* and *Anns* merge together as formal tests; it is the values that are given weight in a case that ultimately decide whether there is proximity or neighborhood. While the motive force behind the move to a test of proximity in economic loss cases is to tie recovery to quasicontractual relationships and to simulate the privity requirement, there is no reason why it could not be used more expansively and accommodate the same values and policy choices as relied on in *Anns*. Accordingly, while the doctrine of economic loss, with its vague distinctions and shallow categorizations, is not quite "a dog's breakfast,"[51] it does not amount to the structured whole that foundationalists project or predict. Indeed, whatever the larger ambitions of jurists, judges seem to have almost given up on the effort to achieve doctrinal integrity. At the very highest level of adjudication, judges can be heard to pronounce that legal principles are merely "convenient labels" for the pragmatic workings of the common law, that proximity "is a black hole into which particular criteria and rules would collapse and from which no illumination of principle would emerge," and that courts should "refuse to accept injustice merely for the sake of doctrinal tidiness."[52] While these comments sustain my nonfoundationalist project, they give little support to the beleaguered efforts of foundationalist jurists (of an internalist or externalist persuasion).

Notwithstanding their failed efforts to rationalize the actual performance of the courts, traditional jurists also seem to be stumped by the challenge of making viable and cogent prescriptions for future judicial endeavors. Even when given a clean slate to write on in their normative theory of choice, tort scholars are at sixes and sevens over the best way to proceed. The fact that there is no one agreed position is of little relevance; the possibility for consensus is so remote as to be fanciful. However, even tort scholars of the same general normative persuasion are divided over an appropriate resolution of economic loss cases. For instance, even among those scholars who subscribe to a law-and-economics approach in which the attainment of "economic efficiency" is paramount, there is very little consensus on what the doctrinal rules for the recovery of economic loss should be: whereas some opt for complete liability, others prefer restricted liability.[53] As well as being of little help over the best doctrinal course to be followed in economic loss cases, this failing points up the considerable bankruptcy of such grand jurisprudential theories generally. While they may be elegant and attractive in their theoretical suggestiveness, they offer indeterminate guidance for the resolution of particular difficulties in concrete circumstances: their normative tilt is often neutralized by the contingent details of situational contexts.

Efforts to rationalize the development and contemporary state of the legal doctrine on recovery for economic loss are not confined to internalist accounts. There is a respectable literature that seeks to demonstrate that while it seems to lack any particular rhyme or reason when viewed from inside the legal project, legal doctrine does conform substantially to an external dynamic or dialectic in the larger social context that frames and intrudes upon the judicial enterprise. It is this kind of jurisprudential claim that this chapter is most concerned to scrutinize and resist. However, before I engage more substantively with these deep-logic theories, some initial observations can be made about their potential application to the doctrinal development of economic loss. The first prerequisite, of course, for such externalist accounts to have any chance of proving their explanatory worth is that legal doctrine possess some semblance of stability and certainty. Without a relative degree of fixity, deep-logic theory will find itself chasing its own tail. Moreover, as regards a Marxist account of law and social relations, if law is supposed to serve the interests of the business community, it will likely guarantee a set of predictable outcomes in the short to medium term. Above all else, commercial entities desire the law to be certain so that they can make plans and establish coping mechanisms that are based on a settled expectation about the likely legal consequences of different business strategies: uncertainty and unpredictability are the bane of commercial planning. However, the progress of tort law in the past decade or so has been far from certain; it is almost as sporadic, shifting, and unpredictable as it can be. Whatever is going on, it is difficult to argue that the pertinent legal rules are stable or determinate.

Also, insofar as deep-logic theories make universalist claims about their theoretical salience, it is reasonable to expect that similar societies will have similar legal doctrines to deal with similar problems. However, a comparison of developments in England and Canada, for example, does little to give deep-logic jurists any reassurance. Although there is some general pattern of increasing liability, Canadian courts have not felt the need or compulsion to repeat the doctrinal contortions of their English counterparts. While Canadian judges showed an early reluctance to treat economic loss the same as any other head of damage, they have remained committed to the elusive search for a principled resolution to the recalcitrant problem of economic loss. Less concerned at the prospect of Tort eclipsing Contract as the primary mode of civil obligation, they have kept faith with the form and substance of the *Anns* decision, notwithstanding its abandonment by the English courts in *Murphy*: pure economic loss is prima facie recoverable, unless there are convincing policy reasons to deny recovery.[54] Accordingly, like English law, Canadian doctrine represents a patchwork of distinctions and exceptions with no convincing holistic pattern, but, unlike English law, the particular stitching together of the various patches is stylistically and substantively different. Of course, deep-logic theorists might want to dismiss these variations as being so subtle as to be irrelevant, or else attribute to them to subtle differences in the prevailing nature of Canadian social relations. Either course of action is predictably dangerous for the foundationalist—while such explanations would increase the theory's accuracy as a descriptive account, they would reduce its value as a predictive tool.

Nevertheless, while such initial comments cast some doubt on the universalist nature of their accounts, they do not dispense with the claims made by deep-logic theorists of a Marxist inclination. Their central thesis is that the general flow of doctrinal history has been determined by the requirements of established interests, the increased division of labor, and the spread of commodification; the details and rationalizations may vary, but the important thrust and tilt of the law are reducible to the logic of class relations and economic inequality under capitalism. In light of the twists and turns in the doctrinal development of recovery for economic loss, the fulfillment of this theoretical task seems a very tall order. However, some intrepid theorists have not flinched from their foundationalist commitments and have sought to show that tort doctrine's trajectory has tracked social history, at least when properly understood in terms of the struggle over and among the social relations of economic production. In short, Marxist-influenced tort scholars maintain that efforts to expand the recovery of economic loss have been haunted by the capitalist ghost of Baron Bramwell, who never seems to tire of preaching the virtues of a sturdy self-reliance that frowns upon whining efforts to shift blame for one's own misfortunes to others.[55]

Missing the Marx

For foundationalists of a Marxist inclination, the most compelling narrative of doctrinal developments around recovery of economic loss is to be found in the judicial efforts, albeit flawed, to respond to the changing needs of the capitalist dialectic. Indeed, according to such accounts, the seesaw struggle between Contract and Tort over the soul of the common law is emblematic of law's systemic tendency to follow the more overtly ideological battles that characterize and energize the larger structure and course of social relations.[56] Traditional contract law, based on an exchange model of nineteenth-century vintage, did not fit well with the more complex economic relations of the mid-twentieth century and the burgeoning rise of the welfare state. Along with the development of tort law generally, the expansion of economic loss in the 1970s and 1980s through *Hedley Byrne* and *Anns* could be seen as part of a judicial campaign to discipline a species of economic relations that such a contract law could no longer hold in check. However, momentarily ignoring its instrumental effects, the courts pursued the intellectual logic of that position to their fateful decision in *Junior Books* and permitted tort law to overshadow contract law. Chastised of the error of their ways, the law lords' retreat in *Murphy* from the radical potential of *Junior Books* can be attributed to the Thatcher-style revival of free-market economics and public deregulation of business transactions in which contract law regained the ascendancy. In this way, therefore, Marxisant critics argue that the path of legal change can be seen to be in step with the capitalist march of social relations.

There is much to this account: it seems to capture and explain, in a much more convincing way than traditional internalist accounts, the broad sweep of social history and doctrinal development. Over the past sixty years or so, there have been some important changes in the ideological alignment of British society. Following the Great Depression, there was a slow shift toward a welfare state that took increasing control over economic matters. However, by the 1970s there had been a Thatcher-inspired preference for a strengthened reliance upon the market as the prime reform for achieving economic freedom and an accompanying distrust of centralized economic planning. Indeed, this contingent success is interpreted by some as the final triumph of liberalism and politics and capitalism in economics; a posthistorical age is upon us.[57] As a matter of symbolic significance, the invisible hand of the Western market has pushed over the Berlin Wall of the Eastern state. In line with these structural changes, it might be expected that after an increasing fondness for greater tort liability, there would be a general preference for promoting contract as the primary mode of incurring obligation to others and a corresponding loss of appetite for imposing liability through the less consensual device of tort law. Moreover, within contractual doctrine itself, there might be a greater willingness to discard the substantive encrustations of the 1960s and early 1970s and to make it conform more closely to the stripped-down formalities of a market-based ethic. And, indeed, this is what has happened.

In schematic terms, there has been a definite realignment of reliance in the choice of legal principles and justificatory rhetoric. In contract law, over the past twenty-five years, the courts have oscillated between different legal ideologies of civil obligation. Up until 1968, the traditional view predominated in which the market place was to be the exclusive site for competitive exchange and law's role was to facilitate consumers' sovereign choice: clarity of expectation and security of transaction were its central principles, with no after-the-fact ad hoc readjustment. However, in the 1970s, courts began to go more intrusively under the veneer of formal fairness and to evaluate the substantive justness of agreements reached. Eschewing unjust enrichment, there was to be proportionality between the seriousness of the breach and the generosity of the remedy; good faith and equitable dealings were to be the guiding lights of this activist intervention. A few years later, the courts were back on the traditional track. They had reaffirmed the sanctity of party autonomy by questioning the pertinence of unconscionability: formal certainty and settled expectations were always to be preferred to the substantive vagaries of good faith dealings.[58] Moreover, as has been shown, a similar pattern occurred in tort law: the bold expansion of tort recovery in the 1970s and early 1980s was matched by a cautious retrenchment in the 1980s. As one senior judge in 1988 dismissively put it in commenting on *Anns* and its progeny, "Negligence began to resemble the proposition that we are all neighbours now, Pharisees and Samaritans alike, that foreseeability is a reflection of hindsight and that for every mischance in an accident-prone world someone solvent must be liable in damages."[59]

Nonetheless, for all its insight and illumination, a Marxist-influenced foundationalist account of law and society is not a complete or exclusive explanation for such events.[60] While the pattern of doctrinal developments over the imposition of civil obligations is consistent with such a foundationalist account of social history, consistency is not enough. From a foundationalist perspective, it is insufficient to show that legal developments are related to political changes in society: all theories recognize such a connection. Also, it is not enough to show that there is a plausible fit between a Marxist account of social structure and its legal superstructure: they must demonstrate that such a fit is both necessary and sufficient in the sense that it supersedes all other plausible hypotheses. In rejecting the validity of these foundationalist assertions, I do not intend to suggest that they have no explanatory or predictive merit but only that they cannot exert the exclusive and primary normative force that foundationalists scholars claim for them. Marxist accounts of doctrinal development can and do provide fruitful insight into the otherwise arcane workings of the legal process. However, the connections between legal doctrine and material interests are often as casual as they are causal and as contingent as they are necessary: they are as likely to be as wide of the mark in explaining or predicting doctrinal developments as they are directly on target. In short, this leads to the banal but important conclusion that law is related to political and social context but in different ways at different times; there is no one overarching or overriding account of that relation that is valid for all time in all places. Accordingly, the Marxist explanation of the doctrinal digressions of tort recovery for economic loss over the past few decades fails because it cannot achieve the appropriate degree of determinacy—it underdetermines the connection between legal doctrine and social relations such that it has no distinctive claim to make, or it overdetermines the connection between legal doctrine and social relations such that it loses any predictive power.

When legal doctrine reflects or serves capitalist interests, Marxists claim that law is operating instrumentally. But when it is not reflecting or serving such interests, they argue that it is operating ideologically as a legitimating device. So whereas *Murphy* is depicted as a direct reflection and implementation of capitalist concerns, *Junior Books* and *Spring* or *White* are considered to be sops to an oppressed majority in order to give the legal process a modicum of justification as a neutral or independent institution of social justice. This response is canny but unconvincing. Under such an account, Marxist theory would or could never be wrong: all possible future doctrinal moves are capable of being rationalized in accordance with its theoretical intimations. By making its account too general, it loses its distinctive quality and analytic power as a Marxist theory. If all eventualities meet the test, then everything and nothing does. For instance, while the Marxist view seems to be that a noncapitalist system would not compensate property loss at all and would leave property owners to insure against loss or damage,[61] this means that any doctrinal shift, including *Junior Books*, that amounted to anything less than a complete abolition of recovery for economic loss would be treated as compatible with a class-based analysis of legal development. Although this proposal for reform might well be meritorious, such a position implies that whatever the attractions of a Marxist jurisprudence as a political critique, it has little to offer as a predictive account of doctrinal development.

Even when there is a seemingly strong parallel between narrow legal doctrine and broader sociopolitical currents, as appears to be presently so in England, there are always precedential flies in the explanatory ointment. For instance, when combined with the cases of *Henderson*, *Spring*, and *White*,[62] the House of Lords' decision in *Smith* v. *Bush* threatens to turn a judicial anomaly into a doctrinal trend. In relying upon the defendants' negligent survey in purchasing a house, the plaintiff sought damages for the cost of unanticipated repairs. The independent survey had been carried out at the urging of a mortgage company, which, along with the defendant surveyors, had disclaimed liability for the accuracy of any survey. In finding for the plaintiff, the court placed considerable weight on his unequal bargaining power and his actual reliance on the professional's advice.[63] The decision to allow tort liability to trump the existence of two separate contractual disclaimers is difficult to reconcile with the general *Murphy* retrenchment from legally enforced social responsibilities; the court's solicitude for ordinary consumers in this instance is not easy to square with its general reluctance to impose liability for economic losses. However, I say *difficult* rather than impossible to reconcile *Smith* v. *Bush* with the entrepreneurial (re)turn in tort doctrine. An alternative reading of the case could be made that justifies it in the rhetorical terms of a more individualistic vision: the imposition of legal liability upon professional surveyors recognizes the need for robust self-discipline and personal responsibility by all sectors of society, especially its more privileged ones. Accordingly, not only does *Smith* v. *Bush* testify to the indeterminacy of individual decisions' justificatory arguments, but it also underlines the shortcomings of any account that strives to reduce the past, present, and future of doctrinal development and legal change to one explanatory dialectic. There is no one foundation that can ground law, politics, and adjudication that is not itself captive to the very context that it claims to explain.

A nonfoundational account of the relation between law and social relations does not dispense with such ideological accounts of law but refuses to be tempted by their scientistic pretensions. As with more general efforts across society, the development of legal doctrine in the courts is better viewed as involving both an ideological and intellectual struggle over the normative terms and material conditions for social life. Behind every doctrinal body of law, there stands a series of social visions of what it means to *play the game*; these create conflict and uncertainty as much as they give life and meaning to it. As such, all lawyers and judges make a commitment to a social vision that helps them grasp the past tradition of political ordering, the present nature of social reality, the future possibilities for transformative action, and the continuing justifications for these understandings. However, there are many different visions at work in the formulation and interpretation of legal doctrine. Lawyers and judges are divided among and within themselves about the appeal and efficacy of these different constructs. For instance, while far from exhaustive of the possibilities, the law of civil obligations is dominated by two central visions—"individualist" and "communitarian"—that have vied for control of the legal imagination. The basic dynamic has been the competition between social regulation and private freedom for normative primacy and organizational control. It is the way each vision balances centralized authority and individual autonomy that gives it its special ambience and character, not the exclusive preference for one over the other. Of course, there is no metavision that is available to integrate or reconcile these visions in any final or settled way.[64] Despite the occasional insistence on visionary purity, the common law is characterized by a pragmatic mixing and-matching mentality and practice. The individualist and communitarian threads are intertwined throughout the historical tapestry of civil obligation's doctrinal development. They appear from case to case, from judgment to judgment, and occasionally within a single judgment.

Accordingly, legal doctrine is not a reflected embodiment of one indwelling and sufficient vision, but it is rather the formal site for the attempted but elusive blending and reconciliation of competing visions. The temporary accommodations made are as much the result of political expediency as moral purity. It is true to state that the path of doctrinal development does tend to follow social developments; sometimes it pulls slightly ahead and sometimes it lags behind. However, this is not the same as showing that it only feeds the desires and designs of those capitalist interests who control the relations of production. In the same way that Thompson announced that "the greatest of all fictions is that the law evolves, from case to case, by its own impartial logic, true only to its own integrity, unswayed by expedient considerations,"[65] the reverse can be proclaimed with equal force—law does not evolve, from case to case, by the partial logic of class struggle, true only to established interests, unswayed by logical considerations. By different measures at different times, the development of law is a mix of the *logical*—in the sense of attempted compliance with law's own generated (and indeterminate) rationality—and the *expedient*—in the sense of responsiveness to society's own political (and indeterminate) demands. Both logic and expediency infiltrate and affect each other's operation; lawyers and judges are neither only the lackeys of established interests nor always the intellectual captives of a professional tradition. Consequently, the relation between law and its larger sociopolitical context is indeterminate and indeterminately so: there is no analytically snug fit between the two because each is itself continuously in flux and, therefore, indeterminate in general structure and design. Whereas the fit between doctrinal development and politics might be particularly close in some areas and at some times, it will be much more tenuous in other areas and at other times. Contingency is the body and soul of law and legal theory.

Conclusion

In working this space between jurisprudential accounts of law as an autonomous entity and as a dependent practice, I have sought to demonstrate that doctrinal development cannot be grounded in any simple or sustained manner. The deficit in justificatory rationality that arises from foundationalist efforts to explain law in its own terms cannot be made good by reference to some off-stage hand who controls the routines and rhythms of judicial marionettes. In contrast, my own nonfoundationalist understanding of the law-and-politics relation is both different from and similar to the understanding of these foundationalist theorists. My view is different from the externalists' in that it recognizes that the law is not exclusively determined by the prevailing socioeconomic context and that judges do have considerable autonomy. But it is also similar in that it concedes that law is significantly influenced by, as it influences, the extant regime of social ordering. On the other hand, my view is different from the internalists' in that it does not think law stands apart from social life and that judges are constrained by the intellectual parameters of law's logical development, but it is similar in that it sees a more multidimensional relation between law and its social-economic milieu. In short, the relationship is both more complicated and more indeterminate than all foundationalists allow. While judges experiment with different ways to play law's language game, they are conscious of the overall social context of which they are part and in which they work: they are political players within the infinite possibilities of law's performative practice. Working in fits and starts, judges respect the intellectual and instrumental limits of their situation as they work to transform them.

9 Playing Politics: Putting Poetry in Motion

......

The dance of renewal, the dance that made the world, was always danced here at the edge of things, on the brink, on the foggy coast.

—Ursula Le Guin, *Dancing at the End of the World*

In demonstrating that adjudication amounts to a playful performance in law's language game, I have insisted that judges and jurists are inevitably and inextricably involved in a political practice—*law is politics*. By this I mean that in making and justifying a decision, judges always have to take a stand that implicates a choice between competing values or a commitment to a particular normative assumption; there is no neutral or uncontroversial way to engage in law and adjudication. This is all by way of insisting that adjudication is a political game in which "anything might go," but not in which "anything goes." However, while a variety of cryptic references have been made throughout the book, I have tended to finesse or sidestep the pressing question of how judges can go about fulfilling that political responsibility and, in particular, how those choices might be evaluated or criticized. It should come as little surprise that a nonfoundationalist approach does not restrict itself to the operation of law and adjudication; this is only one location for its corrosive application. Instead, it insists the search and sighting of solid foundations throughout all social practices is a flawed enterprise. Accordingly, in this chapter, I continue to develop a nonfoundational account of adjudication as a legal game that takes seriously the need to ensure that all the social culture of people's lives is understood as a playful context that can be constantly reconfigured and in which people can constantly reshape themselves.

The chief charge against a nonfoundational approach as a viable mode of political critique is that it possesses no particular set of standards that can be relied upon to guide or energize the reconstructive project that a nonfoundational critique implies; its deconstructive passion debilitates its reconstructive possibilities. Whereas the concern from the *right* is that a nonfoundationalist critique is nihilistic and razes everything to the ground, the worry from the *left* is that it is too precious and leaves everything as it is. While these objections must be taken seriously, they amount to more of a caution than a condemnation. Nothing follows one political way or another from a nonfoundationalist critique: it is neither apocalyptic nor apologetic. When understood properly, a nonfoundational approach can be an effective and viable critical resource in a radical project of transformative politics. Contrary to foundationalists' assertions that such a nonfoundational approach sabotages any possibility of achieving a reliable program of progressive politics, I argue that there is no necessary contradiction between a continuing loyalty to a nonfoundationalist perspective and the practical implementation of a radical political agenda. Indeed, I maintain that a nonfoundational critique is the only critical resource that a progressive (or counterhegemonic) activist can have or need. While it does not provide the ground for a progressive politics, a nonfoundational critique does constitute a complementary strategy for one. The progressive nonfoundationalist critic is not the oxymoronic character nor the inadequate inspiration that foundationalists suggest.[1]

In this chapter, therefore, I intend to explore and defend a nonfoundationalist approach to political critique. After introducing the main thrust of the challenge to such a nonfoundational approach, I develop its basic response by coming to grips with the crucial contribution of Roberto Unger. Next, I play out the implications of a nonfoundational critique for three important strands in modern jurisprudence: the Marxisant critique of social deprivation; the feminist assault on pornography; and the liberal prescriptions of law-and-economics. In each case, the goals are the same—to accept that there is no way of knowing whether the attempt to "do the right thing" might turn out to be another way to "do the wrong thing." Because all strategies are hazardous and all consequences are unpredictable, much will depend on the informing context and precise timing of any particular intervention. In a nonfoundational way of thinking and acting, there are no self-evidently correct actions or easy answers but only difficult choices and questions. Throughout the chapter, therefore, I will emphasize that politics is the poetry that puts law's language game in motion. After all, what is poetry other than the exploration and transformation of language's prosaic practices and possibilities?

It's Too Late to Stop Now

Although law and adjudication are best understood as social practises in an infinite language game, a nonfoundationalist inquiry abandons entirely any transcendental attachment or ambition to fix the foundational conditions for language or its performance; there are no grounded terms by and against which to measure or validate contingent practices. Instead, the task of the nonfoundational critique is to expose the dynamic fluidity and changing character of the temporary practices that allow the routine performances of law, adjudication, and politics to proceed. When law and life are treated as infinite games of endless possibilities and performances, politics and, therefore, adjudication might be viewed more expansively and their transformative possibilities increased. In a social setting in which freedom and constraint are continually renegotiated and resituated, it might be possible to achieve a precarious but exhilarating experience of personal empowerment through which people can confirm themselves in their humanity and its limitless possibilities. None of this, of course, is intended to suggest that there would be an anarchic lack of standards in the playing of law or life that would lead to chaos; there would be new and changing standards that would combine the playful and the serious in a defiantly pluralistic amalgam of style and substance. Within such a nonfoundational understanding, injustice occurs when people's life-chances or sense of self depend not on making a better move or changing the game but on being prevented from participating in the game over what it means to *play the game*. Accordingly, the jurisprudential enterprise will have to undergo a radical reorientation in which philosophy (of law) will cease to be only a technical task of refined description but will also become a political project of opening up the vital play of life and law's game.

In pursuing this particular line of critique, nonfoundationalist jurists face a pressing and persistent challenge: *In the name of what and on behalf of whom is it that the critic speaks?* For many commentators, the failure of a nonfoundationalist approach is that its deconstructive assault is so thoroughgoing that it stymies or negates any reconstructive possibilities. While nonfoundationalist approaches to legal interpretation and adjudicative reasoning are dismissed as radical and nihilistic, their implications for political change are considered complacent and token; they are more intellectually indulgent than politically compelling.[2] By denying the possibility of foundations, it is contended that there is no place from which nonfoundationalists might launch or justify their own positive proposals for social change—how can they ground their own critique if there is no ground on which stand?; and if everything is always open to interpretation, how is it possible to know what is and is not progressive? In short, the contention is that a nonfoundationalist critique will only engender a politics of quietism and irresponsibility that will be long on personal angst and short on social solidarity. Indeed, despite their radical protestations, nonfoundationalists' critical efforts are dismissed as futile and reactionary because they "cannot help but bring comfort, energy, and ideas to the enemy of change."[3] Not surprisingly, foundationalist scholars are at the forefront of this assault upon a nonfoundational approach to political critique and social transformation. Critics from both the traditional Right and Left have insisted that, for political action to be effective, it must be informed and directed by a more grounded and reliable set of normative lights.

For instance, the political right is well represented by Francis Fukuyama, who documents and defends a coherent and universal History of Humankind that inexorably and inevitably leads to liberal democracy: "At the end of history, there are no serious ideological competitors left to liberal democracy." Needless to say, the traditional Left has had little truck with Fukuyama's brand of scholarly proselytizing. The Left condemns its philosophical pretension, suspect history, and ideological apologetics; he contrives to insist, in light of the overwhelming evidence to the contrary, that "America's social and ethnic structures have been sufficiently fluid to prevent the emergence of rigid social classes, significant sub-nationalisms, and linguistic minorities."[4] One of these Left critics is Joel Handler, who is an implacable foe of what he terms "the ideological hegemony of liberal capitalism" and its racist and patriarchal bonds: the motive concern of his work is the need to provide an effective challenge to such a degrading way of living and a bankrupt mode of theorizing. Instead of working to justify the legitimacy of liberal democracy, Handler calls for a "global revolutionary critique" and a "comprehensive political and economic plan" that might invigorate and inform the radical alternative to liberal democracy. Without such a wide-ranging and detailed blueprint for an egalitarian community and nonexploitative economy, the Left will concede the field to the Fukuyamas of the world and the future to the forces of conservative ideology. For Handler, the only way to meet and dislodge one vision is with another, better, and more encompassing vision of the terms and conditions of social life. The blurred vision of liberal democracy must be replaced by the limpid clarity of an egalitarian community that can illuminate the path of a progressive politics: "It is not enough merely to challenge bourgeois hegemony: the Left must create a counter or alternative hegemony."[5]

Yet, as uncompromising as Handler's opposition would be to the substance of Fukuyama's work, he contrives to share the same apocalyptic style and methodological motivations. The problem has as much to do with their foundationalist approaches as with their substantive proposals. Rather than junk entirely this discredited tradition of grand theorizing and cast it onto the scrap heap of failed scholarship, Handler holds on to its broad epistemic framework and historiographical aspirations—the siting and substantiating of a grounding Telos that can guide and judge History in its Progress. The main difference is that whereas Fukuyama wants to sit back and let History run its course, Handler wants to give a tweak to History's tail and point this mythical beast in a more promising direction. Complain as each might, Handler and Fukuyama are members of the same foundationalist family: Handler is the progressive sibling to Fukuyama's reactionary self. As a matter of historical record, both Fukuyama and Handler are on shaky ground. As much as Fukuyama would be hard pressed to demonstrate that recent global events are necessarily attributable to any particular logic or pattern, Handler would be equally flummoxed by the task of showing that such a grand, detailed, and universalizable vision was a necessary precondition of revolutionary change. When people take to the streets of Johannesburg, Prague, Beijing, Moscow, Timisoara, Frankfurt, or Los Angeles, they are rarely motivated by any particular or perfected plans for social renovation. Such uprisings are more often sparked by some local and relatively minor act of official injustice or bureaucratic crassness; they tend to be instinctive, spontaneous, and unpredictable in their timing and intensity. Moreover, if the participants are committed to act in the name of anything, it is the vague but noble desire for human dignity or a stark belief that "enough is enough." People tend not to give their lives for academic musings, nor do revolutions await the final theoretical word from the ivory tower. It is the vague promise of emancipation, not its detailed delineation, that animates people to act.

As a matter of intellectual endeavor, both Fukuyama and Handler want to rescript History by providing a grand narrative of historical justification and social emancipation. The only methodological difference is that while they both engage in a Marxist interpretation of History, Fukuyama's account "leads to a completely non-Marxist conclusion."[6] Where Handler and Fukuyama part company, of course, is on the design and details of this Universal Script. In sharp contrast to Fukuyama's liberal democracy, Handler is dedicated to crafting a blueprint for an egalitarian society that can bring History to an end by force of its own intrinsic appeal and providential rightness. Inspired by such a scholarly vision, Handler imagines that progressive activists can enlighten a dull citizenry, who will compliantly follow the intelligentsia into an egalitarian future. It is a seductive but flawed ambition whose elite means betray its democratic end; such a hegemonic vision cannot transcend the contingent dictates of historical living. As a project of transformative politics, Handler's enterprise must, like Fukuyama's, remain unfulfilled in its theoretical aspirations and practical realization. Accordingly, the challenge is to replace this foundationalist methodology as well as its dubious and self-serving outcomes with a theoretical approach that engenders a more democratic interpretation of history and its redemptive possibilities. Contrary to both Fukuyama and Handler's protestations, this is exactly what a nonfoundational critique does.

As Handler seems unable to accept, the only available option is to abandon entirely the elusive search for grand narratives or grandiose critiques. A nonfoundationalist view of history and its political opportunities is the way to go. There is no one optimistic or pessimistic account of historical destiny. Most important, there is no History or Destiny. While history might not be Shakespeare's "tale told by an idiot, full of sound and fury, signifying nothing,"[7] it is not what Fukuyama thinks it is nor what Handler wants it to be. History cannot be completely got out of or into: its presence is never entirely self-present so that it can be temporarily embraced or summarily evaded. A nonfoundational critique does not denigrate or dismiss the value and truth of historical experience or human suffering—that would be nonsensical and unpardonable. Instead, it avoids essentializing its value or truth; history is both the context for and subject of social study and political interpretation. Historical experience is given relevance by interrogating it and resisting the temptation to reduce it to a new authoritative source of epistemological knowledge or ideological insight.[8] Eschewing any monistic tendency, a nonfoundational critique is robustly pluralistic in its operation and ambition. Indeed, while Handler's catalog of nonfoundational characteristics—anti-essentialism, social plasticity, ironic juxtapositioning, discursive subversion, small-scale insurgency, grassroots organizing, strategic intervention, and the like—is on the mark, his anxiety about them is unnecessary. His fear is that the nonfoundational turn will result in Left politics being steered down a political blind alley in which transformative energies will be exhausted in obsessive and paralyzing odysseys in self-discovery, and from where it will be unable to challenge the oppressive workings of elite institutions: liberal capitalism will have reasserted itself courtesy of its nonfoundational antagonists, and bourgeois hegemony will persist. He is particularly troubled that "without a positive theory of institutions, [a nonfoundational critique] cannot come to grips with institutionally-based power."[9]

Contrary to Handler's (and other Marxisant critics') pessimism, a nonfoundational critique offers all the political firepower that he or anyone else requires. In the next sections, I want to suggest the error of these foundationalist ways by defending a nonfoundational critique as an effective and viable theoretical resource in a radical project of transformative politics. Indeed, not only does a nonfoundational critique allow for talk of justice and betterment, but it provides the most fitting and effective complement to the transformative ambitions of a truly democratic politics. As part of a progressive initiative, a vigorous nonfoundationalist critique is always seeking a better or more just way of proceeding, including a better and more just understanding of what "better" or "just" might mean or require. However, while the nonfoundational task is never complete, it does not reduce to a debilitating nihilism or relativism in which everything and anything is as just or as unjust as anything else. Having abandoned the search for lasting foundations, nonfoundationalist jurists and judges can become all the more political for that; they can begin to take a thoroughly playful and, therefore, political approach to their performances in law's language game. A nonfoundational approach to law and adjudication recognizes the urge to justice but insists that it can never be fully sated. On the contrary, jurists (and political theorists) are best advised to stop worrying about the felt need to construct a full-blown theory of social justice that has lasting appeal and application: this can only lead to paralysis and prevarication. Instead, the focus should shift to concrete efforts to locate and remedy discrete occasions of injustice. As such, I offer an extended meditation on what it might mean "to do the right thing" in a world in which notions of right and wrong are always contestable and contested. The success of political action can never be underwritten, and judges have no easy or obvious way out of their existential predicament.

Doing the Right Thing

The critical challenges to a nonfoundationalist account of law are pressing and significant; they strike at the heart of the critical project. If a nonfoundationalist critique is obliged to exhaust itself in ever more elaborate and precious demonstrations of interpretive and ideological indeterminacy, it will have contributed little to legal and political transformation. Indeed, the status quo will be left untouched, and elite forces will have reasserted themselves courtesy of nonfoundationalists. However, attachment to a nonfoundationalist critique is not as politically enfeebling or intellectually decadent as its foundationalist critics contend. On the contrary, when properly understood, it recommends itself as the most robust and effective companion for a subversive politics that is committed to confronting and confounding the oppressive workings of elite institutions. While a nonfoundationalist approach leads in no necessary direction or to no necessary political program, it is not incompatible with a progressive politics: closure is always contrived, frequently arbitrary, and usually conducive to established power relations. Indeed, an emancipatory impulse informs and energizes a nonfoundationalist account of law. In a world in which the designations of *Right* and *Left* have lost much of their traditional salience, a nonfoundationalist critique ensures that the question of what amounts to a truly radical or progressive politics is treated contextually and contingently; it rejects any reliance on a single or privileged vision of social justice or program of transformative action. There is no place for an enforced orthodoxy or rigid conformity, for "a just society is not a society that has adopted just laws, once and for all, rather it is a society where the question of justice remains constantly open."[10]

Rejecting comprehensive programs and universal positions, the nonfoundationalist critic must attend to local and contingent circumstances of claims to knowledge and to the situated places from which people speak and act. Justice is not a matter of revelation and critique is not apocalyptic. Both consist of a constant interrogation and calling into question of all those ideas and practices that are most familiar and "foundational." It is not possible to make a clean break from inherited tradition, and "one risks ceaselessly confirming . . . that which one allegedly deconstructs."[11] While there is always and already parameters to action, those boundaries must always be part of the struggle: contact and situation are not the same as complicity and saturation. As Derrida defiantly puts it:

> The impression that deconstruction is opposed to politics or is at best apolitical . . . only prevails because all political codes and terminologies still remain fundamentally metaphysical, regardless of whether they originate from the right or the left. The difficulty is to gesture in opposite directions at the same time: on the one hand to preserve a distance and suspicion with regard to the official political codes governing reality; on the other, to intervene here and now in a practical and engagé manner whenever the necessity arises.[12]

While this nonfoundationalist critique rejects the metaphysical privileging of grand theory and metanarratives, it most certainly does not deny the worth of social, historical, or political theorizing as a social, historical, or political praxis. Provided that it is suitably provisional, revisable, and contextual, such reflective activity is at the heart of a transformative political intervention. In rejecting History and Reality, it does not ignore the lessons of history or the realities of suffering. Moreover, in rejecting Telos, it does not ignore the value of criticism. Since all claims are located within a dynamic set of social practices, there is an insistence that all theorizing pay attention to the structural circumstances of that social milieu and, in particular, to theorizing its own embeddedness in such historical contexts. Critical insight is a prelude to transformative action. Understood in this way, a nonfoundationalist perspective neither craves to provide an integrated or finished program for political action nor recoils from the task of struggling toward an enhanced social solidarity and experience of justice. Instead, it points to a renewed engagement and sustained challenge to existing historical conditions. Any theoretically sophisticated or satisfactory account of law and politics must grapple with the extant protocols of power and, in making any proposal for transformative change, must recognize its own revisable and experimental character. The ambition is not to fix an all-encompassing Truth or Justice in a distant metaphysical realm but to pay constant attention to the multiple truths and contextual details of engaged living.[13] Of course, being political, that process will always be open and fluid; meaning will always be provisional and revisable.

Accordingly, the role of nonfoundationalist legal critics is more modest and less removed than that of traditional theorists; what they lose in sweep, they gain in substance. Eschewing both apocalyptic and apologetic styles, they strive to exist in that strange in-between state where they are both inside and outside present society; they must construct an identity for themselves that is more connected than that of the detached philosopher king but less situated than that of the enslaved courtesan. They are neither yea-sayers by habit nor naysayers for the sake of it. They must cultivate "the state of never being fully adjusted, always feeling outside the chatty familiar world inhabited by natives, so to speak, tending to avoid and even dislike the trappings of accommodation and national well-being."[14] Constantly working the seam between the universal and the local, the social and the subjective, the here-and-now and the yet-to-come, this nonfoundationalist brand of intellectual critique is obliged to inhabit the political margins. Nevertheless, because intellectuals cannot be everywhere at once, they must ensure that their interventions achieve optimal strategic effect by revealing the customary habits of mind that blind people to the gap between felt necessity and viable choice. Although change is as much a matter of imagination as anything else, legal intellectuals are always participating within their extant contexts, which they must struggle to change as they play within their constraints: engagement is always tangled and responses are equally complicated. Relieved of the anxiety to craft solutions that are somehow apt for all times and places, they can concentrate on the pressing problems of contemporary society and view social institutions "as experiments in cooperation rather than as attempts to embody a universal and ahistorical order."[15]

The common complaint against a nonfoundationalist critique by Left critics is that it lacks the resources to construct an alternative vision of institutional arrangements that can guide transformative efforts at progressive change. However, if more vision is what is needed, there is nothing in the nonfoundationalist approach that inhibits the exercise of visionary faculties. Indeed, as part of its recommendation to poeticize society and culture, it both allows and encourages such reconstructive insights to take flight; it is traditional legal and political theorizing that clips the wings of the political imagination in the service of foundational truths and other hegemonic projections. What is often forgotten is that legal prose is simply a genre of political poetry that has grown tired and old; it has lost its living connection with its historical milieu. Contrary to received wisdom, poetry is not an aesthetic indulgence that records a romantic escape from the world and its immediate problems. Trading in the politics of responsibility and hope, poets do not betray human suffering but bear radical witness to it. By firing the political imagination, the juristic poet can elevate law and politics from a desultory chatter about institutional technique to an inspired conversation about substantive vision. Once it is understood that judges and jurists inhabit a "realm of contingency," it might become possible to give adjudication a more rhapsodic lease on life and to recognize that "historical sense and poetic sense should not, in the end, be contradictory, for if poetry is the little myth we make, history is the big myth we live, and in our living remake."[16]

Whereas the prosaic tradition of law bids people to endure their given lot with a resigned fortitude, a more poetic and playful jurisprudence might shake this complacency and represent a bold affirmation of the collective and personal responsibility to change the world for the better. In so doing, the ambition is to afford people the opportunity to become their own poetic champions. By revising what counts as The Way Things Really Are, poetry can help to liberate people from the prosaic routines and contingent conventions that constrain their lives and inform their imaginative possibilities. By leaving the risks and responsibilities of reconstruction with real people in real situations, what is good politics or best for the community will always remain contestable. In this way, a nonfoundational account of law and adjudication as a language game of unavoidable political dimensions might be able to contribute to that transformative project. Rather than legitimate their individual performances by reference to the neutrality of the overall adjudicative process, judges will be required to justify law's continuing practice by dint of their rhetorical skills and argumentative maneuvers in each individual performance. As such, judicial poets might rework the prosaic practices of law to further better the prospects and practices of a democratic society.

Foundationalist scholars would be right in thinking that a nonfoundational kind of critical intervention cannot guarantee a politics that will be uniformly progressive or whose practice will be consistently effective. But to think otherwise is to continue in the misguided belief that the establishment of foundational truths is possible and could ground a radical political praxis. The felt need that people have for such solid ground under their critical feet is an effect of traditional theory's mistaken insistence that Truth, History, or Reality—once fixed—will guide and insulate action from error. Disabused of such foundationalist yearnings, people might begin to understand that politics is inside, not outside, history's suzerainty. All that a nonfoundationalist mentality can do is to show that power is never apart from reason: logic and ambiguity, authority and arbitrariness, and universality and contingency are implicated in each other. Truth, individuality, agency, and collective action are problematized—not to discard them from the radical vocabulary of progressive politics but to render them more immediately transformable and politically useful. While there must be talk of egalitarianism's future possibilities, there must also be recognition of oppression's present victims.[17] No theoretical standpoint alone can ensure that the long journey to a better future can be accomplished without struggle, mistakes, and further pain. However, by using rich accounts and critical readings of legal experience to promote political knowledge and action, jurists can play a valuable part in any transformative project.

Nevertheless, a nonfoundationalist temper is not silent on what might generally amount to a progressive politics. It implies, but does not necessitate, a participatory democracy that is egalitarian and pluralist in order to inspire the robust kind of institutional arrangements that will permit the articulation and antagonism of different forms of life by those presently excluded. This espousal of democracy is not to be confused with a loyalty to existing political arrangements that are defended and supported in the name of democracy: this tends to reduce people to walk-on parts in an unfolding drama rather than empower them as active citizens in the poetic struggle to redefine and achieve emancipation. On the contrary, a nonfoundational critique is committed to challenging all forms of totalitarianism, in particular the tendency to sweeping generalizations and an inattention to context and gestures to "a democracy still to come."[18] What has to be measured against this promise are the existing forms of democracy—the gap between the determined and the undetermined, the gap between the here-and-now and the yet-to-come. The familiar totalitarianisms of racism, poverty, sexism, fascism, and the like have no distinct or simple logic that can be opposed to the forces and practices of antitotalitarianism; each blurs with the other and there is no "property so closed and so pure that one may not find any element of these systems in discourses that are commonly opposed to them."[19] The question of what best advances the idea of democratic practice is constantly open to interrogation; it is the problem that can best energize the playful practice of adjudication in law's language game. However, such a commitment will demand the mobilization of popular energies rather than the application of pseudo-expert knowledge. If there is to be adjudication, it must itself become a focus and forum for democratic engagement where politics is open and judgment is contingent. As an occasion for resistance through empowerment, adjudicative exercise must remain piecemeal, situated, responsible, and humble. Without doubt and ambivalence, the temptation to judicial hubris is all too irresistible.

As regards Handler (and other progressive critics), he will have lost nothing and gained much by ditching his foundationalist suppositions. At the cost of abandoning the false lure of universal panaceas, he will have acquired the substantial merit of political relevance. Moreover, he can continue to reap the fruits of socialist thinking, but he must be prepared to cultivate a more diverse crop: "Every project for radical democracy implies a socialist dimension, . . . but socialism is but *one* of the components of a project of radical democracy, not vice versa."[20] Socialism neither exhausts democracy by becoming its total platform, nor is it to be expunged from the radical agenda entirely. In short, Handler can have my nonfoundational critique and his socialism too. Relieved of the anxiety to craft solutions that are somehow apt for all times and places, he can concentrate on the pressing problems of contemporary American society and experiment with local interventions that can best address the prevailing institutional structures and situations of injustice. Indeed, one of the best nonfoundational accounts of political criticism is by Handler himself. His widely and justly acclaimed *The Conditions of Discretion* is devoted to examining and transforming the frustrating interaction between ordinary people and large-scale bureaucracy.

Focusing on Wisconsin's programs for the special educational needs of differently able children, Handler not surprisingly rejects the traditional resort to indeterminate systems of liberal rights and adversarial procedural remedies. For him, the very reasons that gave rise to liberalism's original appeal have become the source of its contemporary failing as a program for progressive change—its universalistic pretensions, unyielding individualism, and pervasive ahistoricality. The whole force and ambition of Handler's project is to replace the formal and abstract logic of rights litigation with situation-specific solutions that are discretionary, local, contingent, experimental, and flexible. In a richly textured and compelling narrative, he articulates the need to nurture a nuanced and revisable power-sharing engagement between parents and administrators that mediates and responds to the interaction of larger structural forces and more local openings for transformative action. As such, Handler's critique and reconstructive proposals are entirely compatible with the spirit and sensibilities of a nonfoundationalist critique:

> Within [various legal, political, social, and structural] constraints and influences, there is room to maneuver, to develop and modify styles and patterns of operation, to create and emphasize certain programs. . . . Thus, in considering the possibilities of organisational response, one must be aware of both contingency and change. Today's solutions will not necessarily be recognisable tomorrow. . . . If we are to take the idea of discretion seriously, then each community must work toward

the conditions of discretion in its own way according to its own particular circumstances. Policy, agencies, social groups, and individuals are fluid and subject to constant change.[21]

As Handler implicitly accepted in *Conditions of Discretion*, the pressing challenge for progressive critics is to move beyond the political stereotyping of traditional ideologies, the false lure of grand theorizing and one-dimensional narratives for transformative action. Totalizing politics are unrealistic and unrealizable. Grassroots engagement is better able to grasp and transform the complex and diverse intersecting forms of oppression. Sexism and racism might be global in existence and sweep, but their dynamism is local in operation and effect. Oppression might be universal, but its modalities are particular. Consequently, Handler's earlier performance strikes all the right chords in the nonfoundationalist register. Abandoning the overweening rhetoric of liberal rights, he concedes that "there are no fixed principles that chart a clear path; there are no laws of nature that will regulate our lives as we wish to lead them; there are no simple truths that will explain the disorders and complexities of life."[22] Instead, he stresses the inevitable struggle with a fluid context of social indeterminacy and extols the virtues of a revisable politics that mediates the micro and macro functionings of power. By so doing, he is able to generate a malleable framework of understanding and empowerment that can be reworked for different settings.

All in all, Handler's work is thoroughly nonfoundational in style and effect. Far from conceding the field, a nonfoundational critique is the best way that those committed to progressive change can occupy the field and begin to challenge "the ideological hegemony of liberal capitalism." Insofar as "an alternative vision of the economy and the polity" is required, Handler and other progressive colleagues can rest assured that there is nothing in a nonfoundational critique that prevents the exercise of visionary faculties. Nevertheless, the pursuit of only *one* "alternative vision of economy and community" is to be resisted.[23] In line with their democratic and pluralistic instincts, nonfoundationalist commentators will reject a belief in any single or accurate vision of social justice; a deconstructive critique must not be allowed to become the last refuge of a foundationalist scoundrel. There is no one way to play law or life's game. Rejecting comprehensive programs and universal positions, nonfoundationalist critics must attend to the local and contingent circumstances of claims to knowledge and to the situated places from which people speak and act. Declining easy answers in favor of better and different questions, foundationalists might begin to recognize that in the never-ending game of life, there will always be playful opportunities to consider (and reconsider) what it means to "do the right thing."

A Poetic Champion

A jurist who has championed the poetic cause is Roberto Mangabeira Unger. Refusing to accept the stultifying conformity and lack of vision of contemporary government, he wants to poeticize the practice and theory of politics so that people can liberate themselves from the prosaic routines and contingent conventions that constrain their lives and inform life's imaginative possibilities. However, he does not aspire to achieve a final resolution of social conflict by poetic fiat, but only to suggest an institutional context in which people can reach their own accommodations with the contingent forces of historical movement. Unger extends an invitation to engage in an "act of hope" that "sets out to execute a program for which no ready-made mode of discourse exists . . . [and which] develops, as it moves forward, a language for a vision." While there is much in Unger's project that warrants close attention, I will concentrate on the extent to which he is able to resolve the tensions between the deconstructive and reconstructive dimensions of the nonfoundational project. Although he claims to be committed to a thoroughly uncompromising nonfoundationalist account of society, his reconstructive proposals are too foundationalist in their programmatic ambition and historical status; his search for a "structure of no-structure" is unwise and unsuccessful.[24] In an important nonfoundational sense, Unger cannot resist the temptation to set the theoretical terms and conditions for life and law's never-ending game of practical politics. In doing so, he allows his foundationalist instincts to cloud his nonfoundationalist judgment.

Unger's central idea is as simple as it is seismic. While many social theorists have insisted upon the idea that society is an artifact, Unger brooks no compromise. For him, there is no aspect of social arrangements that is not open to revision. Emphasizing the need for a contextual, transformative, and nonessentialist approach, the radical project is to complete the rebellion against the foundationalist or naturalistic fallacy (i.e., the confusion of accident with essence and contingency with necessity) and to effect an irrevocable emancipation from false necessity. For Unger, history is the site of social warfare, and the organizational form of particular societies is the truce lines of any interruption or containment of that conflict. However, Unger's unique contribution is his attempt to salvage a reconstructive potential from the deconstructive debris; his social theory is intended to offer "a point of departure that is most constructive precisely where it seems most nihilistic." As society is made, it can be remade. In the attempt to diminish the distance between structure-preserving routines and structure-transforming conflicts and between normal politics and revolutionary struggle, "no hard-and-fast distinction separates criticism and construction." The task is transformation and revision, not dissolution or destruction. In a profound sense, therefore, the insight that everything-is-politics becomes not only an irresistible instrument of social critique but also, in Unger's hands, a tool by which to rebuild society from the raw materials of history. The ambition is "to build a society that is less hostage to itself" and that can give substance to the slogan that "nothing succeeds like plasticity."[25]

For Unger, neither liberalism nor Marxism has made good on its transformative promise because both have fallen victim to the expedient temptation of allowing illusion to pass into prejudice. Whereas liberals confuse the accidents of current democratic and market structures with the essence of true democratic and market ordering, Marxism mistakes contingent trends in social-economic organization for the necessary enactment of world history's script. Rather than reject these deep-structure theories out of hand, Unger deploys the restrained insights of both to inform a radical program of empowered democracy that advances both freedom and equality by completing the liberal war against privilege and by defending a leftist ideal that breaks the spell of deep-logic society theory. In this program, the branches of government would be multiplied, a rotating capital fund from which workers could draw would be established, and a disaggregation of the consolidated property right would occur. An integral dimension of the program would be a system of four basic rights: *immunity* rights would secure basic civil and welfare entitlements; *destabilization* rights would empower individuals to disrupt established institutions and practices; *market* rights would allow people to share in the community's wealth; and *solidarity* rights would entitle individuals to support and loyalty from others.[26]

In sketching out his blueprint for emancipatory democracy, Unger is faced with the obvious challenge of demonstrating why the "structure of no-structure" and "program of empowered democracy" do not contradict the nonfoundationalist thesis. Of course, it is my contention that they do. For instance, throughout Unger's writings, it remains resoundingly the case that "the citizen of the empowered democracy is the empowered individual." For him, individual man stands before (ontologically and chronologically) and above (epistemologically) the community. As such, he remains firmly caught within the limiting presuppositions of liberalism and—it should come as no surprise—is unable to move beyond them. For him, there is no sense in which a community can ever be greater than the sum of its individual parts. Ungerian protagonists seem to believe that they can choose association and obligation through resort to a self-centered imagination and a self-directed instrumentality. Any notion of community within such a scheme can never be more than pale and impoverished. While, of course, there are grave dangers as well as valuable strengths in a strong sense of community—moving in formation does not necessarily mean being on course—it can offer a springboard and a safety net for the social activist. Social progress involves a collaborative and engaged act of social change. It demands not only imagination and "context-breaking brio" but the quiet courage of humility and respect for others.[27] The radical can be more than Springsteen's rebel forever "born to run," whose life can only end in exhaustion and frustration and from which death is the only relief. Social justice can be construed more as a democratic driveway than as a privileged pathway; spontaneity and responsibility might not be antithetical notions but could complement and bolster each other. Whereas dutifulness might set the context for improvisation, extemporization could be energized by obligation. I say all of this not as a matter of theoretical necessity but of political possibility: it is not that "anything goes," but only that "anything might go."

Contrary to the nonfoundational cri de coeur of his whole endeavor, Unger seems to lose his deconstructive nerve at the very point when he most requires it; he seems to want his cake and to eat it too. However, Unger is not immune to this critical charge. He recognizes that his "super-theory" is not the only response to the claim that "everything is politics": an alternative project is that of "ultra-theory," which flatly rejects any attempt to provide a systematic, comprehensive, or reconstructive account of social relations. Such ultra-theorists (like myself) insist that the appropriate nonfoundational response is to abandon the project of Grand Theory entirely and to refuse to compromise on the nonfoundational claim that society is artifactual. Unger's response to these so-called ultra-theorists (or, as I prefer to term them, nonfoundationalists) is generous but unconvincing. Noting their preference for the practical over the theoretical, the local over the comprehensive, the utopian over the transformative, and the existential over the ideal, Unger concedes that such a nonfoundational stance is entirely valid and "is not inherently better or worse than [his own] theoretically aggressive strategy . . . [and] it merely presents a different mix of difficulties, dangers, and opportunities." Apart from highlighting the dangers that ultra-theory risks of sliding into a resigned nihilism or a closet positivism, Unger confirms that "there are . . . no persuasive a priori reasons to prefer either super-theory or ultra-theory as responsive to the contemporary situation of social thought."[28] For a writer who is so uncompromising and relentless in his treatment of other competing views, Unger's lack of any definitive response to a line of argument that cuts to the root of his project is perplexing and lends weight to nonfoundationalist claims.

For myself, I believe that this stark disagreement over the implications of pursuing the claim that "everything is politics" is more serious and more in need of resolution than Unger suggests. It is not the case that each can coexist and work simultaneously, if not together: the thrust of a rigorous nonfoundationalist critique is to deny the viability or efficacy of a foundationalist approach, no matter how stripped down or modest. As I have emphasized, the foundationalist impulse in legal and political theory is understandable, but it must be strenuously and consistently resisted. Of course, in making this point, it is important to remember that it is a nonfoundationalist approach that I am defending, not an antifoundationalist one. Unlike an antifoundationalist critique, a nonfoundational approach does not argue that there are no practices or rules of the game within which we exist and play, but only that those practices and rules have no foundations that are any more secure or stable than the ones accepted in its contingent performance; the rules of the transformative game are both always operative and in play. Whereas Unger seeks higher reconstructive ground than his deconstructive activities will allow and, therefore, falls victim to the foundationalist impulse, antifoundationalist critiques deny there is any extant framework within which to think about, let alone act in or change, the world. In contrast, a nonfoundational approach offers more productive alternatives. Resisting both the hubristic tendencies of foundationalist theorists and the anarchist urges of the antifoundationalist critics, nonfoundationalists might be able to engage in more politically immediate and specific exercises. By working in local and domestic contexts, transformative action becomes a real possibility for disaffected citizens and creates an example that they are capable of replicating in their own lives. The work of prison groups, mental health advocacy groups, and battered women centers and AIDS workers can realize and advance a radical project. Within such a political program, "theory does not express, translate or serve to apply practice: it is practice."[29]

Although Unger's efforts to construct his institutional program of emancipatory democracy or "super-liberalism" are flawed, his work need not be dispensed with altogether: it is far too suggestive and inspired. In line with a rigorous nonfoundational approach, I view the dynamic core of his social theory as a frame of mind or habit of the heart. This critical posture consists of two primary attitudes about *transformative contextuality* and *negative capability*. An adequate appreciation of the formative force, contingent nature, and transformative possibilities of contextuality is at the heart of Unger's work. While all activity is contextual, old contexts can be revised; "the formative contexts of social life are nothing but frozen politics." All sociohistorical contexts establish a framework for routine activity and "put a particular version of society in place of the indeterminate possibilities of social life." However, this does not dictate any necessary logic of social organization. While people can never break entirely "the bonds of contextuality," they can transcend and revise particular contexts. In this sense, Unger's citizens are neither reformers nor revolutionaries but rather subversives and revisionists. They develop an understanding of the existing context as both formative and unnecessary and work to transform it in line with a more open vision of society in which routine and revolution lose their contrasting characteristics. For Unger, this is not the historical contingency of scientific precedents over historical necessity—this itself would be a form of necessitarian social theorizing. Instead, their relation is itself context-specific:

> No ideas about contingency, necessity, or possibility, and no conception of the correct relations among these conceptions, can be defended or even understood outside the setting of a particular view of how things happen in a particular time and place. The intuitive core of the idea of contingency is the notion that all things or some things might be otherwise than they are. . . . There is no fixed list of types of contingency, necessity, and possibility that is anything more than the incomplete summary of an explanation. . . . No invariant scale exists along which conceptions of contingency can vary. Each substantive theory, if it is general or novel enough, changes the relations among the means and senses of necessity, contingency, and possibility. . . . [From an anti-necessitarian perspective,] the point is less to tilt the scales in favour of freedom and against constraint than to change the detailed ways in which we think about the relation between constraint and freedom.[30]

The second and related critical posture is a negative capability. This is a heightened form of empowerment that works to denaturalize and emancipate all forms of social activity from the paralysis of false necessity. Its energy is directed toward loosening rigid hierarchies and entrenched practices at every contextual level from the collectively productive to the privately passionate with the aim of narrowing the gap between routine moves and radical conflicts. By its nature, the actualization of negative capability follows no inherent logic or script and relies on no given set or sequence of institutional instrumentalities. Such a course of action demands indefatigable energy, unquenchable imagination, and an indomitable spirit to remain in permanent defiance of established traditions and to live a life in which routine and struggle endlessly combine in a transformative vocation. In short, "the radical cause concerns the creation of formative institutional and imaginative orderings of social life that . . . diminish the extent to which a pre-established, unchallengeable scheme of social roles and rank shapes our practical or passionate dealings . . . [and] at the same time these valued contexts lay themselves more fully open for identification, challenge, and revision in the midst of our ordinary practical and argumentative activities." Of course, Unger offers no guarantees in waging this war of negative capability. Enlarged revisability increases risk and success is never assured; "the quest for empowerment through plasticity . . . may subject us to a desperatism . . . more thoroughgoing than any yet known."[31] For Unger, it is clearly better to fail in the noble pursuit of radical empowerment than it is to settle for the complacent limits of the status quo.

Accordingly, although Unger is committed to an uncompromising displacement of the traditions of Grand Theory, his work is very much part of that tradition. At the same time that it condemns all positivist contributions to social theory, it strives to manufacture a satisfying response to relativistic critics. Whatever the shortcomings of his offering, Unger's poetic vision is an intellectual adventure of epic proportions: the details may be flawed and his reach may exceed his grasp, but the attempt is monumental. Although overshadowed by the sheer ambition of his emancipatory program, the simple message of his writings is that there is no one cause for our present predicament and, therefore, no one solution. Yet Unger fails to heed his own earlier advice that, "as a normative doctrine, [philosophy's] task is to act as a signpost for politics, not to replace it."[32] As such, the limits of Unger's transformative impulse are also the limits of poetry—the struggle to express in language that which language cannot express. But like any true poetic champion, Unger has pushed our understanding of ourselves and our future possibilities beyond the prosaic horizons of the status quo. It may be that in aching to give expression to the inarticulate speech of the heart, he has spoken in an accent that is too heroic and too programmatic. But in his efforts to wax political, he has cleared a space for others to join and change the conversation of humankind. It is for those previously excluded to give voice.

In Other Words

Law controls sexuality not only by its coercive powers but also through its discursive constructions. While there are other social forces and influences in play, sexual identities and sexual practices are framed within the ample reach of law's linguistic domain. As well as enforcing prevailing moral norms and deciding the scope of socially validated sexual behavior, law also determines what counts as sex in the tableau of human behavior. Although the relationship of law, sexuality, and sex is always ideologically fraught, it is particularly so in regard to graphic representations of sex and sexuality. The debate around this so-called *pornography* hits a very sensitive nerve in the body politic.[33] Indeed, in recent years, few social practices have managed to arouse as much intellectual angst and political anger as pornography. In part, this is because the debate seems to cut across conventional political lines; it sets traditional enemies against each other and fosters strange alliances among them. None of this should be too surprising, since pornography touches profound issues that strike at the very heart of those dilemmas, difficulties, and denials that comprise the human condition. However, I want to place pornography in a much more nuanced and less dogmatic context—in contrast to the theoretical essentialism and practical extremism that presently prevails—in order to get a better handle on the contested notions of sexuality and sex that underlie and energize the academic debate and political furor around it. Concerned as it is with the discursive dimension of social living, a nonfoundational approach has much to recommend it. In other words, I will explore and explain what follows, if anything, from treating pornography as a language game. Far from trivializing or depoliticizing violence against women, this approach underlines the inescapably political, contestable, and, therefore, transformable character of those violent acts and misogynist practices.

One writer who has concentrated on the discursive quality of pornography is Catharine Mackinnon. She espouses a view that language is not a neutral medium through which the world is represented to us but that "society is made of words" and "speech can be an exercise of power which constructs the reality in which people live," and that "social supremacy is made, inside and between people, through making meanings." Nevertheless, despite these promising and convincing assumptions that "society is made of language," MacKinnon seems to forget their force and implications when she moves from statements of general principle to a substantive discussion of pornography. She makes the stark claim that words are never only words: they are actions that cause real and lasting harm to people in the world. This, like her claim that pornography depicts women "as less than human" is hardly novel or controversial: civil and criminal law has long recognized the power of words (defamation and threats) and the need to protect people from the harm that they can do (financial loss and emotional distress). The radical edge of her critique is to be found in her absolute conviction that "unwelcome sex talk is an unwelcome sex act" and that "if there is anything that only pornography can say, that is exactly the measure of the harm that only pornography can do." Indeed, she leaves little doubt of her intent when she insists that "pornography is no less an act than the rape and torture it represents."[34] Accordingly, MacKinnon is clear not only that pornography should be prohibited as a vicious act that causes untold harm to women but also that antipornography legislation ought to be enacted and that it ought not to be constitutionally proscribed because it causes harm.

It is difficult to read MacKinnon's book without believing that, for her, there are a whole set of things—women, men, sex, experience, and oppression—that are real in the sense that they are apprehendable and have meaning outside of language: they are knowable in themselves without interpretation. Contrary to her primary thesis that there are only words, she argues that actions speak not only louder than words but that they speak for themselves in a language that is universal and intelligible to all; only the willfully hard of hearing are deaf to its message. Indeed, she goes as far as to say: "I am asking you to imagine that women's reality is real—something of a leap of faith in a society saturated with pornography, not to mention an academy saturated with deconstruction." It is the affirmation of objective realism on a grand scale. By arguing that "beyond bringing a message from reality, [pornography] stands in for reality: it is existentially being there," MacKinnon adopts a very classical notion of Truth and Reality that is at odds with her discourse-based protestations.[35] She completely eschews any interpretive space between what is said and what there is. This is tantamount to an ontological account of truth (what is true is what exists) that is the philosophical opposite of the pragmatic epistemology (what is true is what can be said) that she claims to hold. For her, the language of pornography has meaning in and of itself; its (bad) nature and effects speak for themselves and need no interpretation. Anyone who fails to recognize this is speaking falsity to truth and is complicit in the violence that pornography does to women.

In driving home her opposition to pornography, MacKinnon has allowed her ideological zeal to compromise her intellectual judgment and, in the process, managed to subvert her own political crusade. The espousal of such a foundationalist epistemology is not only of suspect philosophical validity but of dubious political merit: MacKinnon consigns the meaning of pornography, sex, and oppression to the level of the metaphysical, something that can be named and understood but not challenged or transformed. These acts and situations become part of the Human Condition, beyond the revision of human societies, only to be noted and negotiated around. They are no longer thought of as social constructs for whose making and, importantly, remaking society has to take responsibility. In a perverse turn of events, MacKinnon succeeds in depoliticizing pornography and oppression as the basic theoretical move in her political campaign to eradicate them. In contrast, a nonfoundational account ensures that pornography and the debate around it remain firmly situated on the contested terrain of politics, with all the usual disabling risks as well as the enabling opportunities that attend the play of social and historical forces. Any sexually explicit representation is neither bad nor good, harmful nor ameliorating, abusive nor empowering: the feminist *Not a Love Story* frames sexually explicit images in a context that is very different from the pornographic *Deep Throat*.

Of course, none of this means, as MacKinnon implies, that critics like myself hold that "value can be found in anything" and that a nonfoundational approach "is predicated on obscuring [the normalizing] function in social hierarchy."[36] To conclude that it is *only words* is not to trivialize politics but rather to say the most profound thing that there is to say. MacKinnon has to accept that if words can be acts, then acts not only can be words but must be construed through words if we are to make any sense of them. People do not look at reality through language but always with it and at it. While communicative practices are not the only kind of practices, they do frame and give meaning to other practices and are important for that reason. In other words, when it comes to truth and reality, there are *only words*. Accordingly, my challenge is not to the reality of pornography, sex, or oppression but to the meaning to be attributed to that reality and the reality of that meaning. Whereas MacKinnon presents an account that is ahistorical, universal, and totalizing, I insist that the practices of pornography, sex, and violence are much more historical, contingent, and diffuse. As such, they are much more open to diverse interpretation and, therefore, political disruption. By opening up the discourse of pornography and sexual violence, it becomes possible to work the interpretive spaces to transformative effect. This is not to deny the main gist of MacKinnon's work in its entirety but to restate it in a nonfoundationalist way that makes it more fragmented, less essentialist, and, therefore, more open to interpretation and reappropriation. It does not draw a line in the ground of history and ask people to choose sides in a once-and-for-all way.

Instead, by not treating pornography as static and fixed, a nonfoundationalist critique is better able to understand it as "a process to be analysed and undermined as it occurs."[37] In this way, both women and men can be galvanized to combat women's continued oppression rather than to accept it as an inevitable aspect of contemporary living. While people live in a disciplinary society, they are never entirely disciplined. The conditioning codes of sexual normality are never quite as successful as MacKinnon would have us believe. Although women and men are not the fully free and autonomous choosing selves that liberalism pretends, they are not the fully captive and manipulated foils that MacKinnon implies. Social scripts constrain people's choices, but the choices made transform the scripts and, therefore, people in small yet significant ways. Unlike in MacKinnon's limited political vocabulary, freedom is not about the retrieval of some stifled identity or the revival of a golden age of innocence in which sexual relations were unencumbered by the constitutive culture of pornographic images and patriarchal ideas.

MacKinnon persists in supposing that there is a presocial, supracultural, and free woman, who, laboring under false consciousness, is constantly trying to throw off the yoke of male domination. Her texts and critique are structured around the idea of "women's point of view" and "women's voice," which must be released if society is to give women "really what they want" and "on [their] own terms." In the attempt to give women a voice of their own, MacKinnon insists that it will not be possible until substantive change is made in social arrangements as well as in man and woman's way of thinking, because, at present, "his foot is on her throat."[38] In short, MacKinnon's women reside outside speech in some prelinguistic space and reality, awaiting expressive release.

In a nonfoundationalist discourse, personal freedom is more about the collective establishment of a new social script in which there are roles for men and women that enable them to explore different gendered identities and sexual experiences: "Outcasts invent new moral identities for themselves by getting semantic authority over themselves."[39] The political ambition is for women to construct voices in which they can give expression to the previously inarticulated speech of women's lives and sexuality. There is no core *woman* waiting to be discovered or unearthed. MacKinnon's under-the-feet-of-men women would more likely stay down, since they would have no idea of how to get up or what to do if they did. By resisting the more than uniform history of women's experience and the less than totalizing effect of men's domination, MacKinnon's rhetorical devices and one-dimensional plots inhibit the prospects and possibilities for change. The challenge is to work toward those rare moments in which, as MacKinnon concedes, "sex feeling good . . . may mean that one has glimpsed freedom, a rare and valuable and contradictory event."[40] This does not entail a denial of the fact that such sexual relations take place within a misogynist culture. It accepts that within such a social experience, the only way to transform sexual relations is "by continually rethinking who we are and why we are making the choices we make that we can free ourselves from the belief that our selves are constructed by our sexual identities."[41]

Where does this leave the debate on pornography? And where does it leave MacKinnon's critical ideas and her practical contributions to that debate? The answers are as simple as they are straightforward—where they have always been: on the complex and contested terrain of politics. Nothing will necessarily have been lost or gained. It most certainly does not mean that MacKinnon's writings will have to be discarded. However, in jettisoning her metaphysical baggage, MacKinnon might be prepared to reconsider her essentialist message and absolutist solutions. In doing so, she might deliver a more nuanced and less totalizing account of women's lives that could garner and galvanize greater intellectual and political support: a foundationalist and fundamentalist theory of law and oppression tends to inhibit and compromise a truly transformative politics. Stripped of its essentialist trappings, her reduction of all gender interaction to the universal and irresistible dynamic of female exploitation and male dominance is almost guaranteed to resign people to despair and disempowerment rather than to inspire them to resistance and transformation. Such a monolithic theory of oppression ensures that, to stand any chance of success, the nature of change will have to be revolutionary and tyrannical. This not only makes it highly unlikely, but it runs the risk of curing the illness by killing the patient. While desperate situations require desperate measures, the defeat of tyrannous regimes by tyrannous means is no victory at all. Censorship is an admission of weakness that entrenches the powerlessness of women as much as it strengthens the hand of the patriarchal state. It does not empower women in their own right, nor does it allow the creation of a space within which to resist and realign the misogynist discourse of contemporary society.

Contrary to common expectations, if MacKinnon replaces her classical philosophizing with a more nonfoundationalist approach, it will not inhibit her from arguing that there is truth to women's experience that has been suppressed by the falsity of pornography or from speaking feminist truth to patriarchal power. What it will do is to oblige her to take a less essentialist and more contextual approach to "women's experience," "pornography," "feminist truth," and "patriarchal power." It would oblige her to accept that the idea that there can be an escape to somewhere or something that can give an incontestable foundation to further and future negotiations over feminist truth and patriarchal power is a profoundly political claim that is itself never beyond contestation or debate. There is no nonpolitical place—whether it is science, philosophy, history, experience, human nature, or whatever—to which people can retire to ground their political interventions. Like truth and reality, politics is itself a discursive practice in which the play of power occurs. There is no outside to the world of words and no final escape from the finitude of politics.

However, MacKinnon is right to be concerned that a nonfoundalist approach offers no programmatic or practical prescriptions. There is no nonfoundationalist method or manifesto in the sense of a process that can be followed that will produce and vouchsafe particular results; it is an attitude and a temperament conducive to political engagement. Nevertheless, if by method one means something as prosaic as a way of proceeding, then there are certain lessons for political action and agitation that a nonfoundationalist critique can offer—it denies the univocity of meaning and urges the plurality of interpretation; it realizes that people are never entirely masters of what they say and always partners in the negotiation of meaning; it abandons the preoccupation with universalizable claims and encourages greater attention to social context; it rejects the need for an overarching narrative of political change and accepts the worth of local attempts at transformation; it eschews the taking up of "Right" and "Left" ideological sides and recognizes that politics is diffusely multisided; it does not view freedom as a splendid isolation but as a socially sustained web of relationships; it understands that identity is something that is made and remade, not given and accepted; it emphasizes that while people are always situated and constrained, they are never completely saturated or contained; and it insists that social justice is never a once-and-for-all achievement but a continuing responsibility to keep the question of justice open. All that a nonfoundationalist approach can ultimately do is to reassure people that things need not be the way that they are, that change will always occur, that it is for each person to work for change, and that what amounts to better and worse changes is never incontestable.

A commitment to such a nonfoundationalist perspective is not tantamount to a denial that contemporary society is patriarchal in its sweep and substance or that pornography can be productive of violence against women. But it is to affirm the possibility that society and social life need not be that way. In particular, it reassures people that sex can be more than an aggressive intrusion of a woman by a man and that an erect penis is not always a tool of oppression. As MacKinnon herself demonstrates, such a nonfoundational strategy is no more risky than the present day-to-day business of living for many women in contemporary society. Indeed, a shift to a nonfoundationalist outlook can multiply the sites for resistance to the present order. It is an acknowledgment of pornography's discursive indeterminacy that presents the most viable and effective opportunity for strategic intervention and transformation. Indeed, pornography has occasionally been used as a potent form of dissent from religious and political authority.[42] Its irrepressible openness to multiple interpretations and meanings render it susceptible to alternative readings and deployment against those who presently dominate. Women can begin to explore the discursive possibilities and experiment with new vocabularies that give voice to a broader range of sexual desires and pleasures. Unlike in MacKinnon's account, pornography can be seen as another organic site for continued political struggle and future revalorization rather than only a toxic dump that can only be filled in and kept off limits.

Of course, in saying this, I am not arguing that all sexually explicit representations are good or that they are all bad; that would be to take the same essentialist position as MacKinnon. Depending on the context, some are good and some are bad. To be anti censorship is not to be pro pornography:

this is a ludicrous drawing of ideological lines that distorts and disables any political position. As with all disputed social practices, there is no safe or secure political ground on which to stand or from which to intervene in the pornography debate. As a political engagement, it is always an unstable and shifting medium. Whichever way one turns, there will be trade-offs to be made. To defend sexually explicit representations against legislative prohibition is to be on the side of the pornography industry and its commercialization of all sex. On the other hand, to oppose sexually explicit representations is to be on the side of the Moral Majority and its related campaign against abortion, gays, lesbians, and other groups. Accordingly, the struggle over pornography is not usefully or effectively carried out by prohibiting it entirely. A more progressive and nonfoundationalist strategy is effected by appropriating and revamping the discourse of pornography so that it can be turned into a democratic discourse of political dissent and sexual diversity, not a privileged monologue of men's frustration and women's oppression. The challenge is to rethink and reinvent the nature and diversity of sexual activity by developing more discursive identities and empowering vocabulary that emphasizes "what makes sex a good and positive dimension to our humanity."[43]

Catharine MacKinnon is a little reminiscent of J. D. Salinger's Holden Caulfield. In vain efforts to protect his sister, Phoebe, from obscene graffiti, he goes around erasing them from walls and buildings.[44] Instead of explaining to her why they are there and what discontent they represent, he labors under the naive hope that by effacing them, the obscene ideas and the people who hold them will simply disappear. While Caulfield's and MacKinnon's wish is laudable and defensible, their way of proceeding is misguided and too head-in-the-sand to support or condone. For instance, MacKinnon's plea to reconsider pornography law and sexual practices "in terms of specific experiences, the particularity of history, substantively rather than abstractly" is exactly what is required and exactly what MacKinnon fails to do. Instead of her work being a nuanced and context-sensitive exploration, she commits a flat and sweeping indictment of men, women, and sex throughout history and across societies. Moreover, she seeks to correct it by an equally flat and sweeping solution. She would do much better to pay greater attention to the practices and protocols of power that frame and infuse our experience of sex. If her aim is to create "a context of repose into which thought can expand, an invitation that gives speech its shape, an opening to a new conversation," her work is unlikely to be read as an invitation that can realistically establish a context of repose in which a new conversation can be opened.[45] MacKinnon's approach tends to stifle debate rather than encourage it.

In the most profound sense, a nonfoundationalist approach is the best complement to MacKinnon's political project. It takes seriously the importance of context, speech, and renewed conversation in matters of sex and sexual pleasure. Its commitment is to ensure that the social culture of people's lives is a playful context in which they can constantly reshape themselves and the speech that comprises that culture. The invocation of "play" is, of course, not meant to trivialize sex or violence against women but rather to enlarge the space in which otherness can be encompassed and explored. By treating sex as the ultimate nonfoundationalist space of instability in which the conflicts of power are beyond absolute determination, *jouissance* might be given its fullest expression. In a social space in which freedom and repression are continually renegotiated and resituated, it might be possible to achieve a precarious but exhilarating experience of authentic sexual pleasure that, as MacKinnon puts it, "may mean that one has glimpsed freedom, a rare and valuable and contradictory event."[46] In this way, sexuality might become an activity through which people confirm themselves in their humanity and its limitless possibilities rather than, as MacKinnon suggests, an encounter in which men and women are seemingly obliged to subjugate their own human potential. In life and law's game of sexual relations, it is not so much that "anything goes" but that "anything might go."

Muddling Through

In 1897, a prescient Oliver Wendell Holmes Jr. observed that "for the rational study of the law, the black-letter man may be the man of the present, but the man of the future is the man of statistics and the master of economics."[47] He has been proven right (again). One of the most popular efforts to place law and adjudication on a secure foundational footing is law-and-economics. Its adherents attempt to explain or critique law in terms of economic logic; law is viewed as a series of incentives and disincentives to influence the behavioral choices of people, who are viewed as rational and self-interested maximizers of society's scarce resources. As a mode of positive analysis, it evaluates the empirical impact of different legal rules such as price-setting devices in terms of their allocative efficiency and distributive justice. More controversially, as a mode of normative analysis, it evaluates whether any particular change in legal doctrine will increase *economic efficiency*. Nevertheless, there have been many criticisms of law-and-economics scholarship, including claims that it is conceptually reductionist, politically self-serving, theoretically vague, practically indeterminate, and ethically bankrupt. Yet law-and-economics scholarship does focus attention on the important economic function of legal rules and obliges lawyers to attend to the instrumental consequences of different legal regimes and reforms. Its fatal flaw is that it overreaches itself, and, instead of being content with offering a partial insight into the operation of law and society, it claims to provide a total account of law. As such, it reveals itself to be a political ideology of considerable foundationalist stature as much as a technical critique.

One writer who has sought to do law-and-economics work that is both technically sophisticated and socially sensitive is Michael Trebilcock. In *The Limits of Freedom of Contract* he scrutinizes the claim that the private-ordering paradigm of contracting in a free market is the best institutional arrangement for simultaneously promoting individual freedom and social welfare. He holds that if this claim could be justified, it "would provide a formidable, if not decisive, normative justification for private ordering or other forms of resource allocation in many contexts."[48] To carry out this objective, Trebilcock traverses and evaluates activities as diverse as blood donation, pornography, immigration, prostitution, child custody, racial discrimination, surrogacy, international trade, maternity leave, and, of course, commerce. His standard critical move is to look at the operation of a "free market" in an activity, highlight a particular failure in it (e.g., commodification, coercion, information imperfection, etc.), and suggest the costs and benefits of governmental intervention. In each case, he tries to reach some conclusion about the optimal response, as between allocative and distributional considerations, and about the optimal institutional agency, as between courts and legislation, to achieve this. The result of Trebilcock's analysis in almost all cases is the same—*it is too close to call.* Indeed, despite his avowed foundationalist intention to reduce the frenzy of social life to a fairly simple and overarching explanatory account, Trebilcock manages to give unwitting support to a nonfoundationalist account of law-and-economics.

Some of Trebilcock's best lessons are about indeterminacy and contingency: the social facts are always too unruly to accommodate the economic principles; life is irreducibly complex; and generalization must be avoided. For Trebilcock, economics is not only about making decisions about scarce resources but also about doing so under conditions of historical uncertainty and social instability. As opposed to the scientistic pretensions of mainstream and Marxist economics, there is no one simple and straightforward account that can be given about economics (or law) as a valid description of what goes on and what can be done to change it. The only constant about law, economics, and their interaction is the ceaseless swirl of social forces that defy simple logic and any theoretical attempt to privilege or hypostatize one particular explanation. The theory and practice of law-and-economics are indeterminately political and politically indeterminate; all claims to neutrality are premised on an always undisclosed and often unsensed set of controversial normative commitments about social interaction. This is made plain in Trebilcock's insistent observation that what occurs in one corner of life will have obvious effects on other parts of life; discrete solutions cannot be sanctioned without understanding their larger systemic implications. Consequently, it is important to understand that the introduction of a clearer set of incentives and prohibitions in one area will likely result in greater uncertainty elsewhere. The fact is that the world will not stay still long enough to extract one particular component, then reinsert it in a way that leaves the rest of the world untouched or such that the rest of the world has not since moved on and reconfigured itself into an entirely different set of pressures and problems. As such, the great challenge is not to turn uncertainty into pseudo-certainty, rendering the world determinate and thus perfectly amenable to a once-and-for-all evaluation, but rather to make sense of that uncertainty in such a way that respects it. Modern economics has spectacularly failed to do this and, as Trebilcock himself shows in spite of cautions to the contrary, so has law-and-economics: "*Muddling through* may define our aspirational limits."[49]

Moving from specific issues to more general matters, Trebilcock concedes that such indeterminacy not only exists at the level of operational efficacy, but he grants that "plasticity" is endemic to the guiding principles and controlling concepts themselves; autonomy and efficiency allow for sharp divergences in definition and range. Moreover, there is no "meta-theory that weighs or ranks these various values." However, Trebilcock wants to hold the line at this point and cautions against a slide into a corrosive "nihilism" in which "any set of legal rules that is likely to be constructed for governing the private ordering process is likely to be relatively unprincipled and to reflect the personal normative whims of judges in the case of judge-made law and similar whims on the part of legislators or regulators in framing legislative or regulatory regimes for the contracting process." To guard against such a fate, though, he has only the rather trite observations to offer: "All the values reflected in the various normative perspectives reviewed appear to command wide-spread public support and to be legitimate in their own terms," and "Significant progress can be made at a lower level of abstraction by identifying the institutions or instruments which are best placed, among the array of instruments and institutions available to a community, to vindicate these values." At crucial moments, therefore, Trebilcock loses his nonfoundationalist nerve when he needs it most. For example, in assessing the relative merits of case-by-case adjudication versus legislative regimes for dealing with the pervasive tension between autonomy values and welfare considerations, he cannot resist the temptation to tally up a final accounting and make some decidedly noncontingent recommendations about institutional competence and suitability. Yet the major thrust of his detailed analysis of the relevant data is that such a once-and-for-all reckoning is neither possible nor desirable. When faced with these kinds of basic decisions, Trebilcock's stark injunction is "to think clearly."[50] While this is the best that he is willing to offer, it is unlikely to reap the kind of intellectual dividends that foundationalist theorists crave.

Nonetheless, Trebilcock's work is a strong antidote to those who think that a commitment to law-and-economics is implicitly a commitment to right-wing values. His nonfoundationalist critique, with its emphasis on contingency and indeterminacy, shows that nothing follows, as a matter of necessity, from any particular commitment to some abstract grand-scale values such as equality or liberty. However, this is not to say that a law-and-economics way of thinking about the world does not have certain built-in biases and informing prejudices—as any account will have, including my own. The fatal flaw in Trebilcock's critique is his foundational insistence that it is meaningful to talk about free markets in contrast to schemes of government regulation—that there is some important sense in which a market can be said *not* to be a form of governmental regulation. Indeed, Trebilcock seems to go so far as to suggest that the market is a natural or self-evidently moral arena of social behavior that needs no moral justification but somehow stands as the moral underwriter for what is done in its name: "The perfect market, were it realized, would constitute a morally free zone, a zone within which the constraints of morality would have no place." From a nonfoundationalist perspective, this is an entirely misconceived representation of the market, its relation to governmental regulation, and its moral status. It is never a question of contrasting market allocation with government distribution because the market is one form of government regulation. Contrary to Trebilcock's terms, government regulation is not "an endogenous institutional arrangement"; it is essential to the basic operation of a free market.[51] Without the existence of an authoritative state to define property entitlements, enforce contracts and prevent involuntary transactions, maintain a circulating medium, and curtail monopoly and anticompetitive behavior, there is no market in any real or meaningful sense. Moreover, the choice is never between the allocation of goods by a decentralized market or through centralized government administration. It is a choice between various theories about those choices: "There is no unmeditated epistemological access to something called 'the free market.' "[52]

Many implications flow from Trebilcock's refusal to recognize this vital insight. One is that, by giving critics the burden of justifying intervention, he skews his whole analysis in favor of market-based solutions. Another is that it tends to cast law as a one-dimensional force that only regulates and prohibits activity, rather than as a multifaceted and transformative game through which society continuously reconstitutes itself and expresses its aspirations. Yet the most troubling aspect of this tendency to naturalize the market is its effect upon the all-important question of the nature of market actors and their preference formation. Traditional economics takes preferences as exogenous givens and treats their satisfaction as being presumptively good. Trebilcock, of course, rejects such crude assumptions: "Neoclassical economics essentially has no theory of how preferences are formed . . . [and they] have thus been viewed as exogenous to the exchange process, which simply facilitates their realization." He recognizes that "scholars need to take more seriously the proposition that many individual preferences are socially constructed and are amenable to revision." However, he fails to grasp the corrosive implication of such a recognition in, at least, two important respects.

First of all, although Trebilcock accepts that rich and poor develop their preferences, in part, as a result of their relative positions in the market, he still manages to depict the poor as being poor *outside and independent of* the market. Moreover, he seems to assume that once it is recognized that many individual choices reflect adaptive preferences, the challenge is to predict the kind of choices that people would "make in the absence of social, economic, legal, or other influences that have shaped these preferences."[53] This entirely misses the nonfoundationalist point: people can never be outside or "in the absence of" such influences. Indeed, without such influences, there would be no basis on which to generate preferences or to choose between them; such an account is as deficient as the classical model. People interact with and adapt to their sociohistorical contexts as they struggle to transform and adapt them. The real challenge, therefore, is not to wish away the informing context and then hazard a guess at what hypothetical choices would be made, but to work toward negotiating a context in which people can fully develop and experiment with their preferences. To understand this is to appreciate that freedom, rather than being an absence of constraints, is realized in a particular and changing set of constraints.

Pushed a little further, this insight leads to the second limitation of Trebilcock's analysis. People's identities are affected by their microsocial environments (such as family, friends, colleagues, etc.) and macrosocial environments (such as nationality, class, ethnicity, etc.). Consequently, in a society permeated by economic logic and market imagery, the type of economic arrangements that exist not only influence the substantive preferences that people have but also help shape the kind of persons that people become. For example, within the classic vision of market actors as "preference maximizers" there is little possibility of nurturing a social good that is more than the aggregate of private preferences. Further, it inculcates a consumer mentality and tutors people to be rational economic actors. This is a very sterile and one-dimensional version of human activity and what it means to *play the game*. Market actors are deemed to be cognitively supreme and perfectly rational; they are able to analyze vast amounts of information about alternative courses of action, to prioritize them in terms of their expected utility, and to do so in a perfectly consistent way. Trebilcock is silent on these matters because he fails to appreciate that the market creates this utility monster as much as its acquired preferences. As such, Trebilcock's limited analysis either is truly artificial and thus useless, or it becomes self-evidently trite when it is used to justify any decision by a market actor. It is not that citizens act irrationally but that they follow different and often conflicting rationalities that cannot be reduced to a set of simpleminded directives. Insofar as a market model of human activity simplifies these multiplex calculations, democratic citizens are reduced to little more than fungible consumers: "Once we can convince ourselves that we can picture people evaluating end-states abstracted from their social definition and that we can aspire only to create social institutions that then passively respond to these mysterious end-state judgments, we have moved much too far in the direction of resignation, despairing impotence, and nihilistic skepticism about our capacity to grow."[54]

In contrast to Trebilcock's baseline of a private ordering paradigm, a nonfoundationalist critique suggests an alternative vision of social interaction that is more empowering and enlightened. Rather than taking the market as a given, a nonfoundationalist insists that it needs to be justified as a particular kind of government regulation among a larger mix of schemes and arrangements. It is not exchange in and of itself that should be encouraged but the kind of participation that is not exhausted by an act of market exchange. By reducing participation to exchange, people begin to think of themselves as consumers in all they do, even when they are not in a market situation. My ambition is to ensure that while people are economic consumers some of the time, they are political citizens all of the time.[55] Rather than being about substantive decisions actually made, both civic and market politics recognize that the attempt to legislate what are and are not valid substantive decisions is fraught with historical and ideological difficulty. Accordingly, attention must be focused on the process in and through which people make those substantive decisions. Whereas the market obtains its authority from people's consuming decisions, the practice of citizenship involves a more expanded notion of participation. Markets allow only for differences counted in terms of dollars, and, therefore, the primary difference is between the haves and have-nots. Democratic politics allows for an expanded recognition of differences that can be counted and debated in many different ways. Such a nonfoundationalist commitment does not mean that the future history of economic arrangements will amount to "a random walk in socio-political space."[56] To concede that it is indeterminacy all the way down is not to succumb to an arbitrary or whimsical account of policy making. On the contrary, it affirms the idea that such policy making must become a truly public practice and participatory process. There are only various and competing modes of reasoning that are always part of, not apart from, the debate over policy making. Judges, policy makers, economists, lawyers, and citizens are forever situated in a socioeconomic context that influences them as they strive to influence it.

To achieve his goal of a society that can effectively debate and integrate individual liberty and social equality, Trebilcock needs more than economic language and theory. Otherwise, his world will be economic and nothing else: *homo economicus* rules and is hegemonic in its ambitions. Utilizing the jargon of economics as the language of citizenship tends to make us think of ourselves as only consumers, competitors, enemies, and the like rather than as occasional colleagues, neighbors, friends, and the like. In the same way as all languages, an economic vernacular is not transparent but instead contributes to and constitutes the world in which people live. When people begin to talk of themselves as market actors and consumers, they begin to act out their allotted parts in a game that is not of their own making. In contrast, unlike the individualist cast of Trebilcock's economic liberalism, it might be possible to understand society not only as a crude aggregate of separate things but also as connected players in a thriving game in which individuals are not viewed as universal and abstract moral entities but are situated within a local and concrete context; they are political beings with particular historical and social affiliations. As between people, a sense of belonging and reciprocal responsibility for others might be fostered. Instead of a freedom that is contractual in origin and static in nature, it could be understood more organically and dynamically. If it was sometimes accepted that the social whole was much greater than the haphazard aggregation of its individual parts, personal worth and self-esteem might come to be understood as being embedded in and nourished by affective affiliations. Instead of relying upon transcendent values and abstract rationality, the search for social justice could be based upon a practical reason that is contextual and contingent in character. The political agora and the economic marketplace would cease to be simply arenas for the confrontation of competing wills and the satisfaction of individual wants and might become crucibles in which to forge and reforge common goods.

From a nonfoundationalist perspective, citizenship is more a social activity than an individual status and allows people to inhabit the contested terrain between individual rights and communal Right by colonizing it in the name of democratic performance and play. Neither individualistic nor communitarian, it recognizes that any vision of "the good life" (or what it means to *play the game*) is always provisional and contingent. There is no fixed or final version of what amounts to the best way to live: the good life is to be found in the details of living, socially and privately, which must be constantly reworked and renegotiated. Whereas liberals put representative democracy in the service of private values and Marxists imagine that direct democracy will bring an end to politics, participatory citizens accept that the relation between public virtue and private values is open to revisable articulation and that the attraction of democracy is its promise to keep politics permanently open and fluid. As such, citizenship under radical democracy is not committed to one common good but to an engaged practice of civility in which a good life consists in public-spirited engagement with others over the shape and substance of "the good life." Within this democratic understanding, it is possible to integrate *homo economicus* into a much broader and deeper conversational context. The notion of the "free market" and its abstract denizens would not be outside or beyond political authority; it would be within its bailiwick. Whereas economic actors exist in an abstract realm of optional interactions with anonymous others, the citizen is located at a historical time and in a local place where personal and social living is situated in a web of connections between real people. It might mean that in exercising their rights and making claims, people would take into account their responsibilities to others, particularly those less fortunate and more vulnerable than themselves. Actions and practices would have to be evaluated within the sociohistorical context of the democratic community in which the particular mix of entitlements and responsibilities would always be reconfigurable in light of contingent concerns.

In calling for the abandonment of markets as the theoretical and organizational paradigm for civic interaction, I am not to be taken to be making some commitment to a discredited and disavowed model of a state-planned economy. Any lingering faith in the possibility that a planned distribution of goods and services through bureaucratic channels might be the best alternative to a free market ideology is to be thoroughly debunked and discarded; such polarized thinking is entirely antithetical to a nonfoundationalist and democratic way of proceeding. The mainstream notions of unified economic actors with fixed preferences, instrumental causality, and objective rationality are also preoccupations of Marxian economic thought. Indeed, it sees itself as making up for and correcting the relativism, uncertainty, and indeterminacy of the mainstream models of economic theorizing. However, in the same way that Marxian economists have been quick to overemphasize the disordered and negative nature of capitalist markets, they have exaggerated the ordered and positive consequences of a state-planned economic order.[57] Neither a market-based nor a planned economy is as predictable, rational, or controlled as its apologists contend. This search for a structural and fixed foundation that can account convincingly for present economic behavior and that can forecast confidently for future economic arrangements is misconstrued: contingency is incorrigible and indeterminacy is inextinguishable.

At different times and in different ways, policy makers must be prepared to experiment with a variety of strategies and interventions that draw pragmatically on the imagery of both neoclassical market thinking and its Marxian critique as viewed with a suitably nonfoundationalist optic. At his nonfoundationalist best, Trebilcock recognizes this imperative. He tenders his doctrinal proposals as "provisional and contingent"; they are offered as conditional contributions that were shaped in scholarly debate and will be further revised as that exchange continues. As such, he plays a vital and appropriate role in political engagement: "If everyone takes the position that a provisional view is too presumptuous and disrespectful of other participants in the conversation, there will be a collective silence."[58] However, at his foundationalist worst, Trebilcock ignores the compelling force of a nonfoundational critique at his own and everyone else's peril. While he is willing to debate the thrust and wisdom of particular proposals and initiatives, he seems only prepared to do so within the limited and limiting confines of one particular paradigm of law and policy formation. If Trebilcock were to acknowledge that foundationalist inhibition, he might be more open to recognizing that democratic conversation's ludic possibilities might be found in law-and-economics' lost opportunities.

Conclusion

In this chapter, I have sought to defend a nonfoundationalist approach to politics against charges that it is ineffectual as a mode of progressive critique and, therefore, is necessarily conservative in implication. Drawing examples from both political left and right, I have demonstrated that a nonfoundational account is not only superior to the foundationalist claims of much political theorizing but that it is the most effective complement to a genuine commitment to a truly democratic society. Such a stance ought not to be taken to imply that traditional political theory has nothing to offer or contribute. From a nonfoundationalist perspective, it is possible to learn from Marx without committing to the entire Marxist cause, and to learn from liberals without committing to the entire liberal project. Indeed, it is less about being for or against Marxism or liberalism than about rejecting such accounts as universal programs for human emancipation and empowerment. Eschewing all-encompassing theoretical statements of progressive possibilities to which one must swear allegiance, a nonfoundationalist response is much more pragmatic, piecemeal, and eclectic than that. As played out in the institutional sites of law, the treatment of adjudication as a language game of political sport and consequence enables judges and jurists to "place legal analysis in the service of democratic experimentalism . . . and turn legal thought into a marriage between social realism and social prophecy."[59] Moreover, by understanding that such a democratic commitment demands that the dynamic motion of political poetry not be allowed to calcify into the static duplication of legal prose, judges and jurists can guard against the tendency to allow law's transformative potential to be eclipsed by adjudication's reactive instincts. In this way, it might become possible to grasp that because language is social practice, it will be necessary to develop a way of life that accepts that indeterminacy and transformation are inevitable—the only real choice is whether to concede this understanding regretfully and cling to the status quo or to embrace it enthusiastically and risk today's constraints for tomorrow's freedom.

10 Playing with the Rules: Experiments in Judging

No guru, no method, no teacher.

—Van Morrison, "Poetic Champions Compose"

In defending and elaborating a nonfoundationalist account of law and adjudication, my main focus has been to explain what it is that judges do in deciding cases. In particular, I have been concerned to dismiss the claims of foundationalists (of an internalist and externalist bent) and antifoundationalists as being both descriptively inaccurate and prescriptively unrealizable. While each theory offers various insights that can add to any understanding of law and adjudication, both fail to live up to their own theoretical expectations as the only or best explanation of judicial practice. Too often, the theories run out of critical steam at the very point that they are most needed—in the identification and resolution of so-called hard cases. However, if mainstream jurists could accept the idea that the test of good judging is less about getting it right than about doing it well, jurisprudence might begin to redeem itself. The sooner jurists and judges recognize that the limits and standards of being a good judge are the limits and standards of being a good game player—vision, technique, application, industry, conditioning, insight, openness, fairness, humility, and a willingness to experiment—the better it will be. The hallmark of great judges, as with great game players, is not their encyclopedic knowledge of the rules but their uncommon ability to improvise and transform conventional standards for playing law's infinite game. By taking seriously the injunction that "anything might go," they extend the very idea and practice of what it means to *play the game.*

Within the foundationalist frame of reference, playfulness and lack of closure are marginalized features of law and adjudication. However, even this is more by way of reluctant concession than enthusiastic embrace. Whether this is arrived at from Hart's positivist concern with language or Dworkin's naturalist attention to values, human frailties are considered to prevent judges from perfecting the process of adjudication as a bounded and determinate exercise in legal and/or moral judgment.[1] These jurists argue that while it is possible in theory to imagine the achievement of the foundationalist project, law and adjudication are destined as human enterprises to be imprecise and messy practices. In contrast, I intend to convert the foundationalists' frustration into the nonfoundationalists' triumph. Rather than treat the fact of law's indeterminacy and adjudication's openness as something to be lamented, I will treat it as something to be celebrated. Confirming the understanding of adjudication as a rhetorical performance in law's infinite language game, a nonfoundationalist account places the idea of experimentation at the heart of judicial practice. Moreover, this sense of judicial playfulness is not only encouraged in regard to legal rules; it is also fostered as the best way to deal with political values. By cultivating a healthy sense of humility, judges can be more skeptical about the wisdom of their own values in determining the right thing to do or to decide. Paying attention to context and distrusting broad generalities, nonfoundational judges accept that there is no method or manifesto in the sense of a process that can be followed that will produce and vouchsafe particular results; a nonfoundationalist approach is an attitude and a temperament. In short, judges must have the courage of their legal and political convictions: they must resolve to be "bold spirits" rather than "timorous souls."[2]

In this chapter, therefore, I will supplement my nonfoundational account of what it is that judges do with some suggestions on what it means for judges to do it well. In the first two sections, I will explore the conventional virtues that have been associated with good judging and place them within a nonfoundational frame of reference. While I confirm the traditional emphasis on excellent technique and professional skills, a nonfoundational account demands that these not be treated as sufficient in themselves; they must be placed within a more playful vision of legal craft and politics. Disabused of the foundationalist project's appeal, such ludic judges might come to embrace law's incorrigible indeterminacy and adjudication's openness rather than resist them. In the second half of the chapter, I compare and contrast this "experimental" depiction of the judicial function with the present performance of leading judges. Using the American Supreme Court's decision and judgments in *R.A.V.* as a starting point, I demonstrate that while the judges pay lip service to the foundationalist project, their judgments can be plausibly understood and criticized in nonfoundational terms. In the final section, pushing through on the nonfoundational insight about the need for greater diversity in judicial personnel, I look at the possibilities for further democratization in the legal process by enhancing the role of juries. Throughout the chapter, I contend that judges act most judicially when they do not flinch from the democratic challenge to engage in "courageous and imaginative experimentation."[3]

The Judicial Craft

The debate over what makes a "great judge" and which judicial personalities should be included among its hallowed numbers is as heated and as divisive as any other in the jurisprudential literature. It should come as no surprise to learn that this debate is as contested as the broader engagement over the nature and purpose of law and adjudication; the two are connected in obvious and inextricable ways. The jurists' standards of what counts as a paradigmatic example of good judging will be informed by their commitment to a particular theory of law and adjudication. For instance, whether judges are to be praised for their technical expertise, their political acumen, or both will largely depend on the background understanding about the task in which the judges are supposed to be engaged and the resources that they are expected to utilize: the positivist will be less concerned about the law's moral worth than the naturalist, who will be more concerned about structural coherence than the pragmatist. Fraught with difficulties and disagreements, the whole exercise is not so much a welcome relief from jurisprudential contention as a more focused and less abstract venue and version of it. From a nonfoundationalist perspective, the debate in and around "great judging" is simply one more intellectual location for further engagements over what it means to *play the game*.

Nevertheless, the obvious difficulties of arriving at any neutral or uncommitted account of what makes a great judge and who should be included in its hallowed ranks have not managed to dissuade jurists from engaging in such an exercise. Indeed, developing lists of the essential qualities that great judges should possess and determining which judges meet such exalted standards has become something of an academic parlor game, especially in the United States. For example, a classic and esteemed effort to identify judicial greatness is made by Henry J. Abrahams. He offers a list of the top ten qualities of the Great American Judge that all judges should aspire to and that a small handful of judges actually do embody; whereas Hugo Black and Lewis Powell make the cut, Thurgood Marshall and Learned Hand do not. While his list contains many predictable qualities (like craftsmanship, personal integrity, and proper training) that most observers would accept, it also includes a number of question-begging requirements (like "demonstrated judicial temperament," "absolute fair-mindedness," and "a solid understanding of the proper judicial role of judges under the Constitution") that go to the very heart of the debate over what does make a judge great and, by implication, what the judicial task is all about anyway.[4] Indeed, these criteria do not provide answers to the problem posed but simply rephrase the main questions to be answered—what counts as "demonstrated judicial temperament" and "a solid understanding of the proper judicial role of judges under the Constitution" are the very stuff of jurisprudential debate.

Of course, when viewed from a nonfoundationalist perspective, it will be recognized that the qualities of judicial greatness are historically contingent in that they shift and change over time—what it means to be a great judge is part of the infinite game over what it means to *play the game*. This is not to say that there are no standards at work but only that those standards are always in the play of law's adjudicative and jurisprudential game, not outside its dynamic performances. This means that not only will the qualities of judicial greatness be in the process of constant transition and transformation but also that those judges who are considered to embody most of these select indicia will also switch over time; the heroic judges of one era can become the villains of another. Indeed, a sampling of judicial biographies reveals that they are as much about the appropriate criteria by which to assess judicial achievement as they are about the particular judge(s) under sustained scrutiny. For instance, in his recent tome on Learned Hand (one of the frequent candidates for inclusion in the Judicial Hall of Fame), Gerald Gunther devotes a considerable portion of his lengthy analysis to a comparison of Hand with Holmes. However, in touting the virtues of Hand over those of Holmes, he argues less that Hand has the qualities of a great judge than that the qualities of the great judge are defined by Hand. While Hand's judicial record is marked by "disinterestedness and lack of crusading zeal," this did not condemn him to intellectual impotence, because, according to Gunther, "His decisions were noted for . . . superior craftsmanship and for creative performance within the confines set by the executive and legislative branches."[5]

While being mindful of the nonfoundational admonition about the historical contingency and political partiality of standards for judicial greatness, it is still possible to suggest and defend certain approaches to the judicial task that are more compatible (or, at least, less incompatible) with the insights and imperatives of a nonfoundational account of law and adjudication. The whole idea of "judicial greatness" is a dangerous and dispensable notion, but there are certain general qualities that judges would do well to emulate and enhance if they wanted to perform their responsibilities in a professional and proper manner. Some of these should be apparent from the overall thrust of the nonfoundationalist critique. In particular, judges should look to develop a range of skills and attributes that might further and enrich their capacity to participate in the play of law's language game in a more effective and telling way. As well as industry and intelligence, these qualities might include vision, technique, playfulness, and humility. However, it is important to stress that these general attributes are to be interpreted and substantiated in line with the opportunities and demands of the informing context. Accordingly, it will be for each judge to decide for herself or himself what those qualities require, in what way they can be blended together, and how they are to be deployed in any particular context or situation. As with any aspect of judicial practice, there is no escape from the opportunities and responsibilities of choice.

From a nonfoundationalist perspective, it should be clear from the outset that judicial responsibility is not about unthinking obeisance to external rules; the denial of complexity and ambiguity in the service of the Rule of Law is the epitome of irresponsible behavior. Instead, judges must begin to understand that their institutional duty is best fulfilled not by seeking to avoid or finesse political values but by taking stands on particular rules and being accountable for those choices. Indeed, even a positivist like Hart himself accepted that a nonfoundational approach had two major, beneficial effects for the adjudicative enterprise—the practical and the political. These entail "first, that [judges] should always suspect, although not always in the end reject, any claim that existing legal rules or precedents were constraints strong and complete enough to determine what a court's decision should be without other extra-legal considerations; secondly, that judges should not seek to bootleg silently into the law their own conceptions of the law's aims or justice or social policy or other extra-legal elements required for decision, but should openly identify and discuss them."[6]

In prescient fashion, Hart was hinting—even if he did not concede—that the battery of adjudicative techniques for rule application did not amount to a self-contained technology: they only made sense as part of a larger understanding of law as a rhetorical enterprise. Being a practical activity, adjudication does not consist of a series of formulaic applications in an abstract space but is instead a functional engagement in real time; it is less an occasion for logical operations than an exercise in operational logic. Accordingly, any judge must be well versed in both of the two sets or structures of rules in play—there are not only the legal rules that are the object and substance of the game but also the interpretive rules that stipulate how the game of "playing with the rules" is to be played. Although these competing strategies of adjudication are passed off as ideologically unaligned, they are rhetorical resources in a continuing political struggle for the hermeneutical soul of law. While the impact and success of any particular maneuver or performance will vary with context and audience, judges cannot avoid the opportunities and accompanying responsibility for making political choices. Always a part of and not apart from power, law is a discourse of persuasion, and the judicial craft cannot be reduced to an exclusively professional pursuit. However, there is nothing arbitrary or capricious about this process; values, convictions, and interpretations are no less real or compelling because they are contingent and historical, and they are no more real or compelling because they are underwritten by the spurious logic of some pseudoneutral interpretive strategy. As Fish hooks it, it is not that "all rhetorical constructions are equal, just that they are equally rhetorical."[7] In the nonfoundational almanac, the logic of the law is the rhetorical experience of adapting law to life.

The traditional skills and techniques of the judicial craft are central to the performance of this rhetorical practice. Nonetheless, while the learned knack of using legal materials with adroitness and dexterity is not to be underrated, the effect of such a limited depiction of lawyers' special and distinctive expertise is that it can too easily be used to avoid the democratic responsibility of justifying their power and authority by reference to the real-world pressure of getting the job done. For example, Sunstein defends a modest version of professional craft as the learned ability to make intuitive judgments about fixed points in the legal universe and to fathom ways to render them consistent enough to let legal reasoning proceed. Apart from its foundationalist underpinnings, this account glosses over the more ambitious claims made for it. By insisting that good lawyering must turn on a discipline of restraint and restriction, even the most pragmatic of foundationalists, like Sunstein, turn lawyering into an inward and insular profession.[8] This depiction of the judicial craft artificially and unnecessarily cuts law and adjudication off from the sustaining sociopolitical context and rich historical resources from which they gain their vigor and from the conscience with which they achieve their highest democratic calling. Legal artistry demands more than technical proficiency. The best judicial craftspersons are not those who simply reproduce mechanically and mindlessly old arguments and trite analogies; they are those who can rework legal materials in an imaginative and stylish way. The foundationalist commitment to precedent and the doctrine of stare decisis are craftily observed in their pragmatic breach. A bare legal craft can too easily acquire the elite habits of a Masonic order and fail to meet or sabotage its civic obligations: a job well done is not always its own reward.

As things presently stand, the judicial craft seems designed to serve only its own parochial and foundationalist ends. To be worthy of their professional prestige, lawyers and judges must nurture a sense of social justice and a feel for political vision, unless they are to become only hired hands for vested interests: "Technique without ideals is a menace; ideals without technique are a mess."[9] Adjudication is not carpentry. While judges would do well to inculcate the equivalent judicial pride in their work, they also must be designers and innovators who place their professional craft in the service of political values and ideals. It is true that legal tables will wobble and precedential doors will jam without crafted care and attention, but there is a significant difference between the doors and tables of a torture chamber and those of a hospital ward; a hospital bed is not a torture rack, although it can become one. Politics can be hidden but cannot be done away with altogether. Foundationalist judges and jurists cannot so easily evade taking responsibility for the artifacts and outcomes of their crafted performances by taking refuge in matters of technical consistency and internal coherence. In the same way that a block of wood only has whatever shape and symmetry that it happened to pick up at the last turn of the carpenter's lathe, the law possesses only whatever shape and symmetry that it happened to acquire during the last occasion for legal reasoning.[10]

In insisting that judges must demonstrate a willingness to combine techniques and ideals in order to become gifted and respected performers in law's rhetorical language game, it needs to be remembered that this recommendation is very different in direction and justification from that of foundationalist and antifoundationalist jurists. In particular, the reference to "political ideals and values" is to be understood in a nonfoundational way. Most important, of course, no particular results or consequences necessarily follow from the adoption of such a commitment: there is no one tried-and-true program for political action, because politics itself is always contestable and can never be a privileged ground for anything. Once a nonfoundational critique strives to become doctrinaire or programmatic, it ceases to be nonfoundational. All that a nonfoundational critique can do is to caution judges and jurists that while adjudication cannot be defended or justified as a special apolitical or professional activity, it also cannot be defended or justified as a straightforward working through of a comprehensive ideology. As such, a nonfoundational critique simply promotes "a way of getting rid of some left-over Platonic and Cartesian rubbish" that continues to clutter the legal and political mind.[11] Furthermore, while a nonfoundationalist critique cannot guarantee a politics that will be uniformly progressive or whose practice will be consistently effective, a commitment to what are presently considered to be progressive initiatives is not incompatible with it. Mindful that what counts as progressive will be contextual and open to revision, one can make such an assessment only with attention to the local conditions and the prevailing exigencies of the situation. Consequently, a nonfoundational critique can open spaces for action and increase opportunities for transformation, but it cannot fill those spaces.

A Ludic Style

In articulating the qualities of the "great judge," the foundationalists (of both an internalist and an externalist persuasion) rely on mythical figures who cast long shadows over judicial practice and tend to dominate the jurisprudential scene. The two most well known of these two contending judicial chimeras are *Hercules* and *Hero*. Whereas Hercules is a super-judge who seeks to make the law the best that it can be, Hero is a super-critic who views law as a truncated and discredited mode of politics.[12] Each of them represents a theoretical commitment to a very foundationalist set of premises about law and politics. While Hercules can identify an abiding and all-encompassing political integrity in extant legal materials, Hero can formulate a theoretical program of practical politics that informs the critical transformation of legal doctrine. In contrast to these foundationalist myths, I want to introduce my own suitably nonfoundational breed of judges. I will call them the modest and playful *Ludics*. Ludics are more accepting of law's rule-based existence and less naive about politics' promise of transformation than Hero, and more realistic about judges' real-world capabilities and less fearful of politics' potential for debasement than Hercules. Unlike Hero, Ludics respect the need for institutional deference and, while recognizing its creative possibilities, accept that conventional legal doctrine has its appeal. Unlike Hercules, Ludics maintain that law is neither reducible entirely to unadulterated politics nor capable of being worked up into pure integrity. In short, they recognize that they are bound by an official tradition of legal reasoning but insist that there is ample room to experiment within and with its confines. Consequently, trading in nothing more pretentious than legal reasoning, these judicial players might be able to combine to salvage the legal enterprise from these prevailing hyper-imaginings. At the same time as they experiment with the law to transformative effect, they might be able to restore legal faith in the redemptive power of law's daily rites and rituals.

When judges begin to understand themselves as rhetorical participants in law's infinite language game, they become less troubled by law's incorrigible indeterminacy and adjudication's openness. Indeed, disabused of the foundationalist project's appeal, they might come to embrace those features rather than resist them. Once it is fully accepted that law is a game of infinite possibilities, judges might abandon the beliefs that law and adjudication are closed and determinate practices and that openness and indeterminacy are to be feared. Of course, this does not mean participants are free to do as they wish. They are always participating within their extant context, which they must struggle to change as they play within its constraints. However, once aware of the constructive nature of the boundaries, judges and jurists might realize that their task is less about looking than about seeing. When it comes to law and adjudication, it is people's vision that constrains them, not the legal materials. In this sense, change is as much a matter of imagination as anything else. However, such a realization does not lead into the clutches of the discredited antifoundationalists. Nonfoundational judges will appreciate that, like nonfoundational philosophers, their positive task "is to fecundate [their] analytical skills with dreams and to discipline [their] dreams with analysis." In striving to do this, judges will work with and through the rules, but there will be no governing manual of rules: there is only the continuing responsibility to dream and experiment in reasonable and reasoned ways. And, of course, there are "no rules and regulations for dreaming reasonable dreams."[13]

In going about this experimental work, judges will take a characteristically nonfoundational attitude toward the meaning and merit of past decisions; they recognize that another present way of understanding the past is to imagine a better future. Whereas foundationalist judges and jurists are conservative in the sense that they respect historical continuity for its own sake and treat the doctrinal past as the primary source of future enlightenment, ludic judges seek to make a critical accommodation with the legal tradition by combining heresy and heritage in a playful judicial style. As such, judges should consider themselves neither formalistically bound to perpetuate the wisdom of past decisions nor instrumentally free to craft future decisions; they work the present space between the past and the future. In the experimental spirit of a nonfoundational critique, they might take seriously Holmes's aphorisms that "continuity with the past is only a necessity, not a duty" and that it is "revolting to have no better reason for a rule of law than that it was laid down in the time of Henry IV."[14] So informed, they might begin to push through on the implications of the nonfoundationalist insight that history and its situated reason are not a foundation on which to build but instead a resource site from which to draw. In the nonfoundational thesaurus, yesterday is a foreign country: earlier decisions possess no free-standing or self-justifying precedential value but must continually earn their spurs afresh through dint of their contemporary pertinence to new problems and contexts. Neither historical longevity nor contemporary newness has particular valence in fashioning present solutions to future problems. From a nonfoundationalist point of view, past legal decisions combine to form a valuable institutional almanac of experimental strategies; their relevance and results are to be tested and retested in the service of making society a better place to live, as long as they are understood in a nonfoundational way.

In thinking of law as an institutional laboratory, judges and lawyers ought not to be thought of as scientists, armed with computer spreadsheets and complicated apparatuses, seeking to fathom eternal answers to life's universal mysteries. For instance, foundationalists, like Weinrib and Dworkin, run the grave risk of depicting law and adjudication as practices or games, like chess, that can (at least, in theory) be reduced to a formulaic performance—

coherence resonates with the language of science, not humanity. Indeed, the recent chess contest between grand master Gary Kasparov and the computer Deep Blue intimates the kind of jurisprudential scenario that is unintentionally suggested by the idea that law might be constantly "working itself pure."[15] Whatever a computer's merits or possibilities might be in chess, the problems with law and adjudication are much more severe. Computer programming generally is based on binaries, and they do not allow for what might be called fuzzy logic. The binary tends to work in terms of "if *a*, then do *b*," so it does not cope well with problems or solutions that depend on a condition of "kind of *a*" or "kind of *b*." Logic is of little help in determining such "kind of" issues. While Deep Blue can imitate, it cannot create ex nihilo. In the same sense, the search for "coherence" is only one way among many to play law's language game and must be justified as such—it is neither natural nor pure.

Notwithstanding the technological possibilities in chess, law's intelligence is not reducible to statistical permutations and evaluations. As a finite game, there are limited opportunities for truly creative experimentation and improvisation in chess: a good move is determined only in functional terms of its contribution to winning the game, not by reference to its capacity to thrill or alter how we think about the game and its adaptive possibilities. The real challenge for the (humanly created) computer is whether it can imagine new ways to play chess or create new games entirely. Indeed, the Big Blue phenomenon is not really about a computer against a human in a natural contest but rather about a team of computer-creating humans against one human in a humanly created game: Big Blue won because of the ability of humans to imagine, create, and program such a machine. After all, both chess and Big Blue are human creations. If anything, the victory by Big Blue confirms, not diminishes, the power of human creativity. Compared to chess, the legal game of adjudication is an entirely different kind of playful activity in which the game's rules not only enable the practice but are themselves always in play. When understood in a nonfoundationalist way, adjudication is open to the imaginative move that transforms the game that is being played. Indeed, the judicial imagination is the infinite and unquantifiable variable that simply does not fit into the foundational ambition or scheme of things; it is disruptive and unpredictable in the most profound sense.

In contrast to the scientific imagery of foundationalists, the informing image of nonfoundational judges is that of industrial artists. Working with whatever materials are at hand, they mix and match them in an imaginative way that is a contingent expression of their artistic convictions about truth, beauty, justice, and other ideals in modern society. The excellence of their craft—unhindered by debates about the "true nature" of art or the "correctness" of artistic insight—is found in their connectedness with the world, not some arcane retreat from it.[16] Industrial artists are *industrial* precisely because they do not live exclusively in the studio, do not deal exclusively with paints and canvas, and do not speak exclusively to dealers and critics. Indeed, they are industrial in part because their contribution so often disappears into the product, blended with the contribution of other artists. But it is also bent to the discipline of technology, market constraints, popular tastes, union rules, and other forces that marginalize them and their artistic aspirations and talents. The effect of this, over time, is to habituate them to their role in industry and to cause them to distance themselves from the effete world of Art. But, at the same time, they are making real contributions to industry and changing society by the improvements that they are able to make in the practicality, aesthetics, and cost efficiency of kettles and cars. For such artists and judges, the best accolades are earned not for their technical prowess but for their capacity to engender local hope in the struggle to transform experience, to overcome suffering, and to endow others with opportunities to remake their own world.[17]

Understood in this nonfoundational way, judges will be entitled to be most satisfied with themselves and their work when they are praised not for the legal soundness of their work but for the bold invention of their proposals. Whereas the foundationalist mind is "of a doctrinaire and authoritative complexion: the phrase *must be* is ever on its lips," a nonfoundational judge is more "a happy-go-lucky anarchistic sort of creature" who recognizes both the appeal and responsibility of experimentation.[18] Of course, awareness of the consequences of a decision is an important ingredient in the experimental process. Indeed, judges and jurists must not fall into the foundationalist trap of assessing judicial decisions only in terms of legal craft and rhetorical cogency: the measure of a decision's institutional worth is, as much as anything else, its practical efficacy and social consequences. Nevertheless, ludic judges must perform their imaginative experiments with an intellectual honesty and humility. Paying attention to context and distrusting broad generalities, they must be conscious of their imagination's limitations and guard against the foundationalist tendency to translate personal insight into universal truth. Although expressed in rather grandiloquent terms, the advice of F. J. Stephen seems well suited to the task of ludic judges who have taken to heart the nonfoundationalist critique:

> In all important transactions of life we have to take a leap in the dark. . . . [I]f we decide to leave the riddles unanswered, that is a choice; if we waiver in our answer, that, too, is a choice; but whatever choice we make, we make it at our peril. If a man chooses to turn his back alto-

> gether on God and the future, no one can prevent him; no one can show beyond reasonable doubt that he is mistaken. If a man thinks otherwise and acts as he thinks, I do not see that anyone can prove that he is mistaken. Each must act as he thinks best; and if he is wrong, so much the worse for him. We stand on a mountain path in the midst of swirling snow and blinding mist, through which we get glimpses now and then of paths which may be deceptive. If we stand still we shall be frozen to death. If we take the wrong road we shall be dashed to pieces. We do not certainly know whether there is any right one. What must we do? "Be strong and of good courage." Act for the best, hope for the best, and take what comes. . . . If death ends all, we cannot meet death better.[19]

What would be the qualities of good ludic judges? What kind of people would make the best ludic judges? Emphasis should be placed on the substantive qualities that judges possess as individuals and citizens. It is people who have a diversity of experience, who can open themselves to the situations of others, and who value the worth of compassion, sensitivity, and humanity who would best qualify. While it will not disqualify the hard-headed or the unsentimental, such a revised judicial mandate will require the capacity to be creative and imaginative in the use of rules. In so doing, such judges will not be acting in an arbitrary, idiosyncratic, or ideological way. By working to bring their values and commitments to articulate consciousness in order to understand and interrogate them, they will be acting with the candor that democracy encourages and taking responsibility for what they do in a way democracy expects. By rejecting the hackneyed and unsustainable notion of an entirely differentiated role, judges might begin to gain the respect of the public and themselves. In the same way that "good oratory is a good person speaking well,"[20] so good judging is a good person deciding well. Of course, the notion of what qualities or characteristics go to make up the "good person" is itself always open to debate and disagreement. Similarly, there is no magical guide to be followed as to what judges should do or how they should do it in any specific or conflict-riven situation. Ludic judges will not shy away from a resort to values. As well as always keeping those values in play, they will ensure that the values remain open to reconsideration and that full responsibility is taken for them.

Within this nonfoundationalist frame of reference, the qualities of the great judicial players in law's language game are not so different from those that are exhibited by judges who are traditionally acknowledged to belong to law's judicial pantheon. While good judges are lauded for their technical abilities in parsing cases and rooting out inconsistencies, great judges are celebrated for their vision and inventiveness: "Dealing with great tasks as play . . . is a sign of greatness."[21] The judges who take most seriously the experimental imperative are those who flaunt conventional standards in the process of reformulating them; their judgments are the exceptions that prove the rule. Indeed, some of the great judges of the common law tradition, like Benjamin Cardozo in the United States, Alfred Denning in England, Lionel Murphy in Australia, and Bertha Wilson in Canada, are precisely those who refuse to be hampered by customary habits of judicial mind. For instance, the lasting attraction of Learned Hand's (in)famous judgment in *Carroll Towing*—"The barge owner's duty . . . is a function of three variables: (1) The probability that she will break away; (2) the gravity of the resulting injury, if she does; (3) the burden of adequate precautions. Possibly, it serves to bring this notion into relief to state it in algebraic terms: if the probability be called P; the injury, L; and the burden, B; liability depends on whether B is less than L multiplied by P: i.e., whether $B<PL$"[22]—is not to be found in the substantive wisdom of the decision nor in the fact that he somehow managed to get it right. Instead, from a nonfoundationalist perspective, its canonical quality ought to be found in the ludic example that he set for others by giving other judges the courage to follow their own experimental convictions.

What makes Holmes, Cardozo, Denning, and Wilson great judges is much the same as what makes George Best, Dick Fosbury, Muhammad Ali, and Olga Korbut great players: it is not whether they somehow got it right but that they played with a panache, a style that caught the imagination and changed people's understanding of what it means to *play the game*. By making novel moves, they played the game as much with the rules as within the rules. Such ludic judges recognize that law is not something to be mastered but that it is an infinite game of transformation in which experimentation and improvisation are valued as much as predictability and faithfulness to existing rules and ideas of what it is to *play the game*. At its most audacious, this style of judging demands "the willingness to stay in play, stay with the flux, without bailing out at the last moment . . . [and] in keeping alive that indefiniteness, that possible-who-knows-when, may be-soon, maybe-now, that sense of working on thin ice, without assurance, keeping the play in play, keeping the exposure to the abyss in play, without arresting or tranquillizing it."[23] When played by technically skilled and imaginatively gifted players, adjudication is neither a hubristic effort to bring the game to a perfect end nor an irresponsible attempt to foment chaos; it is an infinitely variable process in which there is never any ultimate victory or performance but only the repeated and unrepeatable working of the space between order and chaos, freedom and constraint, and permanence and contingency.

By celebrating the fact that law is the playful continuation of politics by other rhetorical means, skeptical judges will recognize their inevitable role as agents of political activism. Rather than talk with Weinrib and Dworkin about the common law "working itself pure," judges will be content to know that, through their own efforts and imagination, the law is simply *working itself.* Within this nonfoundational understanding of law and politics, judicial players are capable of imagining and opening themselves up to legal and political possibilities other than those presently available. Such ludic judges do not think of themselves as actors in another's story. Instead, they are committed to being "joyful poets of the story that continues to originate what they cannot finish."[24] In a legal community that understands the force of the nonfoundational critique, the resort to politics will cease to be an aberration or indulgence that judges occasionally choose to do but will instead be something that they will come to live and do as part of the daily routine of their professional lives. Consequently, when involved in the infinite play of rule application, judges and jurists can continue to pretend that they can ignore politics and the burden of choice or they can come clean on their political affiliations in a more open and responsible way. Contrary to foundationalist fears, candor and humility is the best way for judges to fulfill their democratic responsibilities. By taking rules skeptically and by diversifying the judicial ranks, the courts can become one more venue for the infinite game of democratic transformation. Within such a nonfoundationalist society, jurists will not strive to reveal the essence of Law or Social Justice, but they will recognize that the challenge is to make everyone players such that they are participants, in various forms and styles, in the continuing and continual creation and (re)creation of social life; judges can listen to those who speak and strive to hear those who do not.

A Judicial Cross to Bear

In order to illustrate and substantiate these claims about the importance of experimentation in the nonfoundational account of law and adjudication, I intend to concentrate on the controversial American case of *R.A.V.* v. *City of St. Paul.*[25] Dealing with the issue of whether cross burning on other people's property is a constitutionally protected activity, this case placed the judicial process under keen scrutiny from the public and the legal community. However, it is my intention to discuss the decision and judgments in a very focused and particular way. Rather than examine the judicial performances in terms of their political wisdom or rhetorical cogency, I will seek to understand and criticize them as better or worse examples of the nonfoundational imperative to construe law and adjudication as practices in which "anything might go." There were three judgments given in the Supreme Court. While the judgments of Justices Scalia and White are unremarkable in jurisprudential terms, they do provide a convenient occasion to emphasize the nature and style of foundationalist adjudication and its transparency. Although Scalia and White frame and justify their opinions in traditional foundationalist terms, their combined effect is to emphasize the openness of legal doctrine, not its grounded and determinate character; they undermine the foundationalist approach in their attempts to shore up legal doctrine. Justice Stevens's judgment is different. In his rejection of the result reached by the majority and their judicial method, it is possible to glimpse the makings and flavor of a nonfoundational approach to law and adjudication: he seems to grasp, although he does not follow through on, the idea that law is best understood as a playful and contextual practice.

In St. Paul, Minnesota, a teenage gang allegedly assembled a crudely made cross from broken chair legs and burned it inside the fenced yard of a local black family's house. One of the youths, the petitioner R.A.V., was charged under a municipal ordinance that specifically prohibited bias-motivated disorderly conduct: "Whoever places on public or private property a symbol, object, appellation, characterization or graffiti, including, but not limited to, a burning cross or Nazi Swastika, which one knows or ought to know arouses anger, alarm or resentment in others on the basis of race, color, creed, religion or gender commits disorderly conduct." The petitioner sought to have this charge dismissed on the ground that the ordinance was not only overbroad but was also content-based and, therefore, invalid under the First Amendment. While the trial judge found for the petitioner, the Minnesota Supreme Court reversed this decision and held that the ordinance was neither overbroad nor impermissibly content-based, as it was carefully designed to accomplish the compelling government interest in protecting the local community against bias-motivated conduct. Accepting that the ordinance only applied to so-called "fighting words," the United States Supreme Court decided that the ordinance was unconstitutional. While the court was unanimous in its decision, the judges were very divided over the reasons for the decision. Whereas all the judges invalidated the ordinance as overbroad, four of the judges were not prepared to conclude that it was impermissibly content-based under the First Amendment.[26] Most important for my purposes, the three main judgments took very different approaches to their judicial responsibilities in contested matters of constitutional interpretation.

The leading and conflicting judgments of Justices Scalia and White are traditionally foundationalist in ambition and expression. Both judges attempt to engage in a mode of categorical reasoning that involves a taxonomic inquiry into which side of certain bright lines a particular fact situation falls on so that it can be disposed of accordingly. Although they strongly and openly disagree over the appropriate doctrine to apply, they are in tacit agreement on the judicial responsibility to keep faith with the court's constitutional jurisprudence. Forgoing any social or historical analyses of cross burning or hate speech generally, they are adamant that there is a correct and determinate answer that can be gleaned from First Amendment jurisprudence; their analyses remain squarely within the extant legal materials, and they commit themselves to a tidily doctrinaire approach to decision making. In doctrinal terms, their disagreement is over the relation between the "fighting words" doctrine (that are not constitutionally protected) and the "content-based regulation" doctrine (that is constitutionally impermissible). While Scalia and White agree that both doctrines are important components in First Amendment jurisprudence, they disagree markedly over their relative importance and priority.[27] In the process of working through this disagreement, each judge writes as if the only issue at stake was whether the other got it legally right: they elide the obvious fact that different judgments of value and political commitments are being made and tested but not disclosed. More important, in contrast to their legal rhetoric, Scalia and White tend to confirm the nonfoundationalist claim that legal interpretation and decision making are inventive and playful; legal doctrine has no essential or settled meaning—it can be flipped (and flopped) by its judicial exponents.

The gist of Justice Scalia's decision for the court, in which Chief Justice Rehnquist and Justices Kennedy, Souter, and Thomas joined, is simple and straightforward: he gives priority to the "content-based regulation" doctrine over the "fighting words" doctrine. Although cross burning amounted to "fighting words" and, therefore, was generally unprotected by the First Amendment, such expression cannot be selectively regulated on the basis of content-based or viewpoint discrimination, which is constitutionally impermissible: "The government may not regulate use based on hostility—or favouritism—towards the underlying message expressed." If St. Paul had banned *all* fighting words, its ordinance would have been permissible. In reaching this decision, Scalia combines the *Roth* and *Chaplinsky* decisions that "fighting words" are constitutionally unprotected with the *Simon* and *Mosley* decisions that invalidate content-based regulation as constitutionally impermissible. In doing so, Scalia maintains that "a limited categorical approach has remained an important part of our First Amendment jurisprudence." In short, he ranks *Simon* and *Mosley* as being higher in the First Amendment hierarchy and puts *Roth* and *Chaplinsky* in their service. For him, *Chaplinsky* and *Roth* are fixed, but their meaning is not; there is a plasticity to their interpretation and precedential priority. Consequently, he holds that unprotected kinds of speech are not "entirely invisible to the Constitution, so that they may be made the vehicles for content discrimination unrelated to their distinctively proscribable content." Indeed, Scalia goes so far as to say that "fighting words" can be part of a "debate" and that they are protectable. While it is recognized that protection against discrimination is a "compelling interest," the danger of censorship is considered to be a greater evil in the Scalian scheme of constitutional things than the worth of community protection.[28]

White, joined by Justices Blackmun and O'Connor, went along with the judgment of the court, "but not the folly of the opinion." For him, Scalia's judgment amounted to "doctrinal revisionism" and was "an arid, doctrinaire [and mischievous] interpretation, driven by the frequently irresistible impulse of judges to tinker with the First Amendment." White spends most of his judgment challenging Scalia's interpretation and ranking of the relevant fixed precedential points. For him, *Chaplinsky* and *Roth* are to be given doctrinal precedence over *Simon* and *Mosley*; *Chaplinsky* and *Roth* create a category of expression that is denied constitutional protection precisely because of the expression's content, and "within the confines of given classification, the evil to be restricted so overwhelmingly outweighs the expressive interest, if any, at stake, that no case-by-case adjudication is required." White maintains that it is wildly inconsistent to hold that government can ban an entire category of speech because its content is "worthless and undeserving of constitutional protection" but cannot ban a mere subset of that category. While his judgment is archly formalist in both tone and application, he concludes with the clinching political argument that the St. Paul regulation is, "in light of our Nation's long and painful experience with discrimination, . . . plainly reasonable."[29]

However, White saves his strongest criticisms for Scalia's cavalier use of precedent, with its insidious tendency to jeopardize the whole doctrine of stare decisis. He maintains that the court blows hot and cold on the binding force of traditional precedents: "The majority casts aside long-established First Amendment doctrine without the benefit of briefing and adopts an untried theory." According to White, while Scalia raises *Simon* and *Mosley* to an extraordinarily privileged status, he manages to undermine their traditional import by effecting "a general renunciation of . . . a fundamental tool of First Amendment analysis," namely the notion that if narrowly drawn, content-based restrictions on protected speech could survive strict scrutiny: the perverse result is that a wider ban (of all proscribable speech) would be more constitutionally permissible than a narrow ban (of some part of proscribable speech). In particular, White considers Scalia to have given inappropriate meaning and weight to *Roth* and *Chaplinsky*:

> The present court submits that such clear statements "must be taken in context" and are not "literally true." To the contrary, those statements meant precisely what they said: the categorical approach is a firmly entrenched part of our First Amendment jurisprudence. Indeed, the Court in *Roth* reviewed the guarantees of freedom of expression in effect at the time of the ratification of the Constitution and concluded, "in light of this history, it is apparent that the unconditional phrasing of the First Amendment was not intended to protect every utterance."[30]

Insofar as *R.A.V.* is representative or symptomatic of judicial decision making, the two leading judgments reveal that attachment to a foundational approach remains its ruling faith and that tradition and predictability are two of its main tenets. However, Scalia's and White's stark and almost acerbic disagreement over the best and most appropriate way to fulfill the foundationalist calling in such situations indicates that all is not well within law's curial cathedrals and among its judicial clergy. Indeed, it is the force of White's judgment that Scalia is a foundationalist in name and protestation only. White is particularly agitated at Scalia's assertion that while a categorical approach is an important part of the First Amendment jurisprudence, it is "limited" and "not absolute" because it applies differently in different contexts; the state could ban all obscene displays or only those involving minors, but it could not selectively ban only those obscene displays that included offensive political messages.[31] I can agree with White's critique of Scalia's judgment for being a poor exercise in foundationalist judging, but I do not share White's sense of anger and betrayal. From a nonfoundationalist perspective, my more pressing concern is with the fact that Scalia is more inconsistent than mistaken and that he does not have the courage of his intellectual conviction; his sin is hypocrisy, not apostasy.

White's criticisms of Scalia's judgment (it is, he says, "mischievous," "driven by the frequently irresistible impulse of judges to tinker," and, in effect, an effort to "rewrite" established First Amendment doctrine)[32] are intended to chastise and discipline Scalia in an effort to bring him back into the foundationalist fold. In contrast, I maintain that Scalia's failing is not that he reneges on the foundationalist compact but that he remains too committed to it; he needs to abandon entirely his attachment to the foundationalist idea that there is a core or predetermined shape to the First Amendment or any other doctrine. As I have tried to emphasize, the legal materials possess only whatever shape and symmetry that they happened to acquire during the last occasion for legal reasoning; law is an infinite language game whose performances never repeat themselves in any exact or predictable way. For instance, Scalia's efforts to defend his decision against White's assault by arguing that White's "simplistic, all-or-nothing-at-all approach . . . is at odds with common sense" are not helped by Scalia adding that such an approach is at odds "with our jurisprudence as well."[33] Such a rhetorical maneuver will only resonate with those who hold on to a discredited foundationalist account of law and adjudication. Disabused of such a lingering attachment, Scalia would have both the freedom and the obligation to persuade his readers by dint of his legal craft that his use of the legal materials in service of his own political ideals is more cogent and compelling than that of White and his colleagues.

As for White's judgment, although he can claim that he has kept his foundationalist faith in a more rigorous and consistent manner than Scalia, it is very difficult for him to insist that Scalia's use of legal reasoning in reaching his decision is "transparently wrong." For all his righteous indignation about Scalia's "doctrinal revisionism," White is hard pressed to maintain the extreme position that Scalia's arguments and use of precedent are so badly made and presented that they do not deserve to be taken seriously as part of a *judicial* performance.[34] After all, Scalia was able to persuade four of their colleagues that such an exercise in legal reasoning was sufficiently well made and presented as to be worthy of their support and concurrence. Unless White is prepared to make the chilling allegation that Scalia and the majority of the court colleagues were acting in bad faith, there is little else that he can do other than to assume that his own arguments were simply not persuasive enough to sway those colleagues.[35] There is, of course, the alternative argument that all this talk about legal validity and correctness is so much foundationalist pretense and that what actually divides White and the court's majority are the competing pulls of their political visions or values. While such a line of nonfoundationalist critique is very promising, it is not one that is available to White if he wishes to maintain his commitment to the foundationalist understanding of law and adjudication as being primarily legal in scope and operation, not political in derivation and force.

Of course, this is not to suggest that if Scalia, White, and the rest of the court were to effect such an abandonment of the excess and unnecessary foundationalist baggage, it would somehow miraculously change their decisions or force them to reconsider their basic political commitments. However, what it would do is to require them to come cleaner on their informing political visions of speech and democracy. Typically unstated and unacknowledged, what divides Scalia and White is not so much their perception of the formal constraints on their legal role as the substantive cut of their political convictions. Their fractious engagement over stare decisis and doctrinal definition is little more than shadowboxing. Each of them has done enough doctrinally to pass formalist muster; their use of First Amendment doctrine is plausibly judicious and professionally crafted. At bottom, it is the general orientation of their political convictions that pulls them in different legal directions. On the one hand, Scalia is motivated by a conservative conclusion that the marketplace of ideas must be resolutely upheld and that "the danger of censorship" is so debilitating as to prevent a municipality from displaying special hostility to racist activities: "St. Paul has no such authority to license one side of a debate to fight free-style, while requiring the other to follow Marquis of Queensbury Rules."[36] White, on the other hand, leans toward a more liberal stand on the First Amendment that, while protecting a substantial amount of "repugnant" expression, refuses to "legitimate hate-speech as a form of public discussion" and defers "to our Nation's long and painful experience with discrimination."[37]

The more overt traces of a nonfoundational understanding of the judicial function can be found in the judgment of Justice Stevens in *R.A.V.*. He is determined to resist "the allure of absolute principles" that captivate his colleagues. Although Scalia rejects the all-or-nothing nature of the "fighting words" doctrine, Stevens maintains that Scalia enters "something of an adventure in doctrinal wonderland" when "he embraces an absolutism of its own," centered on content neutrality. For Stevens, this is entirely wrongheaded, since the "entire First Amendment jurisprudence creates a regime based on the content of speech." Similarly, while he shares White's conclusion about the constitutional permissibility of the St. Paul's ordinance, he regards White's categoricalist reliance on the "fighting words" doctrine to be unconvincing. In particular, he finds that White's judgment "sacrifices subtlety for clarity and . . . is unsound." Accordingly, he distances himself from both Scalia and White's foundationalist preoccupations:

> The concept of "categories" fits poorly with the reality of expression. Few dividing lines in First Amendment law are straight and unwavering, and efforts at categorisation inevitably give rise to fuzzy boundaries. . . . The quest for doctrinal certainty through the definition of categories and sub-categories is, in my opinion, destined to fail.[38]

In place of such absolutisms, Stevens openly champions the pragmatic virtues of context: "The meaning of any expression and the legitimacy of its regulation can only be determined in context." He maintains that a contextual and multifaceted analysis need not accept that all content-based regulations are equally infirm and presumptively invalid and that all "fighting words" are wholly unprotected by the First Amendment. Instead, Stevens highlights several factors that might be weighed and considered in reaching a nonabsolutist decision on the scope of constitutional protection—the content of the expressive activity in terms of whether it is political, commercial, pornographic, and so on; the character of the expressive activity in terms of whether it is written, spoken, or behavioral; the context of the expression in terms of its location and audience; and the nature of the restriction in terms of its focus, timing, scope, and the like. In light of these considerations, Stevens has little difficulty in concluding that as it was low-value conduct that amounted to "nothing more than a crude form of physical intimidation," cross burning was not constitutionally protected: The judgment "that harms caused by racial, religious, and gender-based invective are qualitatively different from that caused by other fighting words . . . seems to me eminently reasonable and realistic."[39] However, while Stevens hews to a more pragmatic and less doctrinaire line than his absolutist colleagues, his judgment is only suggestive of the shape and substance that a nonfoundational judgment might take.

Being Experimental

While Stevens's judgment points in the right direction, he does not complete a judicial performance that captures the qualities and virtues of a truly nonfoundational judicial player. For judges of a ludic persuasion, Stevens's judgment is much too beholden to the idea that law is an activity that is understandable in its own terms and that legal doctrines have a definite shape and distinctive thrust. He believes that the scope and style of contextualization and experimentation are largely confined to the legal enterprise. For example, for all his rejection of absolutism, Stevens takes Scalia and White to task primarily for their failure to respect the legal traditions of constitutional doctrine. He is particularly harsh on Scalia and notes pointedly that "this new absolutism . . . severely contorts the fabric of settled First Amendment law" and "turns First Amendment law on its head." In a very nonexperimentalist turn of phrase, Stevens considers that Scalia has committed the ultimate judicial sin in that he "wreaks havoc in an area of settled law." As such, Scalia and White are not simply wrong because they are absolutist and noncontingent but because they fundamentally mistake "the very nature of First Amendment jurisprudence."[40] Like his more fundamentalist colleagues, Stevens has not cleared his head entirely of the formalist baggage that still weighs down the judicial mind-set.

Unlike their many pseudo-pragmatic half cousins, judges of the ludic kind would take a more thoroughgoing and iconoclastic approach to context and openness. They are judges who take very seriously the injunction to be legally nonfoundationalist, normatively contextualist, and politically experimental. As their name suggests, they are playful, but they are most definitely situated in their performance and expectations. Unlike *Hercules* and *Hero*, they are not members of any superhuman clan and were not born with the silver mace of justice in their hands: they reject all political orthodoxies and legal dogmas. However, they recognize that, stripped of their theoretical and formalist trappings, prevailing practices have some substantive and selective assistance to offer. It is the general faith in the foundationalist faith that they eschew, not the contingent worth of particular substantive beliefs. In this regard, ludic judges would distance themselves from all or any claims that there is such a thing as "the very nature of First Amendment jurisprudence," such that deviations from its well-settled principles constitute a presumptively incorrect and invalid exercise of judicial power. Indeed, they will realize that all the traditional First Amendment values—individual self-fulfillment, advancement of knowledge, political participation, and communal stability—are capable of justifying all manner of contradictory outcomes; they are hospitable to arguments that place cross burning particularly and hate mongering generally inside and outside the sphere of protected expression. Consequently, ludic judges have no difficulty with conceding that there is nothing to be gained from fruitless quarrels over whether one judgment is more right than another in terms of its interpretive fit and precedential pedigree; they recognize that what counts is a decision's social utility and a judgment's rhetorical success.

Nevertheless, there is much to be gained from appreciating that there is no "very nature" to the First Amendment or any other legal doctrine; the political harvest is increased by the pruning of the legal overgrowth. By acknowledging that the acceptable techniques of legal reasoning can be easily and imaginatively deployed so as to effect almost any outcome or result, ludic judges are able to join issue over the political merit and consequences of different possible decisions; this will make open and candid what is left hidden and unstated by the judges (and jurists) who take a more foundationalist stance. In this way, judges can move beyond endless pseudo-disagreements about analytical truth, legal authority, and doctrinal correctness to meaningful engagement over political alignment and social action. It is naive to pretend that argumentative style is more important than the results reached; judges decide as they presently do in large part because of, and not in spite of, their normative instincts and political assumptions. Nevertheless, while the intellectual act of making these assumptions more visible and self-conscious will not by itself change the decisions reached, their unveiling will oblige judges to be more open about their politics and to provide a more overt defense of them. At the least, it puts the focus of legal analysis and public debate where it should be—on the visions and values that frame and energize the decisions made.

Consequently, a ludic approach to judging will not guarantee the reaching of any particular set of decisions. This is for two reasons. First, a ludic approach will not necessarily recommend more progressive decisions or discourage more reactionary decisions. This inconvenient but important insight is illustrated and confirmed by Scalia's judgment, which protects the vile activity of white supremacists in preference to safeguarding the peaceful security of marginalized black families. There is nothing in the nonfoundational critique that renders any kind of decision more likely than any others. Nevertheless, it might (but only *might*) contribute to a greater democratization in terms of the transparency and candor of that process. Not only will judges not be able to evade responsibility by attributing their decisions to the Law, Truth, or Justice, but it might result in a more diverse range of people being appointed to judicial office.[41] Second, while the nonfoundationalist position is very similar to that of antifoundationalist critics, it is not exactly the same. For instance, when Tushnet argues that the modes of legal reasoning are "so flexible that they allow us to assemble diverse precedents into *whatever pattern we choose*,"[42] he goes one step too far. It is not that law has a fixed pattern, nor that it has whatever pattern judges choose; it is that law's pattern is negotiated and renegotiated in the process of adjudication. In law's language game, it is not that "anything goes" but that "anything might go."

Relieved of the bickering over doctrinal legitimacy, Scalia, White, and Stevens can get on with the more urgent task of debating the worth of their political convictions and, most important, the best legal way to give contingent effect to them. Ludic judges appreciate that, ultimately, what the courts get done is easily as important as what they say, or what they say that they get done. Of course, the difficulty of predicting or measuring the social consequences of legal decisions is notoriously difficult. Ludic judges will not fall into the foundationalist trap of thinking that when courts speak, society does or does not respond and change in the desired way; they will be alert to the possibility that their judicial performance will be put to unintended effect. History is far too messy and complex to isolate any real causes and effects for specific social episodes, let alone to devise a general account of legal causality. Insofar as judicial decisions must combine with broader social forces to be effective, any potential victories can be quickly neutralized by bureaucratic inertia, political intransigence, and judicial complacency. For example, in assessing the efficacy of courts in dealing with issues of racial injustice, ludic judges might consult the record of the civil rights movements, which offers evidence of the limited successes (and substantial dangers) of obliging the political and legal establishment to honor its own halfhearted commitment to the universal dimension of rights talk. Nevertheless, ludic judges will also recognize that the significance of adjudication might have less to do with its functional effect than with its symbolic impact.[43]

Of course, to fulfill such responsibilities, ludic judges will understand the need to go much further than consulting legal materials in heeding the nonfoundational request to pay close attention to context. Mindful that context itself is never entirely fixed and is always reconfigurable, they will look to the social, historical, and economic dimensions of the political context in which any practice of thinking about law must itself be contextualized. They will ensure that they begin with a rigorous effort to understand the social role of cross burning in American society and its political and psychological effects on people of color. At the same time, they will wish to evaluate historically and sociologically claims that banning such activities will actually result in general censorship and a decrease in the extent and openness of political dialogue. In both instances, the inquiry will be as empirical as it is conceptual and as practical as it is theoretical; it will be nonfoundational in scope and ambition. While gathering more information and data about law and its social effects will not alone resolve the immediate challenge of judicial decision making, it is an important undertaking. Such a critical empiricism need not be positivist, determinist, behaviorist, or reductionist: being nonfoundational in practice and purpose, it questions the very activity that it undertakes.[44]

Although ludic judges will not shy away from drawing conclusions and forming opinions, those views will be contingent, provisional, and revisable. Working with the extant legal materials, these experimentalists will strive to illuminate practice, not to pin it down in its essentialness but to make it more pliable for political efforts at interested appropriation. In such an exercise, a doctrinal attachment to stare decisis will be jettisoned as so much excess baggage; the putative loss in predictability and efficiency will be amply compensated for by the real gain in fairness and efficacy. Looking outside legal doctrine, ludic judges will resist the temptation to accept the shibboleths of the political Right or Left on cross burning and hate speech generally. Considering and weighing those views, they will not feel the need to make a leap of faith by way of a once-and-for-all ideological commitment. As well as tolerating a substantial degree of conceptual dissonance and analytic imprecision, they will also experiment with different visions of social justice whose organizing principles will be practical usefulness, not theoretical coherence. However, in the spirit of experiment and improvisation, they will likely pursue a practice of democratic engagement that will be very wary about preventing people from participating in the style and with the substance that they wish. Nevertheless, this does not require that every utterance and action be welcomed, which would not only be impossible but also smack of a fundamentalist and foundationalist position. A commitment to "democratic dialogue" requires a changing and changeable mix of interventions and abstentions. Eschewing sweeping statements and stances, ludic judges would understand that there are no final or right answers but only different options whose exercise and appropriateness will depend upon the particular problem and its socioeconomic context.[45]

Nonetheless, in negotiating the almost limitless possibilities for meeting their judicial responsibilities on law's fields of dreams, ludic judges can safely begin from the assumption that such activities are despicable and dangerous. Not only did Scalia concede that cross burning is "reprehensible," but it is reasonable to assume that the perpetrators of such acts also believe them to be intimidating and harmful, or else they might not do them and might, instead, engage in other more direct actions to terrorize people of color.[46] Ludic judges will ensure that they listen to the voices of those traditionally excluded and those whose experiences are different from their own and from those of their judicial colleagues. While they will give these views and experiences special weight, they will not treat them as an authentic and transparent window on an unabridged Truth and a given Reality. To do more would be to abandon the nonfoundational practice of skeptical knowing, and to do less would be to ignore the situational insights of neglected social knowers. Conscious of their own experience and its pragmatic status, ludic judges might try to put their values out for critical appraisal and scrutiny, with the real possibility that they will be exposed to different views, as strongly held as their own, such that their own views will be amended in the process. Furthermore, ludic judges might attend to the effect of cross burning on people of color in a contemporary world in which racism remains rampant in spite of the United States Constitution's vaunted commitment to eradicating it. As committed democrats, they will be particularly interested in "the feeling of inferiority" that it gives rise to in the "hearts and minds" of people of color.[47]

In reaching a decision, ludic judges will likely concede that although racism is to be combated vigorously and ceaselessly, the legal system should be careful about having a knee-jerk censorial reaction to all speech or activity that has racist overtones; there is a very thin and shifting line between controversial and offensive views. The larger danger is that, no matter how well intended its proponents are, official powers of censorship are difficult to control and monitor; there is a tendency for such powerful weapons to be deployed indiscriminately or against the most vulnerable people in society. Too often, censorship is used as a disciplinary tactic to protect established interests and curb the actions and ideas of those who are devoted to social change, such as antiracist or antisexist activists. In a pluralistic society, there will need to be room for error so that it is possible "to challenge orthodoxy, think imaginatively, experiment boldly."[48] While opportunities for white speech cannot always be allowed to trump occasions of black harm, the threat of black hurt will not always be enough to silence white voices. In a suitably nonfoundational fashion, ludic judges will be more concerned about the practical resolution of particular difficulties than about the theoretical generation of universalizable principles. Consequently, in the case of cross burning in a black family's backyard, they might (or might not) conclude that even if the balance might be different in future and related circumstances, such crass and callous behavior is not worthy of constitutional solicitude and is deserving of collective opprobrium through its criminalization. In reaching this conclusion, ludic judges will find First Amendment jurisprudence and other judges' views to be useful resources and tools for firing and tempering their political imagination and testing the possible social efficacy of their proposed dispositions. But these will not be the constraints or the crutches that the foundationalists pretend that they are.

Ludic judges will not make a vain attempt to check their own voice and values at the courtroom door. While they will not exhaust themselves in vain efforts to integrate their values into a superhuman theory of pure coherence, they will work hard at struggling to bring them to articulate consciousness in order to understand and interrogate them. Cultivating the forgotten talent of empathic listening,[49] ludic judges will scrutinize their own views in light of the litigants' plight and context. It is very difficult—indeed sometimes it might be impossible—to appreciate or understand "alien" views, but there is always the ethical responsibility to listen as empathically as possible to what is being said. This must be done in such a way as to try as best as possible to comprehend those views on their own terms, without translating them into the vernacular of the judge's own tradition (thereby negating their difference) or valorizing them as an exotic but inconsequential alternative to the judge's own worldview (thereby patronizing it as a prelude to dismissing it). By so engaging with the otherness of the Other, it might become possible for judges to grow as citizens and to understand themselves better. In short, it is vital to learn to live with and shift between plural cultures of argument and evaluation. However, while ludic judges must be prepared to take full responsibility for their decision and its consequences, they will, at the end of the day, be left to come to their own conclusion: "The one talent which is worth all other talents put together in human affairs is the talent of judging right upon imperfect materials, the talent if you please of guessing right. It is a talent which no rules will ever teach and which even experience does not always give."[50]

Judges and Juries

None of this should be seen as implying that when released from its allegiance to a foundationalist faith, judicial caution should be thrown to the antifoundationalist wind and that the courts should begin to operate as a clearinghouse for all political disputes and policy making. As some foundationalists rightly note, "Giving away the traditional store . . . would be drastic and dangerous . . . unlikely to help the less powerful members of society."[51] However, the temptation to doctrinaire purity would be resisted with a suitably pragmatic expediency. The nonfoundational challenge would be to transform the courts so that they abandoned their foundationalist ways and began to experiment more candidly with different ways to participate in and transform the performance of law's language game. Along with any efforts to re-envision the judicial craft along nonfoundational lines, it would also be essential to ensure that the institutional sites for such playful transformation were actively multiplied so that a broader range of voices could be heard in society's continuing dialogue about the kind of democratic society it wishes to become. There is only so much that courts can or should do in this process. Nonetheless, insofar as courts are likely to play *some* role in the practice and theory of democratic justice, it would be imperative to work toward a situation in which the personnel of the courts were diversified and democratized.

On the basis that different people bring different experience to the task of applying rules, the need to ensure that the elite ranks of the judicial and legal profession are opened up along more varied class, gender, racial, ethnic, sexual, and political lines is paramount. Of course, the appointment of women, black, and/or gay judges will not guarantee change or make the law more progressive. As I have emphasized throughout, it is a mistake to believe that anything necessarily follows from the identity or experience of a judge.[52] Indeed, it is as wrong to attribute a homogeneity of views to disadvantaged groups as it is to pretend that those views will not be different from those of advantaged groups. Nonetheless, the increased presence of such presently excluded people will increase the likelihood that a different perspective and vision of justice will be brought to bear upon the adjudicative process. While there are not, nor can there be, any metaphysical certainties, the institutional chances of transforming law and adjudication are greatly improved by opening them up to those who have been excluded for so long: robust dialogue is more conducive to the democratic temperament and civic advancement than insulated monologues. This affirmative vision of skeptical judging "is not radical in itself but is radical in the context of the prevailing orthodoxy."[53]

The central importance of participation in the shaping of public values and rules can only be grasped by focusing on an institution that rejects values of expertise and elitism in favor of those of hands-on involvement and self-government. Such an institution is the jury system. Within a nonfoundational legal culture, the role and representation of the jury might be greatly expanded. As an occasion for democratic devolution, jury empowerment would bring a neglected challenge to the aristocratic instincts of legal professionalism and might invigorate the style, range, and direction of the democratic game. Moreover, it would represent a nonfoundational putsch against the legal hierocracy. By changing the civic members of the jury from passive observers to active participants, the legal process might begin to fulfill its democratic commitments. After all, disabused of the foundationalist claim that law is an exercise in reflection and rightness, law could come to be understood as a practical activity that involves the lives and ideals of society's citizens. As such, it is much too important to be left to lawyers. Moreover, by withdrawing the fate of the polity from the clutches of lawyers and jurists, it might become possible for citizens to overcome the dispiriting belief that unless there is something large, powerful, and ahistorical on their side to support their claims—like *the law*—they need not assert their right to govern themselves.[54] Accordingly, a revitalized jury system would be one way to relieve the symptoms of democratic ennui and to prevent further political disempowerment.

To suggest that the jury system represents a paradigm of democratic practice may seem anachronistic or naive. The value of the jury has always been contested. For some, it is a democratic beacon that preserves popular participation in the administration of justice. For others, it is a dubious institution that casts a long shadow of rank prejudice over curial affairs. Indeed, critics on both the political "Right" and "Left" have condemned the jury as a device that legitimates bigotry, ignorance, or racism. These criticisms of the jury parallel those issued against democracy in general; the basic complaints are that these institutions produce decisions that are oppressive and that individual citizens are incapable of making such decisions. Yet, whatever the failings of individual juries, the jury system as a whole embodies to a remarkable degree values of self-government; people become players rather than spectators in law's playful performance. The jury system rejects rule by experts; people assume the responsibility for making important civic decisions on a rotating basis. Discussion and engagement are central to the success of the institution. The jurors neither only meditate on the refined points of legal doctrine nor simply observe the trial and then cast their votes individually in the privacy of a polling booth: they are expected to arrive at a common verdict, through persuasion and argument. Without such debate, "the jury system as a whole would be devalued, and . . . individual jurors would value their own roles less."[55] Viewed in this way, the jury system represents a commitment to the principle that ordinary citizens are competent to debate and decide important issues in the community; they too can be great players in the law's and life's sprawling performance.

While people might disagree with particular decisions or outcomes, the jury offers "a lingering paradigm of an alternative mode of participatory self-government, a nucleus around which analogous modes might grow in our town halls, factories and streets."[56] By multiplying the range of legal players and the sites for their involvement, the jury might not be the salvation of the legal system, but it could make a valuable contribution to the effort to democratize the law and its professional participants.

It is true that the jury can often act as a rubber stamp for prevailing values and prejudices. But it can occasionally be a lamp of liberty that illuminates the darker values of the system and throws light on the potential of ordinary people to take a stand in the name of social justice. In one of the most balanced and rigorous evaluations of the jury system, Valerie Hans and Neil Vidmar amassed all the available evidence to confirm that the jury can be seen as a popularist enclave in an increasingly elite culture. They conclude that "on the whole, the jury behaves responsibly and rationally."[57] While far from perfect, the jury is assessed as having lots of life in it and as deserving of democratic allegiance. They show that only in 3 percent of cases is the jury more severe than the judge, and only in 4 percent of cases less severe. Moreover, general demographic and attitudinal factors are a poor indicator of juries' propensity to reach verdicts in particular situations. Accordingly, despite the increased practice of challenging and vetting juries, lawyers' efforts and objections are based on little more than professional gossip and are largely unreliable. Of course, this general distrust of juries is based on a seeming comparison with the perfect operation of a legal process rather than with the flawed and all-too-human performance of an elite judiciary.

The present weaknesses and potential strengths of an invigorated and expanded jury system can be gleaned from the current debate around the heated issue of racism in the criminal justice system. For instance, in the aftermath of the acquittal of O. J. Simpson and the police officers in the Rodney King beating, juries were condemned as having outlived their usefulness. While both of these particular juries can be harshly criticized and second-guessed, calls to do away with this ancient institution are as misplaced as they are ill thought. The fact that the King jury was not representative of the larger community—it contained no African Americans—speaks to a failing in the process of jury selection, not to the efficacy of the jury system itself. More serious attention must be given to ensuring that all members of the community, including and especially minorities and disadvantaged people, are available and permitted to serve on juries. For every notorious example of an occasion when a jury apparently failed in its duties, such as in the Reuben "Hurricane" Carter case in the United States and the Donald Marshall or the David Milgaard case in Canada, there is always at least one other available instance to counterbalance it. Time and again, the jury has managed to act independently and, in so doing, to reaffirm the value of a popular check on official power.

This continuing debate has been given fresh impetus in Canada by recent developments on racism in the criminal justice system. At long last, the courts have begun to take the jury and racism much more seriously in this country. Members of racial minorities play both large and small roles in the justice system. While they represent a disproportionately high number of people charged and processed through the courts, they comprise only a small portion of the personnel who are relied on to operate the system: the person of color is more often the accused and a white person is more often the judge, jury, lawyer, or police officer. While racial minorities, native Canadians, and low-income tenants are presently on the lists of potential jurors, their actual presence on juries at trials is very limited. Juries tend to be largely white and middle-class in composition. Accordingly, as a crucial democratic institution intended to ensure popular participation in the criminal justice system, the jury in practice fails to represent or reflect in the most rudimentary fashion the cultural, ethnic, and class makeup of society. These stark facts were accepted by the Ontario Court of Appeal in a recent decision on jury vetting. In a candid and refreshing judgment, Justice Doherty concluded:

> Racism, and in particular anti-black racism, is a part of our community's psyche. A significant segment of our community holds overtly racist views. A much larger segment subconsciously operates on the basis of negative racial stereotypes. Furthermore, our institutions, including the criminal justice system, reflect and perpetuate those negative stereotypes. These elements combine to infect our society as a whole with the evil of racism. Blacks are among the primary victims of that evil. In my opinion, there can be no doubt that there existed a realistic possibility that one or more potential jurors drawn from the Metropolitan Toronto community would, consciously or subconsciously, come to court possessed of negative stereotypical attitudes toward black persons.[58]

This belated acknowledgment is a sad but realistic first step in eradicating such a social blight. The next question on the jury agenda is whether, in light of racism's social existence, there should be rules about the racial mix of the jury: Is an all-white jury ever acceptable? Is there a minimum balance required? What weight should local demographics be given? These difficult and divisive issues are presently being grappled with by U.S. courts and have no easy or obvious answers.[59] However, it is only the privileged and protected who can blithely opine that justice is color-blind and that racial considerations have no place in the dispensation of justice. While it is true that racism does cast a shadow over the performance of juries and that jurors have too often been given the benefit of the racist doubt, the appropriate solution is not the abandonment of the jury. On the contrary, if racism in the justice system is to be tackled and rooted out, an expanded role for a more diverse jury would be an important initiative. In an age of rampant professionalization, it is imperative that the value and role of the jury be enhanced: the occasions for popular involvement in official systems must be multiplied, not reduced. Reform of the jury, not its abolition, ought to be the order of the day. To diminish the role of the jury would be to accept the inevitability of racism rather than struggle to eradicate it.

Again, while it would be reassuring to conclude that race, ethnicity, gender, and class background have no connection with values and critical faculties, it flaunts reality to suggest that this is the case in contemporary North Atlantic society. Indeed, a person's racial identity has a significant effect on how he or she understands and evaluates the importance of race in the overall social scheme. Simply put, it is the privilege of the white establishment to pretend that race is not important and that it does not contribute significantly to the kind of lives that people live and, therefore, the values and perceptions that they develop in regard to the shape and experience of social justice. Quite simply, those who have to deal with racism on a day-to-day basis understand it better than those who can ignore or choose to downplay its ravages.[60] Of course, to recognize the need for a truly diverse and mixed jury guarantees nothing. However, it does increase the likelihood that an accused person will receive a fairer, more informed, and more balanced decision that reflects the views of the whole community, not only part of it. Furthermore, the recognition of the part that background and experience play in the formation of values and critical faculties is not to be taken as an invitation to indulge prejudice or to exact revenge. The need for impartiality rather than partiality is still required, provided that impartiality is understood in a suitably nonfoundational way. Impartiality can only be achieved when people—especially those who are historically privileged—accept their own partialities and exhibit a constant willingness to interrogate and question them. In a different (and future) society, it can be hoped that the color of a person's skin will not be important to participation in public institutions and the exercise of democratic power: race and racism are not natural givens. But in a society that is still racist, it is essential that juries be organized so as to reflect the racial, gender, class, and ethnic character of society. The legal system's willingness to make transformative changes is a mark of its democratic commitment to eradicate racism.

Conclusion

In this chapter, I have suggested a style of nonfoundationalist approach that judges (and jurists) might take in fulfilling their professional responsibilities. In advocating a more experimental and playful approach to law and adjudication, I do not intend to trivialize the role that legal craft can play or the need for judges to nurture this professional culture. Instead, a nonfoundationalist account of law and adjudication recommends that legal techniques be placed in the service of political values. However, in insisting upon a fruitful combination of integrity and ideals, it also insists that there is no one way to get the job done and that there is no reason to believe that judges will converge more readily on a particular set of outcomes. While a less diverse judiciary will likely cohere around certain shared commitments, the performance of law's language game will remain indeterminate in operation and unpredictable in outcome. More than anything else, a nonfoundationalist account points to a distinctive attitude or temperament: judges and jurists must approach the infinite game of law's language game in a playful spirit that respects present understandings at the same time that it encourages their reworking. Unlike in other games, the objective is not to win but to keep the game going. Or, to put it another way, the best way to win is to ensure that you contribute to the game in such a way that it challenges others to rethink what it means to *play the game*. Judicial greatness can know no greater achievement or satisfaction.

11 Overtime? A Conclusion

......

Humanity is won by continuing to play in the face of certain defeat.

—Ralph Ellison, *The Invisible Man*

In the mid-1980s, Owen Fiss published an influential essay that lamented the critical turn in jurisprudence. Capturing mainstream jurists' discomfort and disappointment, he regretted that many critical jurists had begun to turn their backs on the law and its adjudicative potential to contribute to the articulation and implementation of a more egalitarian vision of society. For him, the failure of the courts to live up to their transformative promise was cause to redouble efforts at jurisprudential revitalization, not to abandon them. In particular, he chastised critical scholars for trivializing and endangering "the proudest and noblest ambitions of the law" to function, through its curial sites, as an official arena through which to forge and sustain a public morality. Fiss's challenge and complaint are well taken. However, contrary to his account of critical jurisprudence, I do not offer a critical account of law and adjudication that is distinguished by "the purity of [its] negativism." While an antifoundationalist critique of law might be vulnerable to such chastisement, my nonfoundationalist account is neither purely negative nor negatively pure; a ludic understanding of adjudication incorporates both the constructive and deconstructive dimensions of law and also emphasizes the practical and contextual quality of adjudicative practice. Indeed, I agree with Fiss that "what is required is that judges be constrained in their judgment, and that they certainly are."[1] My disagreement is with the nature and force of those constraints, not their existence.

Playing a New Game

As this book has sought to demonstrate, judges are both free and constrained in their efforts to fulfill their institutional responsibilities. Judges do not stand outside the law but inhabit the law in a particular way. Being always situated within a legal context of freedom and restraint, judges (and jurists) are never fully restrained nor ever entirely free. The law-engaged judge is neither context-dependent nor context-transcendent but is situated within a mutually affecting relationship with the law. While there is nothing fixed or determinate about this dynamic interaction, judges will continue to change as they engage in the changing play of difference that constitutes law and its adjudicative practice. In adopting such a playful account of law that takes seriously both the rules' restrictive pull and their interpretation's liberating push, I am not committed to a jurisprudence in which adjudication will be, as Fiss fears, *only* particularistic or exclusively instrumental. Instead, as well as being both particularistic and instrumental, a nonfoundationalist account is able to explain and cultivate a mode of adjudicative performance that best captures its sense as a peculiar professional practice (in which it stands as something of its own thing) and as a profoundly ideological undertaking (in which it is organically related to the larger context of society): it accepts the foundationalist claim that adjudication is a sincere effort to engage with legal materials and, at the same time, holds on to the antifoundationalist claim that law is an exercise in political choice.

The upshot, therefore, of treating adjudication as a playful and experimental performance in law's language game will not be, as Fiss concludes, "law without inspiration." Nor will it be "the death of law . . . as we have come to admire it." A nonfoundationalist account of law and adjudication is both much less pessimistic and much more realistic than the naively optimistic Fiss concludes. While my critical approach might well lead to the "death of law as we have known it throughout history," it can contribute significantly to the rebirth of law as "a generative force of our public life" and the revival of jurisprudence as an "inspiration" to judicial practitioners.[2] A nonfoundationalist account of law, politics, and adjudication does not deliver a public morality, but it does offer a public practice through which to regenerate a morality that respects the playful quality of law and life. Moreover, in a society that still holds to the present institutional arrangements, the courts might (and, of course, might not) become a site for a series of political and transformative practices that people can not only admire but that also might serve to inspire them. Since "anything might go," the value of any judicial or juristic contribution is always up for grabs; the prospect of it being good is always shadowed by the risk of it being bad. Most important, law's adjudicative performances can never transcend the moral qualities and ideological visions of the individuals who are entrusted with this opportunity and responsibility. At the end of the day, the fact that "law is politics" and the need for a diverse group of political players must not be forgotten; democracy demands no less.

In depicting and defending a nonfoundational account of law and adjudication, it will be appreciated that many of the traditional problems and conflicts of jurisprudence are, if not resolved, at least re-presented in more fruitful and less divisive ways. To begin with, a nonfoundational account suggests a very different role for legal theory itself. Legal theory is not in the game of governing or predicting legal practice: to posit such a purpose is to misconceive law as an inorganic clump of prescriptive rules and to mischaracterize adjudication as a technological exercise in normative analysis. It is mistaken and impractical to persist in believing that the role of legal theory is to ground a finite set of fixed rules that result from and inform legal practice but that are somehow apart from legal practice and not entirely reducible to it. The tendency to view law as being the methodological measure of the rational and the task of judges as being the calculation and formulaic application of that metric is the very antithesis of what I maintain that judges do, can do, and should do. Because rules are indeterminate, there can be no rules about the application of rules that do not themselves fall back on the need for judgment; almost all contemporary mainstream jurisprudence is nothing more than "a futile striving to overcome the essential unruliness of judgment."[3] Accordingly, from a nonfoundationalist perspective, all that legal theory can do is to uncover assumptions and illuminate contradictions and make suggestions for improvement, not in the ubiquitous name of Truth or Knowledge but as a part of the continuing challenge to play the political game of law and life.

One upshot of this nonfoundationalist perspective is that law is viewed as performative and that adjudication is understood as a practical activity rather than a theoretical reflection. Treated in this way, judges do not so much put into practice theories of adjudication as engage with the general legal materials at hand and fashion them so as to fit them to the specific requirements of the issue before them in a way that advances justice. In striving to seize the opportunity to effect justice through law, nonfoundationalist judges do not pronounce ex cathedra but creatively reshape old material into new designs: it is the legal past that impels them forward, rather than pulls them back, in their yearning for justice. As such, great judges do not ignore the past nor obsess about it, but they work the past so as to realize its present possibilities for future innovation: they commit themselves to persuading us that the legal materials and the justice that they might give rise to can be and ought to be seen in a very different light and shape. Whether this satisfies the rationalistic fantasies of contemporary jurisprudence is almost besides the point: judges are to be judged by the political merit of their practical performances, not the conceptual coherence of their theoretical reflections.

In contemporary legal thought as elsewhere, too much attention is fixed on the cogency of the answers given rather than on the appropriateness of the questions asked. For instance, when viewed from a nonfoundationalist perspective, the customary standoff between positivists and natural lawyers is revealed to be a pseudo-disagreement. When adjudication is understood as a language game of infinite political possibilities, inquiries about whether law and political morality are necessarily connected and about whether judges' resort to political morality is impersonally determined are no longer pertinent or pressing. As grasped by a nonfoundationalist critique, law is no less about political morality than adjudication is about impersonal determination. By engaging in law and adjudication, its professional participants are involved with political morality in a way that is neither impersonal nor determined; judges and jurists can no more choose to ignore or finesse issues of political morality than they can slough off their responsibility for actually resolving those issues by implicating law's inherent logic. From a nonfoundationalist perspective, there are no "hard cases" in that all cases are both hard and easy in proportion to the (in)stability in social judgments and historical contexts that energize the dynamic interaction of determinacy and indeterminacy in legal language; there is no way to apply the rules to the facts that does not involve ideological choice between competing values and contrasting interpretations. However, this does not mean that judging necessitates or always involves grinding a favored political ax. When they act politically (as they always do), judges can and should remain open and self-critical about their political values, commitments, and biases.

To rephrase Dworkin's famous assessment,[4] law is deeply and thoroughly political as a matter of personal and partisan politics. This simple and fundamental proposition is not a cause for regret. Rather than resist this assessment's normative force, the challenge is get beyond apocalyptic despair or fatalistic resignation and, instead, to turn this fact to democratic advantage. This can be done by recognizing that the insight that "law is politics" is an opportunity to enhance social justice, not an obstacle to its achievement. In making those ideological choices, judges best meet their democratic responsibilities, not by masking their values and commitments but by addressing them candidly. Indeed, they treat their values and commitments in much the same way that they treat legal materials—as resources to be interrogated and reworked in the service of a vision of social justice that is itself always in the process of revision and transformation. The hallmark of the great judge is not to carve out a detailed theory of justice and to cling to it through doctrinal thick and thin; this is the curse of the foundationalist judge who mistakes political hubris for democratic duty. Instead, great judges recognize that while they must assume the responsibility of political choice, they do this in a suitably democratic manner by "keeping questions open, lingering in enlightened confusion, so that [they] do not miss the next insight when it comes."[5]

Furthermore, from such a nonfoundational perspective, the perennial puzzle as to how to make a theoretically justifiable and practically sustainable distinction between the work of judges and legislators in a democratic society begins to take on a very different complexion. This problematic has motivated much contemporary scholarship, but its intellectual parameters have tended to confuse rather than clarify jurists' thinking. A nonfoundationalist approach suggests that the answers given are unconvincing because the questions asked are off the mark. In short, efforts to identify and defend a suitable distinction are doomed because there is none. Or, at least, there is no distinction between adjudicative and legislative practices that can be maintained in a way that is itself foundational or fixed; any such distinctions or practices do not ground or fix debate because they are always part of the debate to be had. As a matter of nonfoundational wisdom, the presumption that decisions of legislatures or governments are necessarily more democratic than those of courts is flawed; courts are "not uniquely subject to the influences of regressive social pressures and the risk of strategies being ineffective or backfiring."[6] The respective responsibilities of judges and legislators cannot be defined outside of the never-ending debate about what democracy demands and what best serves democracy in a particular historical setting and sociopolitical context. In the same way that judges are not constrained in their decisions by legal doctrine in a final or objective sense such that "anything might go," so legislators are not free to make decisions that are unencumbered by institutional constraints such that "anything goes." In both cases, the practices of adjudication and legislation only make sense within a contextual set of legal rules, institutional expectations, interpretive constraints, material conditions, social views, intellectual circumstances, and the like, which both make any decisions possible and also influence the kind of decisions that are made. In an important sense, the legislative and adjudicative games are part of the larger game of life and governance: judges and legislators play out their relative performances within and with democracy's enabling conditions.

For instance, in the cricketing case of *Miller* v. *Jackson*, it will be remembered that a decision had to be made about the relative entitlements of adjacent property owners—whether the interests of the late-arriving Millers could outweigh those of the long-established cricket club. Although all three judges mentioned it in passing, there was a possible but overlooked institutional solution to the problem in that an elected and accountable legislative body had already considered the issue. For example, Lord Denning mentioned the significant matter of planning approval having been required and obtained, only to dismiss its significance to the judicial task:

> I must say that I am surprised that the developers of that housing estate were allowed to build the houses so close to the cricket ground. No

> doubt they wanted to make the most of their site and put up as many houses as they could for their own profit. The planning authorities ought not to have allowed it. The houses ought to have been so sited as not to interfere with the cricket. But the houses have been built and we have to contend with the consequences. . . . [The members of the cricket club] have spent money, labour and love in the making of [the cricket ground]; and they have the right to play on it as they have done for seventy years. Is this all to be rendered useless to them by the thoughtless and selfish act of an estate developer in building right up to the edge of it?[7]

Without speaking to any of the procedural niceties or substantive merits involved, it can be assumed that the development was neither entirely "thoughtless" nor only "selfish"; it benefited many residents on the new housing estate. Before the developers could have proceeded, they would have had to obtain planning permission, and this would (likely) only have been granted in accordance with established regulations, formulated policies, and required procedures. For present purposes, the point of my critical intervention is not to squabble over which body made the best or right decision. All that needs to be pointed out is that the question of which is the more appropriate body to decide the issue and what is the better decision to be made are matters that will depend on the particular context—social, material, intellectual, and institutional conditions—within which the unavoidable balancing and compromise of competing interests takes place. While it is tempting to suggest that a less-than-ideal (elected) municipal board is preferable to an ideal-as-possible (unelected) judicial bench, this kind of generalized and once-and-for-all assessment is not recommended by a nonfoundational perspective. Of course, all commentators and critics will approach specific problems with their own prejudices and presumptions, but they must work to put them in political and judicial play. In participating in democracy's games in good faith, they can avoid the foundationalist tendency to allow generalizable principle to be the enemy of pragmatic good and to resist the antifoundationalist temptation to permit the political end to justify the institutional means. Nonfoundationalist critics recognize and accept that in playing the game, the issue of what it means to *play the game* both defines and is transformed by its continuing performances.

Democracy and Destiny

As the relatively discrete dispute between the Millers and the cricket club suggests, law and games have a way of working far-reaching impacts—for good and bad—on not only their immediate participants but society at large.

Indeed, many commentators and aficionados realize that games of law and, for example, soccer have had enormous historical and social effects: law and soccer have wreaked as much havoc in people's lives as they have occasioned joy. It is no exaggeration to say that soccer has been the catalyst that has sent not only whole countries into ecstatic celebration but also some nations to bloody war. In 1969, a young El Salvadoran woman, Amelia Bolanios, shot herself when the national team lost to a last-minute goal by Honduras in a World Cup qualifying game. After a week of national mourning, the return match took place in El Salvador in a bellicose atmosphere of mob and military intimidation:

> The army surrounded the ground. On the pitch stood a cordon of soldiers from a crack regiment of the *Guardia Nacional*, armed with sub-machine guns. During the playing of the Honduran national anthem the crowd roared and whistled. Next, instead of the Honduran flag—which had been burnt before the eyes of the spectators, driving them mad with joy—the hosts ran a dirty, tattered dishrag up the flagpole. Under such conditions the players from Tegucigalpa did not, understandably, have their minds on the game. They had their minds on getting out alive. "We're awfully lucky that we lost," said the visiting coach, Mario Griffin, with relief. El Salvador prevailed, three-nil.
>
> The same armoured cars carried the Honduran team straight from the playing field to the airport. A worse fate awaited the visiting fans. Kicked and beaten, they fled towards the border. Two of them died. Scores landed in hospital. One hundred and fifty visitors' cars were burned. The border between the two states was closed a few hours later. Luis read about all of this in the newspaper and said that there was going to be a war. He had been a reporter for a long time and he knew his beat. In Latin America, he said, *the border between soccer and politics is vague.*[8]

The next day, war was declared between Honduras and El Salvador: it ended in stalemate after a hundred hours with six thousand dead, more than twelve thousand wounded, and fifty thousand losing their homes and fields. A couple of weeks later, the deciding game of the best-of-three series was played on a neutral ground in Mexico. With five thousand club-wielding police to divide the Honduran and El Salvadoran fans, the game ended in a 3–2 victory for El Salvador: the soccer war was given partial resolution.

Like law and most other games, soccer's appeal is not ultimately to be found in its remarkable capacity to mobilize crowds and to give rise to fanatical devotion. The enduring contribution of soccer has been its capacity to stir people's imagination and to represent, in microcosm, "the drama . . .

of humanity's struggle with destiny." As with law, it is never possible to know exactly how things will work out. Of course, being rule-defined activities, the games of soccer and law are not random or entirely unpredictable in their performances and outcomes; it is not that "anything goes." However, particularly when understood from a nonfoundationalist perspective, both soccer and law celebrate rather than curtail the possibilities for transformative action; it is that "anything might go." Because each new performance takes place under different contextual conditions and never repeats past games in any self-generating way, the need for initiative, experimentation, and strategic choices is inescapable. As befits any activity that aspires to social significance, law and soccer depend upon both individual contribution and collective coordination. Indeed, in the process of play, individual talent and teamwork interact and work to change each other. Like most group games, law and soccer insist upon teamwork, division of labor, commitment, sacrifice, expertise, and common skills. Moreover, as well as requiring effort and discipline, in which individual skill is honed and harnessed to the common goal, law and soccer also require the occasional flash of brilliance and luck. As with all playful activities, all performances in law and soccer contain an element of chance that can neither be eliminated nor controlled. When law and adjudication are understood in a nonfoundational way as playful activities, their performance can, like soccer, help to "reminds us, every day of the week, of the essential truth of an uncertain world—destiny is a perpetual beginning."[9]

More than anything else, a nonfoundationalist critique suggests an entirely different attitude and approach to engagement in law and the responsibilities of adjudication. In playing toward a democracy that takes seriously the critical force of contingency and experimentation, it is no longer appropriate or necessary for judges and jurists to proceed as if their task were to identify those legal structures and doctrines that best reflect and instantiate the natural form and substance of liberal market economies. With the recognition that existing legal rules and arrangements are only the latest in a long line of historical compromises, the judicial and jurisprudential challenge is to undertake the democratic responsibility to continue and facilitate the never-ending process of transformation and renewal.[10] In their case-by-case development of the law, judges will not feel obliged to revere present arrangements or to revise them for the sake of it: they will work to adapt legal doctrine so that it can accommodate to the understanding and practice of social life as a fluid game of dynamic possibilities. Consequently, from a nonfoundationalist perspective, the test of good judging is not whether the judicial players got it right either as a matter of doctrinal logic or legal morality, but whether their decisions contribute to the advancement of a more flexible and less oppressive social structure that is less hostage to itself and more open to transformation. In short, law and adjudication will seek to promote justice by recognizing and acting upon the insight that injustice occurs when people's life-chances or sense of self depend not on making a better move or changing the game but on being prevented from participating in the game over what it means to *play the game.*

For people to have lost faith in the judicial process, at least as presently constituted and practiced, is no bad thing; law and adjudication have failed to live up to their foundationalist expectations and are in danger of falling victim to the antifoundationalist critique. However, this crisis in confidence and legitimacy might galvanize both lawyers and citizens to reassess the theory and practice of law and adjudication. Informed by a nonfoundationalist perspective, they might come to accept that law is both professional and ideological through and through. By understanding themselves as playing both with and within the infinite possibilities of law's language game, its participants might begin to transform themselves as a way of restoring public trust in their capacity for political engagement through law and its propriety. Trading in nothing more pretentious than legal reasoning, judicial players might be able to experiment with the law to transformative effect, and, in so doing, they might be able to reaffirm public faith in the redemptive power of law's daily rites and rituals. The hope is that the recognition that there are no right answers and only difficult choices will energize rather than enervate these players in law's language game. It is only by seizing enthusiastically, if modestly, the political opportunities of their role that judges and jurists can satisfy their highest democratic calling. Indeed, accepting that their work cannot be separated entirely from the material and ideological conditions under which it is constituted and performed, judges and jurists must be prepared to be bold in their actions, responsible in their justifications, humble in their convictions, and pluralistic in their political beliefs.

Whether my proposals are "radical" or not is a matter for debate in the same way that the question of what is and is not "radical" is always an open and contextual question. Indeed, if mainstream jurists were to be believed, it is no longer possible to be a radical unless there is a willingness to countenance some form of wholesale revolution or immediate social reorganization. Furthermore, my arguments and proposals will appear almost anodyne and not at all radical to those who believe that any form or practice of adjudication is problematic. As I have tried to argue throughout, I disagree that only such programmatic or dramatic interventions can count as important radical or progressive (which are not the same thing, of course) contributions to transformative action. Moreover, it would be disingenuous at best, and plain wrong at worst, to insist that there are some necessary practical and political consequences, let alone radical ones, that flow from my theoretical critique: to proclaim such an impact would be to misconceive and contradict the whole critical thrust of a nonfoundationalist approach. While I do not claim that my account has any necessary prescriptive and radical implications for law and adjudication, I do maintain that it does have some important and far-reaching consequences in the prevailing jurisprudential circumstances and political conditions in which foundationalist ideas still hold conservative sway.

My claim is more focused and limited than many mainstream critics can countenance, but it is no more modest or less radical for that. I insist that insofar as adjudication as presently practiced continues to be an important symbolic force and central institution in modern democracies (and the historical evidence suggests that not only will it continue to be but that it will actually increase in significance and scope),[11] my nonfoundationalist account offers the most cogent and compelling explanation of how the judicial task is, can, and should be performed if it is to have any chance of meeting its radical ambitions and fulfilling its democratic role. As such, I have not sought to provide a blueprint for fundamental social reconstruction or to suggest that courts are the most appropriate site to begin that crucial task; there is no one tried-and-tested manifesto that people can simply adopt in a once-and-for-all way. Reconstructive programs, whatever the motivations or credentials of their proponents, soon turn into the same kind of constraints on change that the critiques were originally intended to dislodge. This is particularly the case in regard to transformative actions through the courts: their success or failure will depend on the particular historical concatenation of sociopolitical forces in play. Instead, I have insisted that insofar as courts might be viewed as one place to engage in the political struggle for social justice, a nonfoundationalist account of law and adjudication is the least worst complement to such an endeavor.

Even though a nonfoundationalist approach does not lead inexorably to social enlightenment and political emancipation, it does challenge the idea that things need to be the way that they are and, in so doing, opens up space for possible transformative action: "Every idea is an incitement."[12] Whether a loss of foundationalist faith results in beneficial and/or progressive change is an empirical and historical question. However, there is nothing in my account that precludes or invalidates radical interventions and progressive initiatives, provided that what counts as radical or progressive is understood in a suitably nonfoundational and provisional way. No political strategy can eliminate the risk that it might have the unintended or perverse effect of legitimating the status quo. Indeed, the nonfoundationalist work of Richard

Rorty and Stanley Fish has tended to confirm rather than confound that danger. However, the fact that a nonfoundationalist approach runs that risk does not mean that it must or will result in a quietistic and conservative validation of existing conditions. To move to such a conclusion is to make the mistake that a nonfoundationalist critique is most at pains to warn against—insisting that anything necessarily follows by way of practical action from any theoretical stance. In taking such a line, both proponents and critics of a nonfoundationalist approach have tended to accede too quickly and too easily to the assumption that society is much more stable and inert than it actually is.[13] In contrast, my nonfoundationalist approach insists that social arrangements (and, therefore, law, adjudication, and politics) are much more volatile and contingent than generally assumed: they are in a constant state of flux and reconfiguration. As such, the status quo is more evanescent and less settled than most jurists pretend; it already contains the resources and possibilities for its own transformation. Like law, life at large is a dynamic game in which everything is in play and "anything might go."

Because law and adjudication are institutions that have played a considerable part in maintaining social oppression and stymieing efforts to reduce it, any strategy of resistance and transformation must be alert to the realistic possibility of preemption and co-optation. Again, efforts to debunk thoroughly the foundationalist pretension of those players and participants in the games of law and adjudication lead nowhere in particular other than the nonfoundational realization that there is an inescapable obligation to act in the here and now. Depending on the particular context, action or inaction might be the best tactic to oppose and overcome the stabilizing instincts of the status quo. Moreover, in acting against established interests, it is likely much more radical to resist the allure of false utopias. Instead, it seems much more promising to accept that significant change has less to do with whether lawyers and judges get the jurisprudential theory right than with how well they play the game. In the same way that it is the sign of great players that they exceed the expectations of the greatest coaches in disregarding their instructions, so great judges have an endearing habit of ruining the best-laid plans and recommendations of the greatest jurists. In law's adjudicative game, victories and defeats are temporary; it is the willingness to keep playing and to keep reworking what it means to *play the game* that is the hallmark of democratic players.

The Final Kick?

All in all, taking a nonfoundationalist critique seriously means that citizens, as well as judges and jurists, must pluck up the intellectual and institutional courage to take "leaps in the dark." For citizens, this demands no less than having such confidence in their judicial appointments that they are willing to entrust to them, along with other officials and delegates, the considerable responsibility to make hard decisions in hard circumstances. However, it will be for judges and jurists to earn that opportunity with each and every decision that they reach. Like soccer players, judges are only as good as their last performance. Knowing that they will be called to account before the political bar of democratic governance rather than having to satisfy the philosophical standards of academic authority, judges and jurists might be less inclined to hide behind the professional facade of law's waning prestige. So liberated, citizens and judges could then begin to confirm a democratic belief in themselves and the legal process by adopting a simple nonfoundationalist ethic: "Act for the best, hope for the best, and take what comes."[14] In a society that attempts to embrace the contingency and playfulness of life, there is likely no better way.

Appendix

......

What follows is a standard set of argumentative maneuvers that constantly repeat themselves in legal debate and that can be used to support or undermine each other; it draws heavily on the ideas and inspiration of Duncan Kennedy of Harvard Law School.* This typology is obviously stylized and static. In practice, the better exponents of legal reasoning should be able to weave these different argumentative strategies in an organic and elegant web of persuasive advocacy. I have tried to illustrate their operation by reference to actual cases. In order to appreciate fully the play of these argumentative moves, the reader should read the cases that are referenced. While each pair of arguments might not apply with equal weight and facility to every dispute, almost any legal issue can be worked through using some blend of these techniques. They can be divided into two broad groupings: *Precedent* and *Policy*.

(A) Precedent

The following paired strategies enable lawyers to argue about and reason with rules or past decisions. Contrary to received wisdom, the more expansive or flexible interpretation does not necessarily correlate with the most liberal or progressive outcome, and the more limited or rigid interpretation does not necessarily correlate with the most conservative or reactionary outcome: their effect will depend on the context in which they are used, the particular twist that they are given, and the background of entitlements against which they function.

*D. Kennedy, *A Semiotics of Legal Argument,* 42 Syracuse L. Rev. 75 at 103 (1991), and D. Kennedy, A Critique of Adjudication: fin de siècle 137–56 (1197). See also J. Boyle, *The Anatomy of a Torts Class,* 34 Amer. U. L. Rev. 1003 (1985, and J. Balkin, *The Crystalline Structure of Legal Thought,* 39 Rutgers L. Rev. 1 (9186).

(1) Literal and purposive interpretation

—*Literal*: Interpret the meaning of any particular word or phrase by reference to its abstract and general "dictionary" meaning, and apply it to the facts of the case without reference to the context in which the rule or the facts arise.

—*Purposive*: Posit the purpose or purposes (for there are likely to be multiple and/or conflicting purposes) that the rule arises from or is intended to achieve and elaborate the meaning of the particular word or phrase in light of that purpose and the factual context.

This is a simple maneuver that is commonly used to great effect. Particularly pertinent to statutory analysis, it can function to warrant entirely contradictory outcomes. For example, the meaning of "to use a weapon" under s.267(1) (a) of the Criminal Code can be restricted to the "wielding" and "thrusting" of traditional instruments, such as guns, knives, or even hammers, or, by focusing on the purpose of the object rather than its character, it can be interpreted to encompass the unleashing of a dog or any other animate entity; see *R.* v. *McLeod* (1993), 84 C.C.C.(3d) 336 (YCA).

(2) Narrow and broad interpretations

—*Narrow*: Elaborate the rule or principle in such limited terms that its extension by analogy to any other fact situation will be extremely difficult to pull off and the earlier precedent will have to be distinguished.

—*Broad*: Formulate the rule or principle in such wide terms that its extension by analogy to any other fact situation will be much easier to sustain and the earlier precedent will have to be followed.

This is a run-of-the-mill move that is explicitly relied upon by judges. For example, the famous "neighbor principle" of Lord Atkin can be pitched at many different levels of generality: it can be (and has been) restated in such a way as to support a range of formulations that run from "(a) Scottish manufacturers in the late 1920s of opaque bottles of ginger beer are expected to check that dead snails are not left in them," through "(m) all persons who make goods or offer services to the public must ensure that they are fit for their intended purpose," to "(z) everyone should act with due care in their interactions with others"; see *Donoghue* v. *Stevenson*, [1932] A.C. 562.

(3) General and detailed statement of facts

—*General*: Describe the facts of the case at such a high level of generality and vagueness that they can be made compatible with a variety of different rule formulations.

—*Specific*: Offer an account of the facts of the case at such a low level of detail and specificity that it is very difficult to make them fit almost any rule formulation.

The idea here is to emphasize the way in which the categorization of the facts and the law are manipulated to create better or worse fits between the two (in conjunction with [1] and [2]). Facts and law interrelate; they each determine and refine the other as they are determined and refined by them. Questions of fact are by no means as straightforward or given as they appear in appellate judgments. What is material or relevant will be determined by the law; it is a dialectical relation. For example, in determining issues of foreseeability, it is much easier to support a positive finding when the facts are stated generally (e.g., fireworks and negligent employees) rather than when they are related in fine detail (e.g., carrying fireworks, missing train, helping hand, falling passenger, explosion, unsteady scales, etc.); see *Palsgraf*, 162 N.E. 99 (1928).

(4) Old and modern authorities

—*Old*: The rule or principle is so old that it has become a basic axiom of the entire common law and must be followed, OR it is so old that it has lost contact entirely with the realities of modern society and must be disregarded.

—*Modern*: The rule or principle is so recent that its worth to the law has not been established and it cannot yet be considered to be a stable feature of the common law, OR the rule or principle is so recent that it responds directly to the conditions of modern society and deserves to be taken most seriously on that account.

This maneuver is obvious. There are a host of judicial pronouncements by the same judges that pick and choose among these strategies as it suits them. This is a popular line of argument in property and constitutional law cases.

(B) Policy

While these maneuvers are more openly "political" in nature and sweep, it does not mean that the *precedential* arguments are any less political; they are simply more subtly so. Not only is the choice between the competing pairs of policy arguments not determined by the arguments themselves but the mounting of each argument involves some preference for one value over another (e.g., the positing of a purpose). Also, it is a mistake to assume that one side of each pair will always connect with the same larger political orientation. Apart from the fact that it is not always obvious what is the "Left" or "Right" thing to do in a particular situation, the shifting details of the context will ensure that different arguments have different political spins and implications at different times. At best, each side of a competing pair *tends to tilt generally* in one political direction or the other.

(1) Judicial administration

—*Strict*: A firm or fixed rule is required because it will be easier to administer and enforce; it will enable people to order their affairs with a higher degree of certainty and predictability; and a less firm or fixed rule will lead to outcomes that are inconsistent, confused, arbitrary, and the like.

—*Flexible*: A flexible or variable standard is required because it will be easier to tailor it to an individualized fact situation; it will maintain confidence in the law's status as an institution committed to justice; and a less flexible or variable standard will oblige the courts to reach particular decisions that are mechanical, unfair, unjust, and the like.

This pair of arguments is often used in contract cases. For example, in dealing with the contractual doctrine of "fundamental breach," the courts have swung back and forth between strict rules and broad standards as the most appropriate device to define and monitor the enforcement of unfair agreements—is it better to employ a mechanical and formal rule to establish if the breach has brought the contract to an end or to examine the circumstances in which the contract was made? See *Beaufort Realties*, [1980] 2 S.C.R. 718.

(2) Institutional competence

—*Competent*: The courts are especially suited and able to deal exclusively with this kind of issue because it involves complicated factual matters that require case-by-case resolution; it invites an impartial and experienced act of judgment; and it demands a capacity to respond effectively to rapidly changing social conditions.

—*Incompetent*: The courts are not well situated to deal with this kind of issue, as opposed to the legislature or administrative agency, because it involves matters of social justice that need to be settled by an institution with a broader democratic mandate; it demands resort to specialized knowledge about particular social practices and customs; and it implicates matters that have long-term, structural implications for social ordering.

Although the courts usually proceed without any doubts about their legitimate entitlement to develop or change the law (i.e., the whole of tort law), they occasionally hesitate in certain situations to question whether they should be effecting significant change. For example, the Supreme Court of Canada confidently proceeded to rework most of the rules for the assessment of damages in personal injury litigation but became a little coy about whether it could move from a once-and-for-all lump sum payment to a scheme of periodic payment; see *Andrews*, [1978] 2 S.C.R. 229.

(3) Equality

—*Formal*: A rule or principle should be formulated and applied in such a way that it respects the demands of equality by treating everyone the same without fear or favor; to do otherwise would be to work an injustice on certain groups or individuals.

—*Substantive*: A rule or principle should be formulated and applied in such a way that it respects the demands of equality by treating differently situated groups or individuals differently; to do otherwise would be to compound the inequalities that already exist.

This arises throughout the common law whether it is dealing with the relative capacities of contracting parties (e.g., large bank and poor individual) or the capabilities of differently abled tort-feasors (e.g., the young, old, blind, etc.). However, it is most squarely faced in constitutional cases where courts have to determine the categories and conditions of discrimination; see *Bliss*, [1979] 1 S.C.R. 183.

(4) Morality

Arguments about morality are, of course, manifold. All that one can do is to offer some examples of the general kind of twinned arguments that it is possible to make; much will depend upon the particular substantive matter (e.g., contract, tort, criminal, etc.) that is being considered. Some typical and common examples of such dichotomous pairings include form and substance, individual and community, single instance and multiple series, individualist and altruist, and content and process. A familiar set of arguments are those based around freedom and security.

—*Freedom*: Persons should only be held responsible for those acts that they have chosen to perform, that are blameworthy, that cause foreseeable and intended harm, and that could not have been avoided by others, OR persons should be entitled to engage in activity that does not cause harm to others with a minimum of government interference or regulation.

Security: Persons who are injured or interfered with through no fault of their own are entitled to protection, help, or compensation from other persons or society at large, OR the government has a responsibility to monitor and regulate a person's activities in order to preserve the freedom of others.

These argumentative possibilities arise in most cases; property and criminal law are fertile sources. A particularly stark example of where these possibilties come into play is over whether there is a "duty to rescue." Although the courts work from the general proposition that there is no general obligation to come to the rescue of someone else, they have fashioned an expanded set of exceptions that assume a preexisting relation between parties that warrants the imposition of such a responsibility; see *Horsley* v. *MacLaren*, [1972] S.C.R. 441.

(5) Deterrence

—*Flexible*: A particular standard or rule will encourage good conduct and deter bad conduct because it will allow persons and corporations to respond better to changing social and market conditions; it will facilitate greater interaction and freer competition among persons and corporations; and, as opposed to a less broad and stricter standard, will not inhibit persons or corporations from creative or innovative behavior.

—*Stable*: A particular standard or rule will deter good conduct and encourage bad conduct because it will leave persons and corporations confused as to the limits placed on their behavior; it will stymie open interaction and healthy competition among persons and corporations; and, as opposed to a less broad and stricter standard, it will inhibit persons or corporations from taking chances.

This is a familiar set of arguments in contract and criminal law cases. For example, a continuing challenge that the courts face in contract cases is determining in what circumstances a party is invariably bound to perform certain terms of the contract; see *Hong Kong Fir*, [1962] 2 Q.B. 26 (C.A.). Another approach focuses on the different capacities of different persons and corporations to know the relevant standards and adjust their conduct accordingly; see *Lloyds Bank* v. *Bundy*, [1975] Q.B. 326 (C.A.). This, of course, involves a shift between *formal* assumptions and *substantive* realities.

(6) Cost-benefit analysis

—*Incentives*: A rule or principle will increase or decrease the responsibility on certain persons or corporations to incur certain costs, but these individual expenditures or savings are outweighed by the overall benefits to others and will enhance social utility by encouraging a socially desirable level of activity.

—*Disincentives*: A rule or principle will decrease or increase the responsibility on certain persons or corporations to incur certain costs, but these individual savings or expenditures are not outweighed by the overall benefits to others and will not enhance social utility because they do not encourage a socially desirable level of activity.

Obvious examples of this form of argumentation occur in tort law. For example, in determining the level of resources that must be invested in safety measures, the court must ensure that potential tort-feasors are encouraged to take appropriate steps to safeguard others, but not so that the cost of those steps or the resulting penalties oblige them to withdraw from a useful endeavor; see *Hedley Byrne*, [1964] A.C. 465. Again, it is possible here to move from an abstract analysis to a more concrete discussion by contrasting the *formal* assumptions of economic theorizing (e.g., perfect information, rational actors, etc.) with the *substantive* circumstances of real-world economic activity (e.g., imperfect information, irrational actors, etc.). Also, if the figures are juggled sufficiently, the whole equation of costs and benefits can be stood on its head.

(7) Distributive considerations

—*Redistribution*: A particular rule or principle that places more burdens on one group of persons than another is justified, because that group is better able to afford the costs of that added responsibility, OR because greater opportunities or entitlements will redound to the advantage of a less advantaged group.

—*No distribution*: A particular rule or principle that places more burdens on one group of persons than another is not justified, because that group will usually be able to spread or pass on that burden to other persons, including the very groups that the rule was intended to benefit, OR because such goals are better achieved through the tax or welfare systems.

This set of arguments has particular salience in property law and applies to the whole area of landlord-and-tenant relations, especially the vexed issue of rent control. Also, they have obvious application where the court expects more of one party than another (e.g., unconscionability doctrine in contracts), or places one party under a fiduciary obligation to look after the interests of another party; see *LAC Minerals*, [1989] 2 S.C.R. 574.

(8) Choice

—*Paternalism*: A particular standard that imposes duties or responsibilities on persons is favored because they are in the best interests of those persons, whether or not the persons themselves believe them to be in their own best interests, OR because certain structural conditions prevent those persons from making informed decisions for themselves.

—*Antipaternalism*: A certain standard that imposes duties or responsibilities on persons is not favored because no one is ever in a better position than the persons involved to asses those persons' best interests without imposing their own interests, OR because interfering in one area or instance will only lead to problems and injustices elsewhere.

These maneuvers are invoked in large questions about the scope of tort law generally or the extent of limits on freedom of contract. A particular focus for these considerations is the issue of "consent." For example, they have considerable salience in criminal cases in which the courts are required to decide whether a person can consent to the infliction of actual bodily harm in the course of consensual sexual relations; see *Brown*, [1993] 2 All E.R. 75 (H.L.).

*

Most of these argumentative maneuvers can be brought into play on most legal occasions. In order to demonstrate their relevance and application, I offer an extended Canadian illustration in regard to one particular situation. Take the following hypothetical instance:

> Marie Beaumont throws a large party at her cottage an hour or so out of town. She owns a chain of wineries and supplies most of the alcoholic refreshment herself. Charlie Paylor, a renowned party animal, was invited and drives there with his friend, Jamie Singh. They both drink a considerable amount, and Marie is highly amused at their crazy antics. After midnight, Charlie and Jamie leave. On the way home, they are involved in an accident with Tom in which they are all seriously injured. Is Marie liable in damages to Charlie, Jamie, and Tom?

The most significant authority is *Menow* v. *Honsberger and Jordan House*, [1974] S.C.R. 239, in which a hotel was held partly responsible for injuries caused to a drunken patron who was thrown out of the hotel and later run over by a negligent driver on a busy highway near the hotel. Assume for the purposes of this illustration that it is also the only relevant precedent. While some arguments have more rhetorical bite and cogent force than others, it should be obvious that, with a little imagination and ingenuity, it will be possible to run these permutations of argumentative maneuvers in almost every case that comes up.

On behalf of Charlie, Jamie, and Tom and in favor of liability, it can be argued:

—Although *Menow* was about a hotel, the meaning and reach of any rule imposing responsibility for the care of others is not restricted to "commercial establishments," because its motivating spirit and purpose extends to include private parties.

—The facts of *Menow* were very similar to that of the party (i.e., a host permitted a severely drunken man to drive home) and the likelihood of harm great enough to warrant the imposition of liability.

—The decision in *Menow* is fairly recent and because it represents the prevailing desire to curb drunk driving, it ought to be respected by enforcing it vigorously and widely.

—A broad and flexible standard of liability is suitable because it will allow the courts to adapt the imposition of liability to the particular circumstances and, by imposing liability in this case, to ensure that justice is served.

—The courts act entirely within traditional understandings of their institutional competence by developing the law to meet new challenges and to reflect contemporary expectations.

—Everyone who acts irresponsibly by supplying drivers with excessive amounts of alcohol should be treated similarly regardless of whether they are in business or not.
—Home owners who arrange parties, supply alcoholic refreshment, and invite people with a propensity for drunken revelry should assume responsibility for the safety of such guests.
—A well-formulated rule of responsibility will ensure that antisocial conduct is deterred, so that the kind of wild partying that led to the present accident would be discouraged.
—Marie could have avoided this accident at a very small cost by offering Charlie and Jamie a room for the night or, at least, by arranging for a sober driver or a cab to take them home; this cost pales in comparison to the potential costs of permanently damaged lives.
—Any burden of imposing liability can be readily carried by the home owners, who are in a much better position to avoid it (by being more selective in issuing invitations or by spreading it through insurance) than the random group of drunks and their victims.
—Because Marie invited Charlie and Jamie, at least in part, on the basis of their being renowned party animals, she should have assumed responsibility for their welfare when they became incapacitated.

On behalf of Marie and against the imposition of liability, it can be argued:
—Since *Menow* is about a hotel, the meaning and reach of any resulting rule imposing responsibility for the care of others is restricted to "commercial establishments" and does not extend to private parties.
—The facts of *Menow* were such (i.e., leaving a severely drunken man to walk home in the black of night on a very busy highway with no sidewalk) that the likelihood of harm occurring was much greater than in the present situation, where it was late and the local roads were very quiet and Charlie's car was clearly visible.
—The decision in *Menow* is fairly recent and it would be premature to extend its ambit so quickly without a reasonable chance to evaluate its operation and effect.
—A firm and fixed rule of liability better serves the ends of justice, because it allows a general degree of predictability that will more than compensate for the harsh and inconsistent imposition of liability in situations like this.
—The courts exceed their institutional mandate and infringe on the legislature's prerogative when they extend the law to such an extent that it will have massive effects on people's private behavior.
—Rules of liability should be formulated and applied so that commercial

operators are treated differently and held to a higher standard than private party givers.

—Because Marie did not invite them under false pretenses, Charlie and Jamie knew what they were getting themselves into and were fully able to have taken steps to look after themselves.

—A sweeping rule of liability will have effects that are absurdly wide and will deter activity, like social gatherings, that works to the good of almost everyone in society.

—Charlie and Jamie were in a better position than Marie—or at least as good a one—to take earlier and relatively cheap steps to arrange for transport or to stay at a nearby hotel; this is a much more economical plan than curbing people's willingness to host parties or risking the possibility of drunken accidents.

—The burden of imposing liability will be substantial for social hosts, who, unlike commercial enterprises, will find it difficult to spread potential losses in a relatively cheap way; drivers are much better placed than hosts to provide for their own insurance.

—Although Marie's conduct cannot be entirely condoned, it is unreasonable to expect her to take greater responsibility for the safety of other grown-ups, like Charlie and Jamie, than they would for themselves.

Notes

1 Playing the Game: An Introduction

1 C. Mackinnon, Toward a Feminist Theory of the State 237 (1989). My use of "game" is not to be confused with recent efforts in the law-and-economics literature to deploy game theory as a method for understanding and influencing strategic legal behavior through mathematical modeling. See D. Baird, R. Gertner, and R. Picker, Game Theory and the Law (1994).

2 W. Shankly, Shankly 13 (1976). For anyone who wants to get a sense of this mania, see N. Hornby, Fever Pitch (1993), D. Thomson, 4–2 (1996), and A. Hutchinson, Kicking the Habit: Life, Football, and Other Mysteries (2000). For a good introduction to soccer, see P. Gardner, The Simplest Game: An Intelligent Fan's Guide to the World of Soccer (1994).

3 J. B. Priestley, The Good Companions Bk. 1, ch. 1, 3–4 (1929).

4 *Brown* v. *Allen*, 344 U.S. 443 at 540 per Jackson J. (1953).

5 G. Eliot, Middlemarch 760 (M. Drabble ed. 1985).

6 *Laker Airways* v. *Department of Trade*, [1977] Q.B. 643 at 724 per Lawton L.J. See, generally, J. Frank, Courts on Trial: Myth and Reality in American Justice (1949), and R. Pound, The Causes of Popular Dissatisfaction with the Administration of Justice 12 (1962).

7 See H. L. A. Hart, The Concept of Law (2d ed. 1994). Some commentators have suggested that the contemporary history of jurisprudence amounts to little more than a series of extended footnotes, illustrative appendices, and critical commentaries on Hart's The Concept of Law. One pundit went so far as to describe the first edition as "probably the best book in legal philosophy ever written." J. G. Murphy, Kant: The Philosophy of Right 180 (1970).

8 See The Rule of Law: Ideal or Ideology? (A. Hutchinson and P. Monahan eds. 1986).

9 L. Steyn, *Does Legal Formalism Hold Sway in England?* 49 Current Legal Problems 43 at 58 (1996). See also R. Dworkin, A Matter of Principle 146 (1984).

10 P. Bobbitt, Constitutional Interpretation 24 (1991). While my chosen game is soccer, law has been profitably compared to other sporting activities. See Baseball and the American Legal Mind (S. Waller et al. eds. 1995).

11 T. Eagleton, Ideology: An Introduction 3 (1991).

12 The former tendency is illustrated by R. Dworkin, Law's Empire (1986), and A. Altman, Critical Legal Studies (1990), and the latter tendency by S. Fish, Doing What Comes Naturally: Change, Rhetoric, and the Practice of Theory in Literary and Legal Studies (1989), and P. Schanck, *Understanding Postmodern Thought and Its Implications for Statutory Interpretation*, 65 S. Cal. L. Rev. 2505 (1992). For a general survey of recent jurisprudential

history along these lines, see G. Minda, Postmodern Legal Movements: Law and Jurisprudence at Century's End (1995), and D. Litowitz, Postmodern Philosophy and Law (1997).

13 T. S. Eliot, Little Gidding 5 (1942).

14 S. Fish, Is There a Text in This Class?: The Authority of Interpretive Communities 352 (1980).

15 As quoted in *American Soc. Etc.* v. *Murrray Comms. Inc.*, 547 F. Sup 462 (N.D. Ill. 1982).

16 T. Kuhn, The Structures of Scientific Revolutions (2d ed. 1970).

2 It's All in the Game: Adjudication in a Nonfoundationalist Way

1 L. Wittgenstein, Philosophical Investigations I, s. 65–67 (G. E. M. Anscombe trans. 1953). For a full account of his understanding of language as a game, see ch. 3.

2 See, for example, M. Midgley, *The Game Game*, 49 Philosophy 231 (1974), F. D'Agostino, *The Ethos of Games*, 8 J. of Phil. of Sport 7 (1982), and B. Suits, *What Is a Game?* 34 Philosophy of Science 148–56 (1967). For a tentative account of this idea of "the game within the game" in the jurisprudential context, see B. Jackson, *Towards a Semiotic Model of the Games Analogy in Jurisprudence*, 17–18 Droit et Société 97 (1991).

3 H. L. A. Hart, The Concept of Law 259 (2d ed. 1994).

4 *Ibid.* at 269.

5 See H. L. A. Hart, *American Jurisprudence through English Eyes: The Nightmare and the Noble Dream*, 11 Geo. L. Rev. 969 at 989 (1977).

6 *Supra* note 3 at 252.

7 See, generally, Hart, *supra* note 5 at 989; H. L. A. Hart, *Positivism and the Separation of Law and Morals*, 71 Harv. L. Rev. 593 at 606–7; and H. L. A. Hart, *Problems of the Philosophy of Law* in Essays in Jurisprudence and Philosophy 99 and 144 (H. L. A. Hart ed. 1983).

8 R. Dworkin, Law's Empire 353 and 351 (1986), and R. Posner, The Problems of Jurisprudence 437 (1990).

9 See R. Posner, The Economics of Justice (1981); R. Dworkin, Freedom's Law: A Moral Reading of the Constitution (1996); and C. Sunstein, Legal Reasoning and Political Conflict (1996).

10 R. Unger, What Should Legal Analysis Become? 40 (1996).

11 A. Scalia, *The Rule of Law as a Law of Rules*, 56 U. Chi. L. Rev. 1175 at 1179 (1989). See J. Raz, The Concept of a Legal System (2d ed. 1980), and L. Green, *The Political Content of Legal Theory*, 17 Phil. Soc. Sci. 15 (1987).

12 N. MacCormick, *The Ethics of Legalism*, 2 Ratio Juris 184 at 188 (1989). Other prominent fearmongers are L. Fuller, The Morality of Law 39 (1969); O. W. Fiss, *Objectivity and Interpretation*, 34 Stan. L. Rev. 739 at 749 (1982); H. Edwards, *The Judicial Function and the Elusive Goal of Principled Decisionmaking*, [1991] Wisc. L. Rev. 837 at 838–41; and Scalia, *supra* note 11, at 1182.

13 M. Tushnet, *Does Constitutional Theory Matter? A Comment* 65 Tex. L. Rev. 777 at 782 (1987). See also J. Singer, *The Player and the Cards: Nihilism and Legal Theory*, 94 Yale L.J. 1 (1984). For further discussion, see *infra* ch. 8.

14 J. Derrida, *Force of Law: The "Mystical Foundations of Authority,"* 11 Cardozo L. Rev. 921 at 931 (1990). I have to confess that I have occasionally allowed a debilitating antifoundationalism to get the better of me. See A. Hutchinson, Dwelling on the Threshold: Critical Essays in Modern Legal Thought (1988). This book marks an explicit effort to retain and enhance critical theorizing by distancing it from an antifoundationalist tendency.

15 H. Plessner, Laughing and Crying 77 (J. Churchill and M. Grene trans. 1970).

16 See Hart, *supra* note 3 at 9, 34–35, 40, 56–57, 89, 102, 140–45, 170, 285, 288, and 301.

17 D. Fraser, The Man in White Is Always Right: Cricket and the Law 9, 211, and 52 (1993).

18 See C. Geertz, The Interpretation of Cultures (1973) and Local Knowledge (1983).

19 Fraser, *supra* note 17 at 29.

20 *Ibid.* at 122.

21 For a couple of attempts to place that history in contemporary context, see M. Marqusee, Anyone but England: Cricket and the National Malaise (1994), and G. Wright, Betrayal (1993).

22 Fraser, *supra* note 17 at vii and 66.

23 S. Fish, Is There a Text in This Class?: The Authority of Interpretive Communities 352 (1980).

24 Fraser, *supra* note 17 at 14.

25 *Ibid.* at 272 and 242.

26 *Ibid.* at 273.

27 James P. Carse, Finite Infinite Games: A Vision of Life as Play and Possibility (1986). Carse's ideas, of course, resemble those of other theorists. See H. G. Gadamer, Truth and Method (J. Weinsheimer and D. Marshall trans., 2d ed. 1989), and R. Unger, Politics: A Work in Constructive Social Theory (1987). For an interesting attempt to apply Carse's ideas to business practices, see C. Hampden-Turner and F. Trompenaars, Mastering the Infinite Game (1997).

28 See E. Dunning and K. Sheard, Barbarians, Gentlemen and Players: A Sociological Study of the Development of Rugby Football (1979).

29 Fraser, *supra* note 17, at 272–73.

30 See F. Fukuyama, The End of History and the Last Man (1992).

31 Fraser, *supra* note 17, at 273.

32 F. Nietzsche, *Ecce Homo* in The Philosophy of Nietzsche 853 (1954).

33 J. Caputo, Radical Hermeneutics: Repetition, Deconstruction and the Hermeneutic Project 198–99 (1987).

34 L. Fuller, *The Forms and Limits of Adjudication*, 92 Harv. L. Rev. 353 (1978).

35 *R.* v. *Burns*, [1994] 1 S.C.R. 656 at 664 per MacLachlin J. See also *R.* v. *Secretary of State for the Home Department, Ex Parte Doody*, [1994] 1 A.C. 531. For a general discussion, see M. Taggart, *Should Canadian Judges Be Legally Required to Give Reasoned Decisions in Civil Cases?*, 33 U.T.L.J. 1 (1983), and P. Craig, *The Common Law, Reasons, and Administrative Justice*, 53 Camb. L. J. 282 (1994).

36 Indeed, much of my own work has been, at least in part, devoted to insisting upon the fact that adjudication (again, as presently understood) might well be inimical to a truly democratic society. See A. Hutchinson, Waiting for Coraf: A Critique of Law and Rights (1995).

37 Dworkin, *supra* note 8 at 400–401 (1986). See also J. C. Gray, The Nature and Sources of Law 84 (2d ed. 1921), and O. W. Holmes, *The Path of the Law* in Collected Legal Papers 173 (1920).

38 M. Foucault, Power/Knowledge: Selected Interviews and Other Writings 1 (C. Gordon ed. 1980). See D. Bell, And We Are Not Saved: The Elusive Quest for Racial Justice 25–74, 140–61, and 215–35 (1987), and, generally, G. Rosenberg, The Hollow Hope: Can Courts Bring About Social Change? (1991).

39 See, for example, Hutchinson, *supra* note 36 at 172–83.

40 J.-M. Brohm, A Prison of Measured Time 26 (1978). See also C. Lasch, The Culture of Narcissism 100–24 (1979). For an extended analysis of the Marxist critique of law, see ch. 8.

41 I. Young, *The Exclusion of Women from Sport: Conceptual and Existential Dimensions*, 9 Phil. in Context 44–53 (1979). See also E. Thornburg, *Metaphors Matter: How Images of Battle, Sports, and Sex Shape the Adversary System*, 10 Wis. Women's L.J. 225 (1995).

42 R. West, *Jurisprudence and Gender*, 55 U. Chi. L. Rev. 1 at 2 (1988). See also C. Mackinnon, Feminism Unmodified: Discourses on Life and Law 117–24 (1987).

43 E. Bartlett, *Feminist Legal Methods*, 103 Harv. L. Rev. 829 (1990), and D. Rhode, *Feminist Critical Theories*, 42 Stan. L. Rev. 617 (1990).

44 W. Connolly, Identity/Difference: Democratic Negotiations of Political Paradox (1991). See also J. Derrida, *Afterword* in Limited Inc. 145 (G. Graff and S. Weber eds. 1988).

45 Carse, *supra* note 27 at 56.

46 J.-F. Lyotard, The Postmodern Condition: A Report on Knowledge 67 (G. Bennington and B. Massumi trans. 1984). See also D. Kennedy, Sexy Dressing, Etc. 184 (1993).

47 Derrida, *supra* note 44 at 147.

48 Lyotard, *supra* note 46 at xxiv. See, generally, S. K. White, Political Theory and Postmodernism (1991), and, in law, P. Schlag, The Enchantment of Reason (1998).

49 See R. Rorty, *Solidarity or Objectivity?* in Post-analytic Philosophy 6 (J. Rajchman and C. West eds. 1985).

50 See, for example, H. Arkes, First Things: An Inquiry into the First Principles of Morals and Justice 132–33 (1986), and J. Habermas, The Philosophical Discourse of Modernity 96–97 (F. Lawrence trans. 1987).

51 B. Allen, Truth in Philosophy 6 (1993).

52 *Ibid.* at 182.

53 See R. Rorty, Philosophy and the Mirror of Nature 170–209 (1979), and Fish, *supra* note 23 at 369.

54 O. W. Holmes Jr., Collected Legal Papers 200 (1920).

55 See, for example, *infra* chs. 4, 6, 9, and 10.

56 S. Fish, Doing What Comes Naturally: Change, Rhetoric and the Practice of Theory in Literary and Legal Studies 139, 336, and 321 (1989). Although Fish insists that interpretation is and must be anchored in its social setting, his hermeneutic account is stubbornly ahistorical in content and illustration. For a political critique of Fish's work, see A. Hutchinson, *Gone Fishing* in Dwelling on the Threshold: Critical Essays on Modern Legal Thought 142–63 (1988).

57 *Ibid.* at 27, 14–15, 326, and 28.

58 *Ibid.* at 392. See, also, M. Walzer, *Philosophy and Democracy*, 9 Pol. Theory 379 (1981).

59 See, generally, H. L. Fairland, Critical Conditions: Postmodernity and the Question of Foundations (1994), and G. Wihl, The Contingency of Theory: Pragmatism, Expressivism, and Deconstruction (1994).

60 R. Rorty, Contingency, Irony and Solidarity 39 and 133 (1989).

61 Rorty, *supra* note 53, at 315.

62 S. Fish, *Rhetoric* in Critical Terms for Literary Study 214 (F. Lentricchia and T. McLaughlin eds. 1990).

63 R. Descartes, *Meditations II* (1641) in The Philosophical Works of Descartes 149 (E. Haldane and G. Ross trans. 1967).

3 The Language Game: From Ambiguity to Indeterminacy

1 L. Wittgenstein, Philosophical Investigations I, s. 23 (G. E. M. Anscombe trans. 1953).

2 H. L. A. Hart, The Concept of Law 275 (2d ed. 1994).

3 *Ibid.* at 244. For instance, unlike Hart, Dworkin takes an internal viewpoint on the question of the existence and applicability of law. See R. Dworkin, Law's Empire 65–94 (1986). For a general discussion of this problem, see M. Mandel, *Dworkin, Hart and the Problem of Theoretical Perspective*, 14 Law & Soc. Rev. 57 (1979).

4 *Concept of Law* at 269 and 90.

5 See H. L. A. Hart, *American Jurisprudence through English Eyes: The Nightmare and the Noble Dream*, 11 Geo. L. Rev. 969 at 989 (1977).

6 Hart, *supra* note 2 at 124 and 252. Like Hart, I will use "rule application" to refer to what judges and lawyers do and "rule following" to refer to what citizens (including lawyers and judges in their civic lives) do.

7 *Ibid.* at 131–32 and 262.

8 *Ibid.* at 80 and 135.

9 *Ibid.* at 107, 124, and 107–8.

10 *Ibid.* at 123.

11 H. L. A. Hart, *Positivism and the Separation of Law and Morals*, 71 Harv. L. Rev. 593 at 629 (1958), and *Problems of the Philosophy of Law* in Essays in Jurisprudence and Philosophy 108 (H. L. A. Hart ed. 1983). Although originally written in 1967, these latter words and ideas were republished unchanged in 1983. In 1961 (and, therefore, again in 1994), Hart noted that rule application will work "smoothly . . . over the great mass of ordinary cases," *supra* note 2 at 124.

12 *Supra* note 2 at 251–52.

13 Hart, *Positivism*, *supra* note 11 at 615.

14 Hart, *Problems*, *supra* note 11 at 108.

15 Wittgenstein, *supra* note 1 at I, s. 38.

16 See J. L. Austin, Philosophical Papers 182 (J. O. Urmson and G. J. Warnock eds. 1961) ("Words are not [except in their own little corner] facts or things: we need therefore to prise them off the world, to hold them apart from and against it, so that we can realize their inadequacies and arbitrariness"), and G. Ryle, The Theory of Meaning 144 (1963) ("The meaning of an expression is the role it is employed to perform, not any thing or person or event for which it might be supposed to stand").

17 H. L. A. Hart, *Definition and Theory in Jurisprudence* in Essays in Jurisprudence and Philosophy 31, *supra* note 11 at 31. For earlier efforts along similar lines, see W. Hohfeld, Fundamental Legal Conceptions 35 (1964), and G. Williams, *Language and the Law* (1945) 61 L.Q.R. 71, 179, 293, 384, and (1946) 62 L.Q.R. 387.

18 Hart, *supra* note 2 at 17.

19 *Ibid.* at 125.

20 Hart, *Positivism*, *supra* note 11 at 606–7.

21 Hart, *supra* note 17 at 31 and 23.

22 Hart, *supra* note 2 at 99.

23 Hart, *supra* note 17 at 47.

24 See D. Pears, Ludwig Wittgenstein (1970).

25 Hart, *supra* note 2 at 125.

26 J. Derrida, Specters of Marx: The State of the Debt, the Work of Mourning, and the New International xvii (P. Kamuf trans. 1994).

27 See H. Staten, Wittgenstein and Derrida (1984), and N. Garver and S.-C. Lee, Derrida and Wittgenstein (1994). In this chapter, I concentrate on this vertical aspect. For a discussion of the "play of differences," see *infra* ch. 6.

28 Wittgenstein, *supra* note 1 at I, s. 109 ("Philosophy is the bewitchment of our intelligence

by means of language"). For a critical survey of this philosophical shift, see R. Rorty, The Linguistic Turn: Recent Essays in Philosophical Method 3 (1967).

29 L. Wittgenstein, Tractatus Logico-Philosophicus 6.57 (D. F. Pears and B. F. McGuinness eds. 1961).

30 Wittgenstein, *supra* note 1 at I, s. 192, and T. Kuhn, The Structure of Scientific Revolutions 44–48 (2d ed. 1970). See also W. Quine, From a Logical Point of View 20 (2d ed. 1961), and H. Putnam, Realism with a Human Face 96–104 (1990).

31 R. Rorty, *Inquiry as Recontextualisation* in The Interpretive Turn: Philosophy, Science and Culture 65 (D. Hiley et al. eds. 1991).

32 J. Derrida, Of Grammatology 73 (G. C. Spivak trans. 1976).

33 The metaphorical and nonessential character of language is explored by F. Nietzsche, Early Greek Philosophy and Other Essays 178–79 (M. A. Mugge trans. 1911), and F. Saussure, Course in General Linguistics 65–70 (W. Baskin trans. 1959). For a more modern rendering of these accounts, see G. Peller, *The Metaphysics of American Law*, 73 Cal. L. Rev. 1151 at 1162–70 (1985).

34 C. Geertz, Local Knowledge 184 (1983).

35 *The Queen in Right of British Columbia* v. *Tener et al.* (1985), 17 D.L.R. (4th) 1 (S.C.C.) at 8 (quoting Lord Atkinson in *Attorney-General* v. *De Keyser's Hotel Ltd.*, [1920] A.C. 508 at 542).

36 *Ibid.* at 23 and 25.

37 *Lapierre* v. *Attorney-General of Quebec* (1985), 16 D.L.R. (4th) 554 (S.C.C.).

38 Of course, the fact that Nathalie's action took place in Quebec is extremely relevant, but it does not vitiate or undermine what is to be learned from a comparison of *Lapierre* and *Tener*. Canadian law is characterized by its tolerance of both civil law and common law jurisdictions. The structure and culture of law in each province thus compels the recognition of very different intellectual contexts before it is possible to understand fully any comparison or contrast of the two cases. Nevertheless, the civil law tradition of Quebec and the common law process of British Columbia do not determine the outcomes of these cases. First, the trial judge in *Lapierre*, working within the structure of the Code Civil, could and did provide compensation to Nathalie as had French judges in the early 1960s in similar circumstances. Second, the civilian structure is not monolithic and different judges internalize it to different extents. Common law language and thought, as exhibited in *Tener*, is also not determinative. Again, in *Tener*, the trial judge could and did deny compensation. As well, *Tener* reflects the interpretation of ambiguously worded collections of statutes—and it is fair to say, as the Supreme Court of Canada did, that the internalized structure of private property and ideas about the appropriate role of the state and community were far more important than "technical, legalistic" arguments. Furthermore, *Lapierre* would likely be classified as a *tort* case in common law jurisdictions. This categorization might also have resulted in the dismissal of the lawsuit for several reasons. First, judicial attitudes toward strict products liability and design defects suggest that the judges would have demanded a demonstration of governmental negligence as a precondition of liability. Second, the decision to implement a mass inoculation program with concomitant risks of personal injury would almost certainly have been labeled a "policy" decision and thus beyond judicial review. Finally, the provincial crown proceedings legislation almost uniformly predicates vicarious state liability on the demonstration of a common law tort committed by a particular civil servant. Of course, none of this is to suggest that potential tort liability could not be articulated using common law concepts. See A. Hutchinson and D. Cohen, *Of Persons and Property: The Politics of Legal Taxonomy*, 21 Dalhousie L.J. 20 (1990).

39 R. Savatier, *Responsabilité de l'Etat dans les accidents de vaccination obligatoire reconnus imparables*, Mélange Offerts à Marcel Waline, t. 2 (Paris, 1974) at 752–53, translated at (1985), 16 D.L.R.(4th) 554 at 574–75. The French administrative courts had developed the theory of risk from Rousseauian notions of equality—demanding that individual sacrifice, even in the public interest, represents "a deliberate breach of the equality which should apply between citizens with respect to public burdens, and that equality must be re-established by means of a compensatory payment." Justice Chouinard simply chose to ignore that idea.

40 See W. N. Hohfeld, *Some Fundamental Legal Conceptions as Applied in Judicial Reasoning*, 23 Yale L.J. 16 (1913), and *Faulty Analysis in Easement and License Cases*, 27 Yale L.J. 66 (1917).

41 A. Leff, *Contract as Thing*, 19 Amer. U. L. Rev. 131 at 135 (1970).

42 As in similar discussions of slavery, the Supreme Court still contrives to talk of "justice and humanity" and compensation for "a reduced capital asset" in the same breath. *Andrews* v. *Grand & Toy Alberta Ltd.* (1978), 83 D.L.R.(3d) 452 at 474–75 per Dickson J. (S.C.C.). The language in *Bonne* v. *Eyre* (1777), 1 H.B. l.273; 126 E.R.160, a preeminent "contract" case, which speaks of the lawful possession of Negroes, shows how comfortable such ideas can become to judges.

43 W. Shakespeare, *Romeo and Juliet*, Act I, sc. iv. I agree with Dr. Johnson's refutation of Bishop Berkeley's thesis that only mental experiences are real. Kicking a stone with great force, he recoiled and declared, "I refute it thus." W. Jackson Bate, Samuel Johnson 316 (1975). For an explanation of how there is no way to transfer this nonlinguistic brutality to facts, see R. Rorty, *Texts and Lumps* in Objectivism, Relativism, and Truth: Philosophical Papers 81 (1991).

44 Wittgenstein, *supra* note 1, at I, s. 241 and s. 23.

45 For a defense of the claim that skepticism is not relativistic because relativism is simply one more version of truth stating that skepticism rejects, see R. Rorty, *Solidarity or Objectivity?* in Post-Analytic Philosophy 5–7 (J. Rajchman and C. West eds. 1985) and ch. 2.

46 J. Bruner, Actual Minds, Possible Worlds 64 (1986).

47 A. Leff, *Contract as Thing*, 19 Amer. U. L. Rev. 131 at 157 (1970).

48 Hart, *supra* note 2 at vii.

49 *Ibid.* at 103.

50 Derrida rejects the use of "indeterminacy" and prefers "undecidability." However, because "indeterminacy" is a common term in jurisprudential argot and because I use it in the same way that Derrida uses "undecidability," I have decided to stay with "indeterminacy." See J. Derrida, Limited Inc. 148 (S. Weber trans. 1988). For a contrary reading to my own, see S. Winter, *For What It's Worth*, 26 Law & Soc. Rev. 789 at 810–12 (1992).

51 Hart, *Positivism*, *supra* note 11 at 614. For a similar complaint, see L. Fuller, *Positivism and Fidelity to Law—A Reply to Professor Hart*, 71 Harv. L. Rev. 593 at 663–64 (1958).

52 Hart, *supra* note 2 at 139, 141, and 141.

53 S. Fish, There's No Such Thing as Free Speech 170 (1994).

54 N. MacCormick, Legal Reasoning and Legal Theory 197 (1978).

55 Hart, *supra* note 2 at 132 and 251–52. For a strong defense of Hart and reaffirmation of this positivist commitment, see A. Marmor, *No Easy Cases?* 2 Can. J.L. and Jur. 61 (1990).

56 Derrida, Limited Inc., *supra* note 50 at 147, and *infra* ch. 6.

57 Hart, *supra* note 2 at 126.

58 See D. Lay, Ways of the World: A History of Roads and Vehicles 184 (1992). A bicycle has been considered both inside and outside the definition of "vehicle" for the purposes of determining whether its rider is subject to the statutory rules of the road. In Oklahoma of

1915, it was; see *Tulsa Ice Co.* v. *Wilkes*, 152 P. 1169 (1915). In Maine of 1964, it was not; see *Fowles* v. *Dakin*, 205 A.2d 169 (1964). However, in Maryland of 1975, it was again; see *Richards* v. *Goff*, 338 A.2d 80 (1975).

59 See *White* v. *District of Columbia*, 4 F.2d 163 (1925).

60 *State* v. *One Black Horse Mule*, 92 So. 548 (1922), and *Stanley* v. *Tomlin*, 129 S.E. 379 (1925).

61 On the difference between indeterminacy and predictability generally, see W. Lucy, *Adjudication for Pluralists*, 16 Oxf. J. of Leg. St. 369 at 376–78 (1996). Critics who fail to appreciate this distinction include J. Stick, *Can Nihilism Be Pragmatic?* 100 Harv. L. Rev. 332 at 353 (1986), and L. Solum, *On the Indeterminacy Critique: Critiquing Legal Dogma*, 54 U. Chi. L. Rev. 462 at 471–72 (1987). For more on predictability, see ch. 8.

62 K. Greenawalt, *How Law Can Be Determinate*, 38 U.C.L.A. L. Rev. 1 at 12 (1990). See also C. Sunstein, *Analogical Reasoning*, 105 Harv. L. Rev. 741 (1992).

63 L. Wittgenstein, Zettel 73 (G. E. M. Anscombe and G. H. von Wright eds. 2d ed. 1981).

64 Wittgenstein, *supra* note 1, at I, s. 145, and *infra* ch. 7.

65 Wittgenstein, *supra* note 63 at 303. Picking up on Wittgenstein's ideas, Kripke argues persuasively that it is impossible to establish an authoritative set of philosophical criteria that can test whether a rule is or is not being followed. See S. Kripke, Wittgenstein on Rules and Private Language (1982), and also C. Yablon, *Law and Metaphysics*, 96 Yale L.J. 613 at 633 (1987). In the jurisprudential literature, the tendency has been to deploy Wittgensteinian wisdom to underwrite rather than undermine the positivist project. See B. Bix, *The Application (and Mis-Application) of Wittgenstein's Rule-Following Considerations to Legal Theory*, 2 Can. J.L. and Juris. 107 (1990); F. Schauer, *Rules and the Rule-Following Argument*, 2 Can J.L. and Juris. 187 (1990); and S. Landers, *Wittgenstein, Realism and CLS: Undermining Rule Scepticism*, 9 Law and Phil. 177 (1990). For a good summary of the conclusively inconclusive debate about whether Wittgenstein's ideas can or cannot sustain a skeptical account of legal justification, see A. Arulanantham, *Breaking the Rules? Wittgenstein and Legal Realism*, 107 Yale L.J. 1853 (1998).

66 Hart, *Problems*, *supra* note 11 at 106.

67 See F. Schauer, *Easy Cases* 58 S. Cal. L. Rev. 399 (1985), and R. Dworkin, Law's Empire 351 and 352 (1986).

68 Hart, *supra* note 2 at 123.

69 See Greenawalt, *supra* note 62 at 31.

70 On weird and outrageous cases, see M. Tushnet, *A Note on the Revival of Textualism in Constitutional Theory*, 58 S. Cal. L. Rev. 683 at 688 (1985), and A. D'Amato, *Aspects of Deconstruction: The Easy Case of the Under-Aged President*, 84 Nw. U. L. Rev. 250 (1989).

71 Fuller, *supra* note 51 at 663.

72 See D. Hay, *Property, Authority and Criminal Law* in Albion's Fatal Tree 17–64 (D. Hay et al. eds. 1977). It is not difficult to imagine a repressive regime of the future in which a similar legal sophistry would hopefully arise. See, for example, M. Atwood, A Handmaid's Tale (1985).

73 B. N. Cardozo, Selective Writings of Benjamin Nathan Cardozo 225 (M. Hall ed. 1975).

74 Hart, *supra* note 2, at 139.

4 Playing with Authority: Interpretation and Identity

1 W. Conklin, *The Invisible Author of Legal Authority*, 7 Law and Critique 173 at 186 (1996).

2 See H. L. Gates Jr., Writing and Difference 16 (1986).

3 3R. Barthes, *The Death of the Author* in Image Music Text 142 (S. Heath trans. 1977).

4 W. K. Wimsatt, *Genesis: The Fallacy Revisited* in The Disciplines of Criticism: Essays in Literary Theory, Interpretation and History 222 (P. Demetz et al. eds. 1968).

5 O. W. Fiss, *Objectivity and Interpretation*, 34 Stan. L. Rev. 739 at 763 (1982).

6 W. K. Wimsatt and L. M. Beardsley, *The Affective Fallacy* in The Verbal Icon 22 (W. Wimsatt Jr. ed. 1954). See also M. Moore, *The Semantics of Judging*, 54 S. Cal. L. Rev. 151 at 166 (1981).

7 See C. Fried, *Sonnet LXV and the "Black Ink" of the Framers' Intention*, 100 Harv. L. Rev. 759 at 763 (1987), and H. J. Powell, *The Original Understanding of Original Intent*, 98 Harv. L. Rev. 885 (1985).

8 However, even the conservative House of Lords has recently begun to permit resort to evidence of legislative intent. See *Pepper* v. *Hart*, [1993] A.C. 593. For a sophisticated defense of textualism, see A. Scalia, A Matter of Interpretation (1997).

9 S. Fish, Is There a Text in This Class? The Authority of Interpretive Communities 9 (1980). See also J. M. Balkin, *Ideology as Constraint*, 36 Stan. L. Rev. 1133 (1991).

10 E. D. Hirsch, Validity in Interpretation 216 (1967). See also F. Schauer, *An Essay on Constitutional Language*, 34 U.C.L.A. L. Rev. 797 (1982).

11 See E. Meese, *Original Intent* in The Great Debate: Interpreting Our Written Constitution 9 (1986), and R. Berger, Federalism: The Founders' Design 13–20 (1987). For a balanced and accessible introduction, see D. Farber, *The Originalism Debate: A Guide for the Perplexed*, 49 Ohio St. L.J. 1085 (1989).

12 R. Posner, Law and Literature: A Misunderstood Relation 221 (1988). See also R. Posner, The Federal Courts: Crisis and Reform (1985) and The Problems of Jurisprudence (1990).

13 P. Schlag, *Framers' Intent: The Illegitimate Uses of History*, 8 U. Puget Sound. L. Rev. 283 at 287 (1985).

14 For an excellent account of the difficulty of determining the meaning of "no vehicles in the park" by reference to legislative intent, see P. Brest, *The Misconceived Quest for the Original Understanding* 60 B.U.L.R. 204 at 209–13 (1980).

15 J. Boyle, *The Search for an Author: Shakespeare and the Framers*, 37 Amer. U. L. Rev. 625 (1988). For other general critiques, see M. Tushnet, *Following the Rules Laid Down: A Critique of Interpretivism and Neutral Principles*, 96 Harv. L. Rev. 781 (1983); M. Radin, *Statutory Interpretation*, 43 Harv. L. Rev. 863 (1930); and R. Dworkin, A Matter of Principle 33–57 (1985).

16 R. Dworkin, Law's Empire 225 (1986). For a more thorough coverage of Dworkin's ideas, see *infra* ch. 5.

17 Fiss, *supra* note 5, at 739.

18 *Ibid.* at 746.

19 *Ibid.* at 755.

20 See H. Hart Jr. and A. Sacks, The Legal Process 1201 (W. Eskridge Jr. and P. Frickley eds. 1994). For a good survey of prevailing theories of statutory interpretation, see C. Gonzalez, *Reinterpreting Statutory Interpretation*, 74 N. Carol. L. Rev. 585 (1996).

21 See B. Knapp and W. Michaels, *Against Theory* in Against Theory: Literary Theory and the New Pragmatism 11–30 (W. J. T. Mitchell ed. 1985).

22 J. Balkin, *Deconstructive Practice and Legal Theory*, 96 Yale L.J. 743 at 780 (1987).

23 Barthes, *supra* note 3 at 142.

24 J. Derrida, *Signature Event Context*, 1 Glyph 172 at 192 (1977).

25 M. Foucault, *What Is an Author?* in The Foucault Reader 120 (P. Rabinow ed. 1984). It is instructive to take Foucault's arguments on the role of the author and turn them back on himself as the author of his own text. It is important not for hermeneutical authority but

for political reception. The fact that Foucault was gay helps place his work in some perspective for some purposes. It suggests a context for understanding his work as a revolt against the repressive force of "normalization" and for explaining his preoccupation with the social construction of sexuality. However, it does not offer any magical key to the meaning of that work, nor does it inhibit any particular reading of it. It is a contextual fact whose relevance and significance will vary. See D. Eribon, Michel Foucault 28 (B. Wing trans. 1991).

26 B. Wilson, *Will Women Judges Really Make a Difference?* 28 Osgoode Hall L.J. 507 at 515 and 521–22 (1990). See also C. Gilligan, In a Different Voice: Psychological Theory and Women's Development (1982).

27 C. Mackinnon, Feminism Unmodified: Discourses on Life and Law 88, 91, 160, 195, 83, and 22 (1987). See, also, R. Colker, *Feminism, Sexuality and Self: A Preliminary Inquiry into the Politics of Authenticity*, 68 B.U.L. Rev. 217 (1988), and R. West, *Jurisprudence and Gender*, 55 U. Chi. L. Rev. 1 (1998).

28 D. Fuss, Essentially Speaking: Feminism, Nature and Difference 114 (1989). For an anti-foundationalist critique that claims that it is not possible to offer an anti-essentialist account of identity as long as there are continued efforts to claim that there is a connection between what people do and who they are, see W. Michaels, *Race and Culture: A Critical Genealogy of Cultural Identity* in Identities 61 (K. A. Appiah and H. L. Gates Jr. eds. 1996).

29 R. Chang, *Toward an Asian American Legal Scholarship: Critical Race Theory, Post-Structuralism, and Narrative Space*, 821 Cal. L. Rev. 1241 at 1281 (1993). See also M. Matsuda, *Looking to the Bottom: Critical Legal Studies and Reparations,* 22 Harv. C.R.-C.L. L. Rev. 323 (1997), and J. Williams, *Dissolving the Sameness/Difference Debate: A Post-Modern Path beyond Essentialism in Feminist and Critical Race Theory*, [1991] Duke L.J. 296.

30 M. J. Frug, Postmodern Legal Feminism 107 (1992).

31 E. Said, Representations of the Intellectual 22 (1994).

32 See, for example, *Morgentaler et al.* v. *The Queen*, [1988] 1 S.C.R. 30 at 161–84 per Wilson J.; *Lavallee*, [1990] 1 S.C.R. 852 at 856–97 per Wilson J.; *Symes* v. *Canada*, [1993] 4 S.C.R. 695 at 776–832 per L'Heureux-Dubé J.; *R.* v. *Seaboyer*, [1991] 2 S.C.R. 577 at 597–642 per MacLachlin J. and at 643–713 per L'Heureux-Dubé J.; and *R.* v. *Carosella*, [1997] 1 S.C.R. 88 at 114–55 per L'Heureux-Dubé J.

33 Barthes, *supra* note 3 at 142.

34 M. Tushnet, Red, White and Blue: A Critical Analysis of Constitutional Law 187 (1988).

35 D. Herzog, *As Many as Six Impossible Things before Breakfast*, 75 Cal. L. Rev. 609 at 629 (1987) (discussing Tushnet, *supra* note 34). In an equally witty aside, Kim Lane Scheppele compares the Constitution to a recipe for key lime pie. She reports that judges never confuse the two, and cooks do not assert that recipes reveal rights or the separation of governmental powers. See K. L. Scheppele, Legal Secrets 89–90 (1988).

36 See T. Eagleton, Literary Theory: An Introduction 85 (1983). On the question of what it means to interpret in good faith as opposed to simply ascribing a meaning to a text, see *infra* ch. 7.

37 See *supra* ch. 2.

38 A. Pope, *An Essay in Criticism* in Collected Poems 71 (B. Dobree ed. 1983).

39 S. Fish, Doing What Comes Naturally: Change, Rhetoric, and the Practice of Theory in Literary and Legal Studies 25 (1989).

40 R. Barthes, The Pleasure of the Text 11 (R. Miller trans. 1975).

41 Barthes, *supra* note 3, at 146.

42 T. McLaughlin, *Introduction*, Critical Terms of Literary Study 7 (F. Lentricchia and T. McLaughlin eds. 1990).

43 M. Foucault, *Prison Talk* in Power/Knowledge 93 (C. Gordon ed. 1980). For further discussion on good faith, see *infra* ch. 7.

44 J. Derrida, *The Principle of Reason: A University in the Eyes of Its Pupils*, 13 Diacritics 17 (1983).

45 M. Minow, *Partial Justice: Law and Minorities* in The Fate of Law 58 (A. Sarat and T. Kearns eds. 1991). For a fuller response to this charge, see *infra* ch. 9.

46 T. Moi, Sexual/Textual Politics: Feminist Literary Theory (1985).

47 R. Rorty, *Feminism and Pragmatism* Mich. Q. Rev. 231 at 249 (1990).

48 See, for example, *Adarand Constructors* v. *Pena* (1995), 115 S. Ct. 2097 at 2119. See also *Missouri* v. *Jenkins* (1995), 115 S. Ct. 2038, and *Miller* v. *Johnson* (1995), 115 S. Ct. 2475. See generally G. Loury, One by One from the Inside Out (1996), and J. Rosen, *Moving On* in The New Yorker, April 29, 1996, at 66.

49 W. Allen, Four Films of Woody Allen 13–16 (1982).

50 R. Sennett, Authority 19 (1981).

5 A Pure Way of Playing: The Naturalist Revival

1 R. Dworkin, A Matter of Principle 146 (1984).

2 Learned Hand, *Mr. Justice Cardozo*, 52 Harv. L. Rev. 361 (1938).

3 See, for example, L. Fuller, The Morality of Law (1970). Even Hart maintained that there is "a minimum content of natural law"; see H. L. A. Hart, The Concept of Law 189–95 (2d ed. 1994).

4 *Omychund* v. *Barker* (1744), 26 E.R. 15 at 23.

5 L. Tribe, Constitutional Choices 4 (1985).

6 R. Dworkin, Law's Empire 407 and 400 (1986). See also Fuller, *supra* note 3.

7 E. Weinrib, The Idea of Private Law 3 and 13 (1995).

8 For a political critique of these proposals, see A. Hutchinson, *The Last Emperor?* in Reading Dworkin Critically 45–70 (A. Hunt ed. 1992), and A. Hutchinson, *The Importance of Not Being Ernest*, 34 McGill L.J. 233 (1989).

9 R. Rorty, Philosophy and the Mirror of Nature 392 (1979).

10 See, for example, A. Hutchinson and J. Wakefield, *A Hard Look at "Hard Cases": The Nightmare of a Noble Dreamer*, 2 Oxf. J. of Leg. St. 86 at 91–106 (1982).

11 Dworkin, *supra* note 6 at 354 and 266.

12 H. L. A. Hart, *American Jurisprudence through English Eyes: The Nightmare and the Noble Dream*, 11 Ga. L. Rev. 969 at 982 (1977), and Hart, *supra* note 3 at 275. In the postscript to the posthumous edition of *The Concept of Law*, Hart accepts that Dworkinian principles are indeed part of the law but denies that there is any sharp contrast between nonconclusive principles and all-or-nothing rules: "The distinction is a matter of degree." *Ibid.* at 262. Because a legal system's ultimate criteria of legal validity—the rule of recognition—can easily and legitimately accommodate moral values, Hart insists that there is little to distinguish Dworkin's holistic interpretive criterion of legal integrity from his own recommended judicial way of proceeding. Judges must still offer general justificatory reasons for their decisions and, often proceeding by analogy, "ensure that the new law they make, though it *is* new law, is in accordance with principles or underpinning reasons recognized as already having footing in the existing law." *Ibid.* at 274. Nevertheless, even the most Herculean of judges will occasionally have to fall back "on his sense of what is best and not on any already established order of priorities prescribed for him by law." *Ibid.* at 275.

13 Dworkin, *supra* note 6 at 239, 412, 211, 255, and 222.

14 *Ibid.* at 225 and 413. See also R. Dworkin, Freedom's Law: The Moral Reading of the American Constitution 1–38 (1996).

15 *Ibid.* at 354, 351, 256, and 354.

16 *Ibid.* at 38 and 255. See, for example, R. Sartorius, *Social Policy and Judicial Legislation*, 8 Am. Phil. Q. 151 (1971).

17 *Ibid.* at 255, 352, and 255.

18 B. N. Cardozo, The Nature of the Judicial Process 149 (1921).

19 Dworkin, *supra* note 1, at 146.

20 For other jurisprudential critiques of this precedential chestnut, see Cardozo, *supra* note 18 at 40–43; R. Taylor, *Law and Morality*, 43 N.Y.U.L. Rev. 611 at 626 (1968); I. Ehrlich & R. Posner, *Economic Analysis of Legal Rule-making*, 3 J. Legal Stud. 257 at 259–60 (1974); A. D'Amato, Jurisprudence: A Descriptive and Normative Analysis of Law 93–114 (1984); and D. Patterson, *Law's Pragmatism: Law as Practice and Narrative*, 76 Virg. L. Rev. 937 at 985–87 (1990).

21 Dworkin, *supra* note 6 at 20, 352, and 352.

22 115 N.Y. 506 at 515–17, with whom Danforth J. concurred. Roscoe Pound considered that Earl J.'s judgment in *Riggs* was "the most conspicuous example" of spurious interpretation (i.e., creative lawmaking under the guise of interpretive discovery); see *Spurious Interpretation*, 7 Colum. L. Rev. 379 (1907). Also, it is often overlooked that, as a matter of substantive law, the justice of the decision in this case did not receive universal approval. For instance, Shauck J. said, "the decision in *Riggs* is the manifest assertion of a wisdom believed to be superior to that of the legislature upon a question of policy"; *Deem* v. *Milliken*, 53 Ohio St. 668 (1895). See also *Bird* v. *Planchet*, 139 Conn. 491 (1953), and *Wall* v. *Pfanschmidt* , 265 Ill. 180 (1914). The result, however, did recommend itself to the English courts in *Re Crippen*, [1911] 1 K.B. 149; see H. Harlo, *When Can a Murderer Inherit?* 16 Mod. L. Rev. 100 (1953).

23 *Ibid.* at 511.

24 R. Dworkin, Taking Rights Seriously 26 (1978).

25 Dworkin, *supra* note 6 at 87.

26 Cardozo, *supra* note 18 at 43.

27 Dworkin, *supra* note 6 at 256.

28 R. Barthes, Mythologies 141 (A. Lavers trans. 1972).

29 Dworkin, *supra* note 6, at 444 and 443. In defense of Dworkin's judicial methodology, Andrew Altman has expanded on this point and insisted that "no good reasons" are given as to why particular principles and counterprinciples are "logically incompatible." A. Altman, Critical Legal Studies: A Liberal Critique 124–26 (1990).

30 S. F. C. Milsom, Historical Foundations of the Common Law 11 (1969).

31 Dworkin, *supra* note 6 at 225 and 227–28.

32 *Hong Kong Fir Shipping Co.* v. *Kawasaki Kisen Kaisha Ltd.*, [1962] 2 Q.B. 26 at 71 per Diplock L.J.

33 Dworkin, *supra* note 6 at 255.

34 *Ibid.* at 110–11 and 219.

35 *Ibid.* at 213 and 408. Also, see generally *ibid.* at 23–29, 240–50, and 268–71.

36 See D. Bell, And We Are Not Saved: The Elusive Quest for Racial Justice (1987).

37 Weinrib, *supra* note 7 at 3, 12, 23, 14, and 5 (emphasis added).

38 *Ibid.* at 205–6, 207, and 145.

39 *Ibid.* at 223, 225, and 227.

40 *Ibid.* at 228. See Hutchinson, *supra* note 8.

41 *Ibid.* at 21, 9, and 76.

42 See Fuller, *supra* note 3. For similar criticisms, see H. L. A. Hart, *Book Review*, 78 Harv. L. Rev. 1281 (1965), and G. Hughes, *Positivists and Natural Lawyers*, 17 Stan. L. Rev. 547 (1965).

43 Weinrib, *supra* note 7 at 13.

44 *Ibid.* at 9, 56, 145, and 146.

45 See W. Landes and R. Posner, The Economic Structure of Tort Law (1987); Dworkin, *supra* note 6, at 403; and R. L. Abel, *Torts* in The Politics of Law: A Progressive Critique 180 (D. Kairys ed. 1982).

46 See, for example, R. Epstein, *A Theory of Strict Liability*, 2 J. Legal Stud. 659 (1985), and J. Murphy and J. Coleman, The Philosophy of Law: An Introduction to Jurisprudence 132–8 and ch. 4 (1984). Indeed, a large part of Weinrib's account is devoted to dismissing these competing claims. Weinrib, *supra* note 7 at 171–203.

47 Weinrib, *supra* note 7 at 146. For an interesting acknowledgment of this trend by an enthusiastic supporter of natural law and Aristotelian justice, see J. Finnis, Natural Law and Natural Right 178–79 (1980).

48 *Ibid.* at 21. Although Weinrib does not make this exact statement in The Idea of Private Law, such an opinion runs throughout his discussion; *ibid.* at 145–203.

49 See Hart, *supra* note 3 at 1–6.

50 Weinrib, *supra* note 7 at 14 and 213.

51 *Ibid.* at 21 and 20. For a survey of this record, see A. Hutchinson, *The Canengaustusian Connection* in A. Hutchinson, Dwelling on the Threshold: Critical Essays on Modern Legal Thought 183 (1988).

52 *Ibid.* at 14 and 15.

53 *Ibid.* at 14, 58, and 109.

54 L. R. Hubbard, The Phoenix Lectures (1968). For a wonderful critique along similar lines (positing a "plausible" connection between sleep and sex) of Posner's instrumentalist account of tort law, see J. M. Balkin, *Too Good to Be True: The Positive Economic Theory of Law*, 87 Colum. L. Rev. 1447 (1987).

55 Weinrib, *supra* note 7 at 219, 223–24, and 227.

56 *Lamb* v. *Camden B.C.*, [1981] 2 All E.R. 408 (C.A.).

57 *Ibid.* at 421 (emphasis added) and 419, ed. R. F. V. Heuston quoting Salmond on the Law of Torts 38 (17th ed. 1977).

58 Weinrib, *supra* note 7 at 225, 221, and 221.

59 *Ibid.* at 224 and 225 n. 36. See also E. Weinrib, *Publicness and Private Law* in Proceedings of the Eighth Int. Kant Congress, vol. 1, 191–201 (H. Robinson ed. 1995). For a discussion of "good faith," see *infra* ch. 7.

60 *Ibid.* at 18, 106, and 106. See *infra* ch. 7.

61 G. Hartman, *History-Writing as Answerable Style* In New Directions in Literary History 100 (R. Cohen ed. 1974).

62 John T. Noonan Jr., Persons and Masks of the Law viii–ix (1976). This criticism has been made by other critics; see S. Levinson, *Taking Law Seriously: Reflections on "Thinking like a Lawyer,"* 30 Stan. L. Rev. 1071 at 1106–7 (1978), and T. Pangle, *Discovering Rights*, [1978] Pub. Interest 157 at 160.

6 At Play in the Fields of Law: The Reasoning Game

1 E. Levy, An Introduction to Legal Reasoning 73 (1949).

2 D. Kennedy, *Legal Education and the Reproduction of Hierarchy* in The Politics of Law 47 (D. Kairys ed. 1982).

3 For a general survey, see Pragmatism in Law and Society (M. Brint and W. Weaver eds. 1991) and *Symposium: The Renaissance of Pragmatism in American Legal Thought*, 63 S. Cal. L. Rev. 1569 (1990).

4 C. Sunstein, Legal Reasoning and Political Conflict 135 and 191 (1996).

5 *Ibid.* at 32, 99, 13, 34, and 92.

6 *Ibid.* at 91–92, 195, and 67. As far back as 1837, Francis Lieber claimed that "analogy is the essential means of effecting [legal construction]." F. Lieber, Legal and Political Hermeneutics 46 (1837). Sunstein is in good company in trying to effect such a rehabilitation. See C. Perelman, The Realm of Rhetoric (1982) ("One of the classical arguments of the logic of law"); J. Broekman, *Analogy in Law* in Legal Knowledge and Analogy: Fragments of Legal Epistemology, Hermeneutics and Linguistics 243 (P. Nerhot ed. 1992) ("Analogy is one of the determining forces of legal practice, its regularity and its reasonableness"); and S. Brewer, *Exemplary Reasoning: Semantics, Pragmatics, and the Rational Force of Legal Argument by Analogy*, 109 Harv. L. Rev. 923 (1996) ("Legal interpreters . . . often use exemplary argument as an integral part of that interpretive effort").

7 *Supra* note 4.

8 This is what John Austin labeled "the competition of opposing analogies." See J. Austin, Lectures on Jurisprudence 653 and 1030 (5th ed. 1885).

9 Levi, *supra* note 1 at 2 and 104. See also R. Warner, *Three Theories of Legal Reasoning*, 62 S. Cal. L. Rev. 1523 at 1552–56 (1989).

10 Kennedy, *supra* note 2 at 47.

11 *Brown* v. *Board of Education*, 347 U.S. 483 (1954) and *Roe* v. *Wade*, 410 U.S. 113 (1973).

12 Sunstein, *supra* note 4 at 82 and 75. For a critical account of canon formation in law, see Balkin and Levinson, *The Canons of Constitutional Laws*, III Harv. L. Rev. 964 (1998).

13 *Plessy* v. *Ferguson*, 163 U.S. 537 (1896).

14 *McLoughlin* v. *O'Brian*, [1983] A.C. 410 at 419 per Lord Wilberforce.

15 *Supra* note 4 at 6, 37, 5, and 39. On Herculean adjudication, see R. Dworkin, Law's Empire (1986). Sunstein also draws a comparison between incompletely theorized agreements and Rawls's idea of "overlapping consensus." See J. Rawls, Political Liberalism 133–72 (1993).

16 *Supra* note 4 at 58, 59, 59, and 59.

17 *Ibid.* at 39, 44, and 42.

18 *Ibid.* at 6.

19 For a critical survey of this ludic tradition, see M. Spariosu, Dionysius Reborn: Play and the Aesthetic Dimension in Modern Philosophical and Scientific Discourse (1989).

20 See, for example, P. Feyerabend, Against Method (1975). For an extended account of this "nihilistic" tendency in jurisprudence and its Nietzschean implications, see *infra* ch. 7.

21 J. Derrida, Margins of Philosophy 1–28 (A. Bass trans. 1982) and Positions 39–49 (A. Bass trans. 1982). For introductions to deconstructive critique, see B. Johnson, *Translator's Introduction* in J. Derrida, Dissemination (1981), and J. Balkin, *Deconstructive Practice and Legal Theory*, 96 Yale L.J. 743 (1987).

22 J. Derrida, Of Grammatology 141–64 (1976). For an application of this to law, see G. Frug, *The Ideology of Bureaucracy in American Law*, 97 Harv. L. Rev. 181 (1984).

23 J. Derrida, *Structure, Sign, and Play in the Discourse of the Human Sciences* in The Structuralist Controversy 254 (R. Macksey and E. Donato eds. 1970).

24 *Ibid.* at 248, 264–65, 265, and 260. For Rorty, Derrida is best thought of as "a French Wittgenstein." R. Rorty, *Is Derrida a Transcendental Philosopher?* In Essays on Heidegger and Others: Philosophical Papers, vol. 2, 128 (1991), and *The Banality of Pragmatism and the Poetry of Justice*, 63 S. Cal. L. Rev. 1811 at 1814 (1990). For a more wide-ranging

exchange between Rorty and Derrida on the compatibility of their work, see Deconstruction and Pragmatism: Simon Critchley, Jacques Derrida, Ernesto Laclau, and Richard Rorty (C. Mouffe ed. 1996).

25 See S. Fish, Doing What Comes Naturally 503 (1989) and *supra* ch. 3.

26 See J.-F. Lyotard and J.-L. Thebaud, Just Gaming 28 and 43 (1985).

27 J.-F. Lyotard, The Postmodern Condition: A Report on Knowledge 15 (1984). See also Fish, note 25 at 355–58.

28 *Miller* v. *Jackson*, [1977] Q.B. 966 (CA). In writing the remainder of this section, I benefited enormously from the work in a lecture and unpublished paper by Frank Michelman. See *Miller v. Jackson en critique* (Nov. 1985).

29 Of course, it could be contended that if one of the judges explicitly and exclusively decided the case on the basis that the playing of cricket should be promoted ahead of all other activity, he or she would not have been acting judicially. This is not a particularly devastating charge or interesting revelation. For it to be so, it would have to be demonstrated that the decision was motivated by "nonlegal" considerations and then framed in the conventional rhetoric of legal argumentation. See *infra* at ch. 7. It does not take a cynical or even close reading between the lines to speculate that Denning's judgment might well be an example of such a cricket-loving rationalization.

30 *Supra* note 28, at 981–82. Geoffrey Lane makes passing reference to the need to balance public and private interests and seems to favor private over public interest. See *ibid.* at 986. For an extended critique of the public/private distinction, see A. Hutchinson, Waiting for Coraf: A Critique of Law and Rights 123–53 (1995).

31 *Ibid.* at 982, 981, and 982.

32 *Ibid.* at 978, 981, 976, 981, and 977 (quoting *Bolton* v. *Stone*, [1951] A.C. 850 at 867 per Lord Reid).

33 Michelman, *supra* note 28 at 5.

34 *Supra* note 28 at 984, 983, 989, and 986–87.

35 *Ibid.* at 987 and 988–89.

36 Michelman, *supra* note 28 at 14. See also J. Dewey, The Quest for Certainty 213 (1929).

37 J. Derrida, *Force of Law: The Mystical Foundation of Authority* in Deconstruction and the Possibility of Justice 3 (D. Cornell et al. eds. 1992).

38 Deconstruction and Pragmatism, *supra* note 24 at 87.

39 This distinction bears a passing resemblance to Hart's between primary and secondary rules, but it is very loose and nontechnical. See H. L. A. Hart, The Concept of Law 79–99 (2d ed. 1994) and *supra* ch. 2.

40 For an illustrated inventory of the extant rules, see *infra* appendix.

41 B. Slattery, *Are Constitutional Cases Political?*, 11 Sup. Ct. L. Rev. 507 at 515 (1989). In 1837, Francis Lieber noted that writing a book on legal reasoning was "like writing a recipe of a cookery book." See The Life and Letters of Francis Lieber 116 (T. Perry ed. 1882). See also K. Polanyi, Personal Knowledge (1962), and R. Posner, The Problems of Jurisprudence 405 (1990).

42 J. Wisdom, *Gods* in Philosophy and Psychoanalysis 157 (1953).

43 J. Derrida, Speech and Phenomena 135 (D. Allison trans. 1973).

44 M. Radin, *Reconsidering the Rule of Law*, 69 B.U.L. Rev. 781 (1989).

45 F. Lentricchia, Criticism and Social Change 81 (1983).

46 H. Baker Jr., Blues Ideology and Afro-American Literature: A Vernacular Theory 8 (1984). On such a scenario, Jacques Derrida is like a Parisian John Coltrane. At 89.

47 D. Kennedy, *A Semiotics of Legal Argument*, 42 Syracuse L. Rev. 75 at 103 (1991).

7 Playing by the Rules: A Good Faith Approach

1 *Duport Steels Ltd.* v. *Sirs*, [1980] 1 W.L.R. 142 at 168 per Lord Scarman.

2 J.-F. Lyotard, The Postmodern Condition: A Report on Knowledge 41 (1984).

3 L. Tribe, *Taking Text and Structure Seriously: Reflections on Free-Form Method in Constitutional Interpretation*, 108 Harv. L. Rev. 1221 at 1225, 1227, 1288, 1230, 1224, 1285, and 1232 (1995). The substantive focus of Tribe and Ackerman's disagreement is over the meaning to be attributed to the treaty clause of the American Constitution and, in particular, what kind of congressional majority is required to approve major international agreements, like NAFTA or GATT. Although Tribe draws on the whole of Ackerman's constitutional writings, he concentrates on an article that Ackerman cowrote with David Golove. See B. Ackerman and D. Golove, *Is NAFTA Constitutional?*, 108 Harv. L. Rev. 799 (1995).

4 *Ibid.* at 1227 and 1302.

5 W. Waluchow, Inclusive Legal Positivism 259 (1994). This is not an isolated view. See O. W. Fiss, *The Death of Law?* 72 Cornell L.Q. 1 (1986); F. Schauer, Playing by the Rules: A Philosophical Examination of Rule-based Decision-making in Law and in Life 192 (1991); Tribe, *supra* note 3, at 1221; and E. Weinrib, The Idea of Private Law 106 (1995).

6 Carrington, *Of Law and the River*, 34 J. Legal Stud. 224 at 227 (1984).

7 *Supra* note 3 at 1234.

8 D. Kairys, *Politics and Law*, 52 Geo. Wash. L. Rev. 243 at 244, 247, 245, and 247 (1984). It seems appropriate to point out that some of my own earlier writing can be read as promoting such a position. See, for example, A. Hutchinson, Dwelling on the Threshold: Critical Essays on Modern Legal Thought 85–90 (1989).

9 J. Frank, Law and the Modern Mind 100 and 131 (1936). There are passages in Frank's work that can be read as approving of rationalization in certain circumstances. *Ibid.* at 128 and 130.

10 C. Sunstein, *Analogical Reasoning*, 105 Harv. L. Rev. 741 at 779, n. 130 (1992).

11 See F. Nietzsche, *Thus Spake Zarathustra* in The Portable Nietzsche 103 (W. Kaufman ed. 1954) and *supra* ch. 6. For more on Nietzschean adjudication, see S. Levinson, *Law as Literature*, 60 Texas L. Rev. 373 (1982).

12 J. Butler, *Contingent Foundations: Feminism and the Question of Postmodernism*, 11 Praxis Int. 150–65 at 156 (1991). See also D. Kennedy, *The Phenomenology of Adjudication* in The Rule of Law: Ideal or Ideology 141–67 (A. Hutchinson and P. Monahan eds. 1987); S. Fish, Doing What Comes Naturally (1989); and *supra* ch. 6.

13 H. L. A. Hart, The Concept of Law 142 and 145 (2d ed. 1994).

14 *Ibid.* at 145 and 144.

15 *Ibid.* at 244. I offer no account of the psychological basis of "bad faith"—how judges explain to themselves what they are doing when they are judging, especially in response to the charge that they are acting ideologically rather than legally, is not my concern. See D. Kennedy, A Critique of Adjudication: fin de siècle 180–212 (1997). In arguing that "adjudication is best described as ideological choice . . . carried on by actors many of whom are in bad faith," he includes any judge who existentially denies that adjudication is so practiced; see *ibid.* at 4. Kennedy is addressing much more than those judges who cheat deliberately and willfully by following their ideological predisposition without an attempt to fit it to the available legal materials. I tend more toward the view that "nobody would claim that their own thinking was ideological just as nobody would habitually refer to themselves as Fatso. . . . Ideology like halitosis is in this sense what the other person has." T. Eagleton, Ideology: An Introduction 3 (1991).

16 *Ibid.* at 91.

17 See F. Rabelais, Gargantua and Pantagruel chs. 39–40 (1963).

18 S. Carter, Integrity 7 (1996). See also M. Benjamin, Splitting the Difference: Compromise and Integrity in Ethics and Politics (1990); S. Bok, Lying: Moral Choice in Public and Private Life (1978); and L. McFall, *Integrity*, 98 Ethics 19 (1987).

19 See S. Fish, *Play of Surfaces: Theory and the Law* in Legal Hermeneutics: History, Theory, and Practice 297 at 302 (G. Leyh ed. 1992).

20 See J. Passmore, Serious Art 65 (1991).

21 Kennedy, *supra* note 15 at 4, 197, and 203 (1997). His sources include Sartre, Being and Nothingness (H. Barnes trans. 1965) 89–90 and A. Freud, The Ego and the Mechanisms of Defence (C. Baines trans. 1937). See also P. Schlag, *Contradiction and Denial*, 87 Mich. L. Rev. 1216 (1989), and S. Altman, *Beyond Candor*, 89 Mich. L. Rev. 296 (1990).

22 Until amended in 1993, "nonfrivolous argument" used to read "a good faith argument." See *Nemeroff* v. *Abelson*, 620 F. 2d 339 (2d Cir. 1980), and *Kinee* v. *Abraham Lincoln Fed. Saving & Loan Assoc.*, 365 F. Supp. 975 (E.D.Pa. 1973).

23 D. Risinger, *Honesty in Pleading and Its Enforcement: Some "Striking" Problems with Federal Rule of Civil Procedure* 11, 61 Minn. L. Rev. 1 at 57 (1976). For a more jurisprudence-oriented discussion, see S. Levinson, *Frivolous Cases: Do Lawyers Really Know Anything at All?* 24 Osgoode Hall L.J. 353 (1987).

24 *C.U.P.E. (Local 963)* v. *New Brunswick Liquor Corp.*, [1979] 2 S.C.R. 227 at 237 per Dickson J. However, as one might expect, there has been considerable doctrinal backsliding in subsequent cases. See J. Evans et al., Administrative Law 573–98 (4th ed. 1995). A similar deferential position has been adopted by the American courts. See *Chevron U.S.A. Inc.* v. *Natural Resources Defense Council*, 467 U.S. 837 (1984).

25 *Canada (Attorney-General)* v. *Mossop*, [1993] 1 S.C.R. 554 at 634 per L'Heureux-Dubé J.

26 See generally R. Simon, Sports and Social Values 64–74 (1985), and W. Brown, *Ethics, Drugs and Sport*, 7 J. Phil. of Sport 15 (1980).

27 For further discussion of what might be entailed in judges striving to "do the right thing," see *infra* ch. 9.

28 S. Burton, Judging in Good Faith 163 (1992).

29 *R.* v. *Sussex Justices, Ex parte McCarthy*, [1924] 1 K.B. 256 at 259 per Hewart L.J.

30 *R.* v. *Secretary of State for the Environment, ex p. Brent London Borough Council*, [1982] 2 W.L.R. 693 at 731–32 per Ackner L.J.

31 See *Dimes* v. *Proprietors of the Grand Junction Canal* (1852), 10 E.R. 301 (H.L.), and *Old St. Boniface Resident Assoc.* v. *Winnipeg (City)*, [1990] 3 S.C.R. 1170.

32 See R. Dworkin, Law's Empire (1986), and C. Sunstein, Legal Reasoning and Political Conflict (1996). For a full discussion, see *supra* at 000.

33 See *Brown* v. *Board of Education* (1954), 347 U.S. 483; *Morgentaler* v. *The Queen*, [1988] 1 S.C.R. 30; and *Donoghue* v. *Stevenson*, [1932] A.C. 572.

34 M. Tushnet, *Does Constitutional Theory Matter? A Comment* 65 Tex. L. Rev. 777 at 782 (1987). For an account that highlights nihilism but only to resist its debilitating specter, see J. Singer, *The Player and the Cards: Nihilism and Legal Theory*, 94 Yale L.J. 1 (1984).

35 For a full discussion, see *supra* ch. 3.

36 The Constitutional Court began its first sessions in February 1995. The court consists of eleven judges, in 1995 nine men and two women, who serve for seven years. All eleven judges hear every case. The court does not hear evidence or question witnesses. It does not decide directly whether accused persons are guilty or whether damages should be awarded to an injured person: these are matters for the ordinary courts. Its function is to determine

the meaning of the constitution in relation to matters in dispute. The constitution makes it possible for a wide range of individuals and public and private bodies to raise a constitutional question. However, anyone wishing to bring a constitutional case before the court must start in the Supreme Court, which will either refer the matter to the Constitutional Court or, if it has the power to do so, decide the matter itself. Appeals can be lodged with the Constitutional Court, but cases are not heard automatically; it is for the court to decide if an important question of principle relating to the interpretation of the constitution has been raised. Also, any judge of the Supreme Court may refer a matter directly to the Constitutional Court. If there is a constitutional question involved, the hearing of the case will be suspended by the judge until the Constitutional Court has given its decision. Finally, the court also had a special role in the process of drafting a new and final constitution for South Africa. Sitting as the Constitutional Assembly, Parliament produced a constitutional text, and then the court had to certify that all thirty-four constitutional principles agreed upon in advance by the negotiators of the interim constitution had been complied with.

37 *State* v. *Zuma and Others*, [1995] 4 B.C.L.R. 401.

38 *Mhlungu and Four Others* v. *The State*, [1995] 3 S.A. 867 at 874, 902, and 874 (quoting *Minister of Home Affairs [Bermuda]* v. *Fisher and Another*, [1980] A.C. 319 at 329 per Lord Wilberforce).

39 Kentridge A. J. recognizes that, on the facts of this particular case, it would not be difficult to fudge the question by stipulating that proceedings did not begin until the serving of the second indictment in May, after the coming into force of the constitution. However, like his colleagues, he takes a more general approach in order to resolve the overall issue for the "tens of thousand" cases that could be said to be "pending." See *ibid.* at 895–96 per Kentridge A.J. and 910–11 per Kriegler J.

40 *Ibid.* at 896, 900, and 904–5. Kentridge A.J. offers *Hunter et al.* v. *Southam Inc.* (1984), 9 C.R.R. 355 at 364–65, and *Government of the Republic of Bophuthatswana and Others* v. *Segale*, [1990] 1 S.A. 434 at 448–49 as contrasting examples.

41 *Ibid.* at 902, 900, and 902 per Kentridge A.J. For an uncompromising defense of the minority position, see E. Fagan, *The Longest Erratum Note in History*, 12 S. Afr. J. Hum. Rts. 79 (1994). See, more generally, E. Fagan, *In Defence of the Obvious: Ordinary Meaning and the Identification of Constitutional Rules*, 11 S.A.J. of H. Rgts., 545 (1995).

42 *Ibid.* at 872, 873, 874, 874, 876, and 879–80 per Mahomed J.

43 *Ibid.* at 885 and 889 per Mahomed J.

44 *Ibid.* at 906, 908, 908, and 909 per Kriegler J.

45 *Ibid.* at 911, 916n.32, 911, 912, and 918 per Sachs J.

46 J. Derrida, Positions 63 (A. Bass trans. 1981).

47 See *supra* ch. 4. While four of the white judges comprised the minority, the other three combined with the black judges to form the majority: one joined Mahomed's judgment and two wrote separate concurring judgments. Although the distinction between black and white judges is paramount in the context of recent South African history and politics, it is important to remember that the formation and attribution of identity is no simple or straightforward matter. Racial identity is mediated by other factors. For instance, Sachs is white, but he is also Jewish and spent a large part of his life in exile as an African National Congress (ANC) activist. Similarly, Kentridge is white, but he is also Jewish and had a prominent career at the bar representing anti-apartheid activists, like the Garment Workers' Union and the family of Stephen Biko. Racial identity counts, but in no entirely predictable or reliable way.

48 *Supra* note 3 at 1250, 1224, 1279, and 1302.

1 J.-F. Lyotard, The Postmodern Condition: A Report on Knowledge xxiv (1984). Lyotard's work is a reaction to the alleged sterility of Marxism. See also J. Baudrillard, The Mirror of Production (1974).

2 See D. Kennedy, A Critique of Adjudication: fin de siècle 225–26 (1997).

3 H. Kelsen, The Pure Theory of Law 1 (1967). Weinrib is a possible exception. See *supra* ch. 5.

4 See R. Unger, Social Theory: Its Situation and Its Task (1987).

5 See, for example, J. Fudge, *Marx's Theory of History and a Marxist Analysis of Law* in Canadian Perspectives on Legal Theory 151–75 (R. Devlin ed. 1991); C. Mackinnon, Toward a Feminist Theory of the State (1989); D. Bell, Faces at the Bottom of the Well: The Permanence of Racism (1993); and F. Fukuyama, The End of History and the Last Man (1992).

6 Exactly what Marx himself thought, let alone what modern Marxists maintain, is difficult to fix with any certainty. Throughout his life's work, there are conflicting views on whether law was autonomous or epiphenomenal. See, for example, M. Cain and A. Hunt, Marx and Engels on Law (1979). It is no longer fruitful to argue any version of the claim that "Marxian theory is at bottom. . . ." This is not simply a mistake of Marxian theorists but a flawed approach to the reading of any particular political theory. The Marxian canon has always been subject to debate and transformation. See Whither Marxism? Global Crisis in International Perspective (B. Magnus and S. Cullenberg eds. 1995).

7 K. Marx, *Preface to a Critique of Political Economy* in Karl Marx: Selected Writings 389 (D. McLellan ed. 1977). For a more modern but consistent account, see C. Sypnowich, The Concept of Socialist Law (1990).

8 R. Abel, *Torts* in The Politics of Law: A Progressive Critique 186 and 188 (D. Kairys ed. 1982).

9 Fukuyama, *supra* note 5 at 131, 139, 211, and 48.

10 See, for example, H. Collins, Marxism and Law 50 (1982), and *supra* ch. 3.

11 G. A. Cohen, Karl Marx's Theory of History 233 (1978).

12 See G. Frug, *The Ideology of Bureaucracy in American Law*, 97 Harv. L. Rev. 1276 (1984).

13 C. Mackinnon, Feminism Unmodified: Discourses on Life and Law 151 (1987). See also A. Dworkin, Intercourse (1987), and C. Littleton, *Feminist Jurisprudence: The Difference That Method Makes*, 41 Stan. L. Rev. 751 (1989).

14 *Ibid.* at 4. On the idea of sex as violence, see MacKinnon, *supra* note 5 at 172–83.

15 For a different account of this claim from a heterosexual male perspective, see D. Kennedy, Sexy Dressing Etc. 137 (1993).

16 J. Butler, Gender Trouble: Feminism and the Subversion of Identity 28 (1990).

17 MacKinnon, Feminism, *supra* note 13 at 205. A similar view is offered in A. Dworkin, Right-wing Women 227–31 (1982) and Intercourse 143 (1987).

18 See E. Jackson, *Catharine MacKinnon and Feminist Jurisprudence: A Critical Appraisal*, 19 J. Law & Soc'y 195 at 202 (1992).

19 C. Mackinnon, Only Words 37 (1993).

20 For a general critique of such causal claims about pornography, see Women against Pornography (V. Burstyn ed. 1985), Sex Exposed: Sexuality and the Pornography Debate (L. Segal and M. MacIntosh eds. 1993), and Dirty Looks: Women, Pornography, Power (P. Gibson and R. Gibson eds. 1993).

21 See T. McCormack, *If Pornography Is the Theory, Is Inequality the Practice?* 23 Phil. of Soc. Sciences 298 (1993).

22 See B. Quistgaard, *Pornography, Harm and Censorship: A Feminist (Re)Vision of the right to Freedom of Expression*, 52 U. T. L.J. 132 (1993).

23 See Pornography: Women, Violence and Civil Liberties 201–398 (C. Itzin ed. 1992).

24 R. West, *The Feminist-Conservative Anti-Pornography Alliance and the 1986 Attorney General's Commission Report on Pornography*, [1987] A.B.F. Res. J. 686 at 696. See also New Lesbian Criticism: Literary and Cultural Readings (S. Munt ed. 1992), and B. Cossman et al., Bad Attitudes on Trial (1997).

25 MacKinnon, *supra* note 19 at 37.

26 See S. Fish, There's No Such Thing as Free Speech 31–50 (1994), and *supra* ch. 4.

27 See C. Smart, *Law's Power, the Sexed Body, and Feminist Discourse*, 17 J. Law & Soc'y. 194 at 208 (1990).

28 Unger, *supra* note 4 at 88. For a confident account of "the structure and logic of capitalist social relations," see J. Bakan, Just Words: Constitutional Rights and Social Wrongs 7–8 and 145–47 (1997).

29 P. Gabel and J. Feinman, *Contract Law as Ideology* in The Politics of Law: A Progressive Critique 173 and 175–76 (D. Kairys ed. 1982). See also A. Gramsci, The Prison Notebooks (Q. Hoare ed. 1973).

30 See, for example, M. Mandel, *Marxism and the Rule of Law*, 35 U.N.B.L.J. 7 (1986).

31 R. Gordon, *Law and Ideology*, 3(1) Tikkun 14 at 15 (1988).

32 In this sense, it remains particularly pertinent to embrace the notion that the best way to remain faithful to the spirit of Marxism is by critiquing Marx. By doing so, it makes sense to conclude that "men and women, all over the earth, are today to a certain extent the heirs of Marx and Marxism." J. Derrida, Specters of Marx: The State of the Debt, the Work of Mourning, and the New International 91 (P. Kamuf trans. 1994).

33 E. P. Thompson, Whigs and Hunters: The Origins of the Black Act 260, 262, and 263 (1976).

34 D. Kennedy, *Legal Education as Training for Hierarchy* in The Politics of Law 50 (D. Kairys ed. 1982). See also D. Kennedy, *Form and Substance in Private Law Adjudication*, 89 Harv. L. Rev. 1685 (1976), and R. Unger, The Critical Legal Studies Movement (1986).

35 See, for example, P. Macklem, *Of Texts and Democratic Narratives*, 41 U. T. L.J. 639 (1991), and A. Hunt, *Living Dangerously on the Deconstructive Edge*, 26 Osgoode Hall L.J. 869 (1988).

36 *Donoghue* v. *Stevenson*, [1932] A.C. 562 at 592 per Lord Atkin.

37 *Ibid.* at 582 per Lord Buckmaster. Other judicial chants also echo throughout the modern doctrine. Lord Abinger's warning that if privity of contract were relaxed, "the most absurd and outrageous consequences, to which I cannot see the limit, would ensue," renders Atkin's bold advice that "when the ghosts of the past stand in the path of justice clanking their medieval chains, the proper course for the judge is to pass through them undeterred" easier said than done. See *Wright* v. *Winterbottom* (1842), 152 E.R. 402 at 405 per Lord Abinger, and *United Australia Ltd.* v. *Barclays Bank Ltd.*, [1941] A.C. 1 at 2 per Lord Atkin. See, generally, J. Smith, *Economic Loss and the Common Law Marriage of Contracts and Tort*, 18 U.B.C. L. Rev. 95 at 101 (1984).

38 Abel, *supra* note 8 at 185, and M. Rabin, *The Historical Development of the Fault Principle: A Reinterpretation*, 15 Ga. L. Rev. 925 (1982).

39 *Cattle* v. *Stockton Waterworks Co.* (1875), L.R. 10 Q.B. 453. While this decision is still considered the leading authority, it ought not to be forgotten that it was decided over fifty years before the modern law of negligence was born.

40 *Hedley Byrne & Co. Ltd.* v. *Heller & Partners Ltd.*, [1964] A.C. 465 at 530 per Lord Devlin.

41 *Spartan Steel & Alloys Ltd.* v. *Martin & Co.*, [1973] Q.B. 27. In a strong, though since

ignored dissent, Lord Edmund Davies allowed recovery for all the lost profits because they were foreseeable and direct. See also *Weller & Co.* v. *Foot and Mouth Institute*, [1966] 1 Q.B. 569; *Electrochrome Ltd.* v. *Welsh Plastic Ltd.*, [1968] 2 All E.R. 205; and *S.C.M. (U.K.) Ltd.* v. *W. J. Whittall & Son Ltd.*, [1970] 3 All E.R. 245.

42 *Dutton* v. *Bognor Regis U.D.C.*, [1972] 1 Q.B. 373.

43 *Anns* v. *Merton Borough Council*, [1977] 3 All E.R. 492 at 498 per Lord Wilberforce.

44 *Ross* v. *Caunters*, [1979] 1 A.C. 193 at 199 per Megarry V.C.

45 *Junior Books Ltd.* v. *Veitchi Co.*, [1983] A.C. 520 at 545 per Lord Roskill.

46 *Greater Nottingham Co-operative* v. *Cementation*, [1988] 3 W.L.R. 396 at 407 per Purchas. J. See also *Muirhead* v. *Industrial Tank Specialities Ltd.*, [1985] 3 All E.R. 705, and *Caparo* v. *Dickman*, [1990] 2 W.L.R. 358 at 362–65 per Lord Bridge, 374 per Lord Roskill, and 379–81 per Lord Oliver.

47 *Junior Books*, *supra* note 45 at 551. See also *The Aliakmon*, [1986] A.C. 785.

48 *Murphy* v. *Brentwood District Council*, [1990] 3 W.L.R. 414 at 432 per Lord Keith.

49 *Henderson* v. *Merret Syndicates Ltd.*, [1995] 2 A.C. 145; *Spring* v. *Guardian Assurance PLC*, [1992] 2 A.C. 296; and *White* v. *Jones*, [1995] 2 A.C. 207.

50 J. Steele, *Scepticism and the Law of Negligence*, [1993] Camb. L.J. 437.

51 A. W. B. Simpson, A History of the Common Law of Contract 325 (1975). In attempting to justify the developing doctrine on economic loss, the courts have fallen back on a battery of argumentative strategies. For a critical catalog of these justifications, see A. Hutchinson and R. Maisey, *Blurred Visions: The Politics of Civil Obligations* in Tort Theory 276 (K. Cooper-Stephenson and E. Gibson eds. 1993).

52 *Caparo*, *supra* note 46 at 618 per Lord Bridge. See also *Bryan* v. *Maloney* (1995), 128 A.L.R. 163 at 192 per Brennan. J.

53 See, for example, P. Cane, Atiyah's Accidents, Compensation and the Law 74 (4th ed. 1987); B. Feldthusen, Economic Negligence (2d ed. 1989); R. Bernstein, Economic Loss (1993); and B. S. Markesinis and S. F. Deakin, Tort Law 86–118 (3d ed. 1994).

54 See, for example, *Kamloops* v. *Nielson*, (1984), 31 C.C.L.T. 1; (1984), *A.G. of Ontario* v. *Fatehi*, 10 D.L.R. (4th) 641 (S.C.C.); *Just* v. *B.C.*, [1989] 2 S.C.R. 1228; *Rothfield* v. *Manolakos*, [1989] 2 S.C.R. 1259; *Edgeworth Construction* v. *Lea* (1993), 107 D.L.R. (4th) 169 (S.C.C.); *Norsk Pacific Steamship Co.* v. *C.N.R.*, [1992] 1 S.C.R. 1021; and *Winnipeg Condominium Co.* v. *Bird Construction*, [1995] 1 S.C.R. 85.

55 *Holmes* v. *Mather* (1875), L.R. 10 Ex. 261.

56 See, for example, J. Conaghan and W. Mansell, The Wrongs of Tort 94–99 (1993), and R. Abel, *A Critique of Torts*, 37 U.C.L.A. L. Rev. 785 (1990).

57 See Fukuyama, *supra* note 5.

58 See J. Adams and R. Brownsword, *The Ideologies of Contract Law*, 7 Legal Studies 205 (1987), and H. Collins, The Law of Contract (1986). The prominent stages in this doctrinal history include *Suisse Atlantique*, [1967] 1 A.C. 36; *Lloyds Bank Limited* v. *Bundy*, [1975] Q.B. 326; *Photo Production Limited* v. *Securicor Transport Limited*, [1980] A.C. 827; *Morgan* v. *National Westminster Bank Limited*, [1985] A.C. 687; and *Walford* v. *Miles*, [1992] 2 W.L.R. 174 (H.L.).

59 *C.B.S. Songs Limited* v. *Amstrad P.L.C.*, [1988] 1 A.C. 1013 at 1059 per Lord Templeman.

60 See D. Howarth, *Negligence after Murphy: Time to Re-Think*, 50 Camb. L.J. 58 at 66–68 (1991).

61 Abel, *supra* note 56 at 823.

62 See *supra* note 49.

63 *Smith* v. *Bush*, [1990] A.C. 811. It should be noted that the House of Lords relied upon a statute to invalidate the disclaimers.

64 By vision, I do not simply mean an all-embracing narrative that provides an explanation of the past, a blueprint for the future, and a connecting thread between the two. My version is much more modest. See *infra* ch. 9.

65 Thompson, *supra* note 33 at 250.

9 Playing Politics: Putting Poetry in Motion

1 See A. Hunt, *The Big Fear: Law Confronts Postmodernism*, 35 McGill L.J. 507 (1990), and G. Binder, *What's Left?* 69 Texas L. Rev. 1985 (1991).

2 See P. Goodrich, *Sleeping with the Enemy: An Essay on the Politics of Critical Legal Studies in America*, 68 N.Y.U. L. Rev. 389 at 396 (1993).

3 F. Lentricchia, *The Return of William James*, 53 Partisan Rev. 2 at 253 (1986), and also Ariel and the Police (1988). See also T. Eagleton, Literary Theory: An Introduction (1983); E. Said, The World, Text, Critic (1983); and J. Habermas, The Philosophical Discourse of Modernity (F. Lawrence trans. 1987).

4 F. Fukuyama, The End of History and the Last Man 211 and 118 (1992).

5 J. Handler, *Non-Foundationalism, Protest and the New Social Movements*, 26 Law & Soc'y Rev. 695 at 719, 727, 720–21, 722, and 722 (1992).

6 Fukuyama, *supra* note 4 at 131. See also, *supra* ch. 8. For a powerful effort to imagine a nonfoundationalist account of Marxism that emphasizes the contingent over the universal and the emancipatory over the deterministic, see A. Janmohamed, *Reconfiguring Values, Power, Knowledge* in Whither Marxism? Global Crisis in International Perspective 35 (B. Magnus and S. Cullenberg eds. 1995).

7 W. Shakespeare, Macbeth Act V, sc. v.

8 See M. Matsuda, *Looking to the Bottom: Critical Legal Studies and Reparations*, 22 Harv. C.R.-C.L. Rev. 323 at 325 and 324 (1987). In her later work, she seems to have put any essentialism behind her. See M. Matsuda, *Pragmatism Modified and the False Consciousness Problem*, 63 S. Cal. L. Rev. 1763 (1990).

9 Handler, *supra* note 5 at 724.

10 C. Castoriadis, *Socialism and Autonomous Society*, [1980] Telos 91 at 104.

11 J. Derrida, *The Ends of Man* in The Margins of Philosophy (A. Bass trans.) 135.

12 J. Derrida, *Deconstruction and the Other* in Dialogues with Contemporary Continental Thinkers 119–20 (R. Kearney ed. 1984). See also J. Derrida, Positions 93 (A. Bass trans. 1981) ("[I]t is not *neutral*. It *intervenes*"), and T. McCarthy, *The Politics of the Ineffable: Derrida's Deconstructionism*, 21 Phil. Forum 146 (1989).

13 See A. Harris, *Race and Essentialism in Feminist Legal Theory*, 42 Stan. L. Rev. 581 (1990), and M. Radin, *Pragmatism and Feminism*, 63 S. Cal. L. Rev. 1699 (1990).

14 E. Said, Representations of the Intellectual 53 (1994).

15 See R. Rorty, *Priority of Democracy to Philosophy* in The Virginia Statute for Religious Freedom 274 (M. Peterson and R. Vaughan eds. 1988). Rorty reiterates this radical commitment in urging that we have "faith in ourselves—in the utopian hope characteristic of a democratic community—rather than asking for reasons or back up from outside." R. Rorty, *Education without Dogma*, [1989] Dissent 198 at 201. See also R. Rorty, Achieving Our Country: Leftist Thought in Twentieth-Century America (1998).

16 R. P. Warren, *America and the Diminished Self* in Democracy and Poetry 3–37 (1975). See also S. Heaney, The Government of the Tongue (1988); M. Heidegger, *What Are Poets For?* in Poetry, Language, Thought 94 (A. Hofstadter trans. 1971); and M. Oakeshott, *The Voice of Poetry and the Conversation of Mankind* in Rationalism in Politics and Other Essays 197–247 (1962).

17 See H. L. Gates, *Statistical Stigmata*, 11 Cardozo L. Rev. 1275 at 1289 (1990).

18 J. Derrida, Specters of Marx: The State of the Debt, the Work of Mourning, and the New International 64–89 (P. Kamuf trans. 1994).

19 J. Derrida, *Like the Sound of the Sea Deep within a Shell: Paul de Man's War*, 14 Critical Inquiry 590 at 645 (1989).

20 E. Laclau and C. Mouffe, Hegemony and Socialist Strategy: Toward a Radical Democratic Polity 178 (1985).

21 J. Handler, The Conditions of Discretion: Autonomy, Community, Discretion 10, 12, and 15 (1986). For a similar approach, see L. White, *Subordination, Rhetorical Survival Skills and Sunday Shoes: Notes on the Hearing of Mrs. G.*, 38 Buff. L. Rev. 1 (1990).

22 Conditions of Discretion, at 303–4.

23 Handler, *supra* note 5 at 727.

24 R. Unger, Social Theory: Its Situation and Its Task 9 and 46 (1987). See also False Necessity: Anti-necessitarian Social Theory in the Service of Radical Democracy (1987) and Plasticity into Power: Comparative-Historical Studies on the Institution of Conditions from Economic and Military Success (1987).

25 Social Theory, *ibid.* at 87, 143, 45, and 198.

26 False Necessity, *ibid.* at 508–39. While Unger has begun to resist the foundationalist tendency to be programmatic, he still has not managed to disabuse himself entirely of the need to develop a full-blown theory of social explanation and just relations. See R. Unger, What Should Legal Analysis Become? 130–34 (1996).

27 False Necessity, *ibid.* at 579 and 583. For a critique of the heroic, male, and elitist slant of Unger's work, see A. Hutchinson, *A Poetic Champion Composes: Unger (Not) on Women and Ecology*, 40 U. T. L.J. 271 (1990).

28 False Necessity, *ibid.* at 8, and Social Theory, *ibid.* at 169. Although Unger offers no names, the most prominent ultra-theorist in law is Duncan Kennedy. See P. Gabel and D. Kennedy, *Roll Over Beethoven*, 36 Stan. L. Rev. (1984), and D. Kennedy, A Critique of Adjudication: fin de siècle (1997). See also A. Freeman, *Truth and Mystification in Legal Scholarship*, 90 Yale L.J. 1229 (1981). For an excellent examination of this tendency, see J. Boyle, *The Politics of Reason: Critical Legal Theory and Local Social Thought*, 133 U. Pa. L. Rev. 685 (1985).

29 M. Foucault, *Interests and Power* in Language, Counter-Memory, Practice 208 (D. F. Bouchard ed. 1977).

30 Social Theory, *supra* note 24 at 145; False Necessity, *ibid.* at 58 and 578; and Social Theory, *ibid.* at 173–74.

31 Social Theory, *ibid.* at 209, and False Necessity, *ibid.* at 592.

32 R. Unger, Knowledge and Politics 289 (1975).

33 The term "pornography" is itself part of the problem; there is something very essentialist and judgmental about it because it is used to connote what is already considered to be harmful and deviant. It would be more effective to talk about sexually explicit representations, which, like any other kind of representations, are neither intrinsically good nor bad. What is and is not a pornographic representation (as opposed to, say, erotica) involves a context-specific and constantly contestable political assessment; it does not have the universalized and incontestable thereness of traditional assertions. See M. J. Frug, Postmodern Legal Feminism 145–53 (1992).

34 C. Mackinnon, Only Words 30, 31, 31, 106, 62, and 122 (1993). For a critical account of MacKinnon's view of social relations, see *supra* ch. 8.

35 *Ibid.* at 7 and 25. For a more general critique, see *supra* ch. 2.

36 *Ibid.* at 88 and 123.

37 I. Marcus, *Fighting Bodies, Fighting Words: A Theory and Politics of Rape Prevention* in Feminists Theorize the Political 388 (J. Butler and J. Scott eds. 1992).

38 C. Mackinnon, Feminism Unmodified: Discourses on Law and Life 88, 91, 160, 195, 83, 22, 74, and 75 (1987). See also R. Colker, *Feminism, Sexuality and Self: a Preliminary Inquiry into the Politics of Authenticity*, 68 B.U.L. Rev. 217 (1988).

39 R. Rorty, *Feminism and Pragmatism*, Mich. Q. Rev. 231 at 249 (1990).

40 MacKinnon, *supra* note 38 at 218.

41 Frug, *supra* note 33 at 107. For a powerful and eloquent, though a little naive, antidote to MacKinnon's pessimism, see S. Tisdale, Talk Dirty to Me: A Personal Philosophy of Sex (1994).

42 See The Invention of Pornography: Obscenity and the Origins of Pornography 1500–1800 (L. Hunt ed. 1993).

43 B. Cossman et al., Bad Attitudes on Trial: Pornography, Feminism and the Butler Decision 144 (1997).

44 J. D. Salinger, Catcher in the Rye (1945).

45 MacKinnon, *supra* note 34 at 109 and 110.

46 MacKinnon, *supra* note 38 at 218.

47 O. W. Holmes Jr., Collected Legal Papers 187 (P. Smith ed. 1920).

48 M. Trebilcock, The Limits of Freedom of Contract 242 (1994).

49 *Ibid.* at 126. Similarly, after discussing paternalism in public policy making, not only does Trebilcock acknowledge that "it is impossible to sustain a sharp and clear divide between the domains of public and private ordering," but he reaches a conclusion that places faith in sensible ad hockery and that "does not seem strikingly dissimilar from that espoused by Duncan Kennedy." *Ibid.* at 163. See D. Kennedy, *Distributive and Paternalistic Motives in Contract and Tort Law*, 41 Maryland L. Rev. 563 (1982), and *supra* ch. 8. This notion of "muddling through" echoes the nonfoundationalist views of Rorty: "I think of justice as muddling through—in the way judges do when they decide hard cases." R. Rorty, *Response to Simon Critchley* in Deconstruction and Pragmatism 42 (C. Mouffe ed. 1996).

50 *Ibid.* at 246, 247–48, 250–60.

51 *Ibid.* at 29 and 60.

52 P. Schlag, *The Problem of Transaction Costs*, 62 S. Cal. L. Rev. 1661 at 1698 (1989). For more on the indeterminacy of economic theory and the futile effort to canonize any single form of economic regulatory organization, see P. Schlag, *An Appreciative Comment on Coase's* The Problem of Social Cost: *A View from the Left*, [1986] Wis. L. Rev. 919.

53 Trebilcock, *supra* note 48 at 147, 267, and 243.

54 M. Kelman, *Comment on Hoffman and Spitzer's Experimental Law and Economics*, 85 Colum. L. Rev. 1037 at 1047 (1985).

55 An objection that must be faced is that the market, warts and all, is still the least worst alternative, compared to, for example, modern Cuba, recent U.S.S.R., medieval France, and so on. See Fukuyama, *supra* note 4. Yet even a cursory glance around the world shows that starvation, mass unemployment, social unrest, ethnic wars, race riots, environmental despoliation, and other problems have not been eradicated or tamed by liberal democracy's hegemony. See Derrida, *supra* note 18.

56 J. Buchanan, The Limits of Liberty: Between Anarchy and Leviathan 167 (1975). For an application of these ideas to issues around racism in the marketplace, see A. Hutchinson, *Michael and Me: A Postmodern Friendship*, 33 Osgoode Hall L.J. 237 at 252–58 (1995).

57 J. Amariglio and D. Ruccio, *Postmodernism, Marxism, and the Critique of Modern Economic Thought*, 7 Rethinking Marxism 7 at 21 (1994). This is also the case from a feminist

economic perspective. Several writers identify and reject the totalizing, constructed, and male tendencies of traditional neoclassical theories. See S. Feiner and B. Roberts, *Hidden by the Invisible Hand: Neoclassical Economic Theory and the Textbook Treatment of Race and Gender*, 4 Gender and Society 159 (1990), and J. Nelson, *Gender, Metaphor, and the Definition of Economics*, 8 Economics and Philosophy 103 (1992).

58 M. Trebilcock, *Critiques of* The Limits of Contract: *A Rejoinder*, 33 Osgoode Hall L.J. 353 at 364 (1995).

59 Unger, Legal Analysis, *supra* note 26 at 23.

10 Playing with the Rules: Experiments in Judging

1 See *supra* ch. 3 and ch. 5.

2 See *Candler* v. *Crane, Christmas & Co.*, [1951] 2 K.B. 164 at 178 per Denning L.J. (C.A.).

3 R. Rorty, *Feminism and Pragmatism*, 30 Mich. Q. Rev. 231 at 242 (1990). See also R. Rorty, *Intellectuals and the End of Socialism*, 80 Yale Rev. 1 (1992).

4 H. J. Abrahams, preface in Great Justices of the U.S. Supreme Court: Ratings and Case Studies xviii (W. Pederson and N. Provizer eds. 1993). See also E. White, The American Judicial Tradition (1976).

5 G. Gunther, Learned Hand: The Man and the Judge xvi and 166 (1994).

6 H. L. A. Hart, *American Jurisprudence through English Eyes: The Nightmare and the Noble Dream*, 11 Geo. L. Rev. 969 at 977–78 (1977).

7 S. Fish, *Rhetoric* in Critical Terms for Literary Study 214 (F. Lentricchia and T. McLaughlin eds. 1990). See also K. Polanyi, Personal Knowledge (1962).

8 See C. Sunstein, Legal Reasoning and Political Conflict (1996), and *supra* ch. 6.

9 K. Llewellyn, *The Adventures of Rollo*, 2 U. Chi. L. Sch. Rec. 3 at 23 (1952).

10 See R. Rorty, *The Pragmatist's Progress* in U. Eco, Interpretation and Overinterpretation 97 (1992).

11 R. Rorty, *The Professor and the Prophet*, 52 Transition 70 at 75 (1992), and *infra* ch. 10.

12 See J. Harris, *Unger's Critique of Formalism in Legal Reasoning: Hero, Hercules, and Humdrum*, 52 Mod. L. Rev. 42 (1989). It will be obvious that Hercules and Hero are the creations of Ronald Dworkin and Roberto Unger, respectively. See R. Dworkin, Law's Empire (1986), and R. Unger, The Critical Legal Studies Movement (1986).

13 S. Rosen, The Limits of Analysis 260 (1990).

14 O. W. Holmes, Collected Legal Papers 270 (P. Smith ed. 1920), and O. W. Holmes Jr., The Common Law 5 (1881). See also T. Hobbes, Leviathan 180–82 (1651).

15 See Dworkin, *supra* note 12 at 401, and E. Weinrib, The Idea of Private Law 13 (1995), both quoting *Omychund* v. *Barker*, 26 E.R. 15 at 22 (1744). See also *Can Machines Think?* Time, April 1, 1996, at 50, and *Our Machines, Ourselves* in Harper's Magazine, May 1997, at 45–54.

16 See *supra* ch. 9.

17 Rorty, *supra* note 3 at 239.

18 W. James, Pragmatism 124 (B. Kuklick ed. 1978).

19 F. J. Stephen, Liberty, Equality, Fraternity 353 (2d ed. 1874).

20 Quintilian, Institutio Oratoria, Bk. 12, s. 1.1 (H. E. Butler trans. 1961).

21 Nietzsche, *Ecce Homo* in The Philosophy of Nietzsche 853 (1954).

22 *U.S.* v. *Carroll Towing Co.*, 159 F.2d 169 (2d Cir. 1947).

23 J. Caputo, Radical Hermeneutics: Repetition, Deconstruction and the Hermeneutic Project 198–99 (1987).

24 James P. Carse, Finite and Infinite Games: A Vision of Life as Play and Possibility 149 (1986). For a fuller discussion of this political challenge, see also *supra* ch. 9.

25 *R.A.V.* v. *City of St. Paul*, 112 S. Ct. 2538 (1992).

26 For the purposes of this analysis, I ignore Justice Blackmun's judgment, which is more of a footnote to White and Stevens. Also, I leave aside the issue of overbreadth and assume that, with a narrow construction, the law applies only to speech unprotected by the First Amendment. On the overbreadth of the overbreadth doctrine, see R. Fallon, *Making Sense of Overbreadth*, 100 Yale L.J. 853 (1991).

27 Many outcomes and ways of reaching them were available to the court. For a survey of the choices available, see K. Sullivan, *The Justices of Rights and Standards*, 106 Harv. L. Rev. 22 at 41–43 (1992). A likely list of "fixed points" on the shifting terrain of the First Amendment might include: *Schenck* v. *U.S.*, 249 U.S. 47 (1919); *Chaplinsky* v. *New Hampshire*, 315 U.S. 568 (1942); *Terminiello* v. *Chicago*, 337 U.S. 1 (1949); *Roth* v. *U.S.*, 354 U.S. 476 (1957); *New York Times Co.* v. *Sullivan*, 376 U.S. 254 (1964); *Ginsberg* v. *New York*, 390 U.S. 629 (1968); *Watts* v. *U.S.*, 394 U.S. 705 (1969); *Brandenburg* v. *Ohio*, 395 U.S. 444 (1969); *Cohen* v. *California*, 403 U.S. 15 (1971); *Police Dept. of Chicago* v. *Mosley*, 408 U.S. 92 (1972); *Miller* v. *California*, 413 U.S. 15 (1973); *Hudgens* v. *N.L.R.B.*, 424 U.S. 507 (1976); *Virginia Bd. of Pharmacy* v. *Virginia Citizens Consumer Council Inc.*, 425 U.S. 748 (1976); *Texas* v. *Johnson*, 491 U.S. 397 (1989); and *Simon & Schuster, Inc.* v. *Members of N.Y. State Crime Victims Bd.*, 112 S. Ct. 501 (1991).

28 See *R.A.V.*, *supra* note 25, at 2545, 2543, 2548, and 2549. It should be added that Scalia J. is clear that there would have been no constitutional difficulty with convicting the petitioner under more generic criminal offenses, like trespass or property damage; it was the "bias-motivated" character of the ordinance that was at issue.

29 *Ibid.* at 2560, 2555, 2560, 2552 (quoting *Chaplinsky*, *supra* note 27 at 768–69), and 2556. Not all commentators agree that "fighting words" should not receive full constitutional protection. See F. Haiman, Speech and Law in a Free Society 148–56 (1981).

30 *R.A.V.*, *ibid.* at 2551. White is particularly bemused in light of the fact that in the decisions immediately preceding *R.A.V.*, the Supreme Court declined to overturn long-standing but controversial decisions; see *Allied Signal, Inc.* v. *Director, Division of Taxation*, 112 S. Ct. 2251 (1992), and *Quill Corp.* v. *North Dakota*, 112 S. Ct. 1904 (1992). In particular, he points to the decision in *Burson* v. *Freeman*, 112 S. Ct. 1846 (1992), in which the court, joined by two of the five justices in the majority in *R.A.V.*, went the opposite way from the decision in *R.A.V.*.

31 *R.A.V.*, *ibid.* at 2543, 2545, and 2546 per Scalia J.

32 *Ibid.* at 2560, 2560, and 2558 per White J.

33 *Ibid.* at 2543 per Scalia J.

34 *Ibid.* at 2551 and 2555.

35 For a discussion of "bad faith," see *supra* ch. 7.

36 *R.A.V.*, *supra* note 25 at 2549 and 2548 per Scalia J. For instance, it is naive to believe that Robert Bork lost his nomination to the Supreme Court because of his interpretive methodology: it was the substance of his political views that made all the difference. See R. Bork, The Tempting of America: The Political Seduction of the Law (1990).

37 *Ibid.* at 2559, 2554, and 2556 per White J. For an interesting discussion of the confusing judicial politics of *R.A.V.*, see K. Sullivan, *supra* note 27 at 44–45 and 103–7.

38 *R.A.V.*, *ibid.* at 2561, 2562, 2563, and 2566. For other examples of Justice Stevens' opposition to categorization, see *New York* v. *Ferber*, 458 U.S. 747 at 777 (Stevens J. conc.); *California* v. *Carney*, 471 U.S. 386 at 395 (Stevens J. diss.); *Johnson*, *supra* note 27 at 2555 (Stevens J. diss.); and *Lucas* v. *South Carolina Coastal Council*, 112 S. Ct. 2886 at 2919 (1992).

39 *R.A.V.*, *ibid.* at 2566, 2569, and 2565.

40 *Ibid.* at 2564, 2566, and 2563. See also Blackmun J., *Ibid.* note 25 at 2560–61.

41 See *supra* ch. 4 and ch. 5.

42 M. Tushnet, Red, White and Blue: A Critical Analysis of Constitutional Law 192 (1988), and *supra* ch. 7.

43 See K. Crenshaw, *Race, Reform, and Retrenchment: Transformation and Legitimation in Antidiscrimination Law*, 101 Harv. L. Rev. 1331 (1988). For a general survey of law's instrumental efficacy, see G. Rosenberg, The Hollow Hope (1992), and R. Epstein, *The Social Consequences of Common Law Rules*, 95 Harv. L. Rev. 1717 (1982).

44 See D. Trubek, *Where the Action Is: Critical Legal Studies and Empiricism*, 36 Stan. L. Rev. 509 at 581 (1984), and Coombe, *Room for Manoeuvre: Toward a Theory of Practice in Critical Legal Studies*, 14 Law & Soc. Inq. 69 (1989).

45 See A. Hutchinson, Waiting for Coraf: A Critique of Law and Rights 210–17 (1995).

46 See Scalia, J. *supra* note 25 at 2550, and M. Matsuda, *Public Response to Racist Speech: Considering the Victim's Story*, 87 Mich. L. Rev. 2320 at 2326–41 (1989).

47 *Brown* v. *Board of Education*, 347 U.S. 483 at 494 (1954). See D. Bell, And We Are Not Saved (1987), and P. Williams, The Alchemy of Race and Rights (1991). Of course, who and what I am—a white, English, once-working-class-now-middle-class, middle-aged, divorced, remarried, father, and so on—will influence the way that I think about the problem and its possible solution. While identity cannot be escaped from, it can be constantly reviewed and reassessed. See A. Hutchinson, *Identity Crisis: The Politics of Interpretation*, 26 New Eng. L. Rev. 1173 (1992), and *supra* ch. 4.

48 J. Rauch, *In Defence of Prejudice; Why Incendiary Speech Must Be Protected*, Harper's Magazine, May 1995, 37 at 39. For a good survey of this history, see D. Downs, The New Politics of Pornography (1989), and B. Cossman et al., Bad Attitudes on Trial: Pornography, Feminism and the Butler Decision 4–41 (1997).

49 See M. Minow, Making all the Difference (1990).

50 Stephen, *supra* note 19 at 352.

51 S. Burton, Good Faith in Judging 237 (1992). See also F. R. Kellogg, *Legal Scholarship and the Temple of Doom: Pragmatism's Response to Critical Legal Studies*, 65 Tulane L. Rev. 15 at 18 (1990).

52 See *supra* ch. 4.

53 P. Goodrich, Reading the Law: A Critical Introduction to Legal Method and Techniques 216 (1986).

54 See Rorty, *supra* note 3 at 254.

55 M. Walzer, Spheres of Justice: A Defense of Pluralism and Equality 309 (1983).

56 E. P. Thompson, Writing by Candlelight 170 (1980).

57 V. Hans and N. Vidmar, Judging the Jury 163 (1986).

58 *R.* v. *Parks*, (1993), 15 O.R. (3d) 324 at 342 (C.A.).

59 See *Developments in the Law—Jury Selection and Composition*, 110 Harv. L. Rev. 1443 (1997).

60 See R. Chang, *Toward an Asian American Legal Scholarship: Critical Race Theory, Post-Structuralism, and Narrative Space* 821, Cal. L. Rev. 1241 at 1281 (1993).

11 Overtime: A Conclusion

1 O. W. Fiss, *The Death of the Law?* 72 Cornell L. Rev. 1 at 1, 9, and 11 (1986).

2 *Ibid.* at 16, 16, 16, and 15. See also M. Nussbaum, *The Use and Abuse of Philosophy in Legal Education*, 45 Stan. L. Rev. 1627 (1993).

3 P. Nonet, *Judgment*, 48 Vand. L. Rev. 987 at 989 (1995).

4 R. Dworkin, A Matter of Principle 146 (1984).

5 L. Meyer, *Is Practical Reason Mindless?* 86 Geo. L.J. 647 at 652 (1998).

6 J. Bakan, Just Words: Constitutional Rights and Social Wrongs 145 (1997). While I agree with Bakan that too much constitutional scholarship assumes uncritically that "constitutional law is central in people's lives" (*ibid.*), I stick by my assessment that, under present sociohistorical circumstances (at least, in Canada), there is more to be lost than gained in perpetuating lawyers' knee-jerk tendency to litigate social problems. A. Hutchinson, Waiting for Coraf: A Critique of Law and Rights 175–78 (1995).

7 *Miller* v. *Jackson*, [1977] Q.B. 966 at 976 and 978 (C.A.). See also *infra* ch. 6. For more on the relation of democracy and the courts, see A. Hutchinson, "The Rule of Law Revisited: Democracy and Courts" in Recrafting the Rule of Law: The Limits of Legal Order (D. Dyzenhaus ed. 1999).

8 D. Kennedy, A Critique of Adjudication: fin de siècle 374 (1997).

9 R. Kapuscinski, The Soccer War 158–59 (1991). For more on the link between soccer and antisocial behavior, see B. Bufford, Among the Thugs (1990), and J. King, The Football Factory (1996).

10 C. Bromberger, *Do You Like Soccer?* 103(3) Queen's Quarterly 471 at 471 and 475 (1996).

11 D. Beatty, Constitutional Law in Theory and Practice (1995).

12 R. Unger, What Should Legal Analysis Become? 115 (1996).

13 See M. Burton, *Determinacy, Indeterminacy and Rhetoric in a Pluralist World*, 21 Melb. U. L. Rev. 544 at 581–83 (1997).

14 J. F. Stephen, Liberty, Equality, Fraternity 270 and 271 (2d ed. 1874).

Index

Allan C. Hutchinson is Professor of Law at Osgoode Hall Law School, York University, Toronto. He is the author of *Waiting for Coraf: A Critique of Law and Rights* (1995) and *Dwelling on the Threshold: Critical Essays on Modern Legal Thought* (1988), and the editor of many more books.

Library of Congress Cataloging-in-Publication Data
Hutchinson, Allan C.
It's all in the game : a nonfoundational account of law and adjudication / Allan C. Hutchinson.
Includes index.
ISBN 0-8223-2428-8 (cloth : alk. paper)
1. Law—Philosophy. 2. Law—Methodology. 3. Judicial process. 4. Law and politics. I. Title.
K230.H88A35 2000
340'.1—dc21 99-33752 CIP